CHAPTER 1: YOU'RE NEVER GONNA MAKE IT

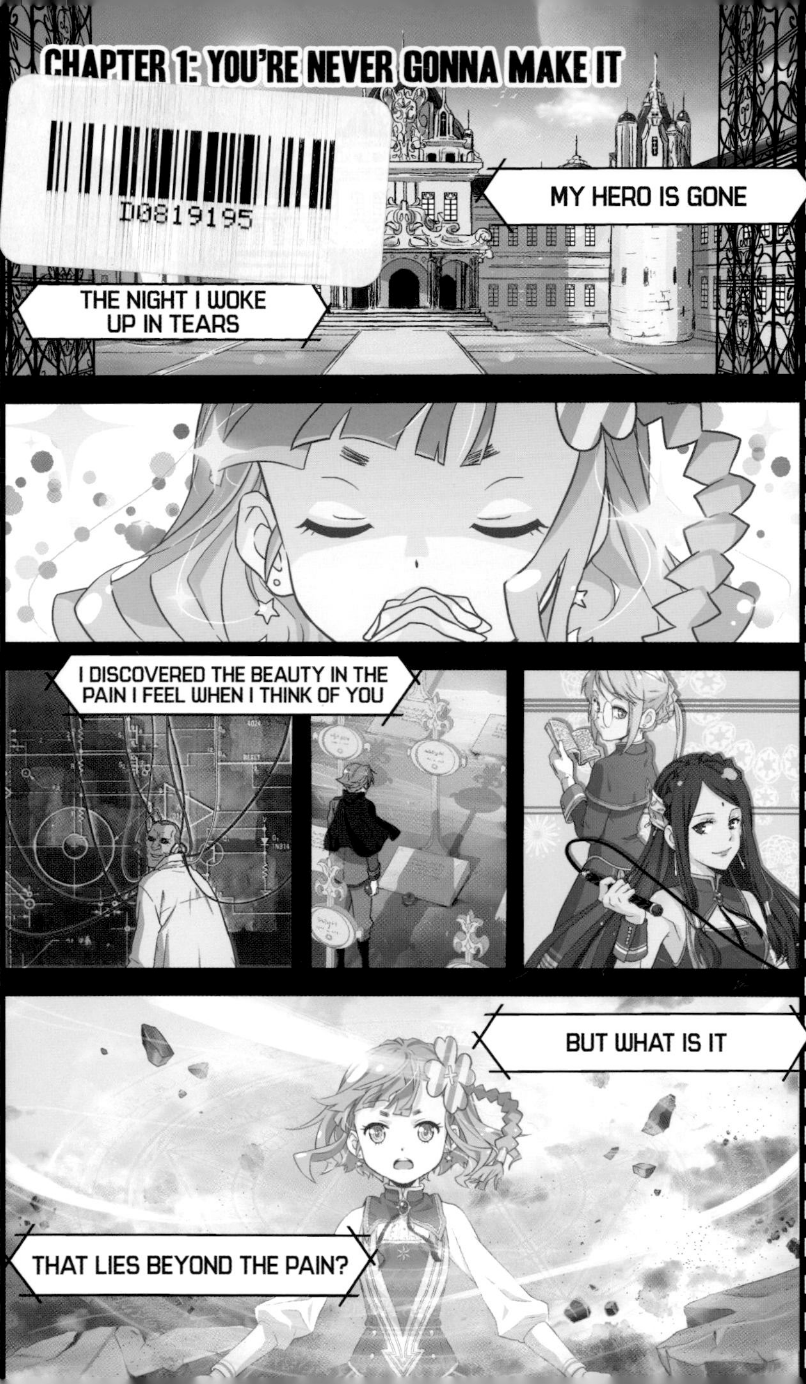
MY HERO IS GONE
THE NIGHT I WOKE UP IN TEARS
I DISCOVERED THE BEAUTY IN THE PAIN I FEEL WHEN I THINK OF YOU
BUT WHAT IS IT
THAT LIES BEYOND THE PAIN?

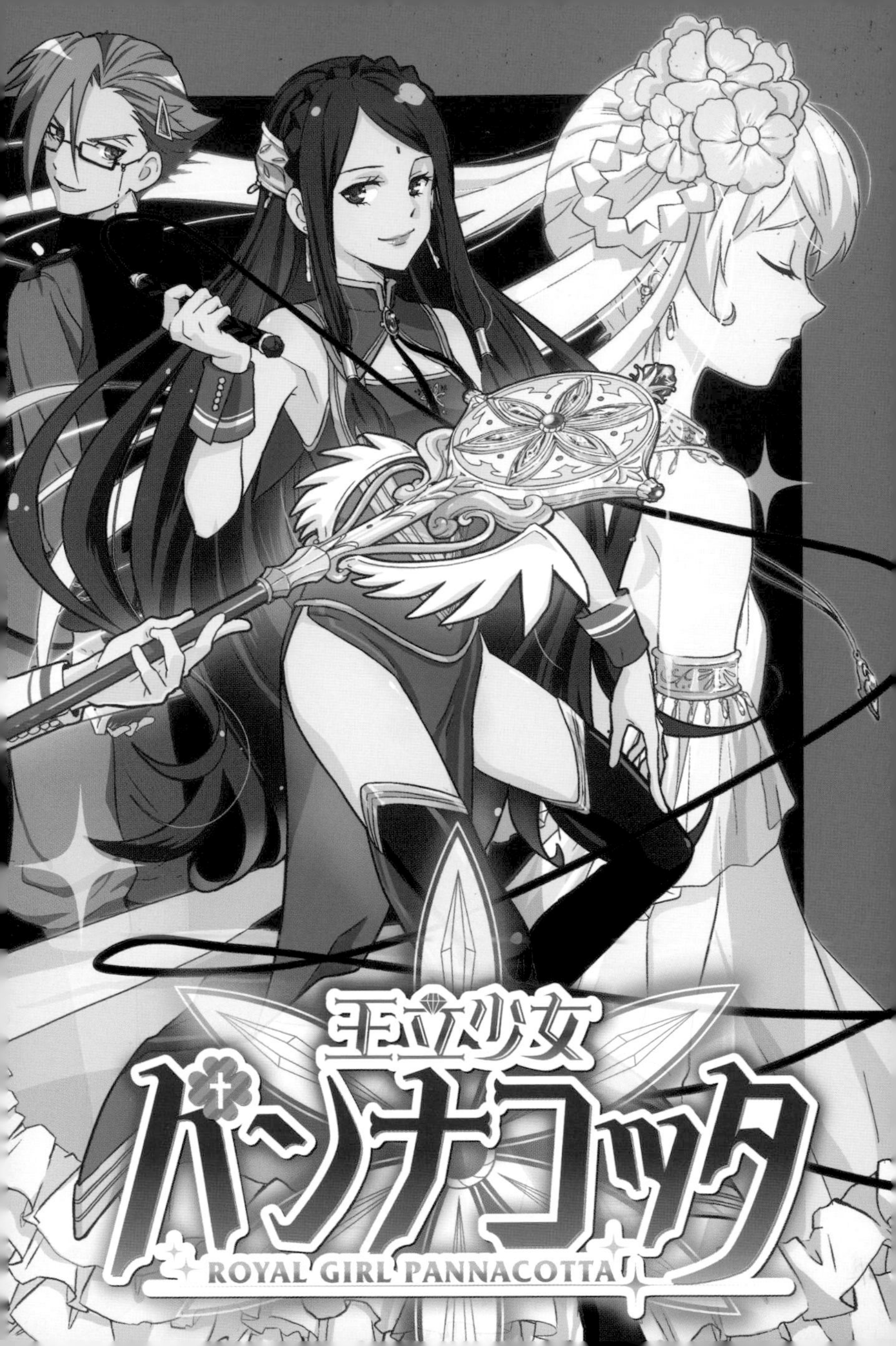

王立少女
パンナコッタ
ROYAL GIRL PANNACOTTA

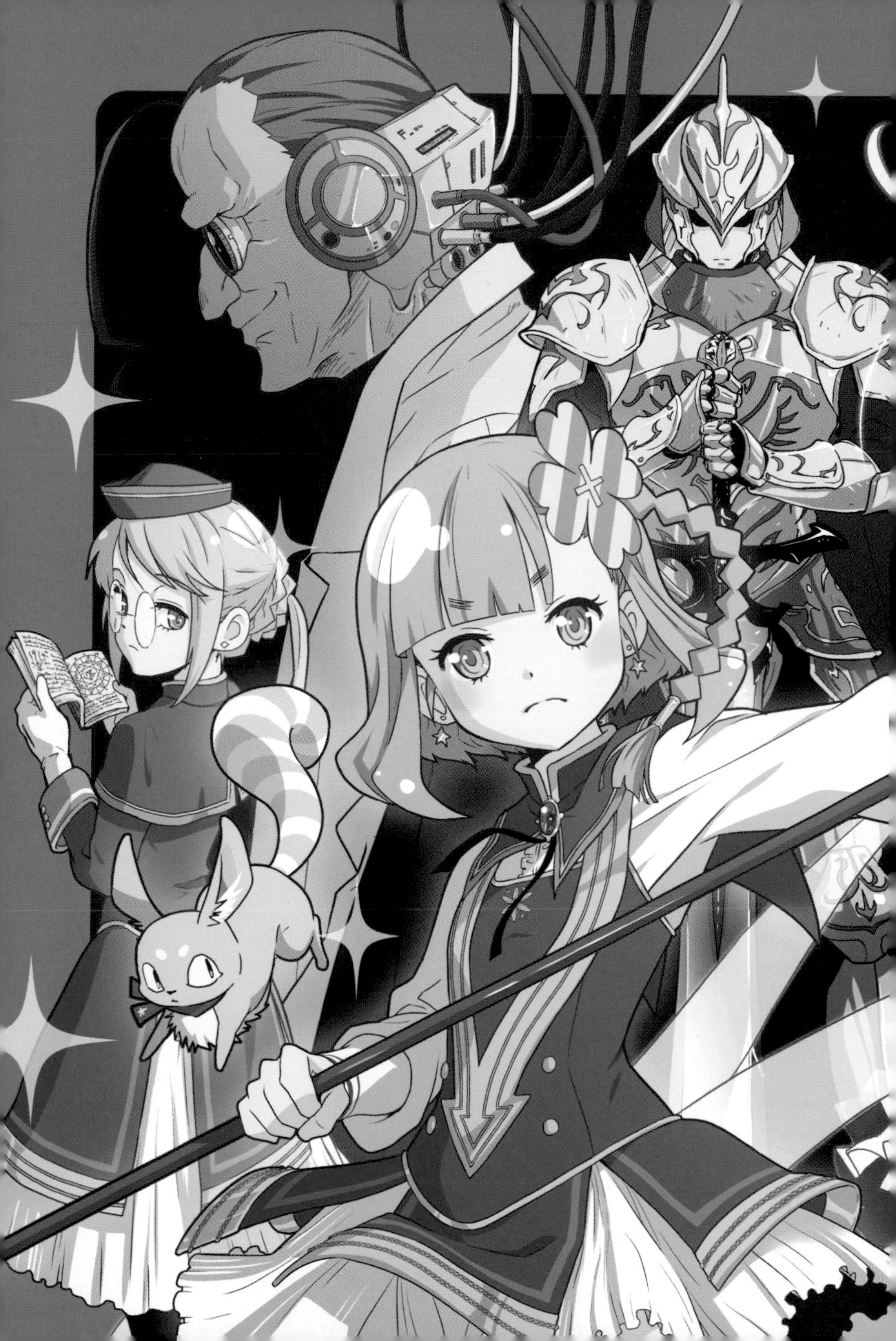

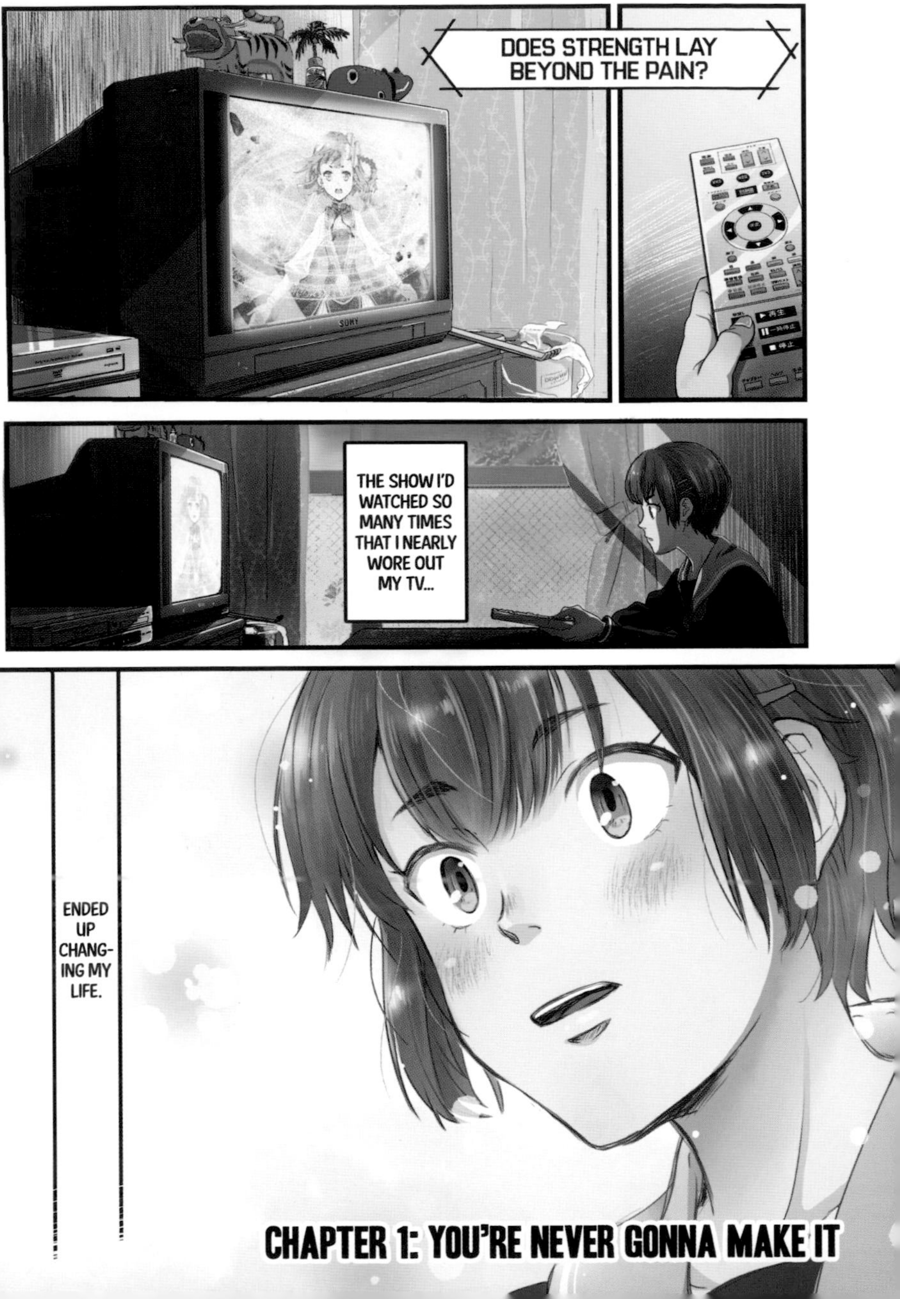
DOES STRENGTH LAY BEYOND THE PAIN?
THE SHOW I'D WATCHED SO MANY TIMES THAT I NEARLY WORE OUT MY TV...
ENDED UP CHANGING MY LIFE.

CHAPTER 1: YOU'RE NEVER GONNA MAKE IT

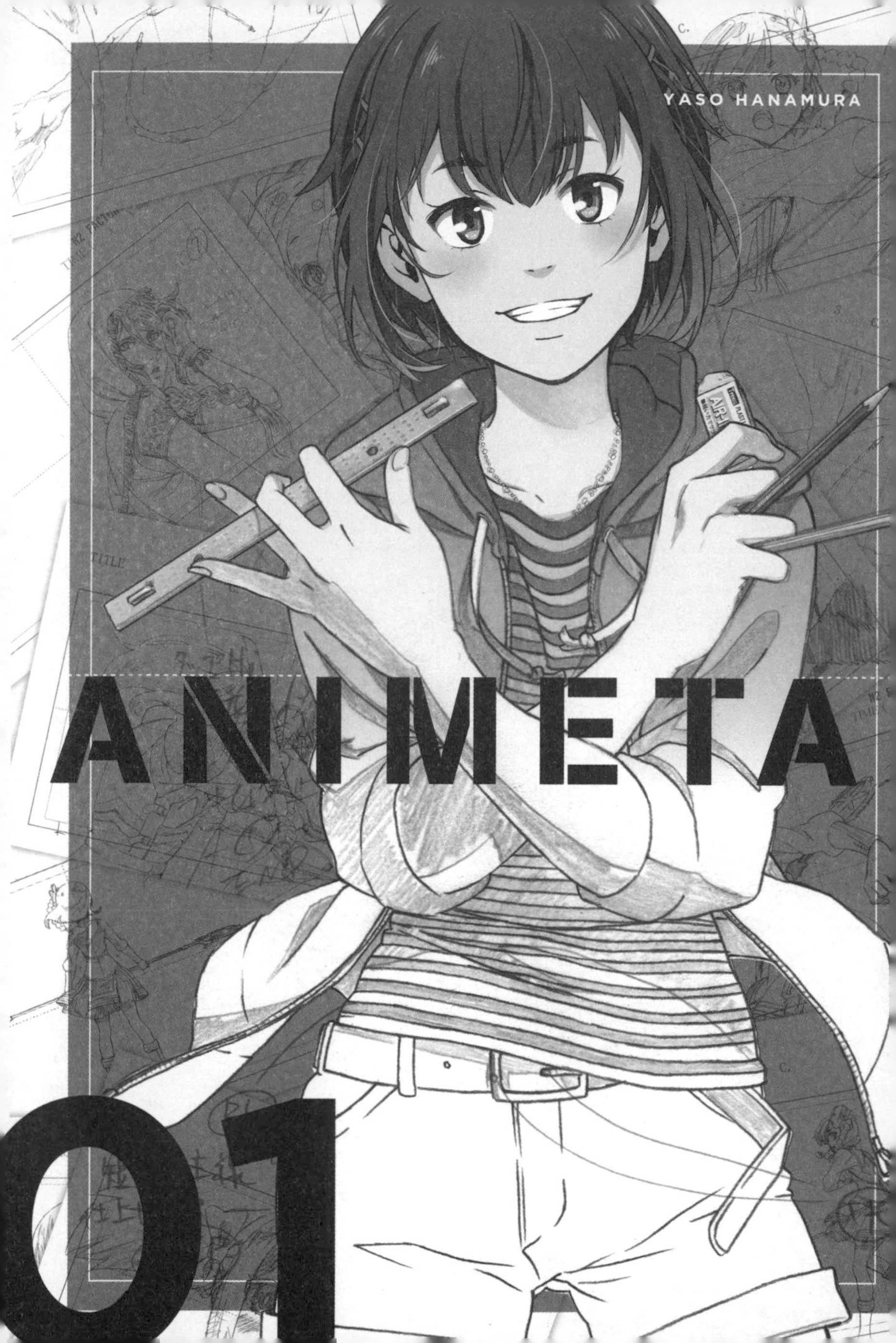
YASO HANAMURA
ANIMETA
01

ANIMETA!

YASO HANAMURA

01

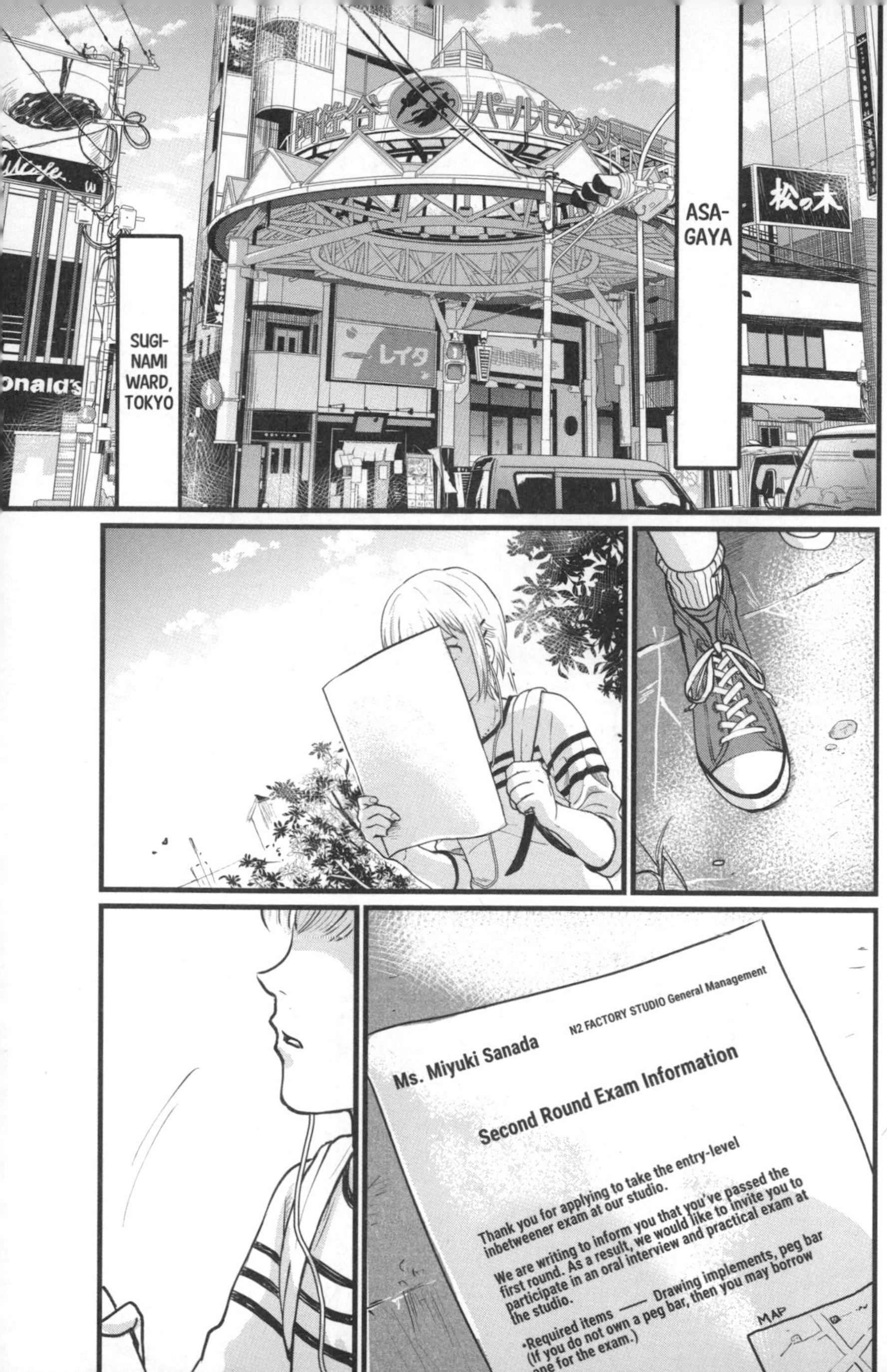
ASA-GAYA
SUGI-NAMI WARD, TOKYO
松の木
阿佐谷
N2 FACTORY STUDIO General Management
Ms. Miyuki Sanada
Second Round Exam Information
Thank you for applying to take the entry-level inbetweener exam at our studio.
We are writing to inform you that you've passed the first round. As a result, we would like to invite you to participate in an oral interview and practical exam at the studio.
•Required items —— Drawing implements, peg bar (If you do not own a peg bar, then you may borrow one for the exam.)
MAP

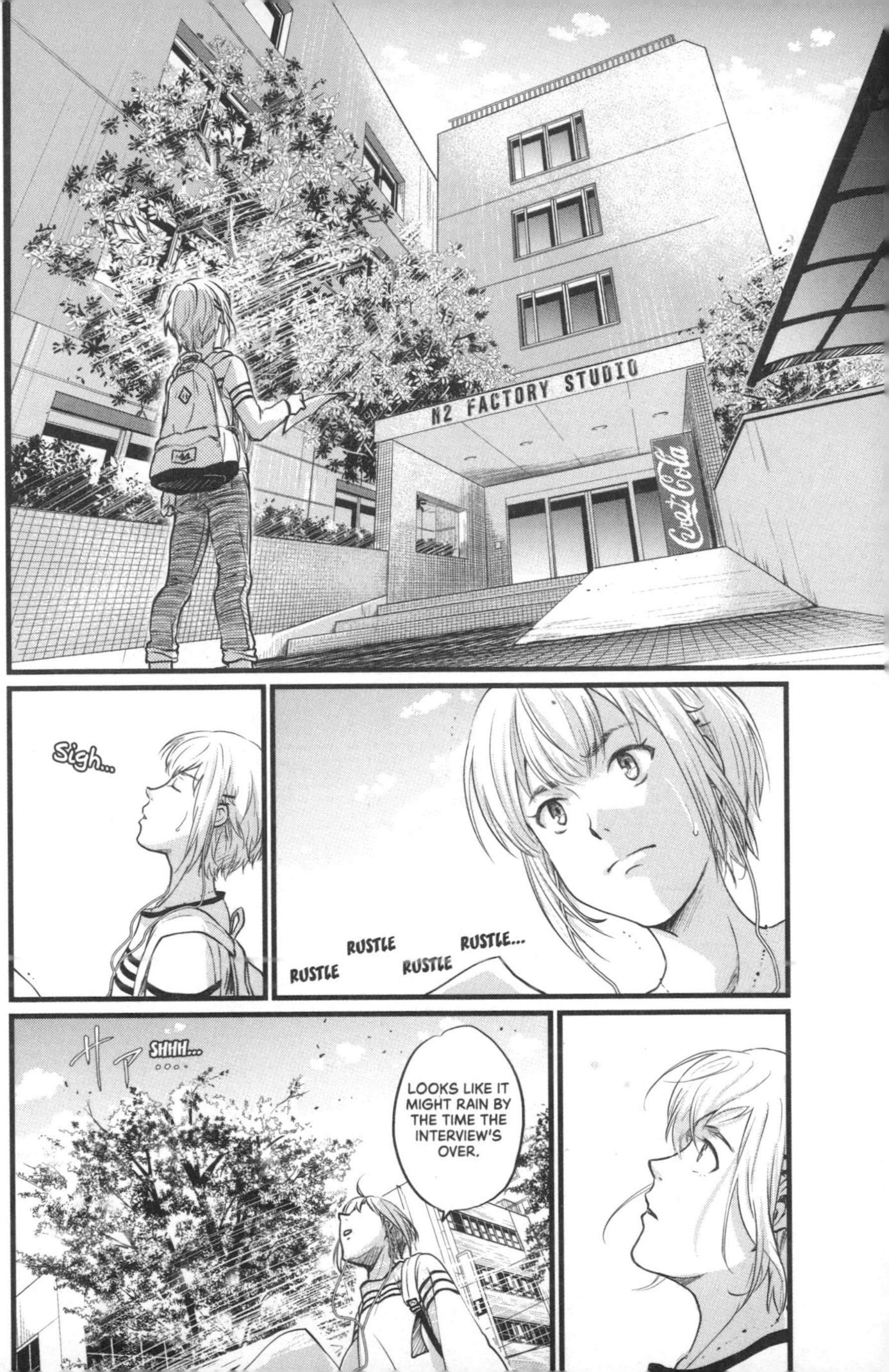
N2 FACTORY STUDIO
RUSTLE...
RUSTLE
RUSTLE
RUSTLE
Sigh...
サァ
SHHH...
LOOKS LIKE IT MIGHT RAIN BY THE TIME THE INTERVIEW'S OVER.

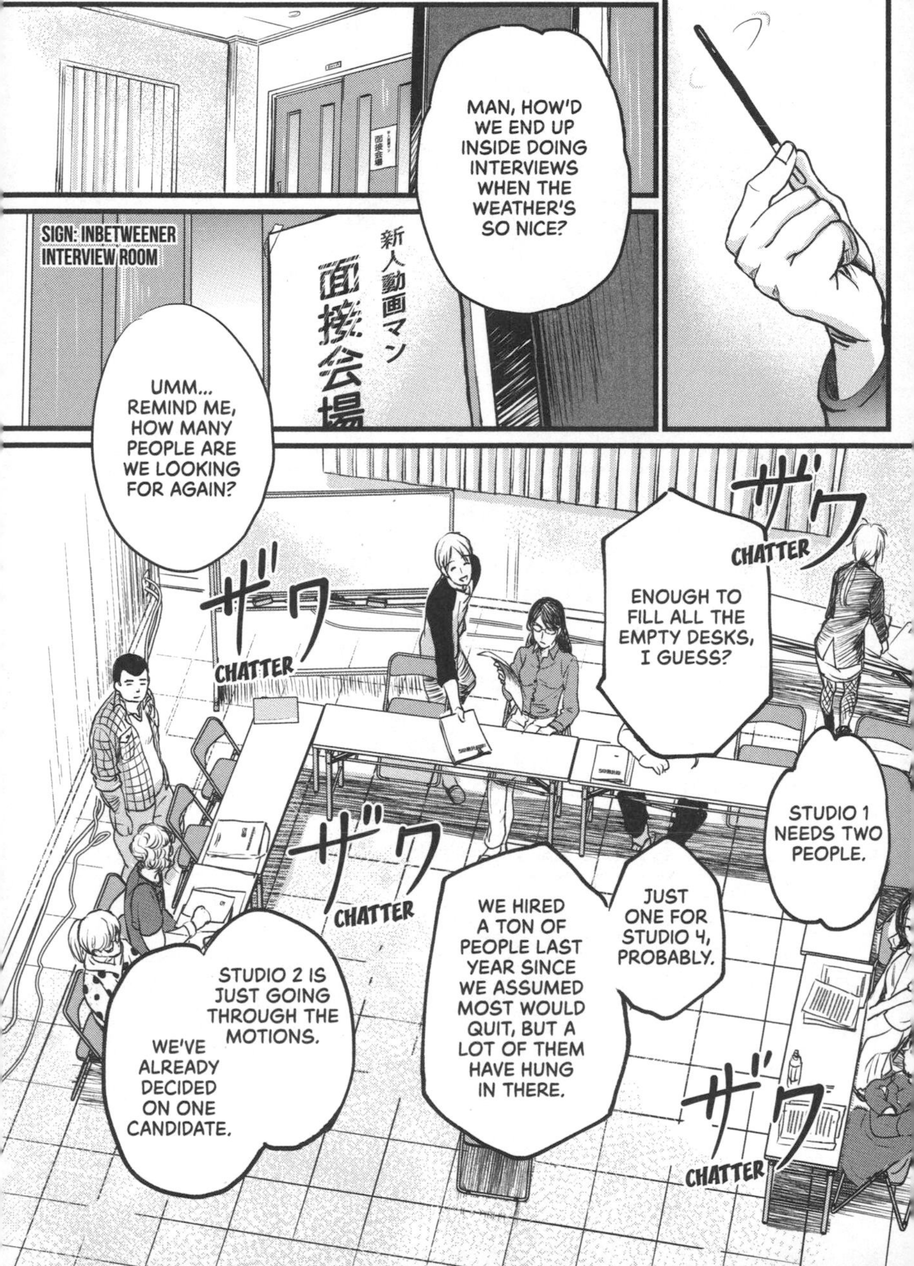
MAN, HOW'D WE END UP INSIDE DOING INTERVIEWS WHEN THE WEATHER'S SO NICE?
SIGN: INBETWEENER INTERVIEW ROOM
新人動画マン
面接会場
UMM... REMIND ME, HOW MANY PEOPLE ARE WE LOOKING FOR AGAIN?
ザワ
CHATTER
ENOUGH TO FILL ALL THE EMPTY DESKS, I GUESS?
ザワ
CHATTER
STUDIO 1 NEEDS TWO PEOPLE.
JUST ONE FOR STUDIO 4, PROBABLY.
ザワ
CHATTER
WE HIRED A TON OF PEOPLE LAST YEAR SINCE WE ASSUMED MOST WOULD QUIT, BUT A LOT OF THEM HAVE HUNG IN THERE.
ザワ
CHATTER
STUDIO 2 IS JUST GOING THROUGH THE MOTIONS.
WE'VE ALREADY DECIDED ON ONE CANDIDATE.

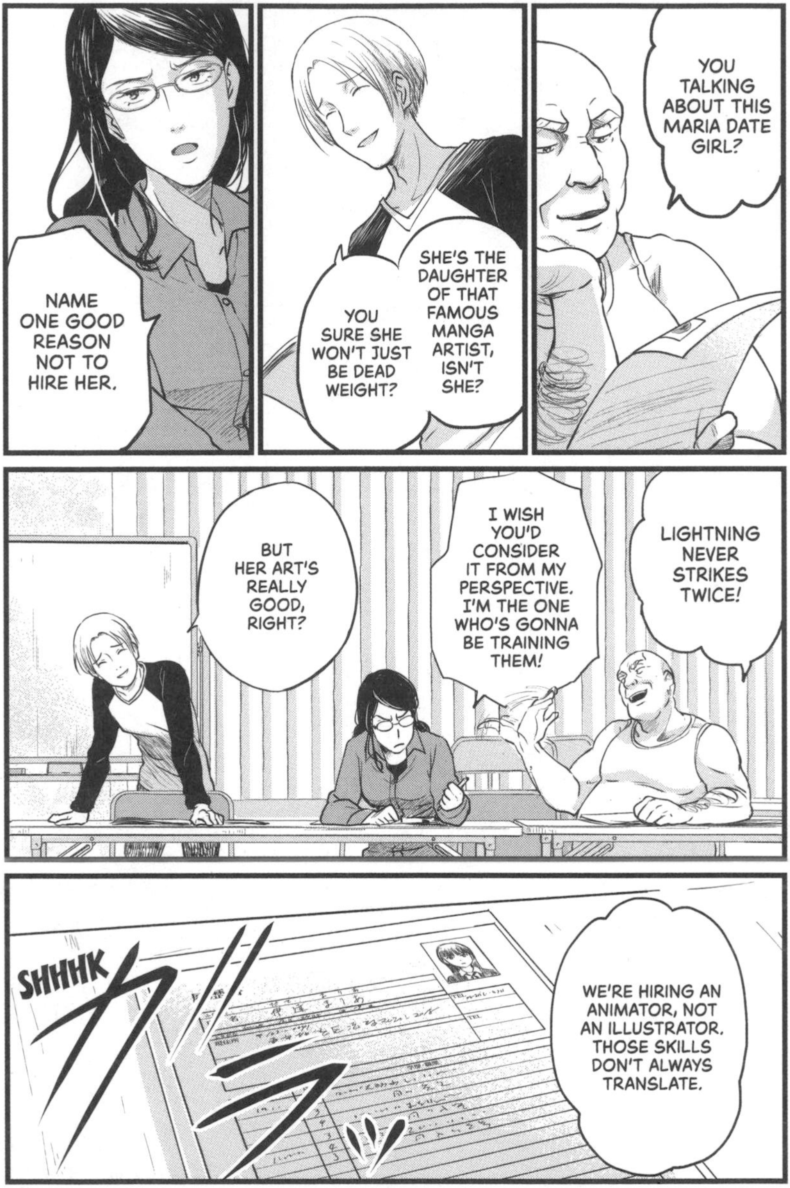
YOU TALKING ABOUT THIS MARIA DATE GIRL?
SHE'S THE DAUGHTER OF THAT FAMOUS MANGA ARTIST, ISN'T SHE?
YOU SURE SHE WON'T JUST BE DEAD WEIGHT?
NAME ONE GOOD REASON NOT TO HIRE HER.
LIGHTNING NEVER STRIKES TWICE!
I WISH YOU'D CONSIDER IT FROM MY PERSPECTIVE. I'M THE ONE WHO'S GONNA BE TRAINING THEM!
BUT HER ART'S REALLY GOOD, RIGHT?
WE'RE HIRING AN ANIMATOR, NOT AN ILLUSTRATOR. THOSE SKILLS DON'T ALWAYS TRANSLATE.
SHHHK

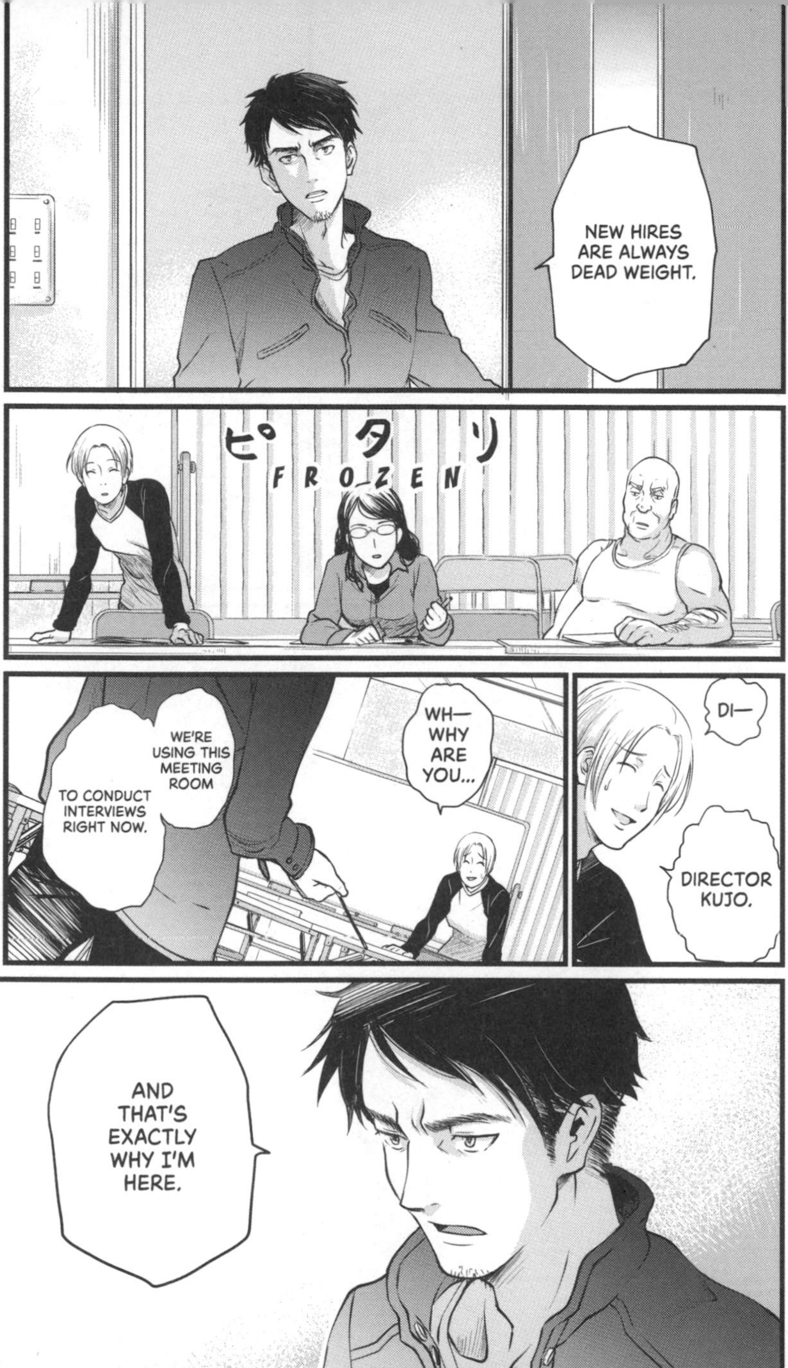
NEW HIRES ARE ALWAYS DEAD WEIGHT.
ピタリ
FROZEN
DI—
DIRECTOR KUJO.
WH— WHY ARE YOU...
WE'RE USING THIS MEETING ROOM
TO CONDUCT INTERVIEWS RIGHT NOW.
AND THAT'S EXACTLY WHY I'M HERE.

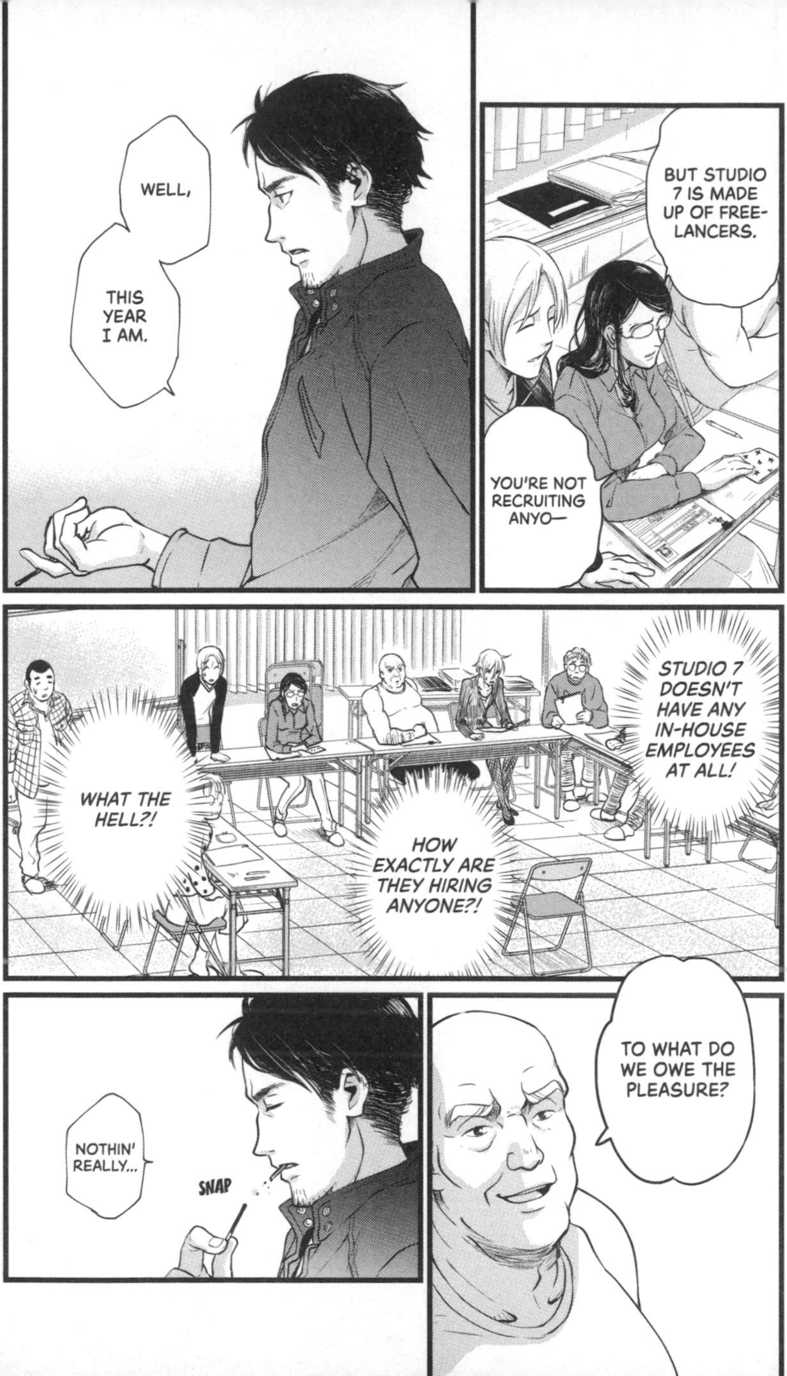
BUT STUDIO 7 IS MADE UP OF FREE-LANCERS.
YOU'RE NOT RECRUITING ANYO—
WELL,
THIS YEAR I AM.
STUDIO 7 DOESN'T HAVE ANY IN-HOUSE EMPLOYEES AT ALL!
HOW EXACTLY ARE THEY HIRING ANYONE?!
WHAT THE HELL?!
TO WHAT DO WE OWE THE PLEASURE?
NOTHIN' REALLY...
SNAP

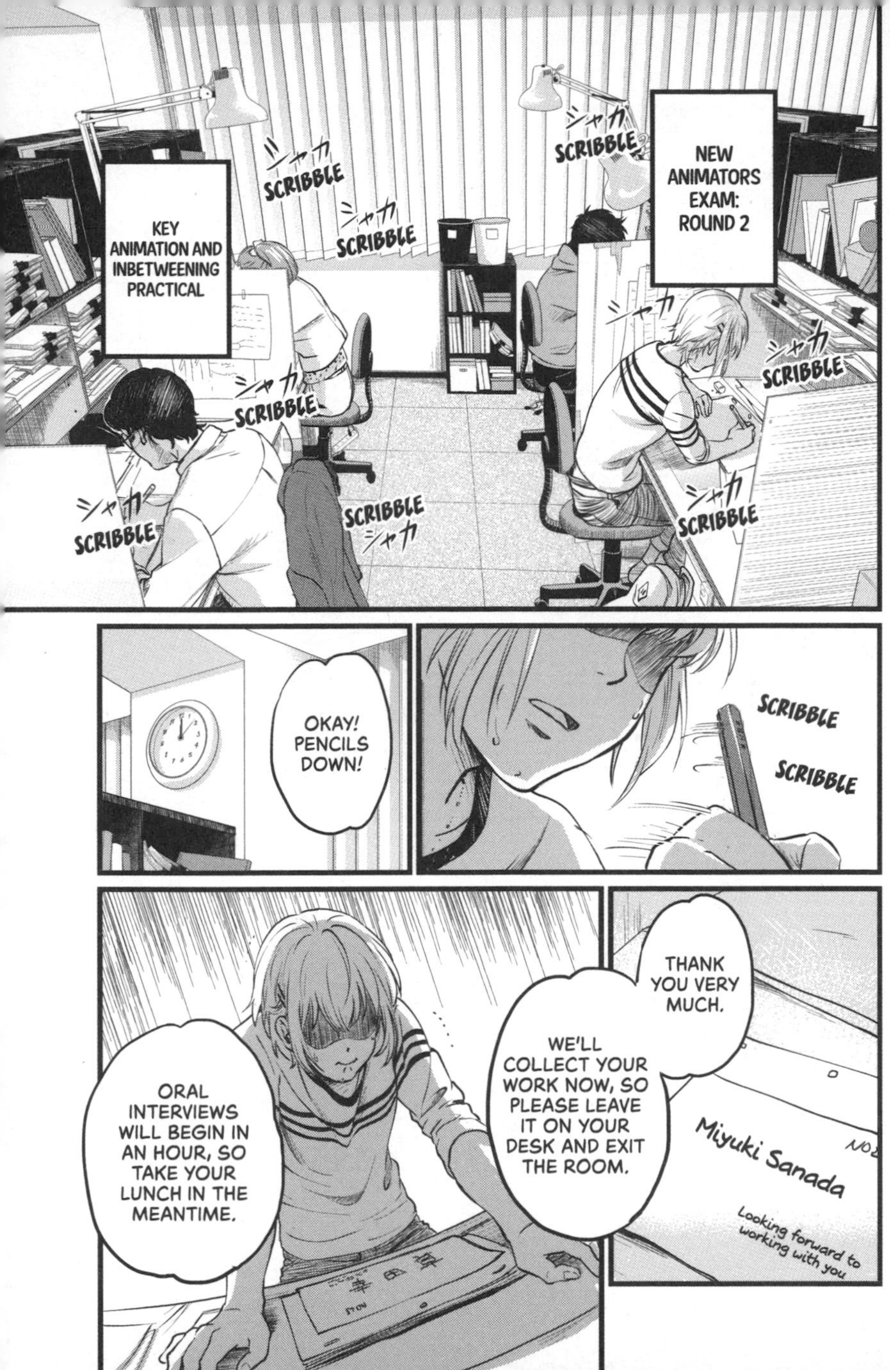
NEW ANIMATORS EXAM: ROUND 2
KEY ANIMATION AND INBETWEENING PRACTICAL
シャカ SCRIBBLE
シャカ SCRIBBLE
シャカ SCRIBBLE
シャカ SCRIBBLE
シャカ SCRIBBLE
シャカ SCRIBBLE
シャカ SCRIBBLE
SCRIBBLE シャカ
シャカ SCRIBBLE
SCRIBBLE
SCRIBBLE
OKAY! PENCILS DOWN!
THANK YOU VERY MUCH.
WE'LL COLLECT YOUR WORK NOW, SO PLEASE LEAVE IT ON YOUR DESK AND EXIT THE ROOM.
Miyuki Sanada
Looking forward to working with you
ORAL INTERVIEWS WILL BEGIN IN AN HOUR, SO TAKE YOUR LUNCH IN THE MEANTIME.

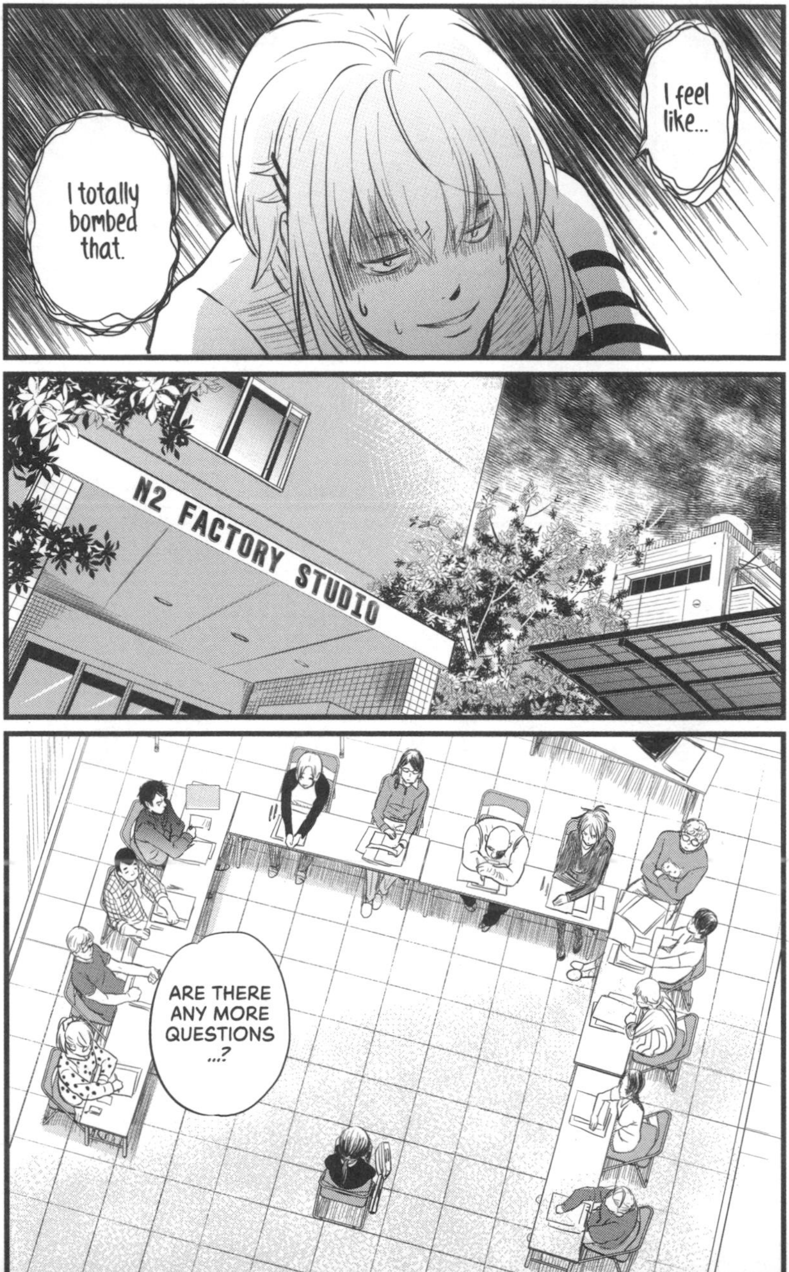
I feel like...
I totally bombed that.
N2 FACTORY STUDIO
ARE THERE ANY MORE QUESTIONS ...?

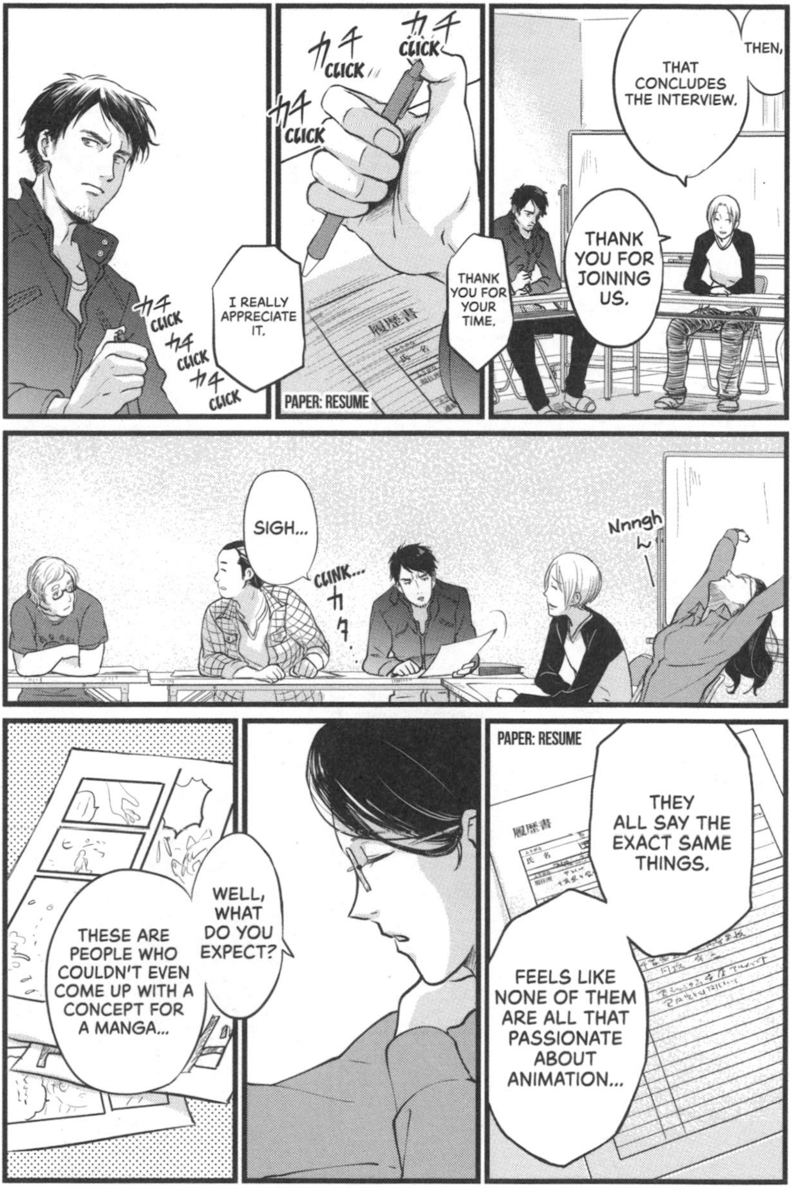
THEN,
THAT CONCLUDES THE INTERVIEW.
THANK YOU FOR JOINING US.
THANK YOU FOR YOUR TIME.
カチ CLICK
カチ CLICK
カチ CLICK
I REALLY APPRECIATE IT.
PAPER: RESUME
カチ CLICK
カチ CLICK
カチ CLICK
Nnngh ん
CLINK... カタ
SIGH...
PAPER: RESUME
THEY ALL SAY THE EXACT SAME THINGS.
FEELS LIKE NONE OF THEM ARE ALL THAT PASSIONATE ABOUT ANIMATION...
WELL, WHAT DO YOU EXPECT?
THESE ARE PEOPLE WHO COULDN'T EVEN COME UP WITH A CONCEPT FOR A MANGA...

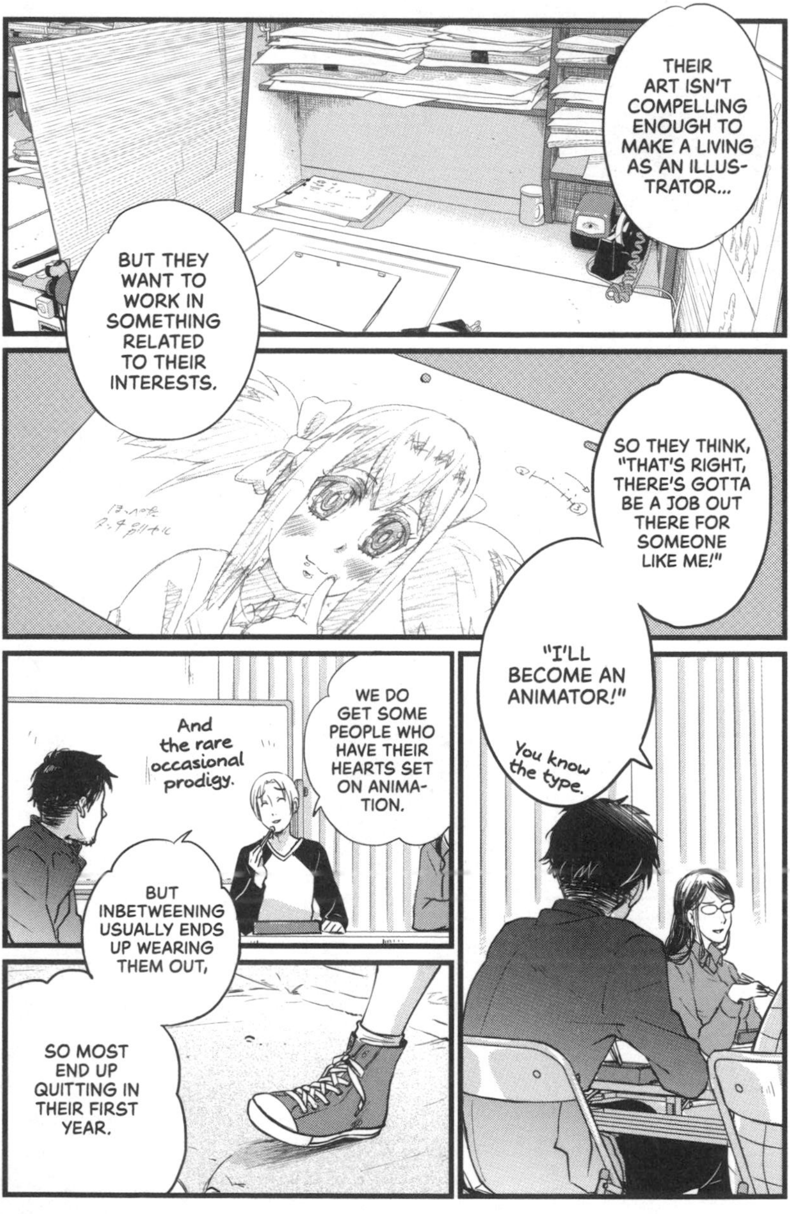
THEIR ART ISN'T COMPELLING ENOUGH TO MAKE A LIVING AS AN ILLUS-TRATOR...
BUT THEY WANT TO WORK IN SOMETHING RELATED TO THEIR INTERESTS.
SO THEY THINK, "THAT'S RIGHT, THERE'S GOTTA BE A JOB OUT THERE FOR SOMEONE LIKE ME!"
"I'LL BECOME AN ANIMATOR!"
You know the type.
WE DO GET SOME PEOPLE WHO HAVE THEIR HEARTS SET ON ANIMA-TION.
And the rare occasional prodigy.
BUT INBETWEENING USUALLY ENDS UP WEARING THEM OUT,
SO MOST END UP QUITTING IN THEIR FIRST YEAR.

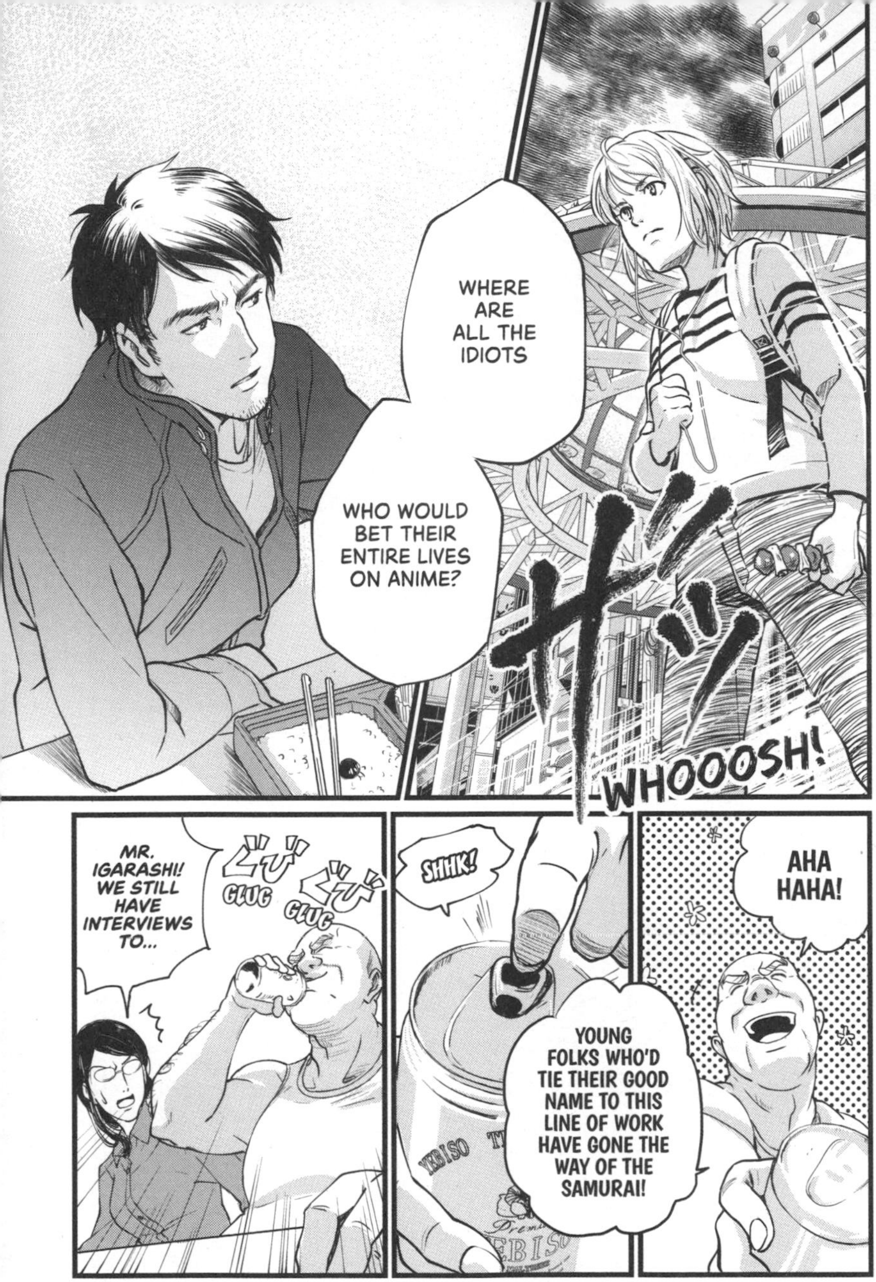
WHERE ARE ALL THE IDIOTS
WHO WOULD BET THEIR ENTIRE LIVES ON ANIME?
ザッ
WHOOOSH!
AHA HAHA!
YOUNG FOLKS WHO'D TIE THEIR GOOD NAME TO THIS LINE OF WORK HAVE GONE THE WAY OF THE SAMURAI!
SHHK!
MR. IGARASHI! WE STILL HAVE INTERVIEWS TO...
GLUG
GLUG

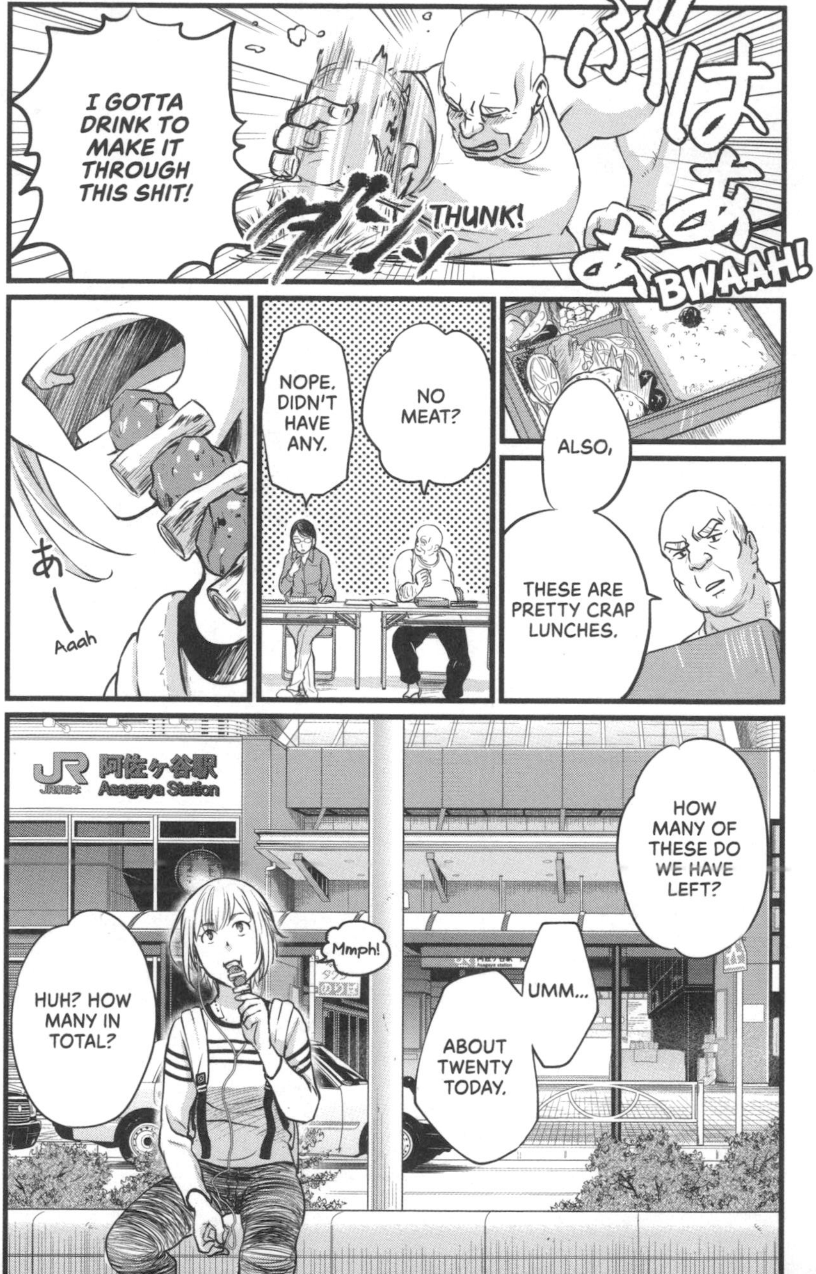
ぶはあぁ
BWAAH!
I GOTTA DRINK TO MAKE IT THROUGH THIS SHIT!
ダンッ
THUNK!
ALSO,
THESE ARE PRETTY CRAP LUNCHES.
NO MEAT?
NOPE. DIDN'T HAVE ANY.
あー
Aaah
HOW MANY OF THESE DO WE HAVE LEFT?
JR 阿佐ヶ谷駅
Asagaya Station
UMM...
ABOUT TWENTY TODAY.
Mmph!
HUH? HOW MANY IN TOTAL?

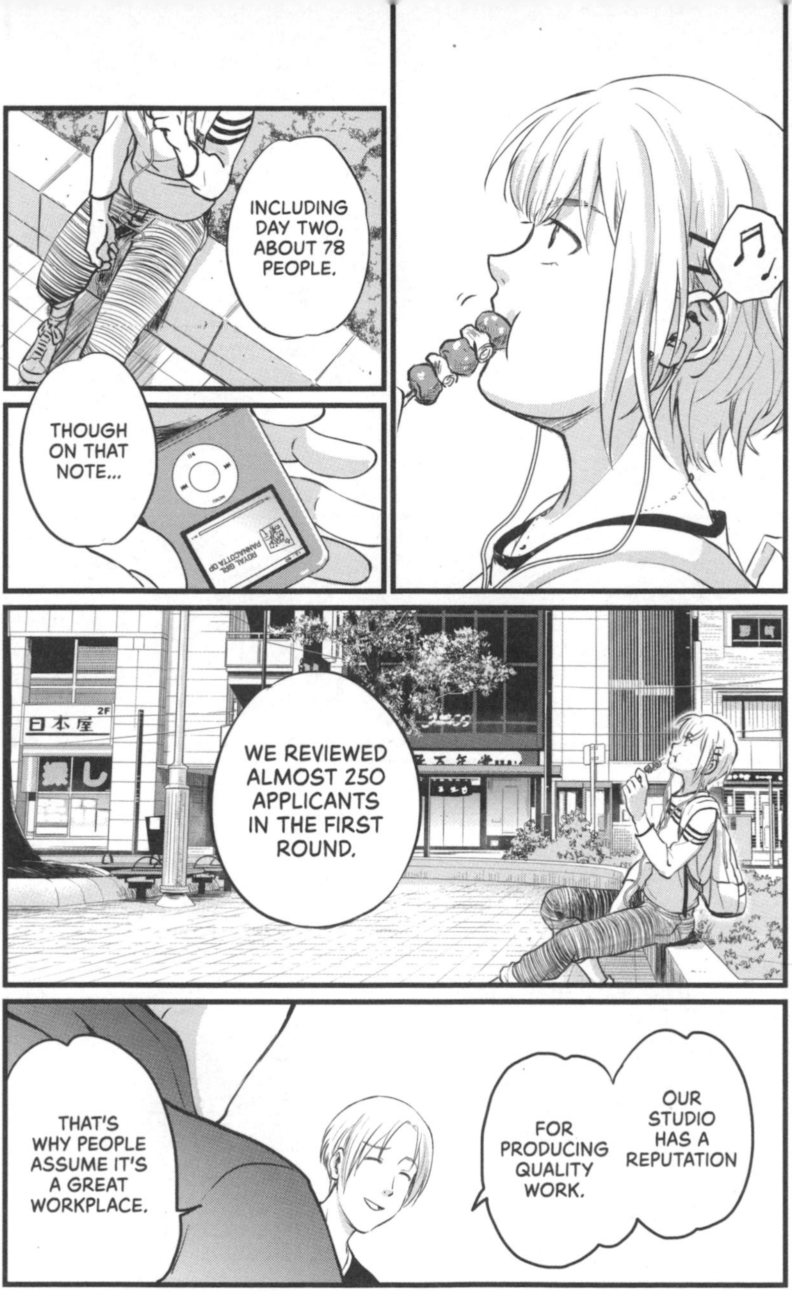
INCLUDING DAY TWO, ABOUT 78 PEOPLE.
THOUGH ON THAT NOTE...
WE REVIEWED ALMOST 250 APPLICANTS IN THE FIRST ROUND.
OUR STUDIO HAS A REPUTATION FOR PRODUCING QUALITY WORK.
THAT'S WHY PEOPLE ASSUME IT'S A GREAT WORKPLACE.

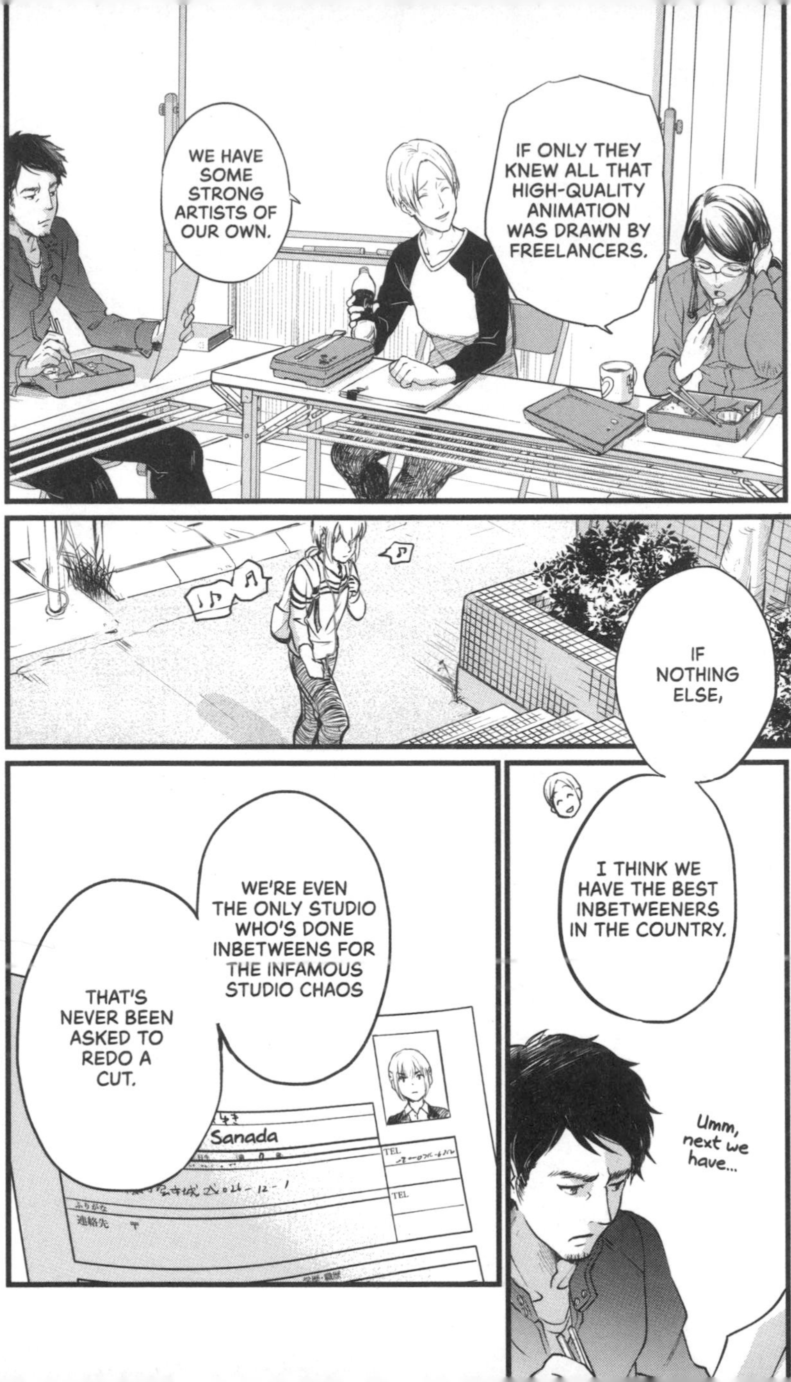
IF ONLY THEY KNEW ALL THAT HIGH-QUALITY ANIMATION WAS DRAWN BY FREELANCERS.
WE HAVE SOME STRONG ARTISTS OF OUR OWN.
IF NOTHING ELSE,
I THINK WE HAVE THE BEST INBETWEENERS IN THE COUNTRY.
Umm, next we have...
WE'RE EVEN THE ONLY STUDIO WHO'S DONE INBETWEENS FOR THE INFAMOUS STUDIO CHAOS
THAT'S NEVER BEEN ASKED TO REDO A CUT.
Sanada
TEL
TEL
ふりがな
連絡先 〒

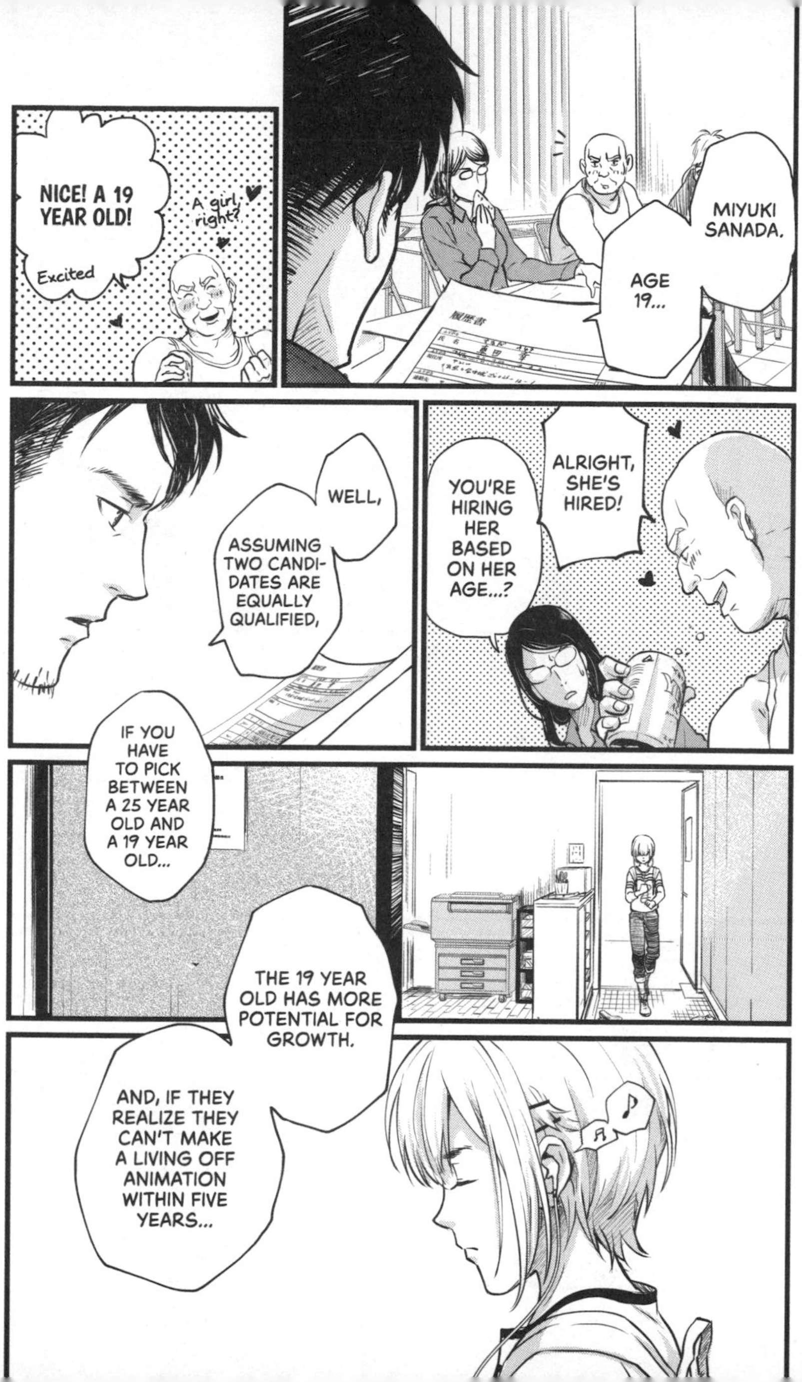
MIYUKI SANADA,
AGE 19...
NICE! A 19 YEAR OLD!
A girl, right?
Excited
ALRIGHT, SHE'S HIRED!
YOU'RE HIRING HER BASED ON HER AGE...?
WELL,
ASSUMING TWO CANDIDATES ARE EQUALLY QUALIFIED,
IF YOU HAVE TO PICK BETWEEN A 25 YEAR OLD AND A 19 YEAR OLD...
THE 19 YEAR OLD HAS MORE POTENTIAL FOR GROWTH.
AND, IF THEY REALIZE THEY CAN'T MAKE A LIVING OFF ANIMATION WITHIN FIVE YEARS...

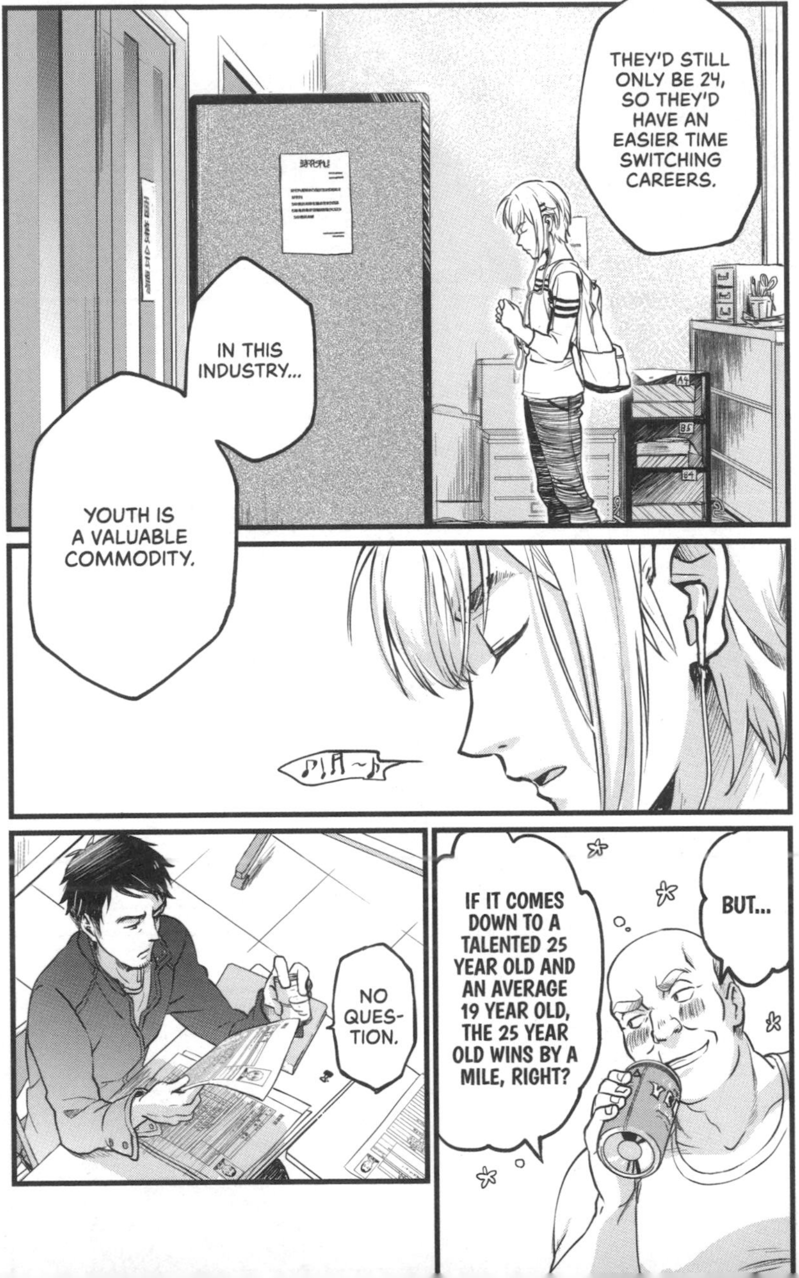
THEY'D STILL ONLY BE 24, SO THEY'D HAVE AN EASIER TIME SWITCHING CAREERS.
IN THIS INDUSTRY...
YOUTH IS A VALUABLE COMMODITY.
BUT...
IF IT COMES DOWN TO A TALENTED 25 YEAR OLD AND AN AVERAGE 19 YEAR OLD, THE 25 YEAR OLD WINS BY A MILE, RIGHT?
NO QUES-TION.

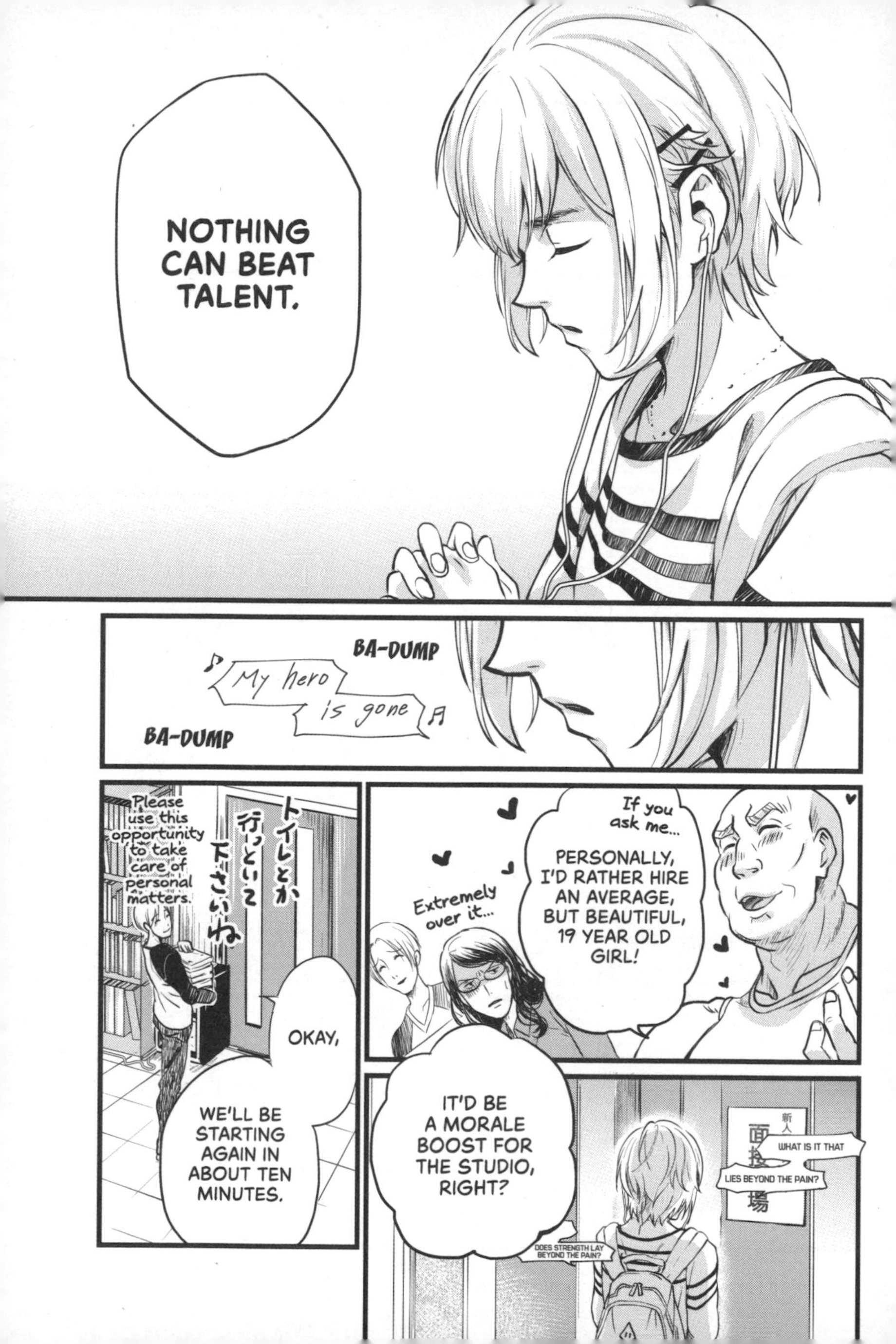
NOTHING CAN BEAT TALENT.
BA-DUMP
My hero is gone
BA-DUMP
If you ask me...
PERSONALLY, I'D RATHER HIRE AN AVERAGE, BUT BEAUTIFUL, 19 YEAR OLD GIRL!
Extremely over it...
IT'D BE A MORALE BOOST FOR THE STUDIO, RIGHT?
新人
面接場
WHAT IS IT THAT
LIES BEYOND THE PAIN?
DOES STRENGTH LAY BEYOND THE PAIN?
Please use this opportunity to take care of personal matters.
トイレとか行っといて下さいね
OKAY,
WE'LL BE STARTING AGAIN IN ABOUT TEN MINUTES.

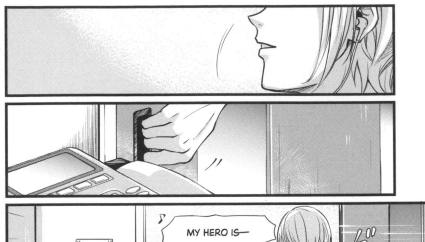

MY HERO IS—

GONE!

SHHK

THE NIGHT... I...

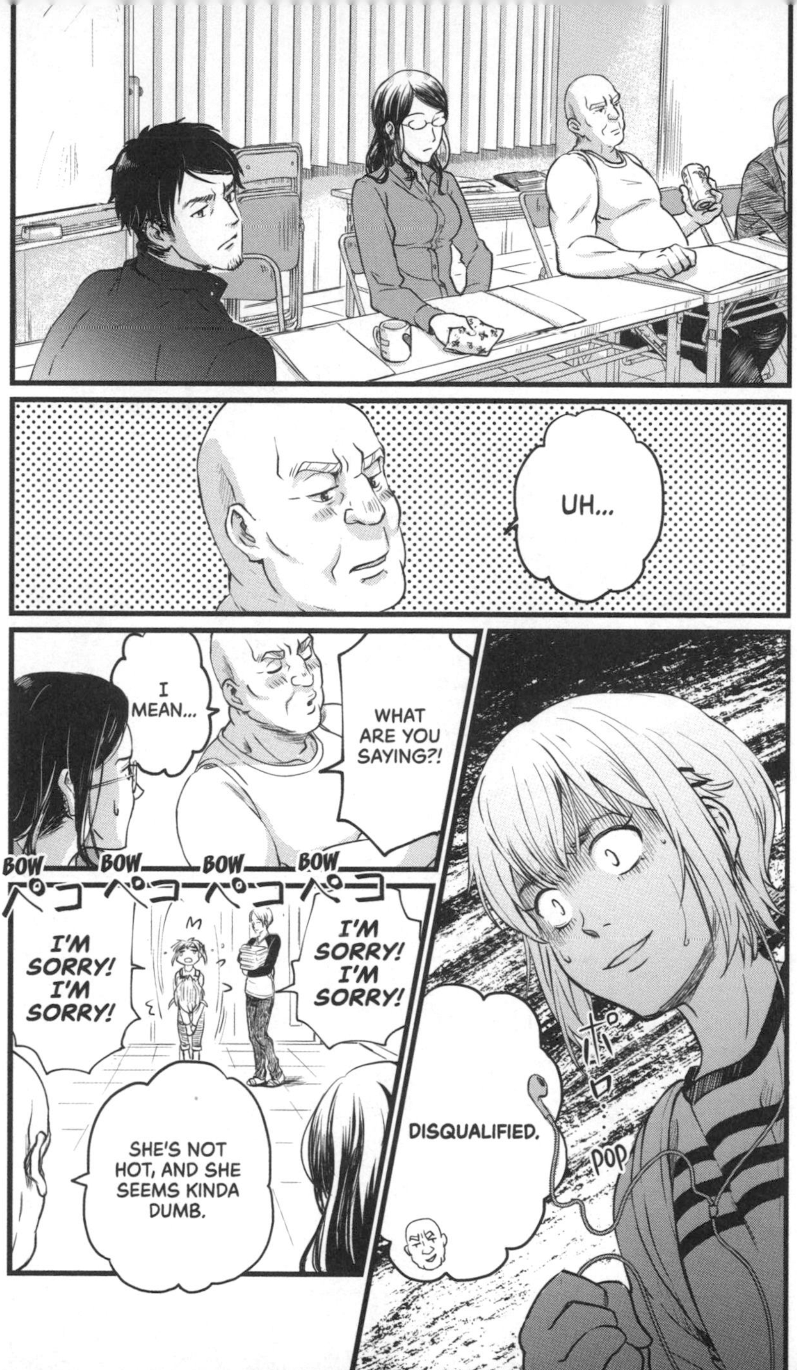

UH...
DISQUALIFIED.
ポロ
POP
WHAT ARE YOU SAYING?!
I MEAN...
BOW BOW BOW BOW
ペコ ペコ ペコ ペコ
I'M SORRY! I'M SORRY!
I'M SORRY! I'M SORRY!
SHE'S NOT HOT, AND SHE SEEMS KINDA DUMB.

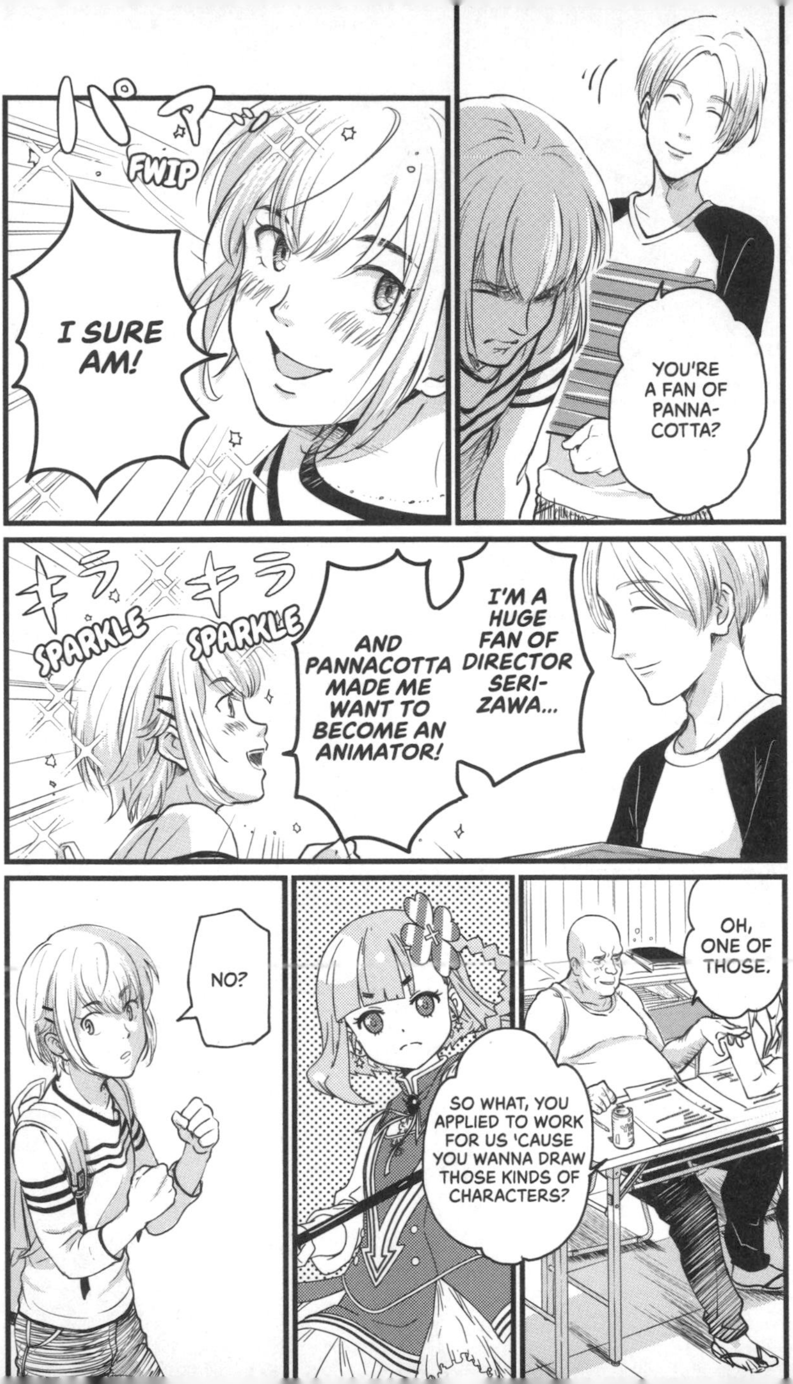

YOU'RE A FAN OF PANNA-COTTA?
パア
FWIP
I SURE AM!
I'M A HUGE FAN OF DIRECTOR SERI-ZAWA...
AND PANNACOTTA MADE ME WANT TO BECOME AN ANIMATOR!
キラ
SPARKLE
キラ
SPARKLE
OH, ONE OF THOSE.
SO WHAT, YOU APPLIED TO WORK FOR US 'CAUSE YOU WANNA DRAW THOSE KINDS OF CHARACTERS?
NO?

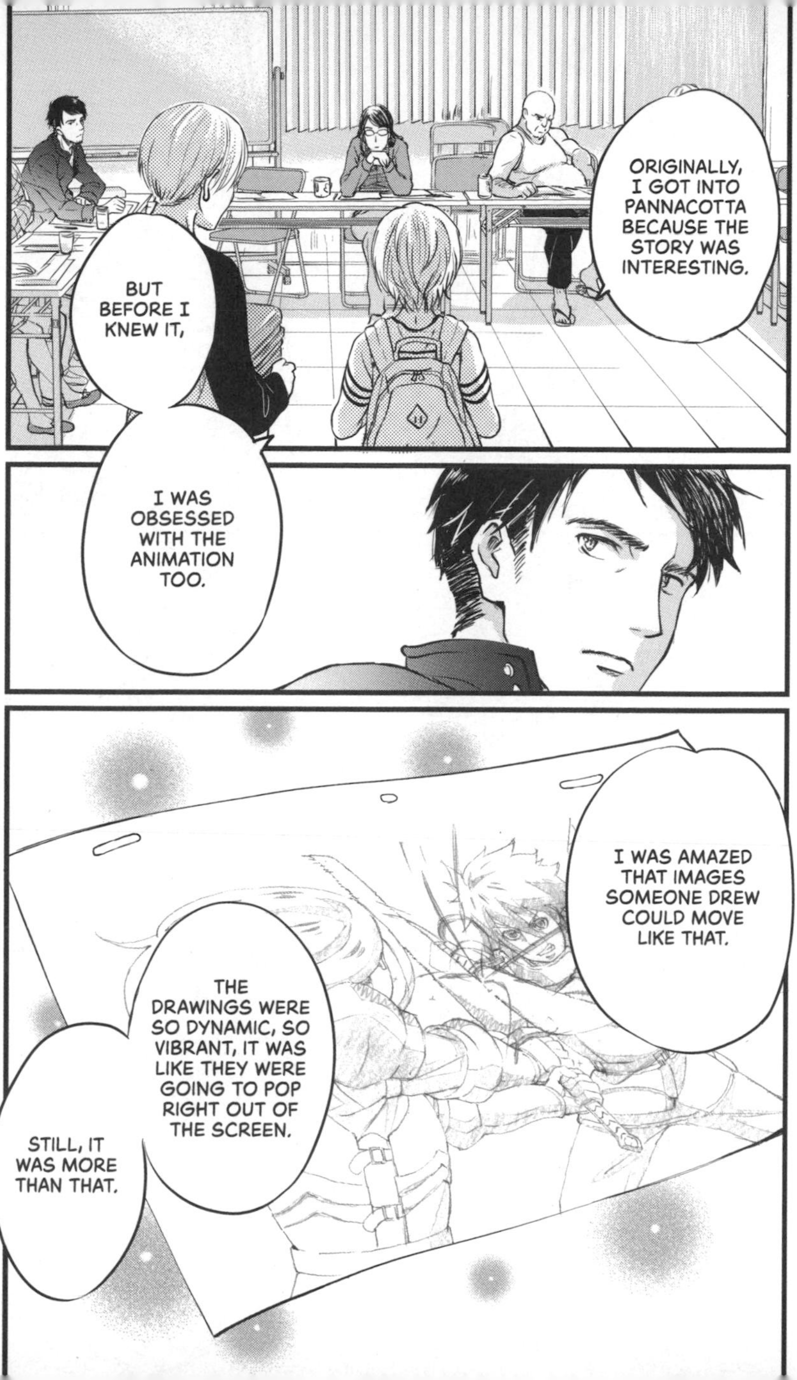
ORIGINALLY, I GOT INTO PANNACOTTA BECAUSE THE STORY WAS INTERESTING.
BUT BEFORE I KNEW IT,
I WAS OBSESSED WITH THE ANIMATION TOO.
I WAS AMAZED THAT IMAGES SOMEONE DREW COULD MOVE LIKE THAT.
THE DRAWINGS WERE SO DYNAMIC, SO VIBRANT, IT WAS LIKE THEY WERE GOING TO POP RIGHT OUT OF THE SCREEN.
STILL, IT WAS MORE THAN THAT.

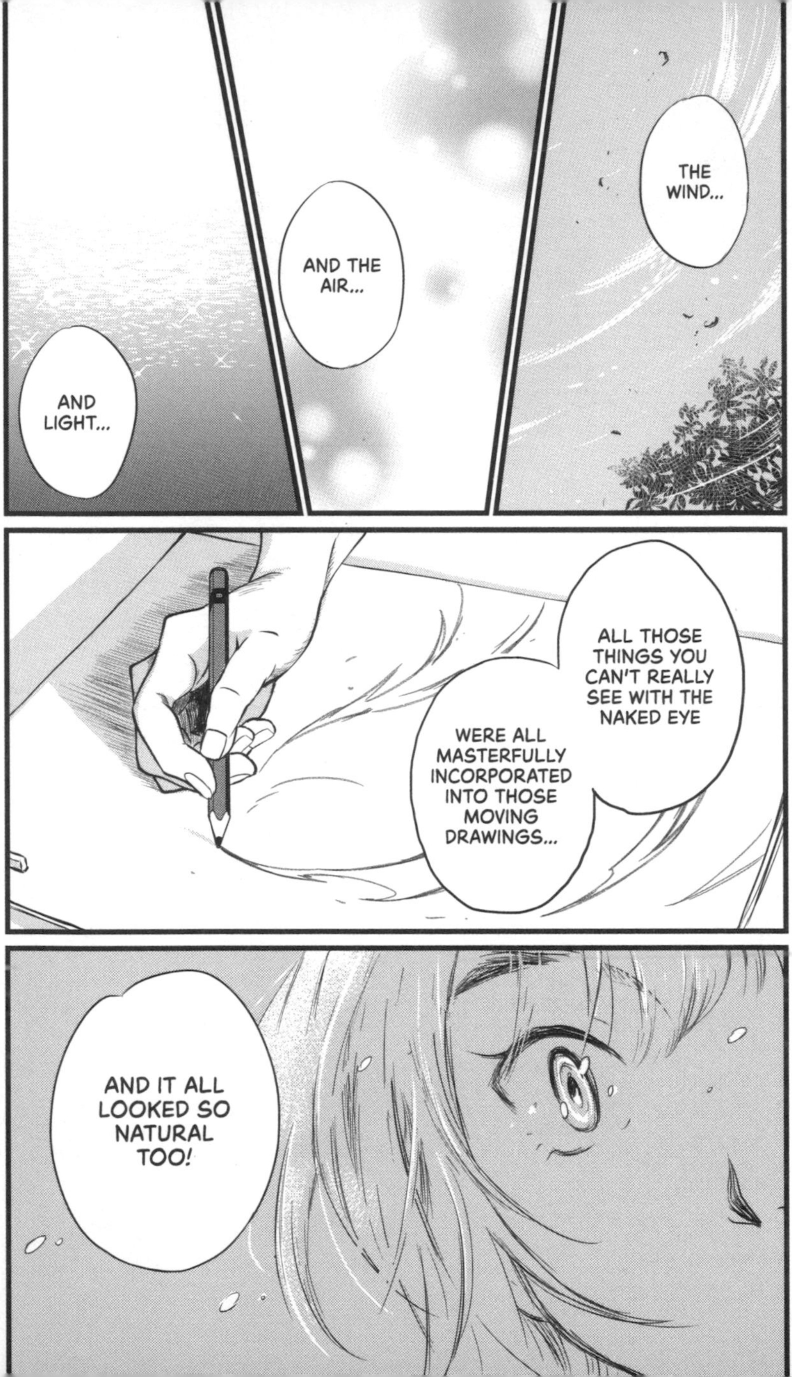
THE WIND...
AND THE AIR...
AND LIGHT...
ALL THOSE THINGS YOU CAN'T REALLY SEE WITH THE NAKED EYE
WERE ALL MASTERFULLY INCORPORATED INTO THOSE MOVING DRAWINGS...
AND IT ALL LOOKED SO NATURAL TOO!

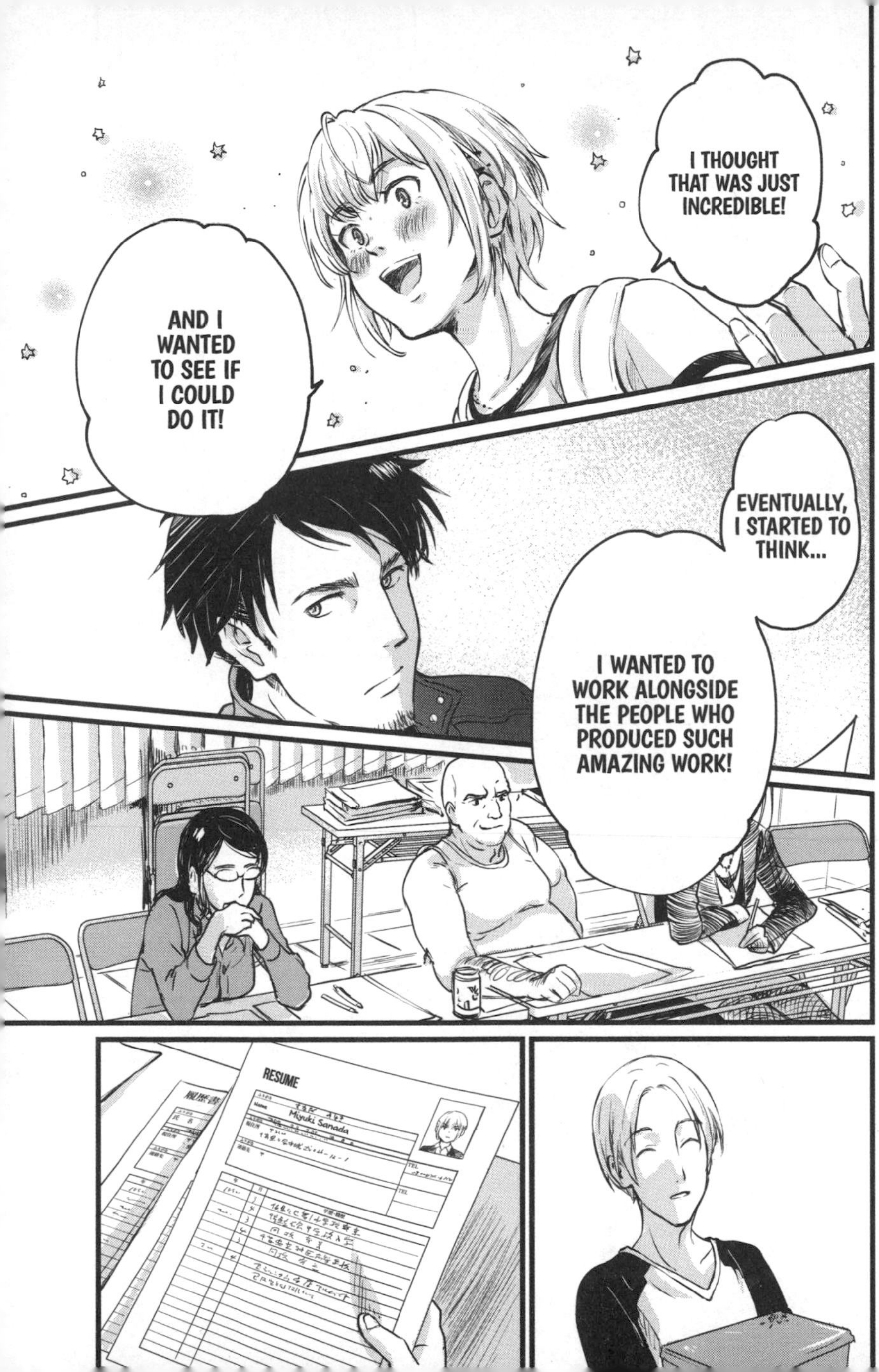
I THOUGHT THAT WAS JUST INCREDIBLE!
AND I WANTED TO SEE IF I COULD DO IT!
EVENTUALLY, I STARTED TO THINK...
I WANTED TO WORK ALONGSIDE THE PEOPLE WHO PRODUCED SUCH AMAZING WORK!
RESUME
Miyuki Sanada
TEL
TEL

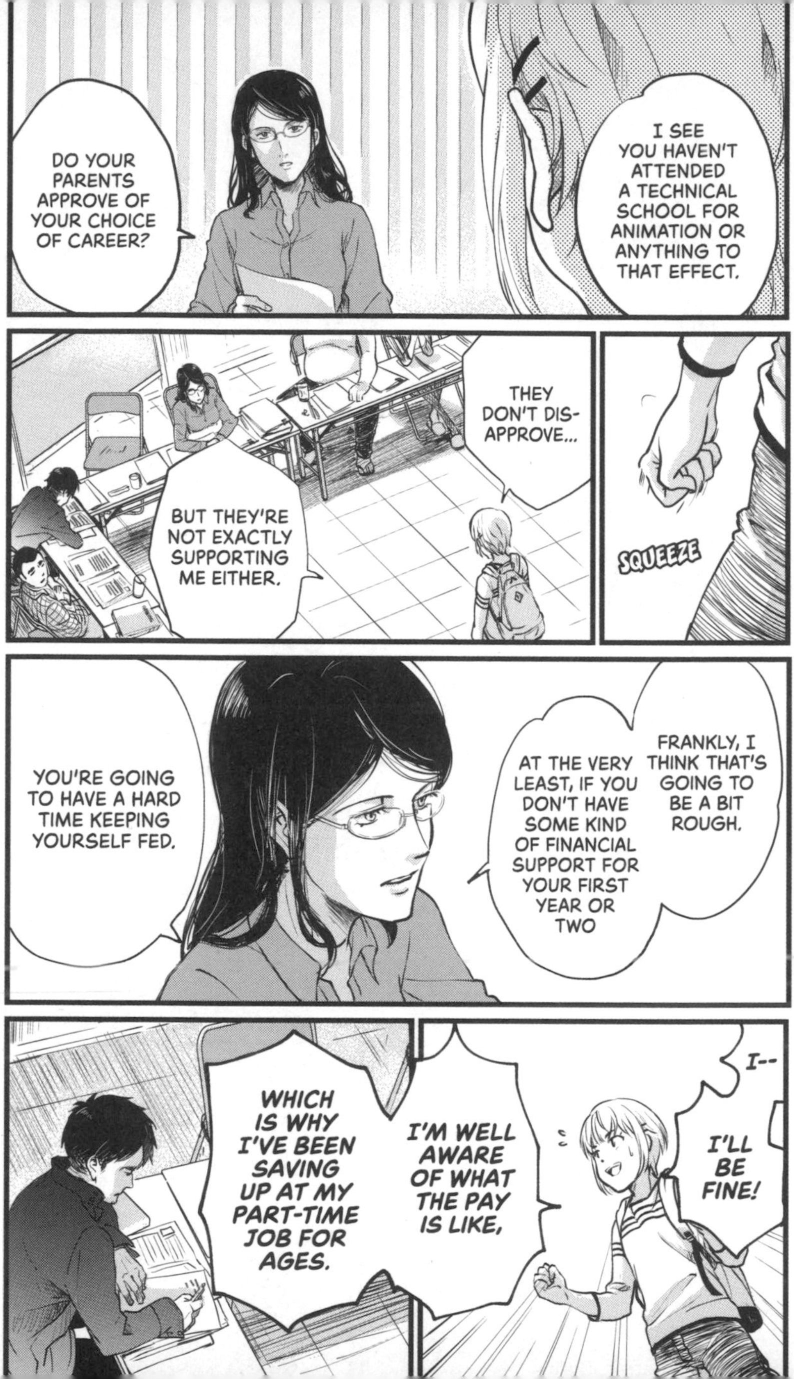
I SEE YOU HAVEN'T ATTENDED A TECHNICAL SCHOOL FOR ANIMATION OR ANYTHING TO THAT EFFECT.
DO YOUR PARENTS APPROVE OF YOUR CHOICE OF CAREER?
SQUEEZE
THEY DON'T DIS-APPROVE...
BUT THEY'RE NOT EXACTLY SUPPORTING ME EITHER.
FRANKLY, I THINK THAT'S GOING TO BE A BIT ROUGH.
AT THE VERY LEAST, IF YOU DON'T HAVE SOME KIND OF FINANCIAL SUPPORT FOR YOUR FIRST YEAR OR TWO
YOU'RE GOING TO HAVE A HARD TIME KEEPING YOURSELF FED.
I--
I'LL BE FINE!
I'M WELL AWARE OF WHAT THE PAY IS LIKE,
WHICH IS WHY I'VE BEEN SAVING UP AT MY PART-TIME JOB FOR AGES.

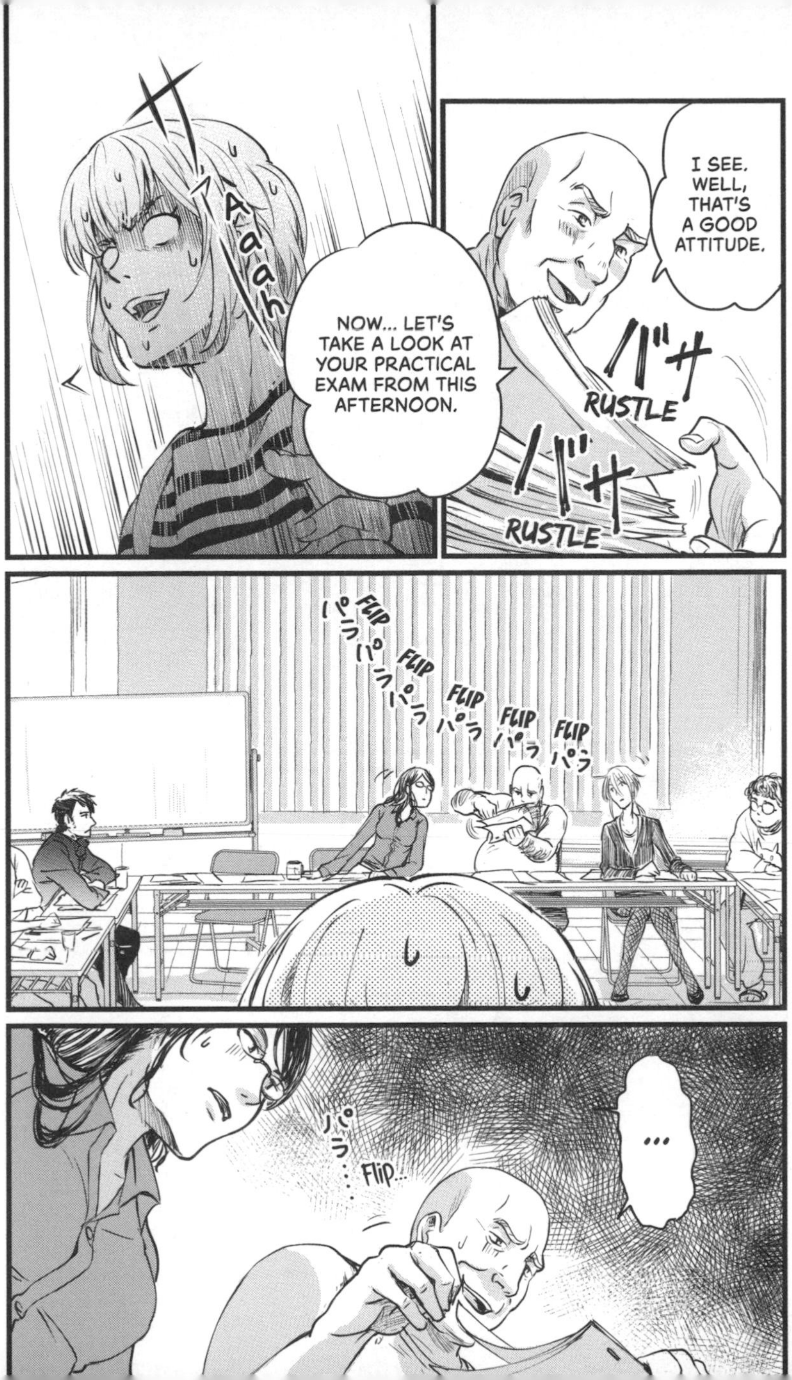

I SEE. WELL, THAT'S A GOOD ATTITUDE.
NOW... LET'S TAKE A LOOK AT YOUR PRACTICAL EXAM FROM THIS AFTERNOON.
バサ
RUSTLE
バサ
RUSTLE
Aaah
FLIP
パラ
FLIP
パラ
FLIP
パラ
FLIP
パラ
FLIP
パラ
パラ
...
パラ...
Flip...

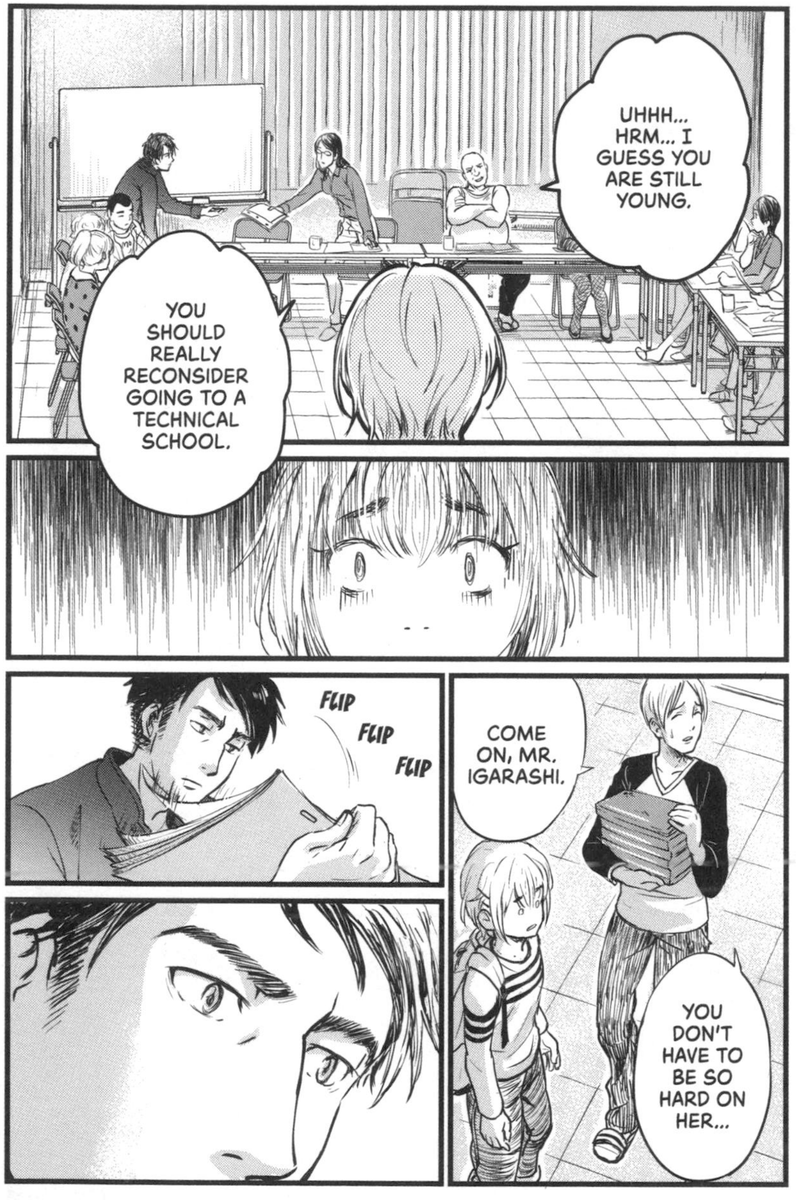
UHHH... HRM... I GUESS YOU ARE STILL YOUNG.
YOU SHOULD REALLY RECONSIDER GOING TO A TECHNICAL SCHOOL.
COME ON, MR. IGARASHI.
YOU DON'T HAVE TO BE SO HARD ON HER...
FLIP
FLIP
FLIP

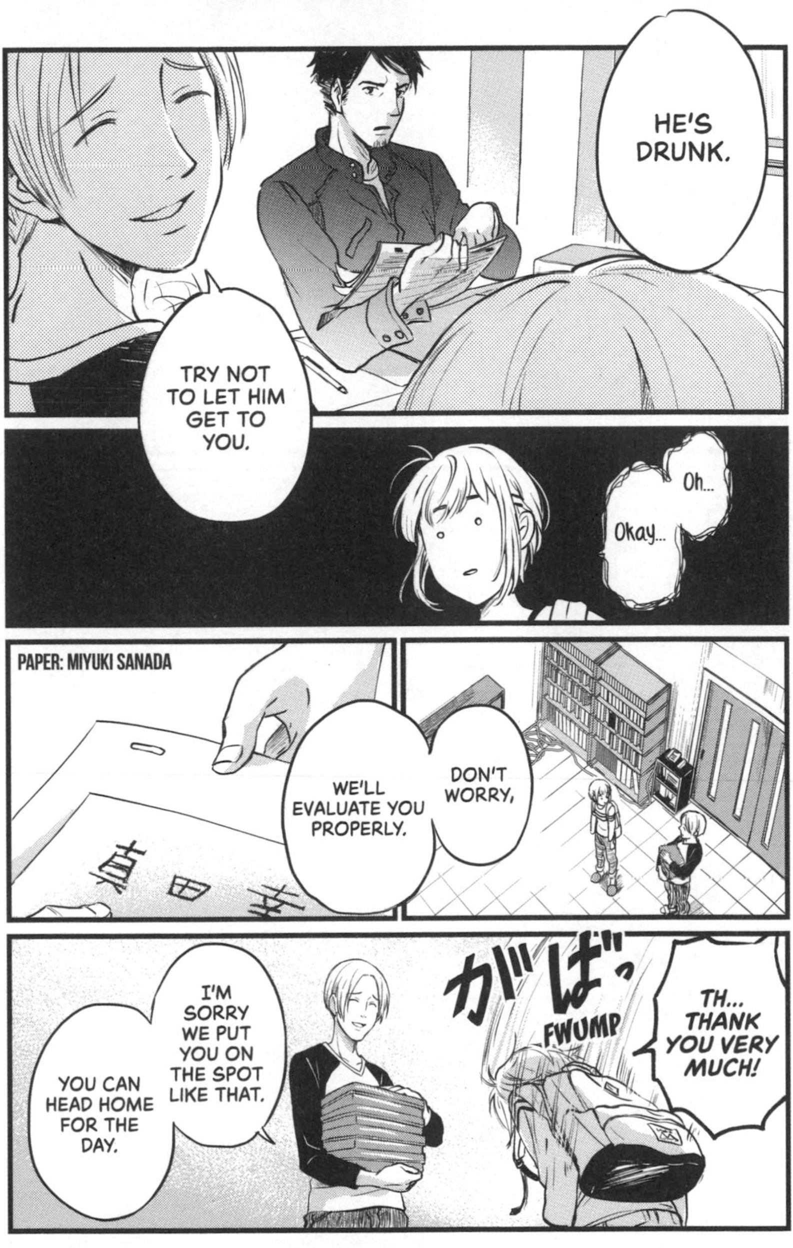
HE'S DRUNK.
TRY NOT TO LET HIM GET TO YOU.
Oh...
Okay...
DON'T WORRY,
WE'LL EVALUATE YOU PROPERLY.
PAPER: MIYUKI SANADA
真田幸
TH... THANK YOU VERY MUCH!
がばっ
FWUMP
I'M SORRY WE PUT YOU ON THE SPOT LIKE THAT.
YOU CAN HEAD HOME FOR THE DAY.

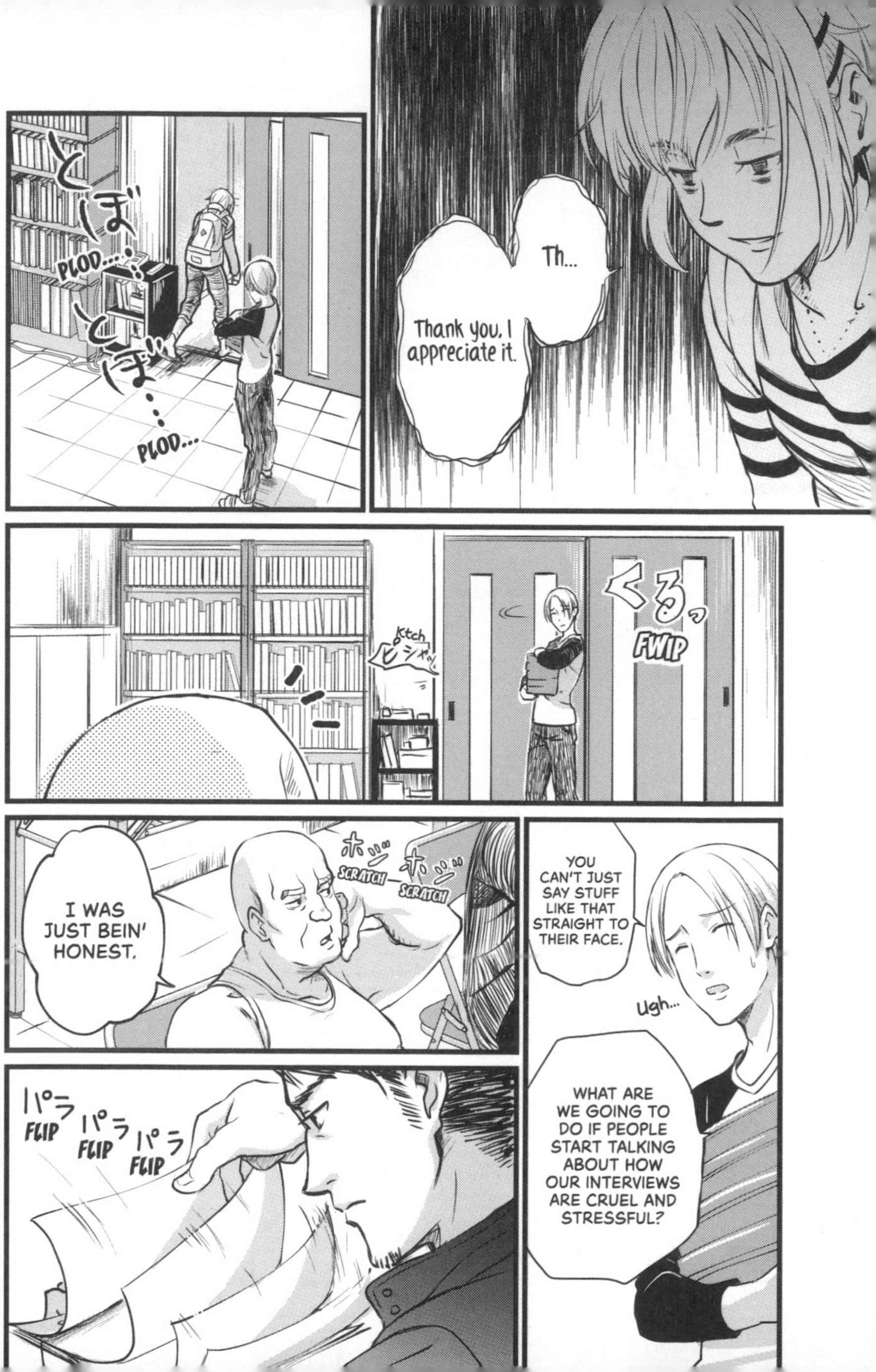
Th...
Thank you, I appreciate it.
とぼ
PLOD...
とぼ
PLOD...
くるっ
FWIP
ピシャッ
Ktch
YOU CAN'T JUST SAY STUFF LIKE THAT STRAIGHT TO THEIR FACE.
Ugh...
WHAT ARE WE GOING TO DO IF PEOPLE START TALKING ABOUT HOW OUR INTERVIEWS ARE CRUEL AND STRESSFUL?
I WAS JUST BEIN' HONEST.
SCRATCH
SCRATCH
パラ
FLIP
パラ
FLIP
パラ
FLIP

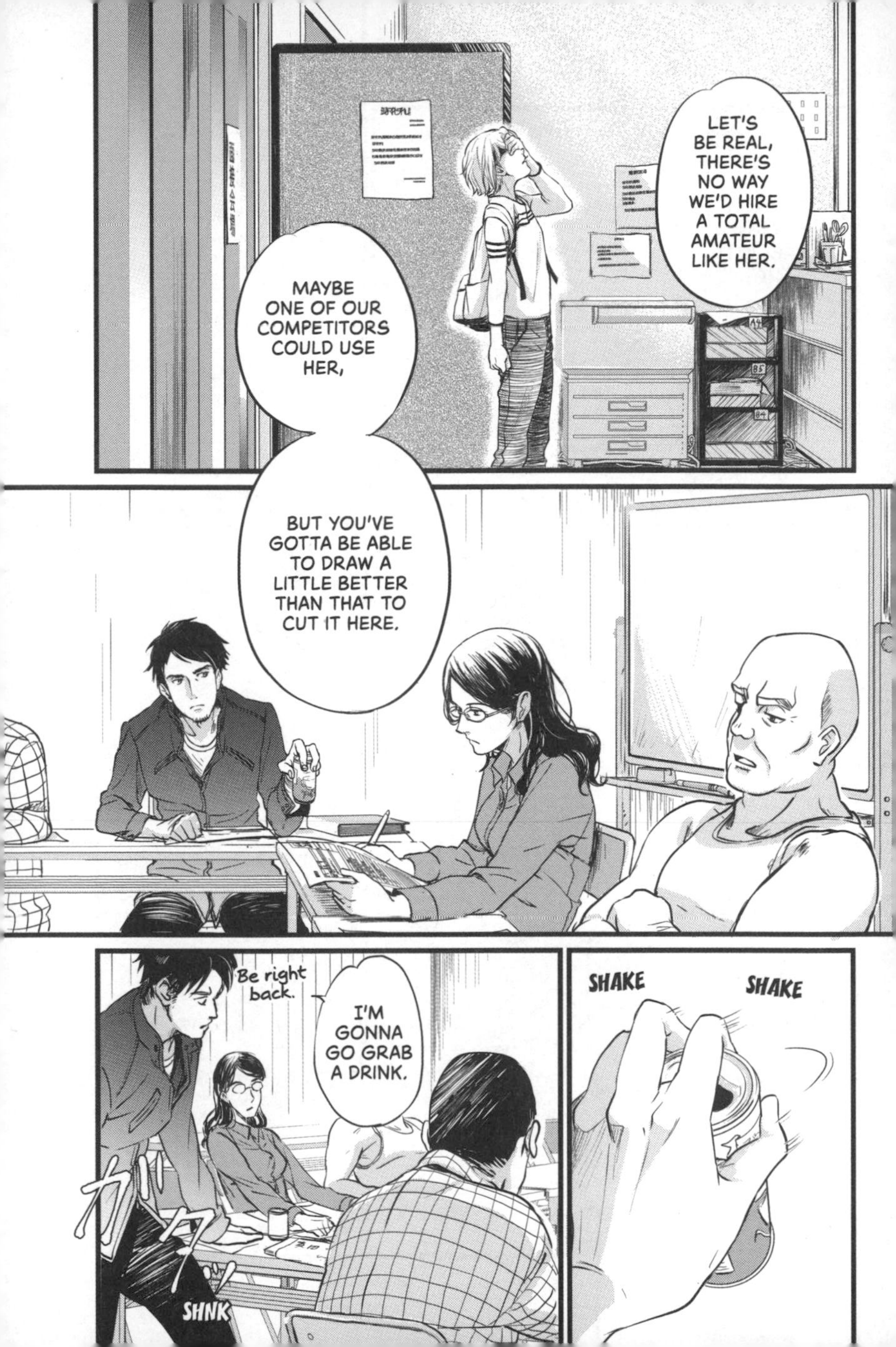
LET'S BE REAL, THERE'S NO WAY WE'D HIRE A TOTAL AMATEUR LIKE HER.
MAYBE ONE OF OUR COMPETITORS COULD USE HER,
BUT YOU'VE GOTTA BE ABLE TO DRAW A LITTLE BETTER THAN THAT TO CUT IT HERE.
SHAKE
SHAKE
I'M GONNA GO GRAB A DRINK.
Be right back.
SHNK

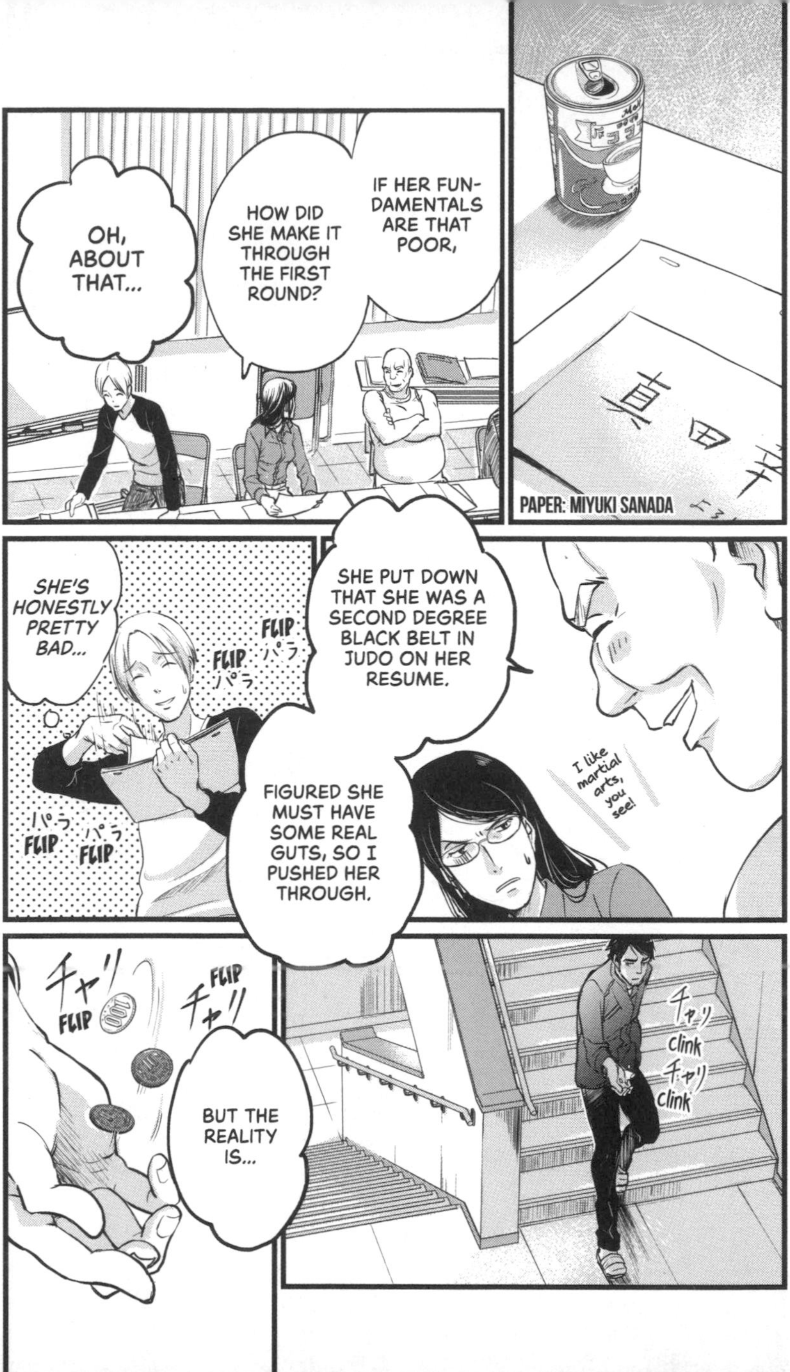

PAPER: MIYUKI SANADA
IF HER FUN-DAMENTALS ARE THAT POOR,
HOW DID SHE MAKE IT THROUGH THE FIRST ROUND?
OH, ABOUT THAT...
SHE PUT DOWN THAT SHE WAS A SECOND DEGREE BLACK BELT IN JUDO ON HER RESUME.
I like martial arts, you see!
FIGURED SHE MUST HAVE SOME REAL GUTS, SO I PUSHED HER THROUGH.
SHE'S HONESTLY PRETTY BAD...
FLIP パラ
FLIP パラ
パラ FLIP
パラ FLIP
チャリ clink
チャリ clink
チャリ FLIP
FLIP チャリ
BUT THE REALITY IS...

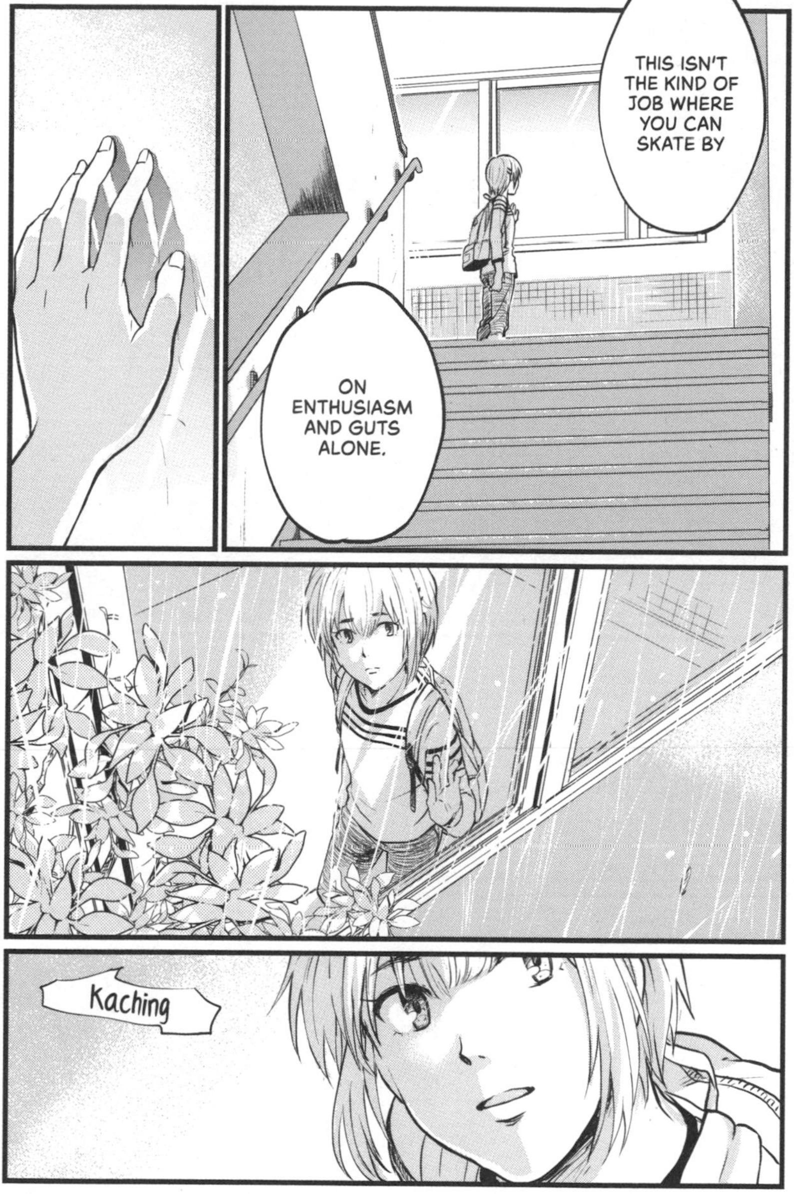
THIS ISN'T THE KIND OF JOB WHERE YOU CAN SKATE BY
ON ENTHUSIASM AND GUTS ALONE.
Kaching

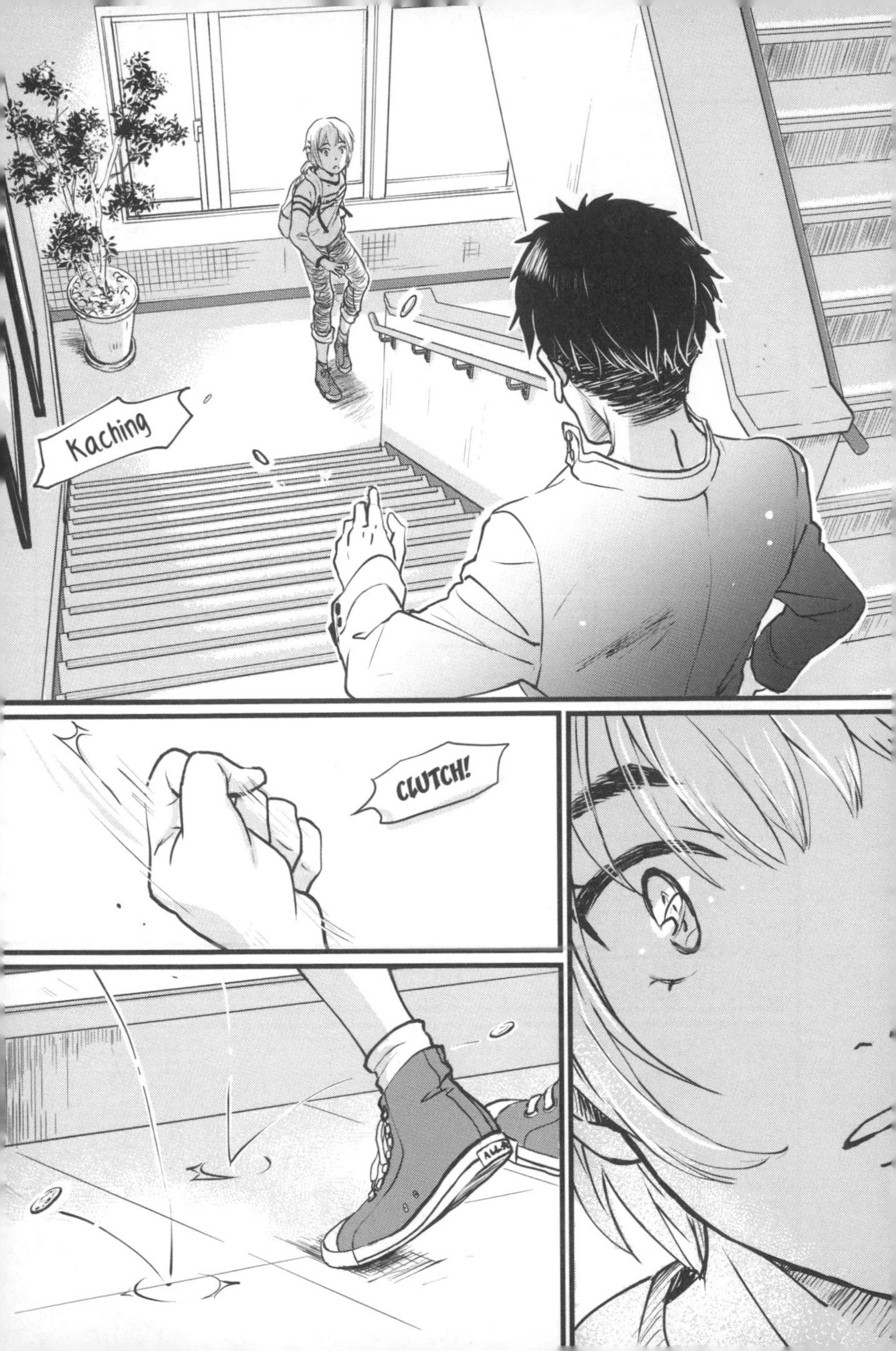
Kaching
CLUTCH!

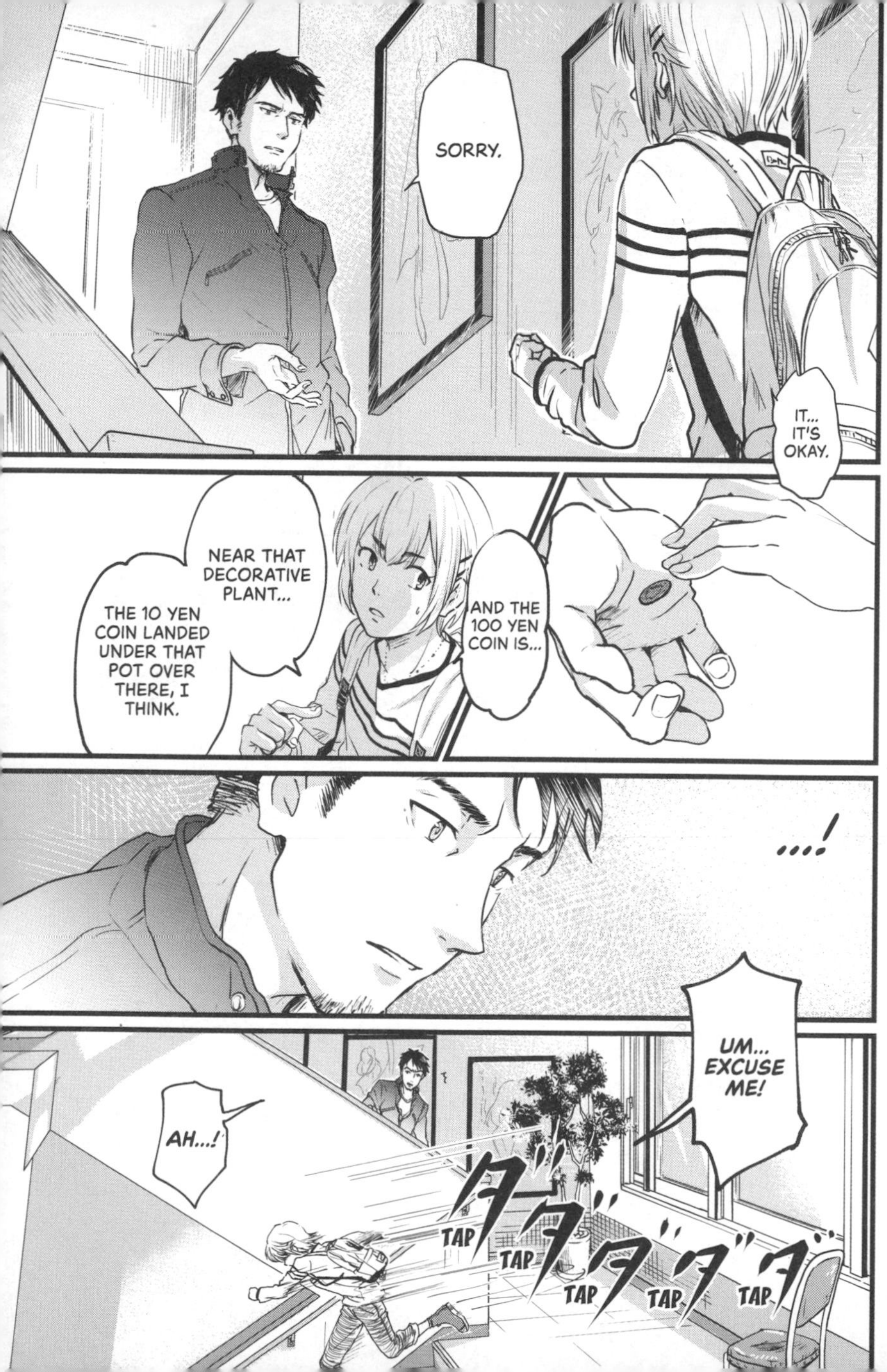
SORRY.
IT... IT'S OKAY.
AND THE 100 YEN COIN IS...
NEAR THAT DECORATIVE PLANT...
THE 10 YEN COIN LANDED UNDER THAT POT OVER THERE, I THINK.
...!
UM... EXCUSE ME!
AH...!
TAP
TAP
TAP
TAP
TAP

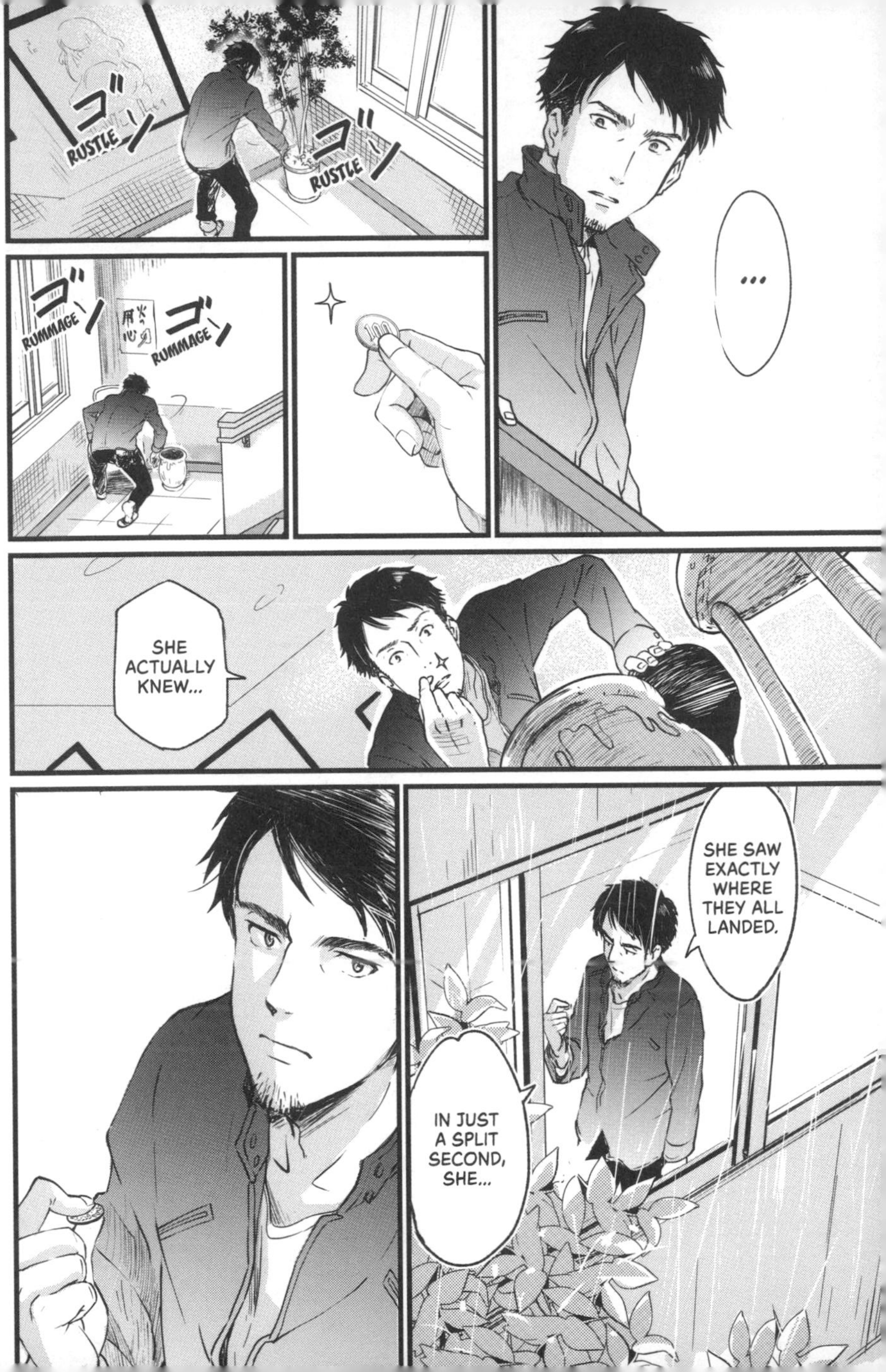
...
ゴソ
RUSTLE
ゴソ
RUSTLE
ゴソ
RUMMAGE
ゴソ
RUMMAGE
SHE ACTUALLY KNEW...
SHE SAW EXACTLY WHERE THEY ALL LANDED.
IN JUST A SPLIT SECOND, SHE...

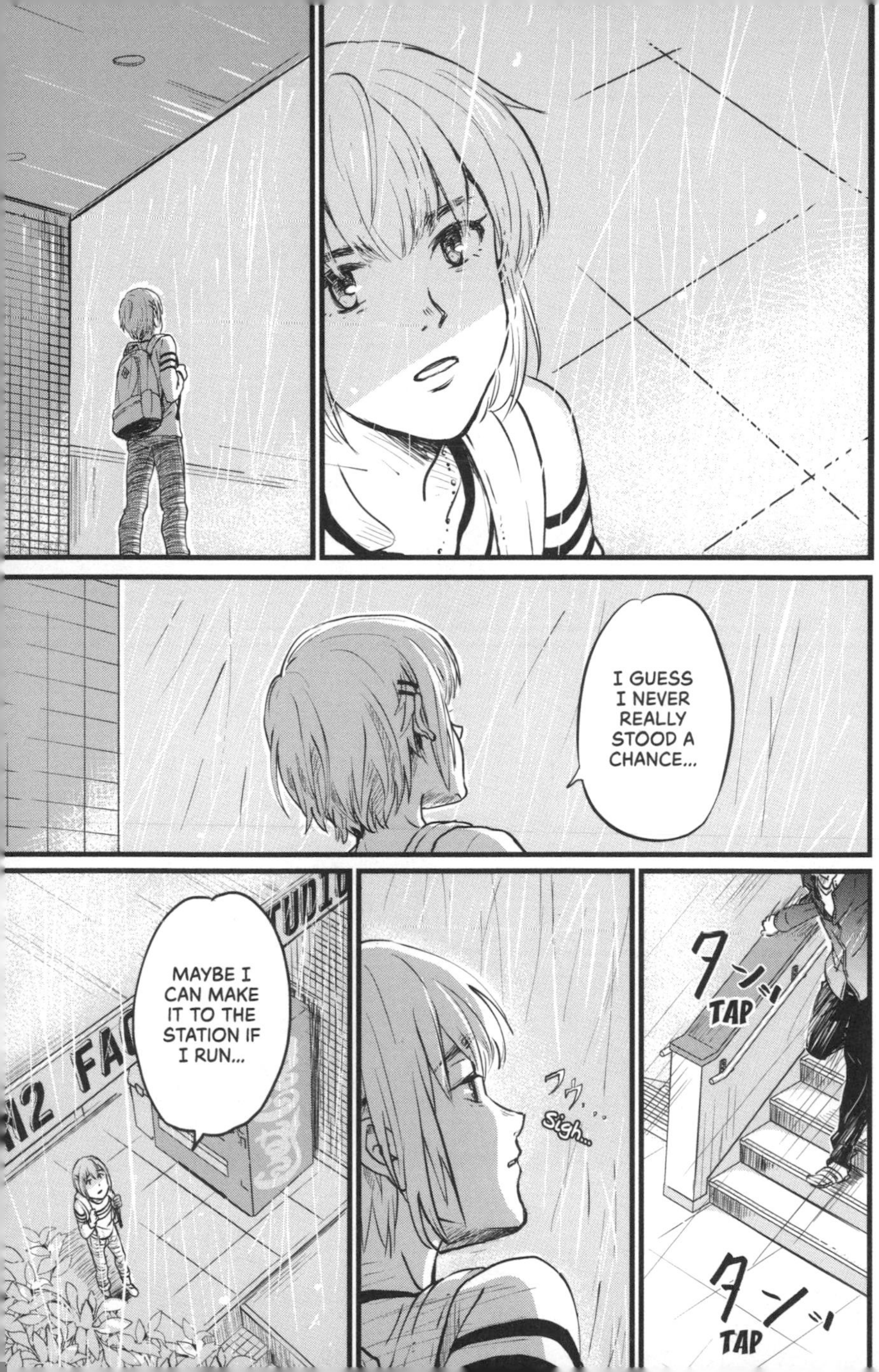
I GUESS I NEVER REALLY STOOD A CHANCE...
タンッ
TAP
タンッ
TAP
フウ..
Sigh...
MAYBE I CAN MAKE IT TO THE STATION IF I RUN...

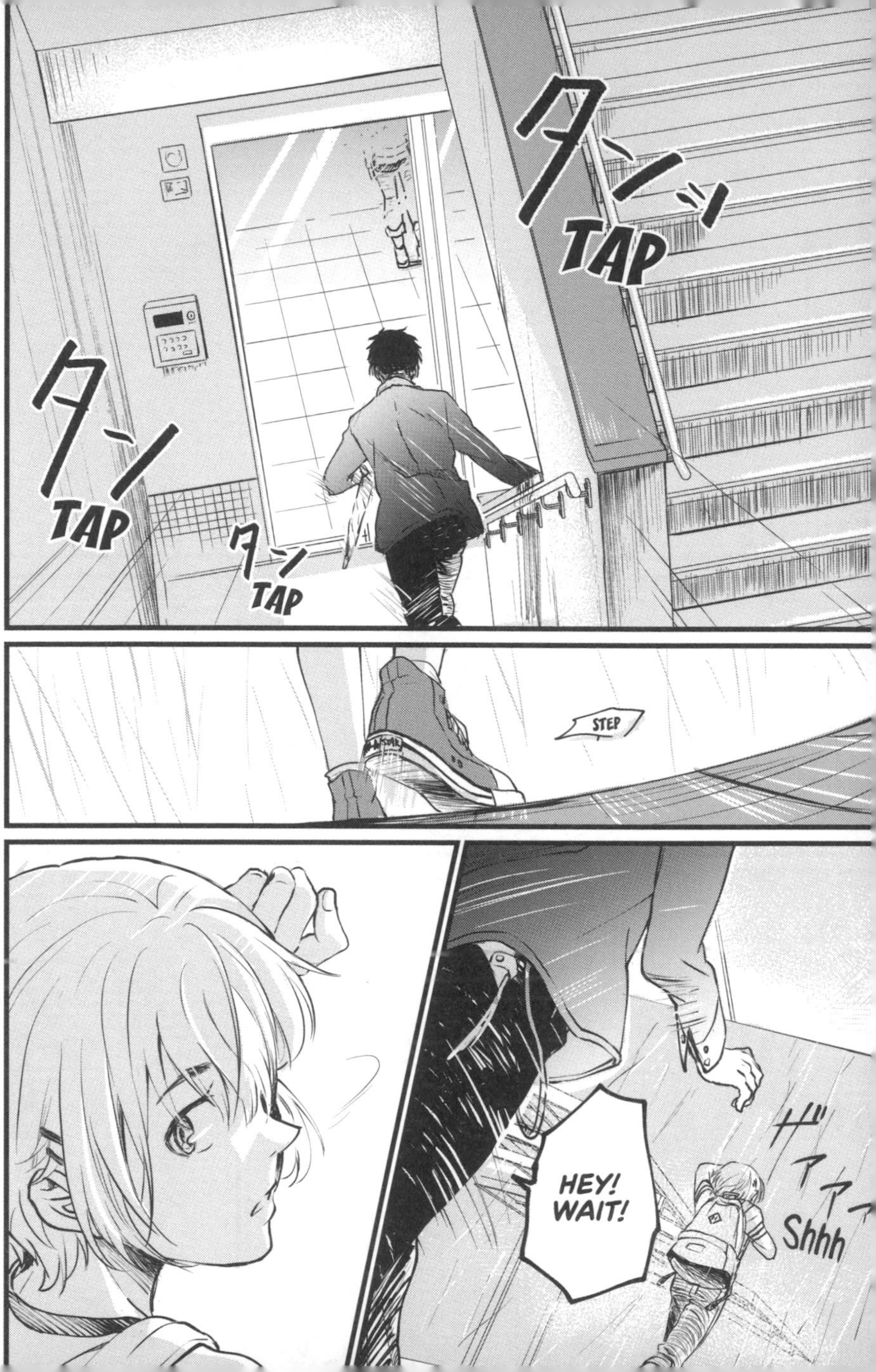
タンッ
TAP
タン
TAP
タン
TAP
STEP
ザァア
Shhh
HEY! WAIT!

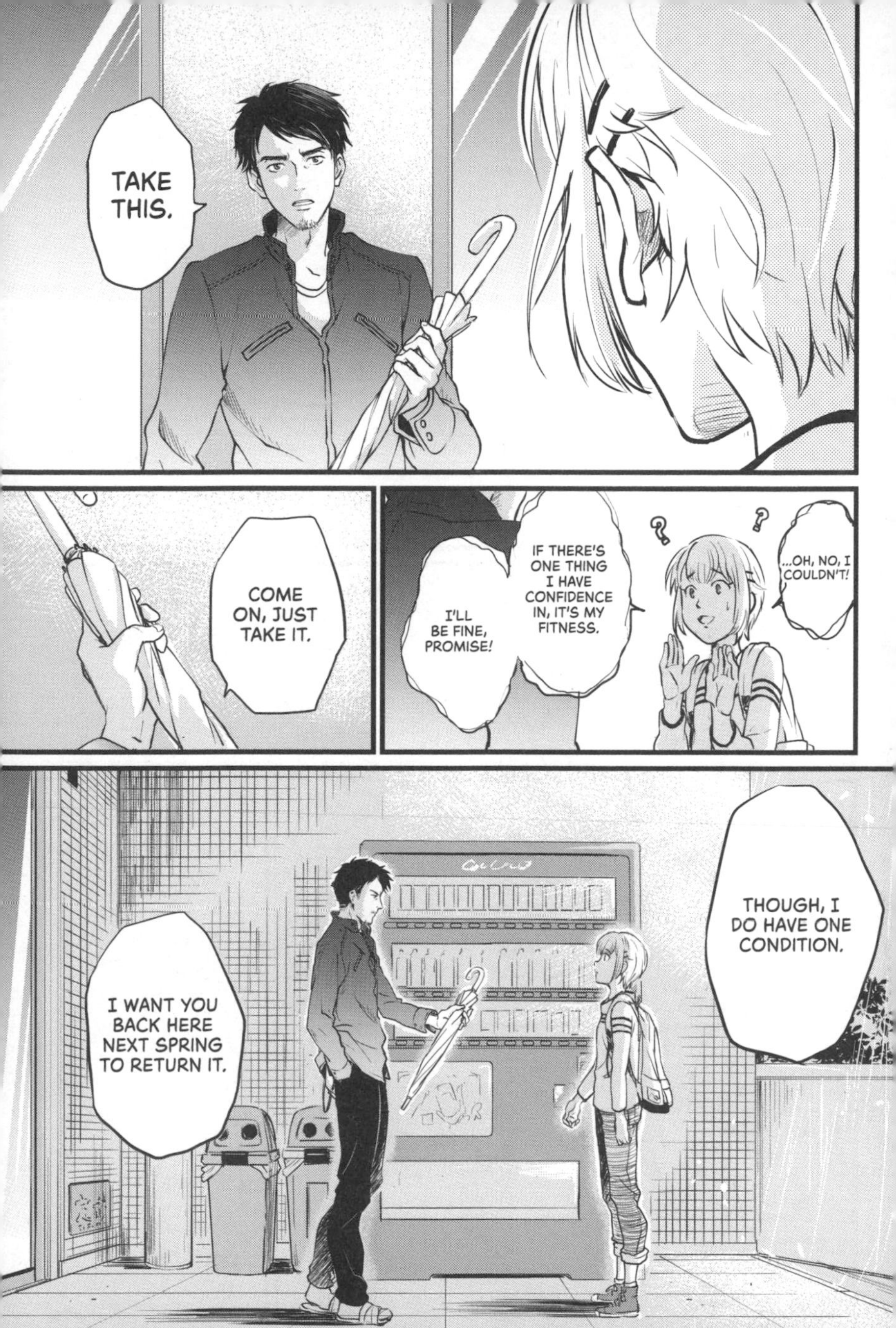
TAKE THIS.
...OH, NO, I COULDN'T!
IF THERE'S ONE THING I HAVE CONFIDENCE IN, IT'S MY FITNESS.
I'LL BE FINE, PROMISE!
COME ON, JUST TAKE IT.
THOUGH, I DO HAVE ONE CONDITION.
I WANT YOU BACK HERE NEXT SPRING TO RETURN IT.

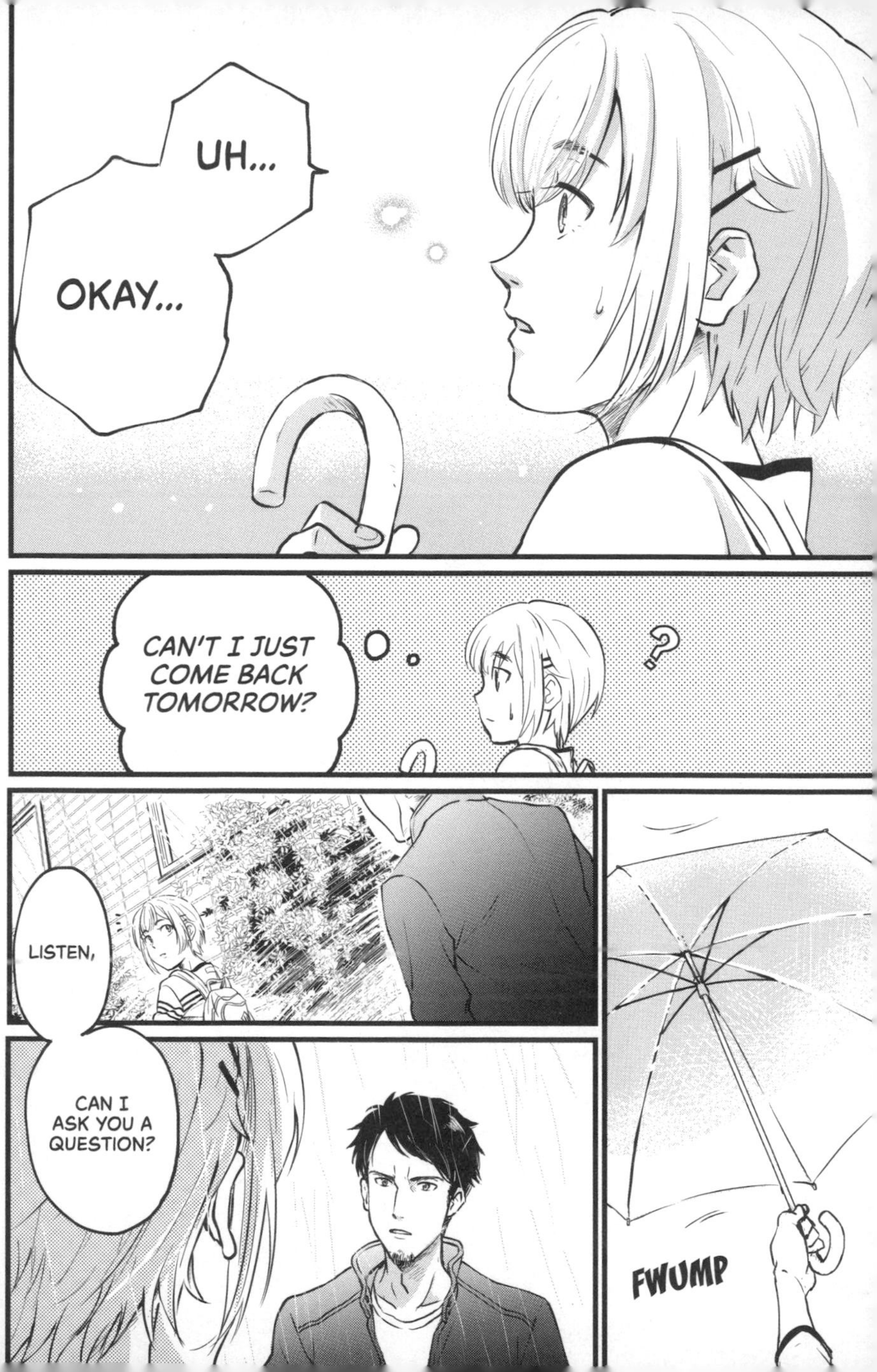
UH...
OKAY...
CAN'T I JUST COME BACK TOMORROW?
FWUMP
LISTEN,
CAN I ASK YOU A QUESTION?

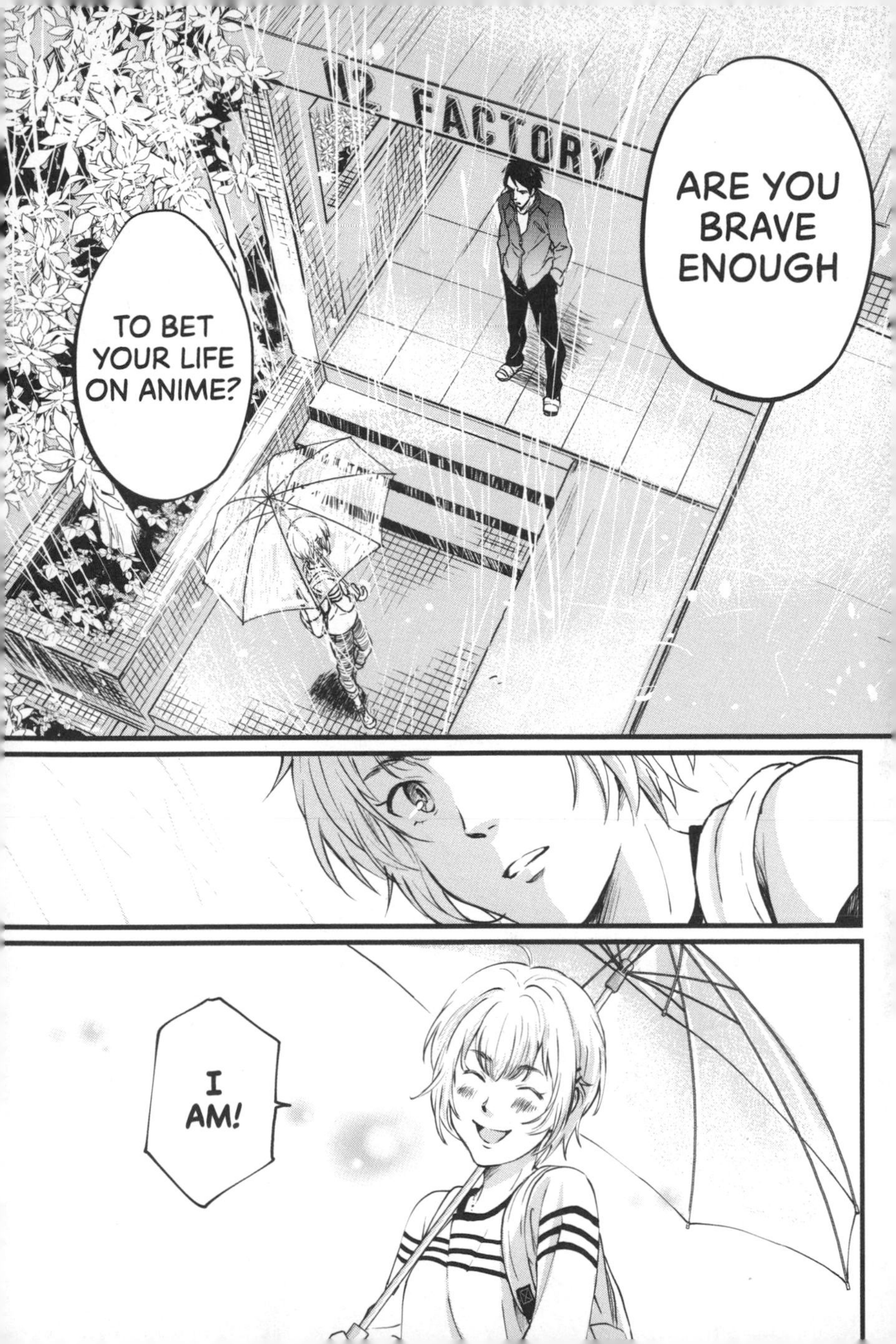
FACTORY
ARE YOU BRAVE ENOUGH
TO BET YOUR LIFE ON ANIME?
I AM!

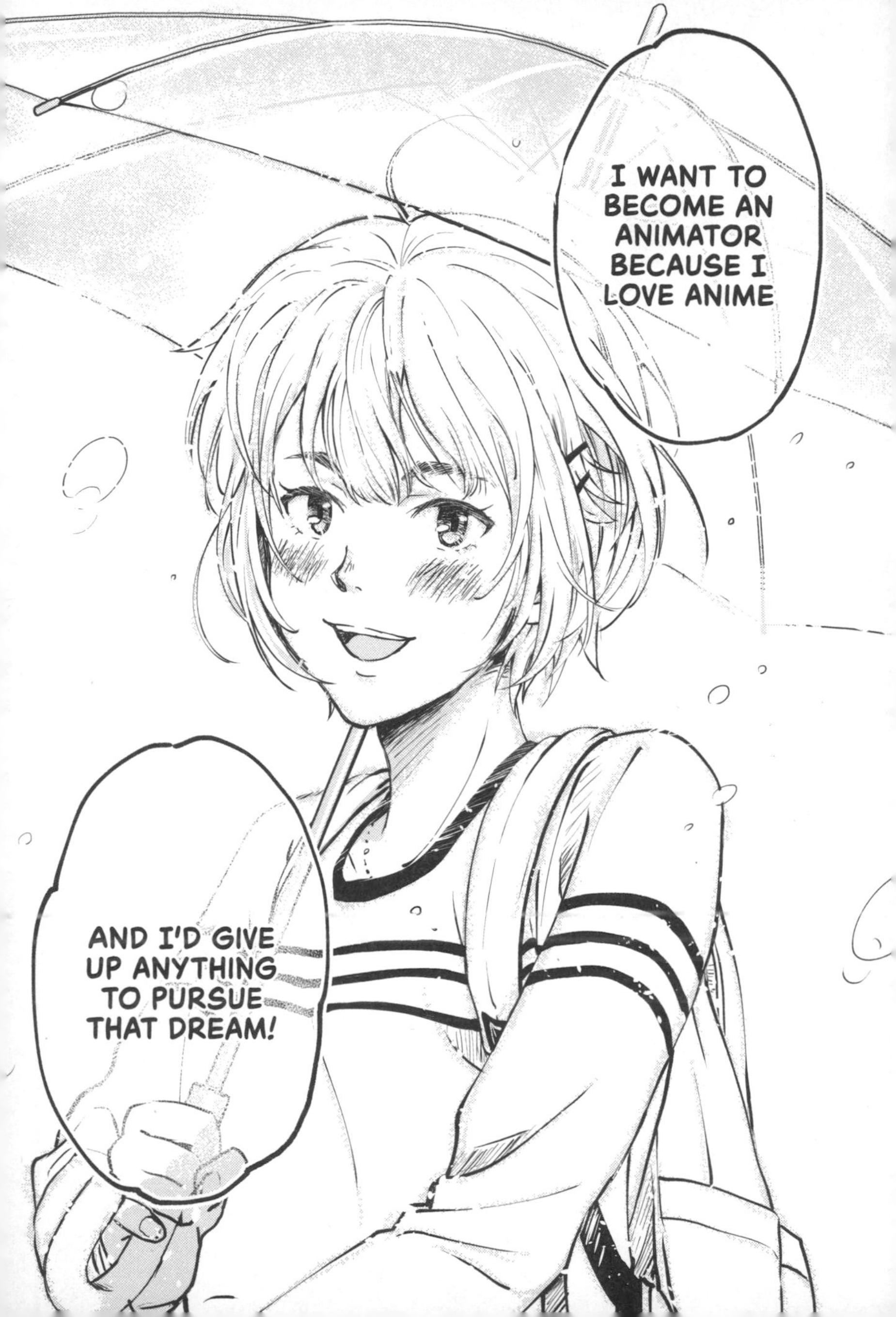
I WANT TO BECOME AN ANIMATOR BECAUSE I LOVE ANIME
AND I'D GIVE UP ANYTHING TO PURSUE THAT DREAM!

AN IDIOT'S GUIDE TO PRODUCING ANIME

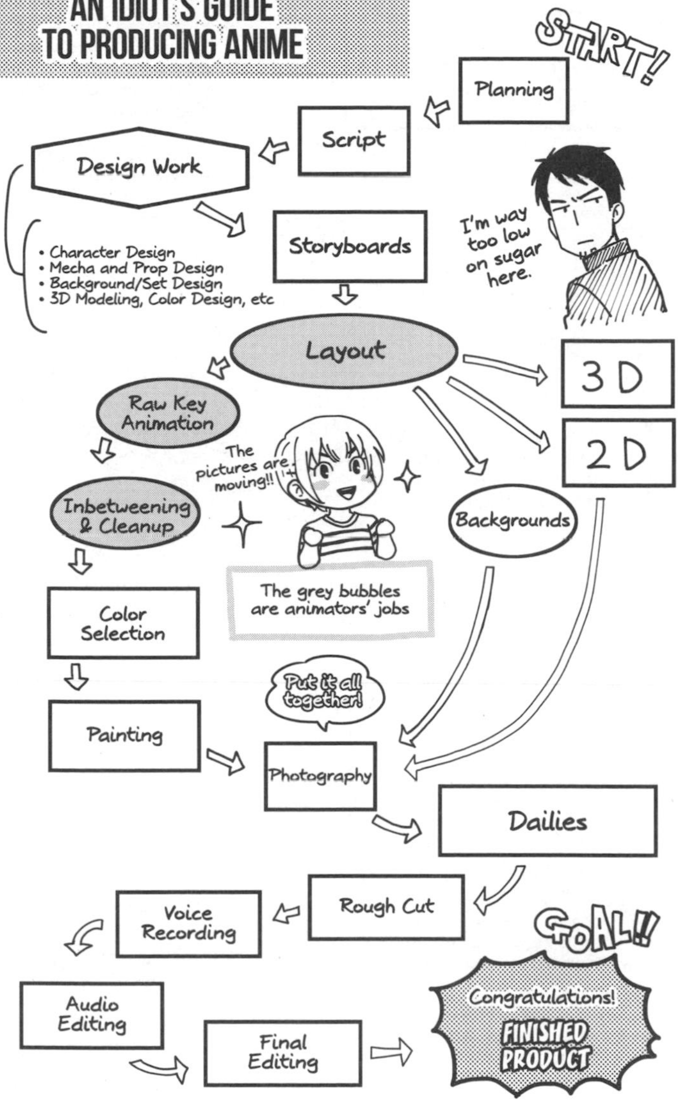
START!
Planning
Script
Design Work
• Character Design
• Mecha and Prop Design
• Background/Set Design
• 3D Modeling, Color Design, etc
Storyboards
I'm way too low on sugar here.
Layout
3 D
2 D
Raw Key Animation
The pictures are moving!!
Inbetweening & Cleanup
Backgrounds
The grey bubbles are animators' jobs
Color Selection
Put it all together!
Painting
Photography
Dailies
Rough Cut
Voice Recording
GOAL!!
Audio Editing
Final Editing
Congratulations!
FINISHED PRODUCT

N2 FACTORY STUDIO ENTRY LEVEL INBETWEENER FIRST ROUND EXAM

• You mail a sketchbook full of sketches and studies that illustrate your artistic ability to the studio.

• It's best if you include original work featuring both backgrounds and figures.

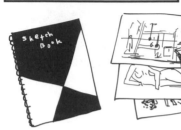

*On rare occasions people pass the first round because of eye-catching hobbies or special skills listed on their resume.

Wow... She's a 2nd degree blackbelt at 19.

Resume

SECOND ROUND

Practical exam (tweening a running sequence + key animation)

After you inbetween from A1 to A2, you're asked to make the character move however you like.

THERE IS A 2.5 HOUR TIME LIMIT.

2.5 hours...

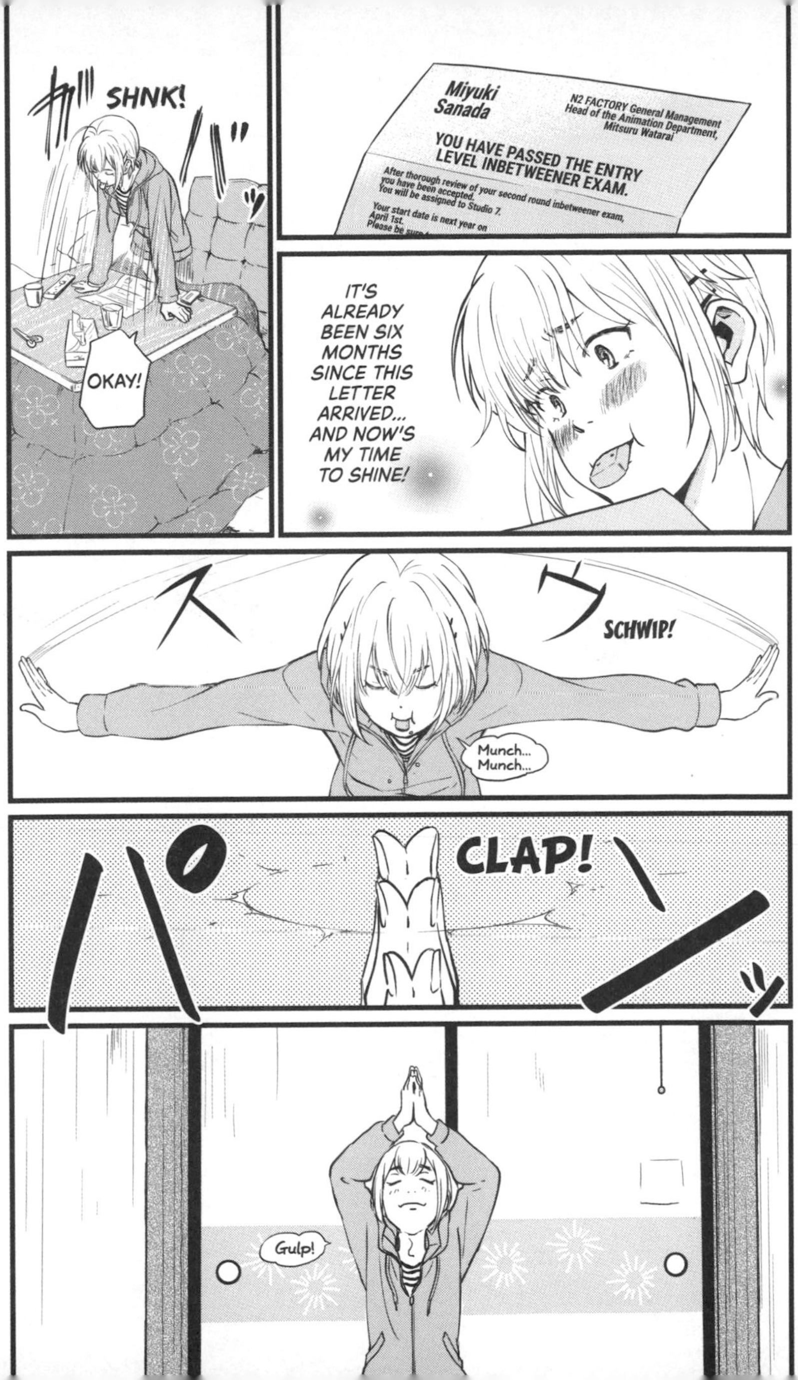
Miyuki
Sanada
N2 FACTORY General Management
Head of the Animation Department,
Mitsuru Watarai
YOU HAVE PASSED THE ENTRY LEVEL INBETWEENER EXAM.
After thorough review of your second round inbetweener exam, you have been accepted.
You will be assigned to Studio 7.
Your start date is next year on April 1st.
IT'S ALREADY BEEN SIX MONTHS SINCE THIS LETTER ARRIVED... AND NOW'S MY TIME TO SHINE!
SHNK!
OKAY!
SCHWIP!
Munch... Munch...
CLAP!
Gulp!

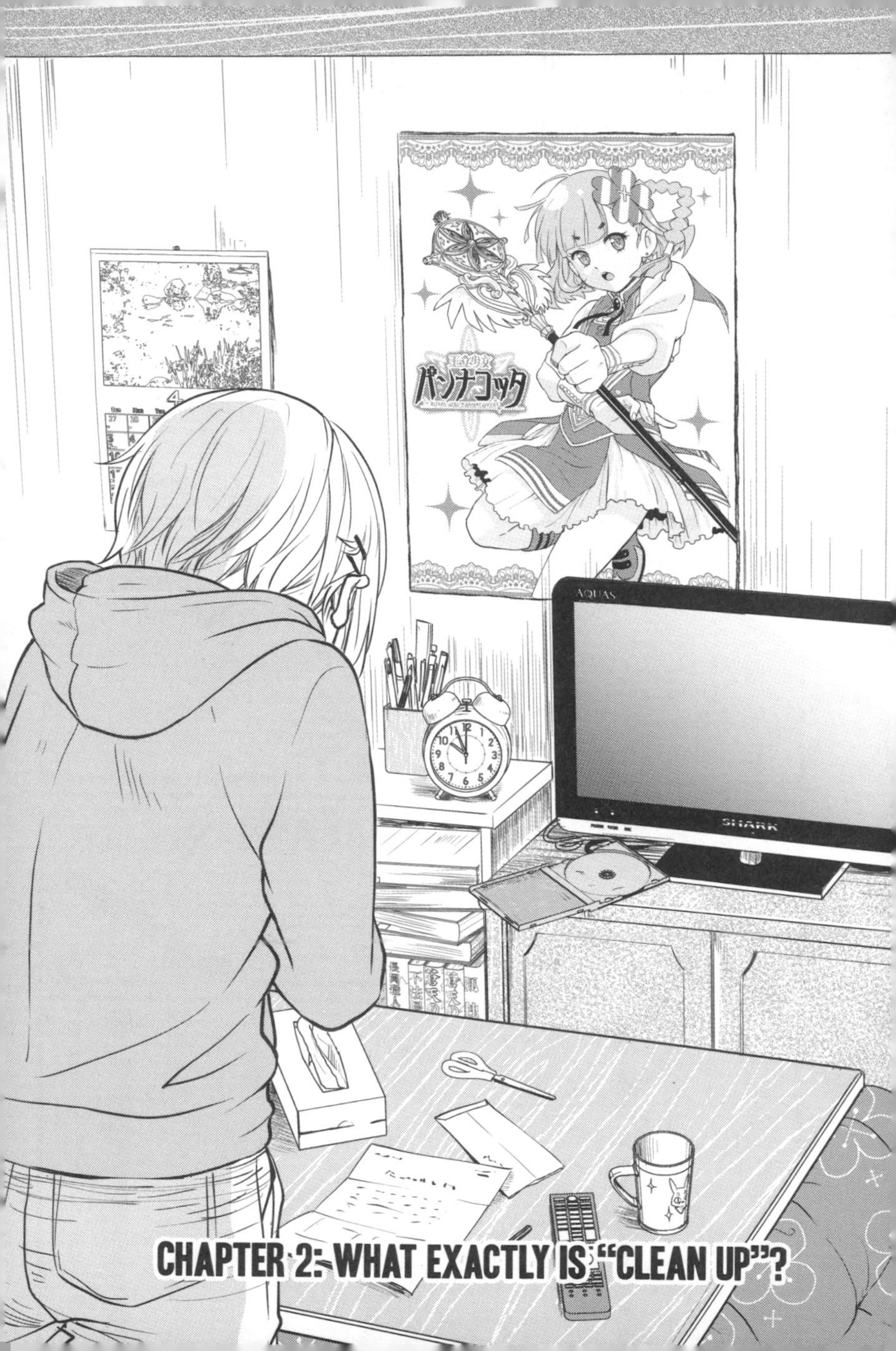
パンナコッタ
AQUAS
SHARK

CHAPTER 2: WHAT EXACTLY IS "CLEAN UP"?

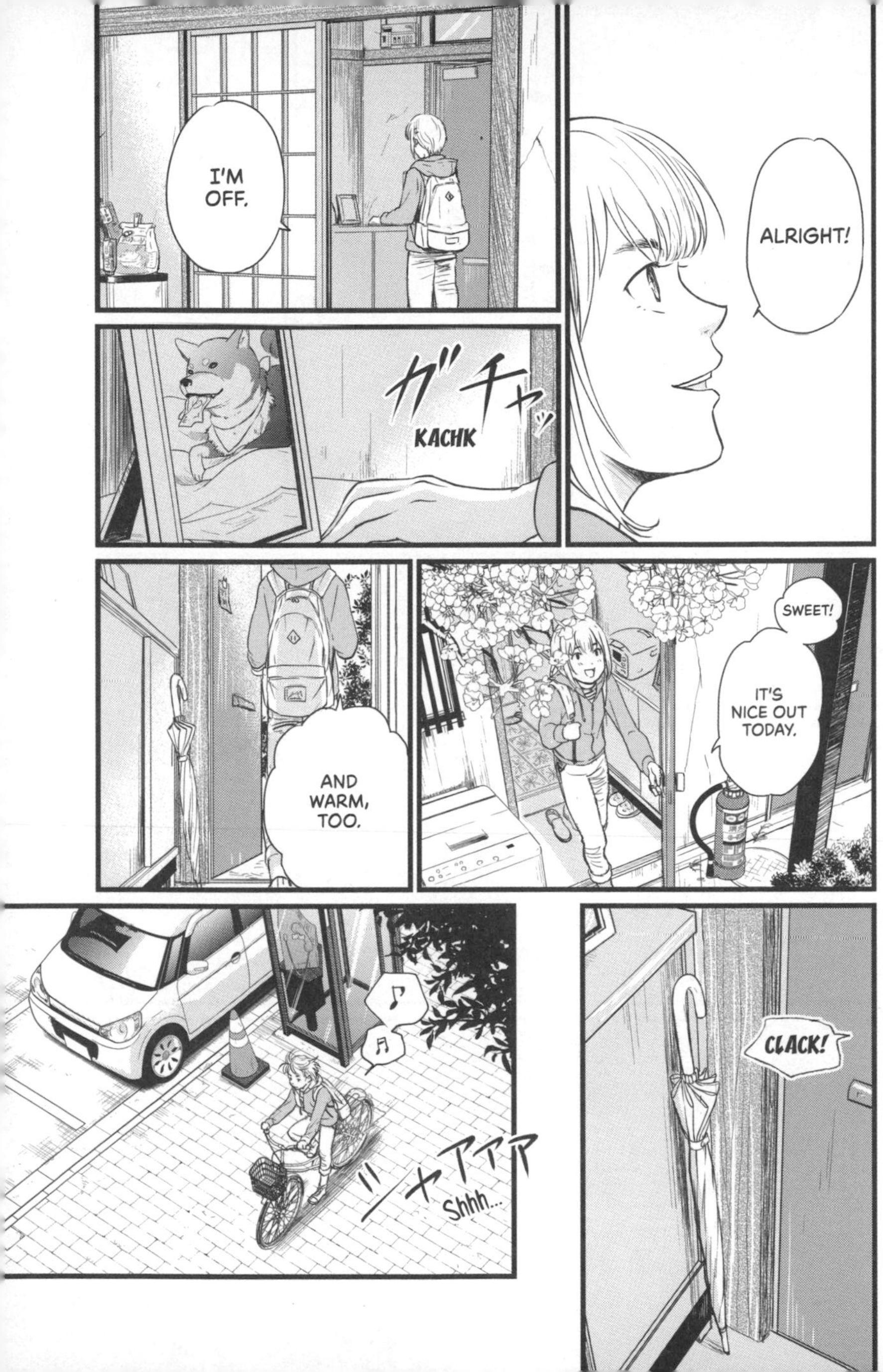
ALRIGHT!
I'M OFF.
ガチャッ
KACHK
SWEET!
IT'S NICE OUT TODAY.
AND WARM, TOO.
CLACK!
♪
♫
シャアアア
Shhh...

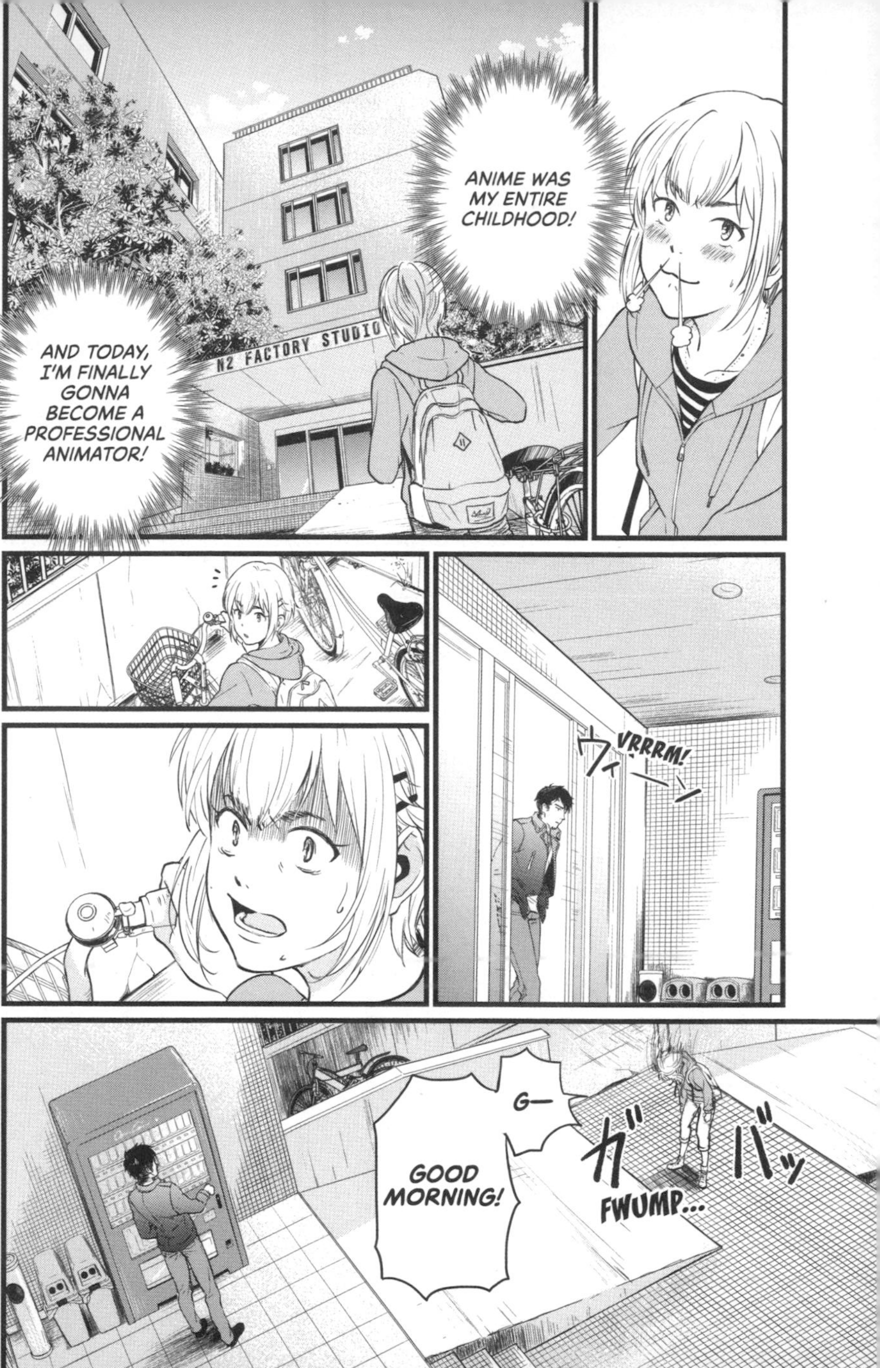
ANIME WAS MY ENTIRE CHILDHOOD!
N2 FACTORY STUDIO
AND TODAY, I'M FINALLY GONNA BECOME A PROFESSIONAL ANIMATOR!
ウィーン
VRRRM!
G—
GOOD MORNING!
ガバッ
FWUMP...

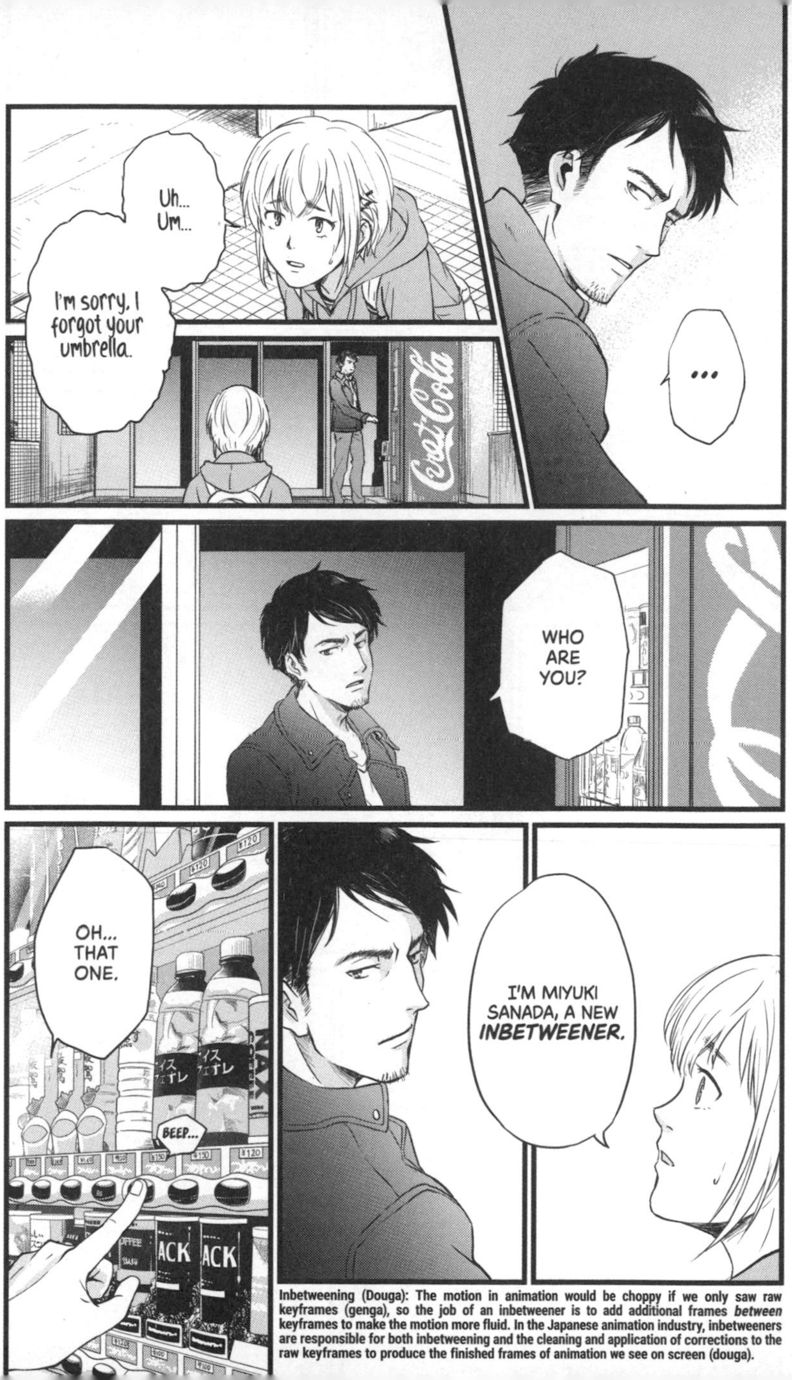
...
Uh... Um...
I'm sorry, I forgot your umbrella.
WHO ARE YOU?
I'M MIYUKI SANADA, A NEW ***INBETWEENER.***
OH... THAT ONE.
BEEP...

Inbetweening (Douga): The motion in animation would be choppy if we only saw raw keyframes (genga), so the job of an inbetweener is to add additional frames *between* keyframes to make the motion more fluid. In the Japanese animation industry, inbetweeners are responsible for both inbetweening and the cleaning and application of corrections to the raw keyframes to produce the finished frames of animation we see on screen (douga).

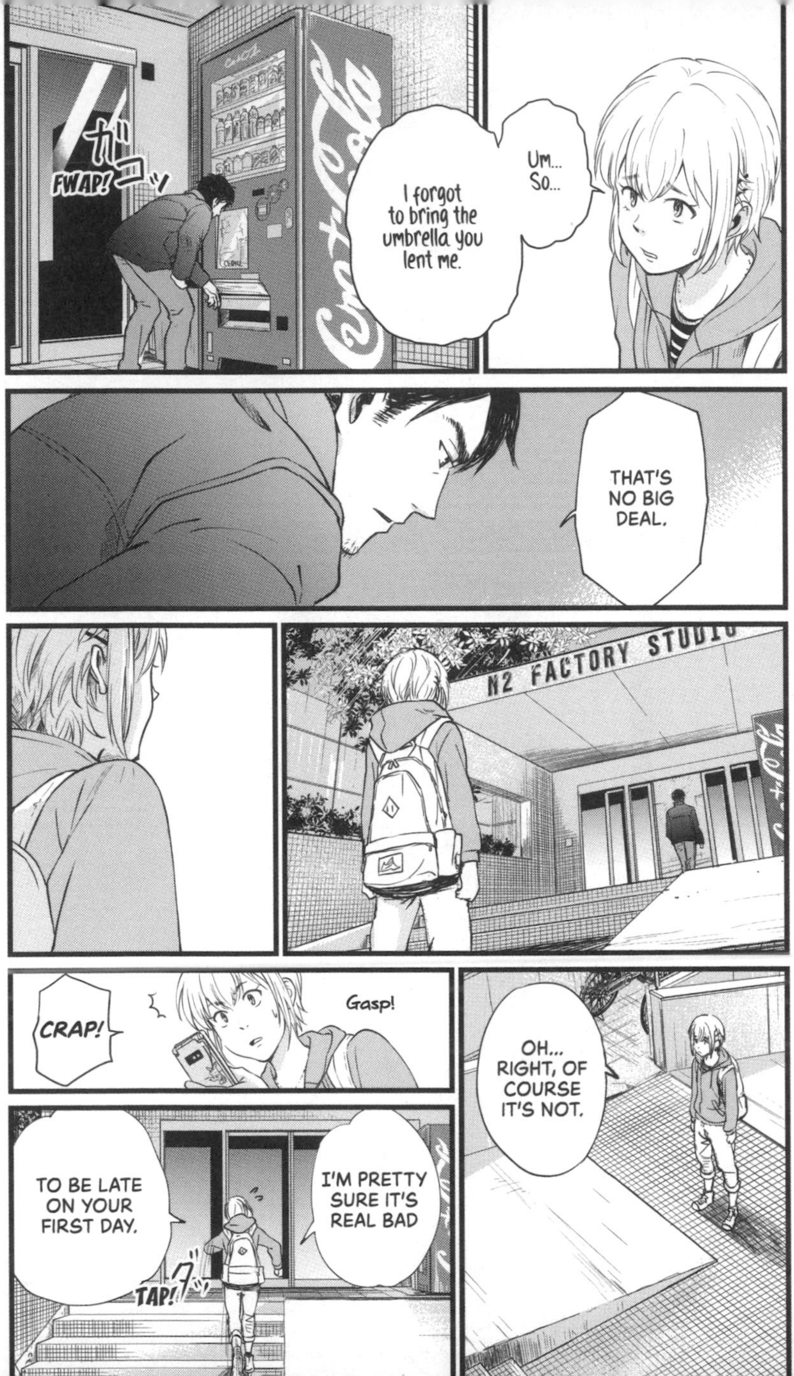

Um... So...
I forgot to bring the umbrella you lent me.
ガコッ
FWAP!
THAT'S NO BIG DEAL.
N2 FACTORY STUDI
OH... RIGHT, OF COURSE IT'S NOT.
Gasp!
CRAP!
I'M PRETTY SURE IT'S REAL BAD
TO BE LATE ON YOUR FIRST DAY.
タッ
TAP!

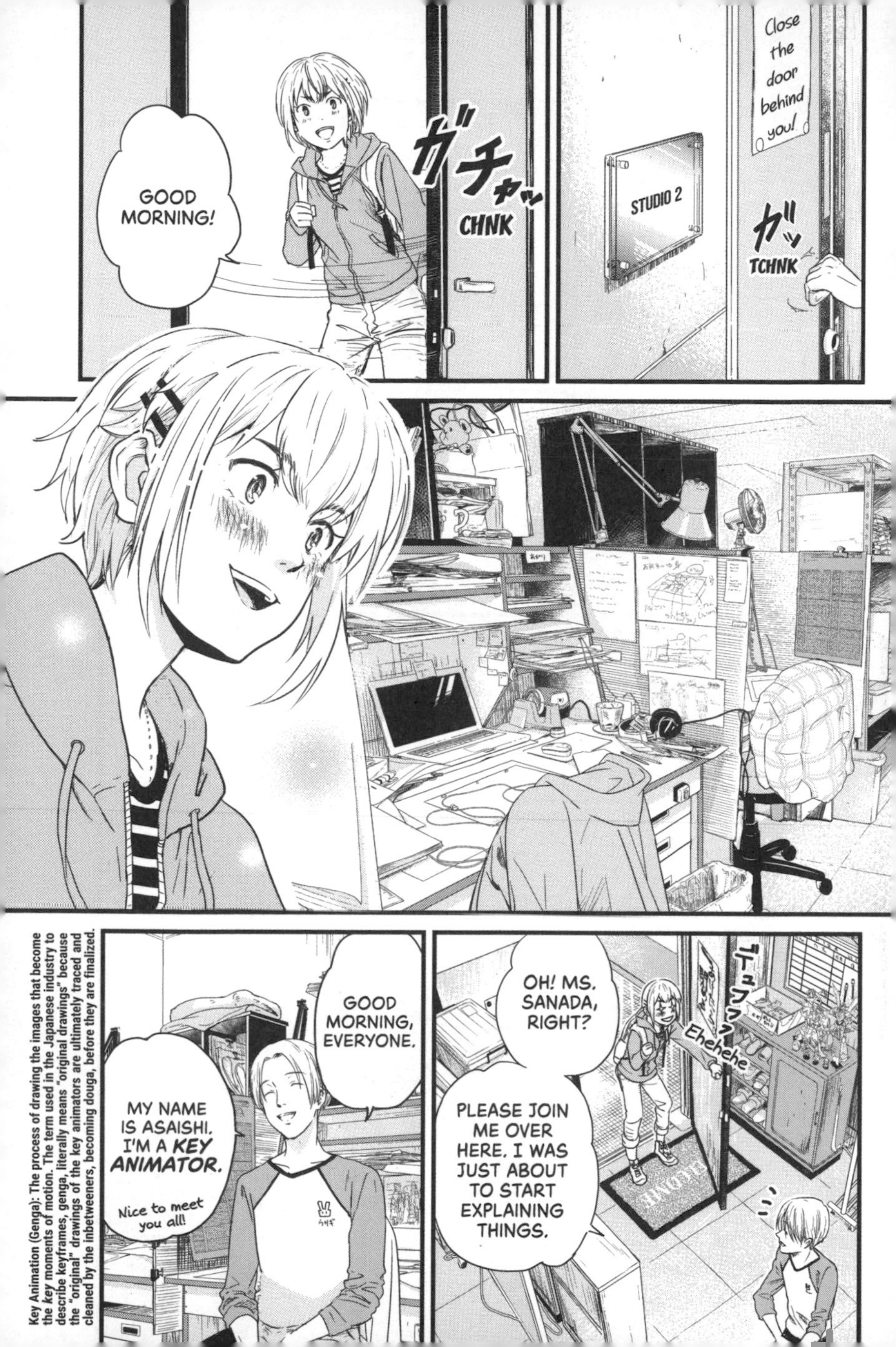

Close the door behind you!
STUDIO 2
ガッ
TCHNK
ガチャッ
CHNK
GOOD MORNING!
OH! MS. SANADA, RIGHT?
デュフフ
Ehehehe
PLEASE JOIN ME OVER HERE. I WAS JUST ABOUT TO START EXPLAINING THINGS.
GOOD MORNING, EVERYONE.
MY NAME IS ASAISHI. I'M A ***KEY ANIMATOR.***
Nice to meet you all!

Key Animation (Genga): The process of drawing the images that become the *key* moments of motion. The term used in the Japanese industry to describe keyframes, genga, literally means "original drawings" because the "original" drawings of the key animators are ultimately traced and cleaned by the inbetweeners, becoming douga, before they are finalized.

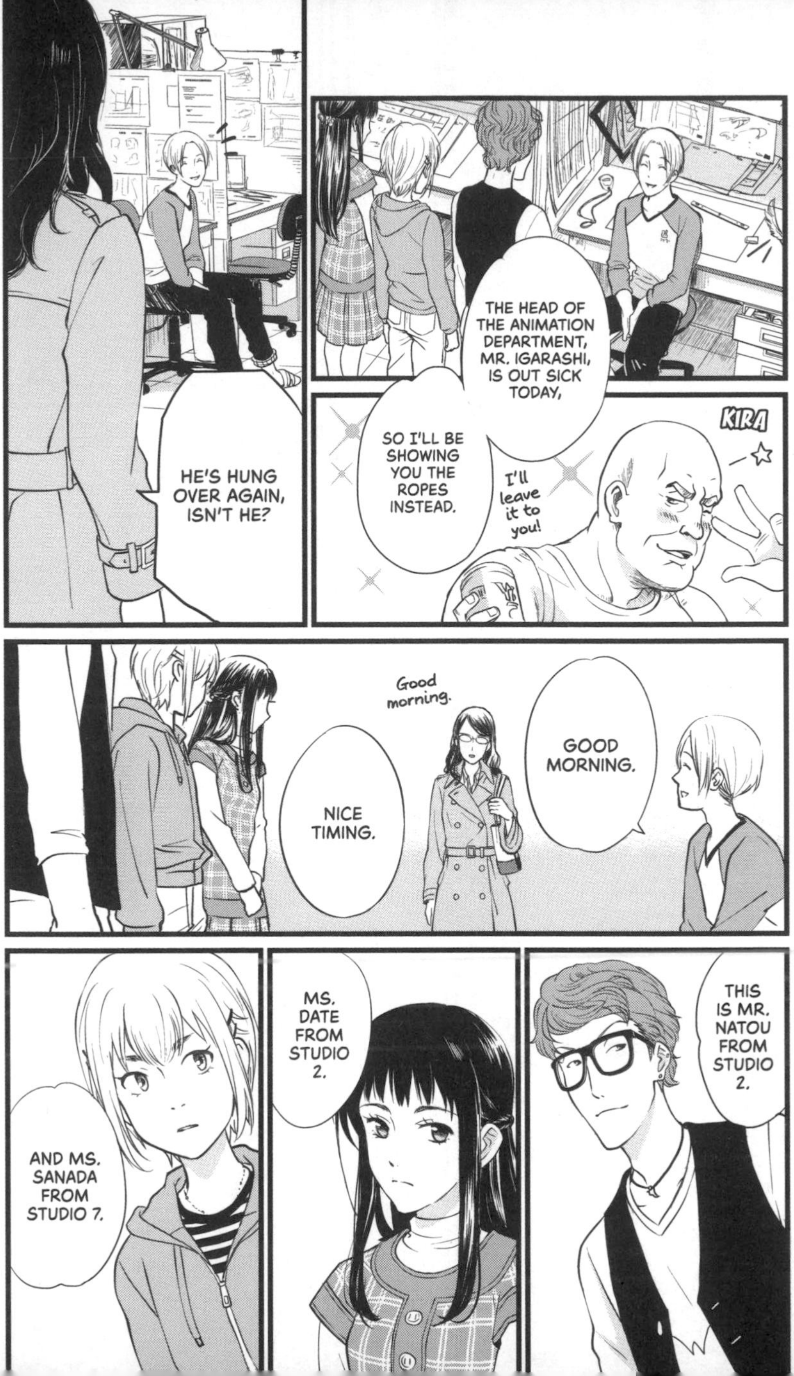

THE HEAD OF THE ANIMATION DEPARTMENT, MR. IGARASHI, IS OUT SICK TODAY,
SO I'LL BE SHOWING YOU THE ROPES INSTEAD.
KIRA
I'll leave it to you!
HE'S HUNG OVER AGAIN, ISN'T HE?
GOOD MORNING.
Good morning.
NICE TIMING.
THIS IS MR. NATOU FROM STUDIO 2.
MS. DATE FROM STUDIO 2.
AND MS. SANADA FROM STUDIO 7.

Inbetween Check (Douga Kensa, sometimes abbreviated to Douken): The job of ensuring that the inbetweens are neat and the motion smooth. Similar to the job of the Animation Director (sakuga kantoku), but for inbetweens and cleanup rather than key animation.

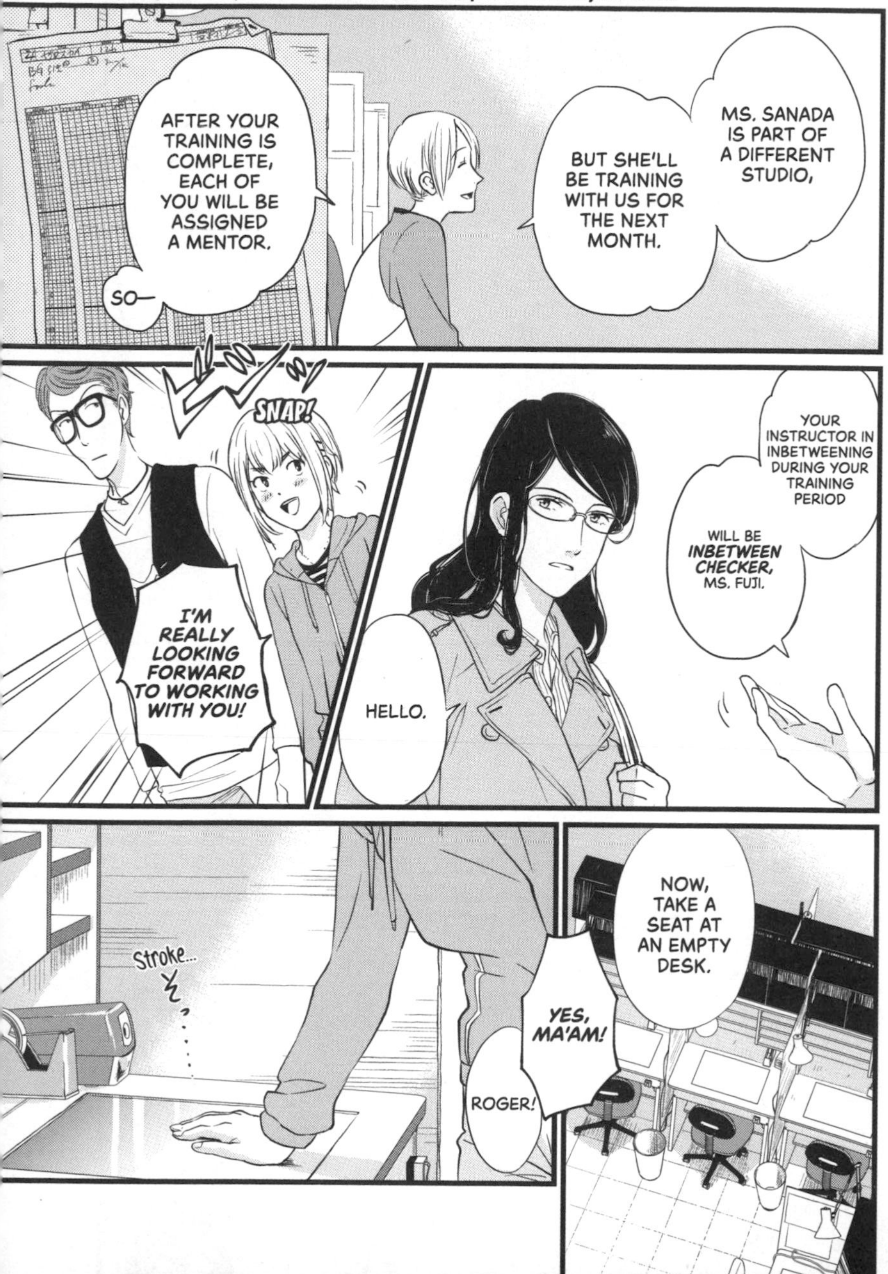
MS. SANADA IS PART OF A DIFFERENT STUDIO,
BUT SHE'LL BE TRAINING WITH US FOR THE NEXT MONTH.
AFTER YOUR TRAINING IS COMPLETE, EACH OF YOU WILL BE ASSIGNED A MENTOR.
SO—
YOUR INSTRUCTOR IN INBETWEENING DURING YOUR TRAINING PERIOD
WILL BE *INBETWEEN CHECKER,* MS. FUJI.
HELLO.
SNAP!
I'M REALLY LOOKING FORWARD TO WORKING WITH YOU!
NOW, TAKE A SEAT AT AN EMPTY DESK.
YES, MA'AM!
ROGER!
Stroke...

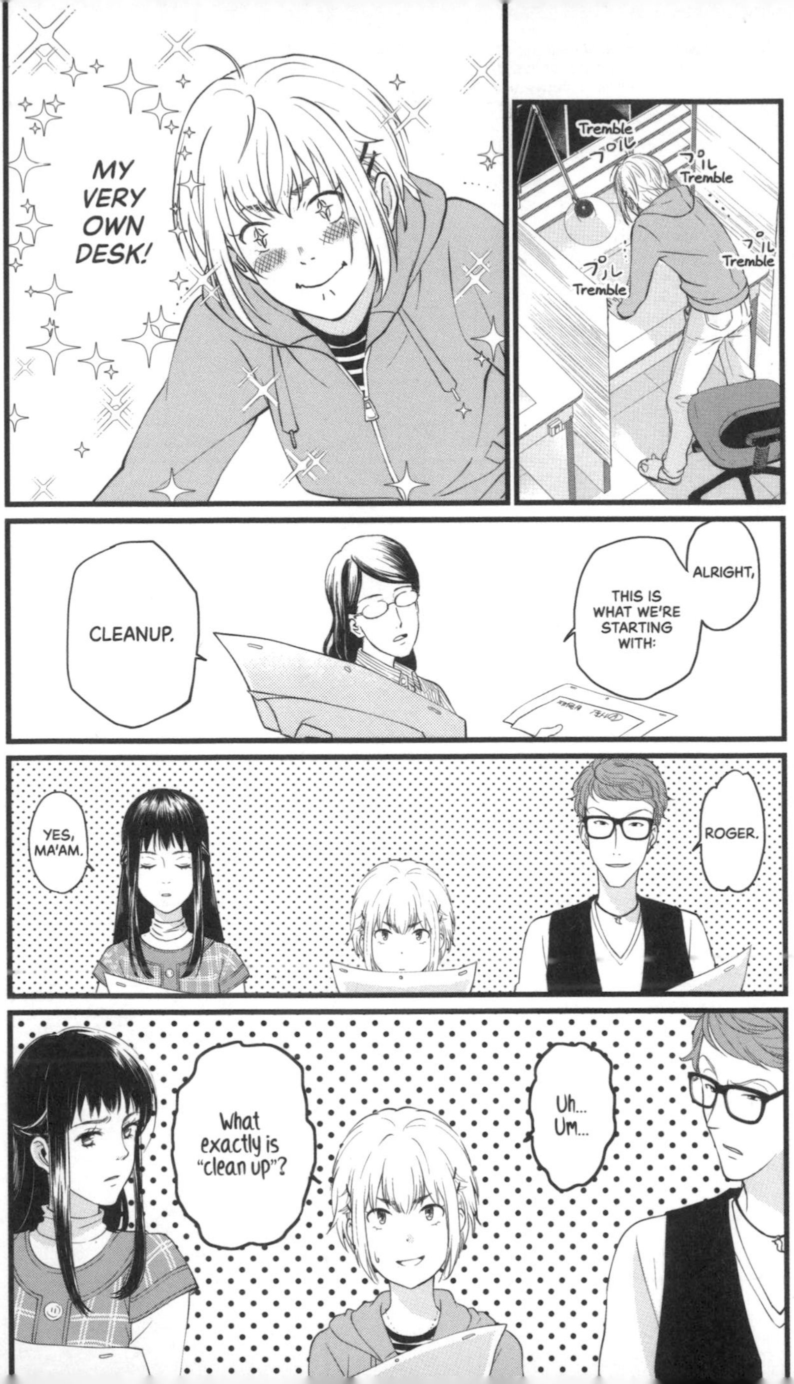

プル Tremble
プル Tremble
プル Tremble
プル Tremble
MY VERY OWN DESK!
ALRIGHT, THIS IS WHAT WE'RE STARTING WITH:
CLEANUP.
ROGER.
YES, MA'AM.
Uh... Um...
What exactly is "clean up"?

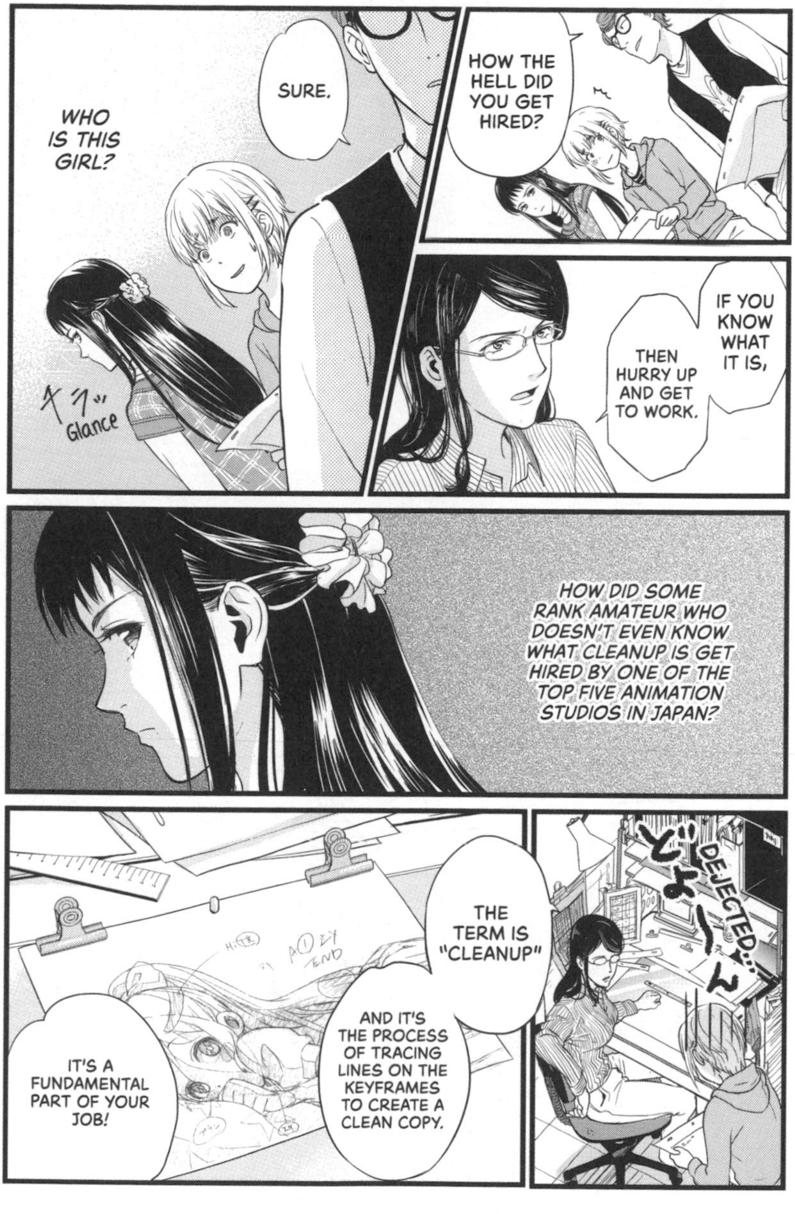
HOW THE HELL DID YOU GET HIRED?
IF YOU KNOW WHAT IT IS,
THEN HURRY UP AND GET TO WORK.
SURE.
WHO IS THIS GIRL?
Glance
HOW DID SOME RANK AMATEUR WHO DOESN'T EVEN KNOW WHAT CLEANUP IS GET HIRED BY ONE OF THE TOP FIVE ANIMATION STUDIOS IN JAPAN?
DEJECTED...
THE TERM IS "CLEANUP"
AND IT'S THE PROCESS OF TRACING LINES ON THE KEYFRAMES TO CREATE A CLEAN COPY.
IT'S A FUNDAMENTAL PART OF YOUR JOB!

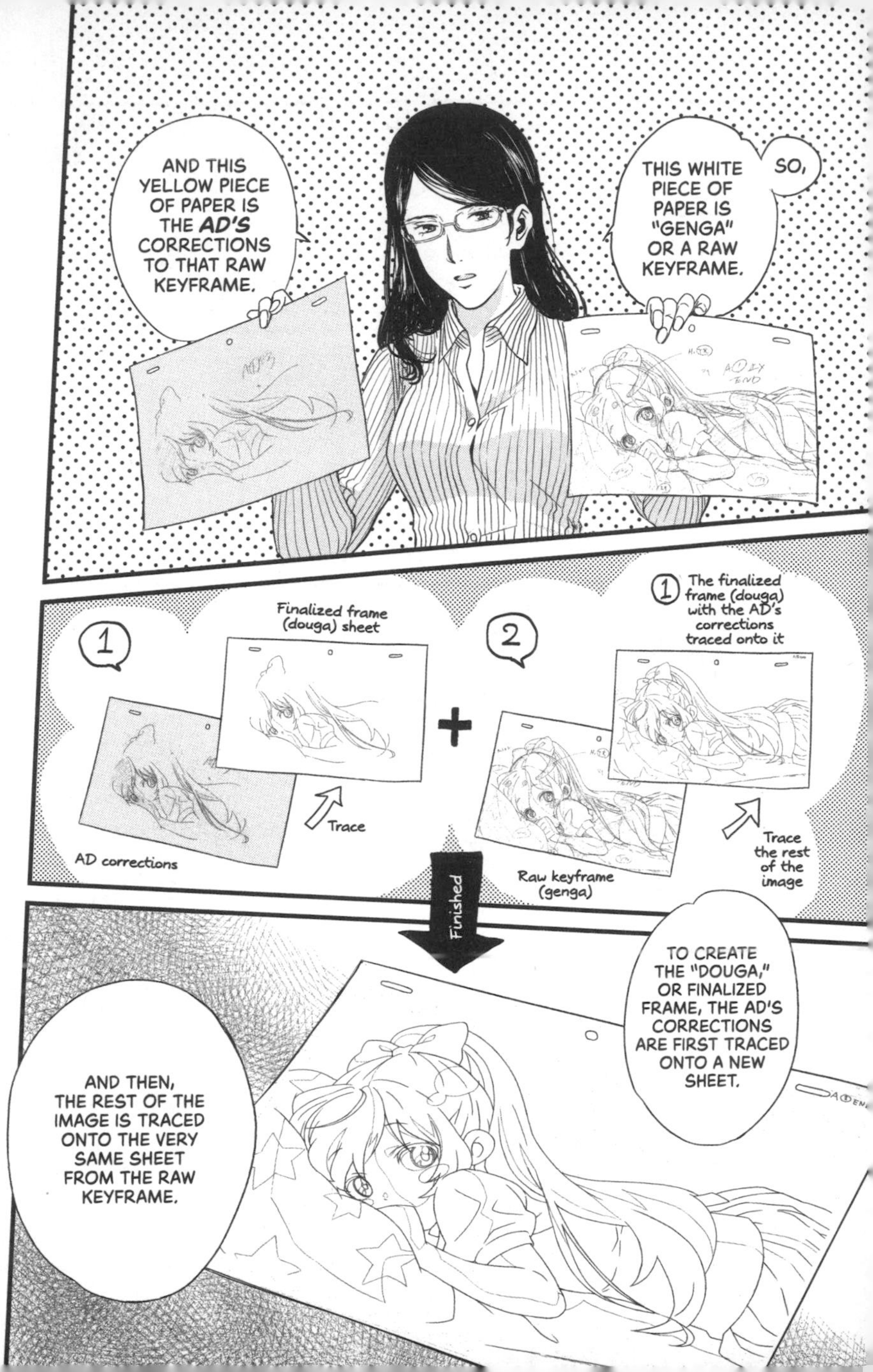
SO,
THIS WHITE PIECE OF PAPER IS "GENGA" OR A RAW KEYFRAME.
AND THIS YELLOW PIECE OF PAPER IS THE AD'S CORRECTIONS TO THAT RAW KEYFRAME.
① The finalized frame (douga) with the AD's corrections traced onto it
2
Trace the rest of the image
Raw keyframe (genga)
Finished
1
Finalized frame (douga) sheet
Trace
AD corrections
TO CREATE THE "DOUGA," OR FINALIZED FRAME, THE AD'S CORRECTIONS ARE FIRST TRACED ONTO A NEW SHEET.
AND THEN, THE REST OF THE IMAGE IS TRACED ONTO THE VERY SAME SHEET FROM THE RAW KEYFRAME.

AD (Sakkan): Short for Animation Director (sakuga kantoku). The AD's job is to correct keyframes to ensure uniformity in the art of a production.

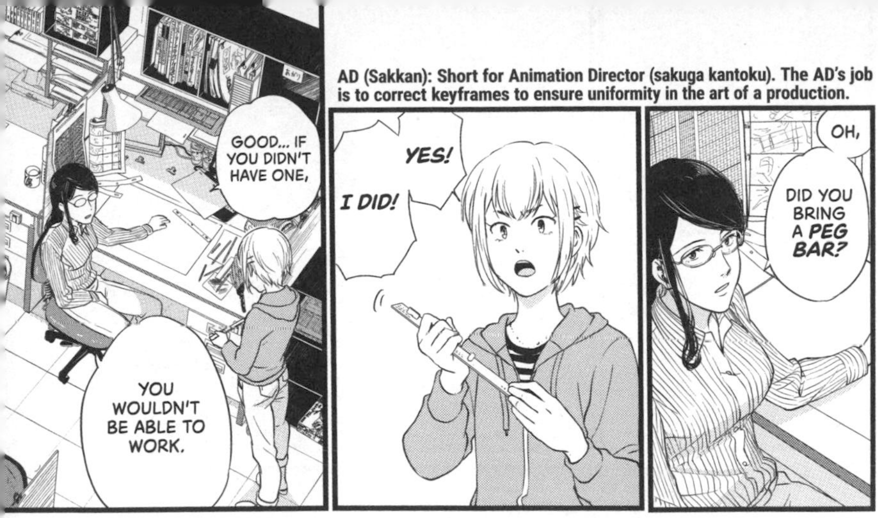
OH,
DID YOU BRING A PEG BAR?
YES!
I DID!
GOOD... IF YOU DIDN'T HAVE ONE,
YOU WOULDN'T BE ABLE TO WORK.

SIGN: STUDIO 7

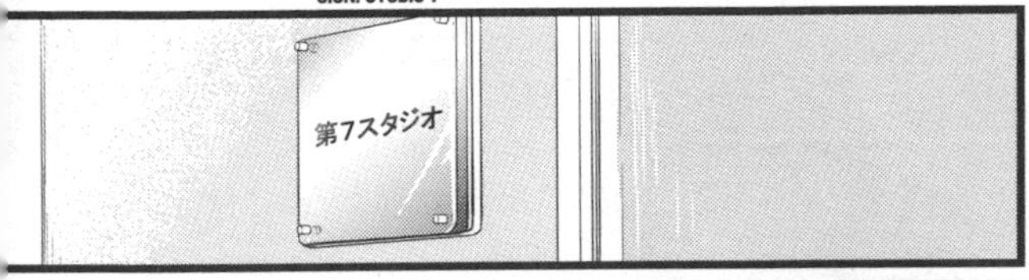
第7スタジオ

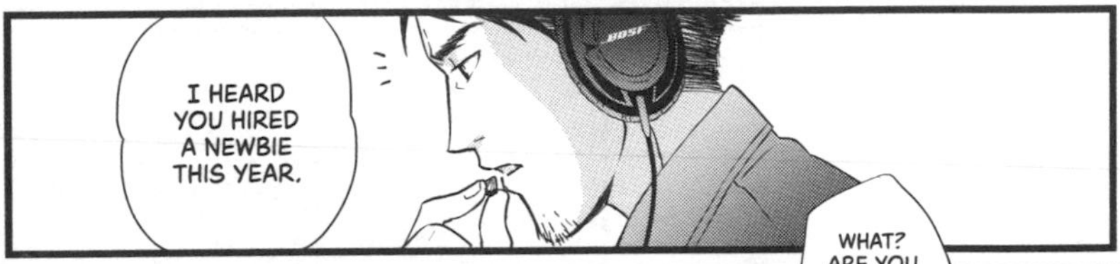
I HEARD YOU HIRED A NEWBIE THIS YEAR.

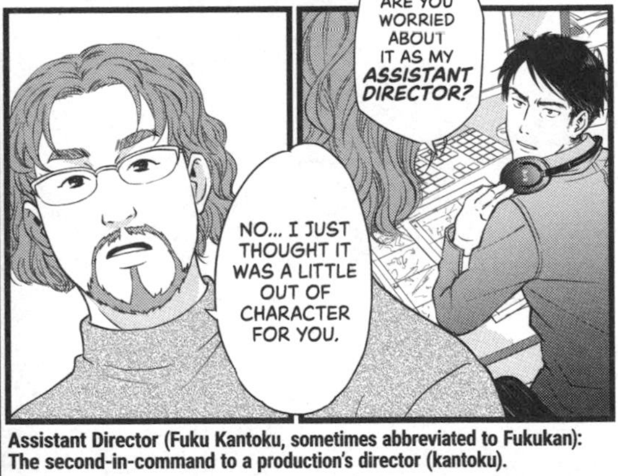
WHAT? ARE YOU WORRIED ABOUT IT AS MY ASSISTANT DIRECTOR?
NO... I JUST THOUGHT IT WAS A LITTLE OUT OF CHARACTER FOR YOU.

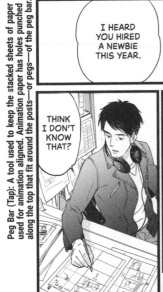

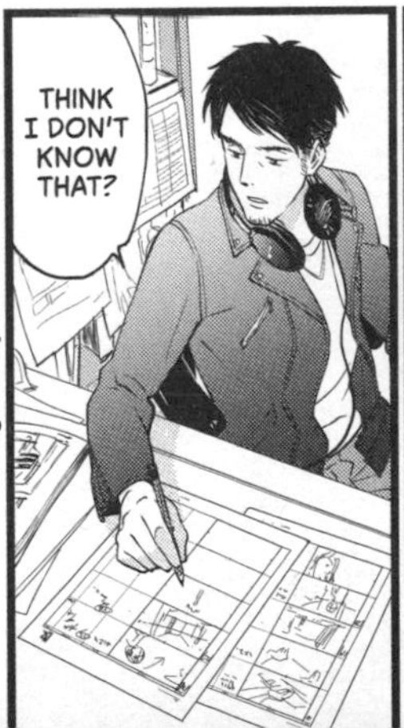
THINK I DON'T KNOW THAT?

Peg Bar (Tap): A tool used to keep the stacked sheets of paper used for animation aligned. Animation paper has holes punched along the top that fit around the posts—or pegs—of the peg bar.

Assistant Director (Fuku Kantoku, sometimes abbreviated to Fukukan): The second-in-command to a production's director (kantoku).

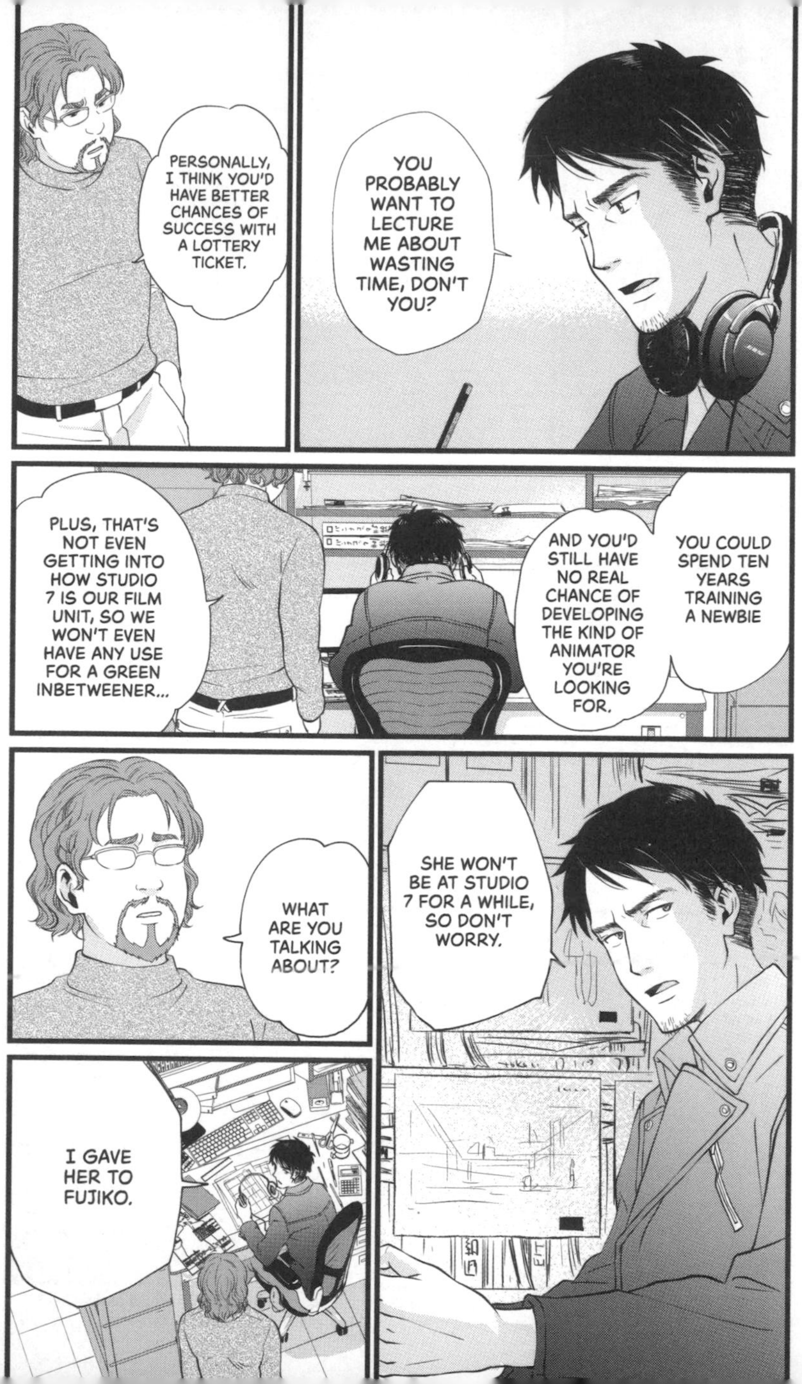
YOU PROBABLY WANT TO LECTURE ME ABOUT WASTING TIME, DON'T YOU?
PERSONALLY, I THINK YOU'D HAVE BETTER CHANCES OF SUCCESS WITH A LOTTERY TICKET.
YOU COULD SPEND TEN YEARS TRAINING A NEWBIE
AND YOU'D STILL HAVE NO REAL CHANCE OF DEVELOPING THE KIND OF ANIMATOR YOU'RE LOOKING FOR.
PLUS, THAT'S NOT EVEN GETTING INTO HOW STUDIO 7 IS OUR FILM UNIT, SO WE WON'T EVEN HAVE ANY USE FOR A GREEN INBETWEENER...
SHE WON'T BE AT STUDIO 7 FOR A WHILE, SO DON'T WORRY.
WHAT ARE YOU TALKING ABOUT?
I GAVE HER TO FUJIKO.

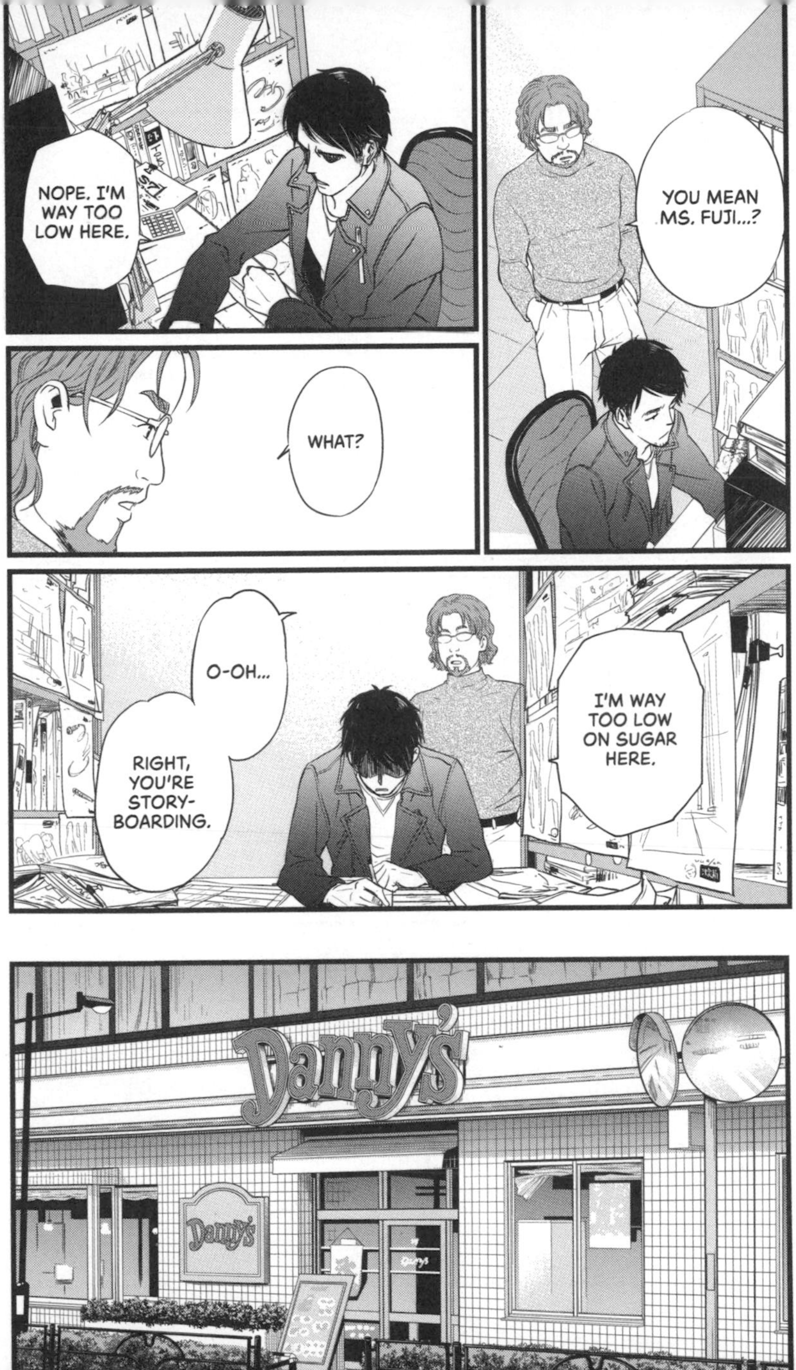
YOU MEAN MS. FUJI...?
NOPE. I'M WAY TOO LOW HERE.
WHAT?
I'M WAY TOO LOW ON SUGAR HERE.
O-OH...
RIGHT, YOU'RE STORY-BOARDING.
Danny's
Danny's

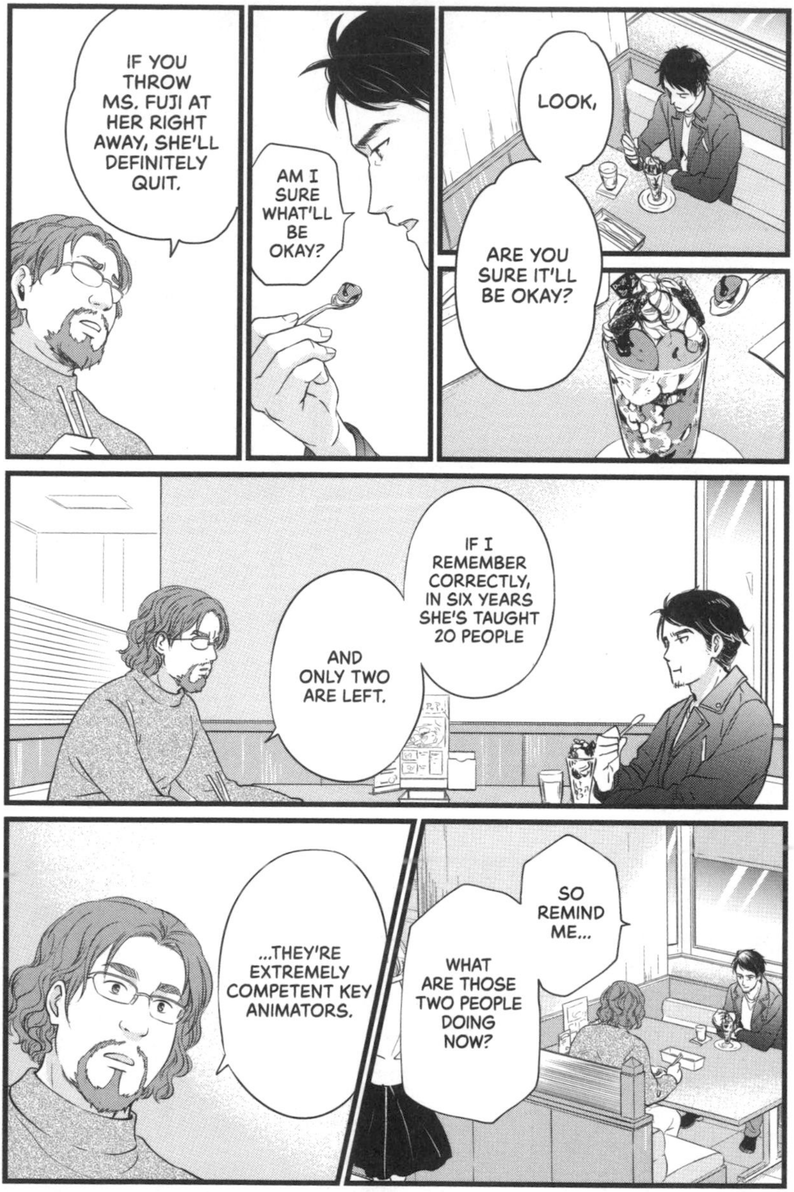
LOOK,
ARE YOU SURE IT'LL BE OKAY?
AM I SURE WHAT'LL BE OKAY?
IF YOU THROW MS. FUJI AT HER RIGHT AWAY, SHE'LL DEFINITELY QUIT.
IF I REMEMBER CORRECTLY, IN SIX YEARS SHE'S TAUGHT 20 PEOPLE
AND ONLY TWO ARE LEFT.
SO REMIND ME...
WHAT ARE THOSE TWO PEOPLE DOING NOW?
...THEY'RE EXTREMELY COMPETENT KEY ANIMATORS.

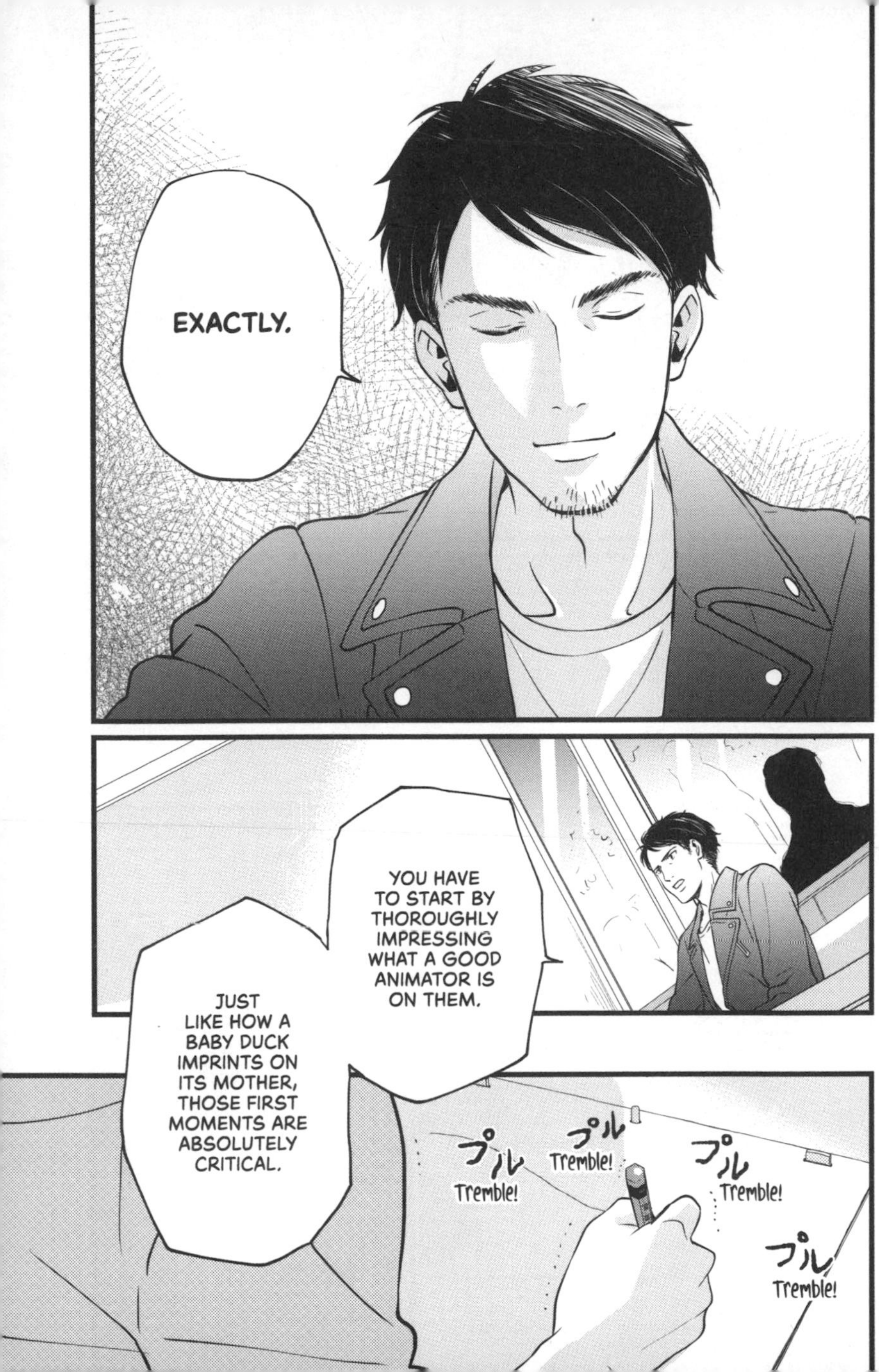
EXACTLY.
YOU HAVE TO START BY THOROUGHLY IMPRESSING WHAT A GOOD ANIMATOR IS ON THEM.
JUST LIKE HOW A BABY DUCK IMPRINTS ON ITS MOTHER, THOSE FIRST MOMENTS ARE ABSOLUTELY CRITICAL.
プル Tremble!
プル Tremble!
プル Tremble!
プル Tremble!

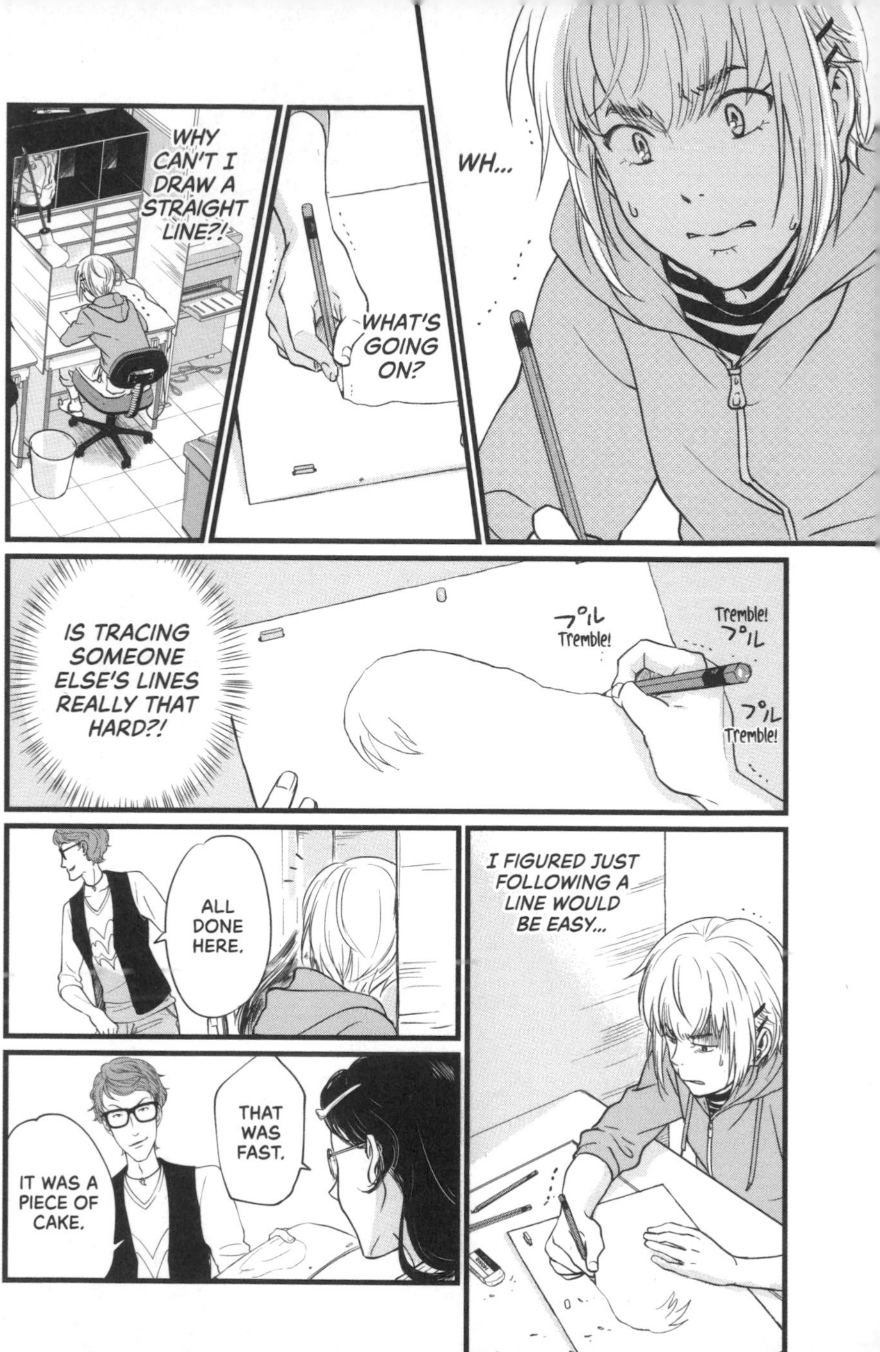
WH...
WHAT'S GOING ON?
WHY CAN'T I DRAW A STRAIGHT LINE?!
Tremble! プル
プル Tremble!
プル Tremble!
IS TRACING SOMEONE ELSE'S LINES REALLY THAT HARD?!
I FIGURED JUST FOLLOWING A LINE WOULD BE EASY...
ALL DONE HERE.
THAT WAS FAST.
IT WAS A PIECE OF CAKE.

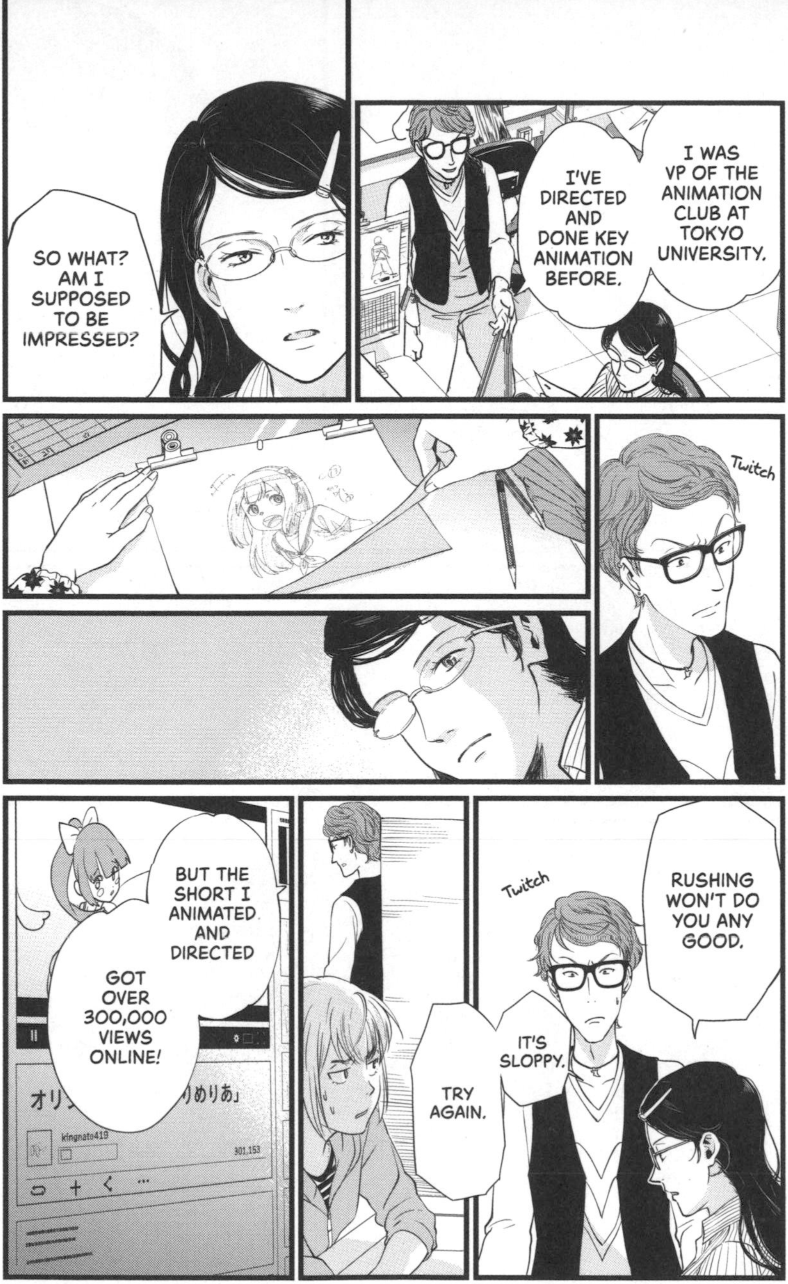
I WAS VP OF THE ANIMATION CLUB AT TOKYO UNIVERSITY.
I'VE DIRECTED AND DONE KEY ANIMATION BEFORE.
SO WHAT? AM I SUPPOSED TO BE IMPRESSED?
Twitch
RUSHING WON'T DO YOU ANY GOOD.
Twitch
IT'S SLOPPY.
TRY AGAIN.
BUT THE SHORT I ANIMATED AND DIRECTED
GOT OVER 300,000 VIEWS ONLINE!
kingnato419
301,153

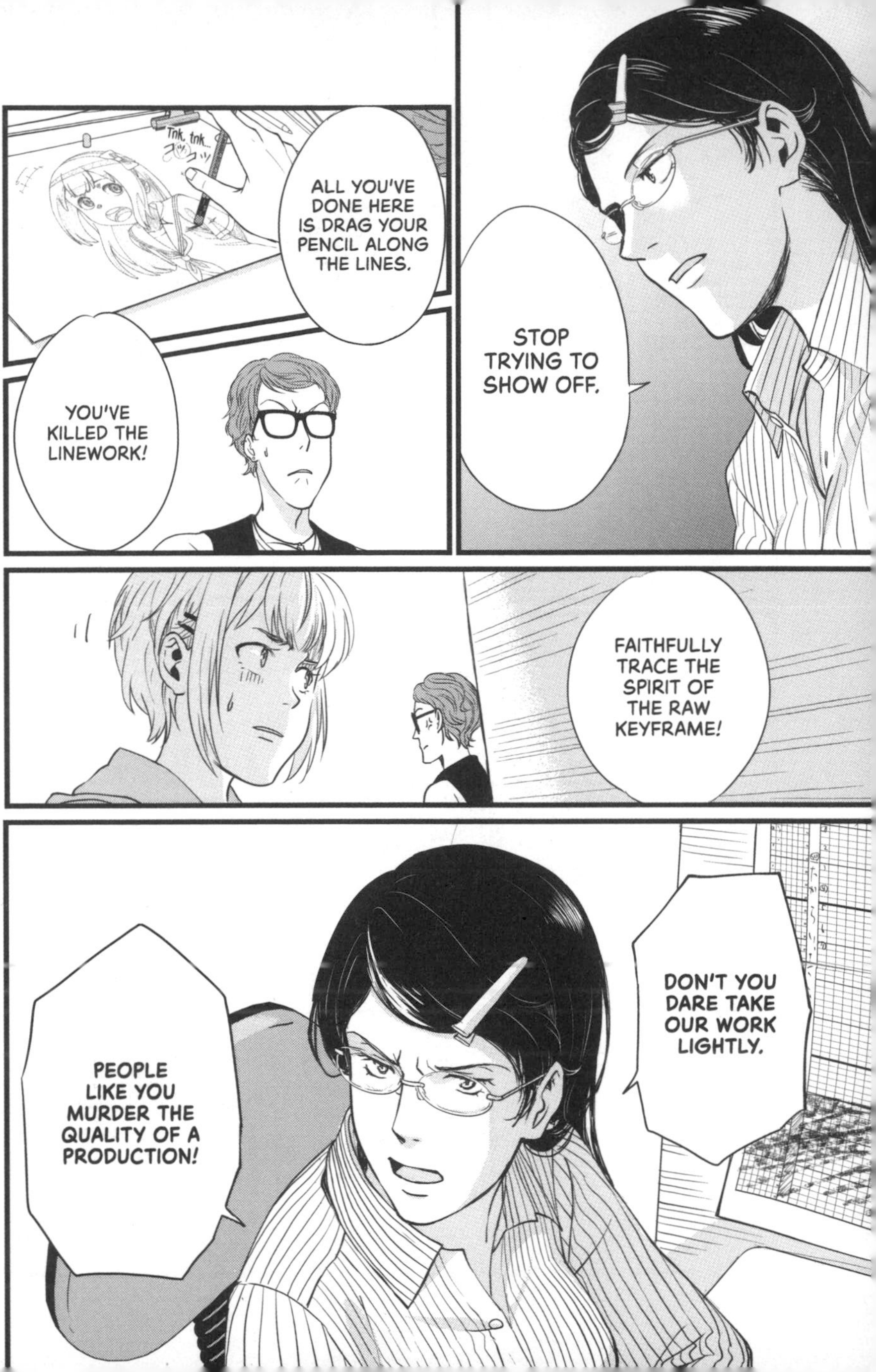
STOP TRYING TO SHOW OFF.
Tnk, tnk...
ALL YOU'VE DONE HERE IS DRAG YOUR PENCIL ALONG THE LINES.
YOU'VE KILLED THE LINEWORK!
FAITHFULLY TRACE THE SPIRIT OF THE RAW KEYFRAME!
DON'T YOU DARE TAKE OUR WORK LIGHTLY.
PEOPLE LIKE YOU MURDER THE QUALITY OF A PRODUCTION!

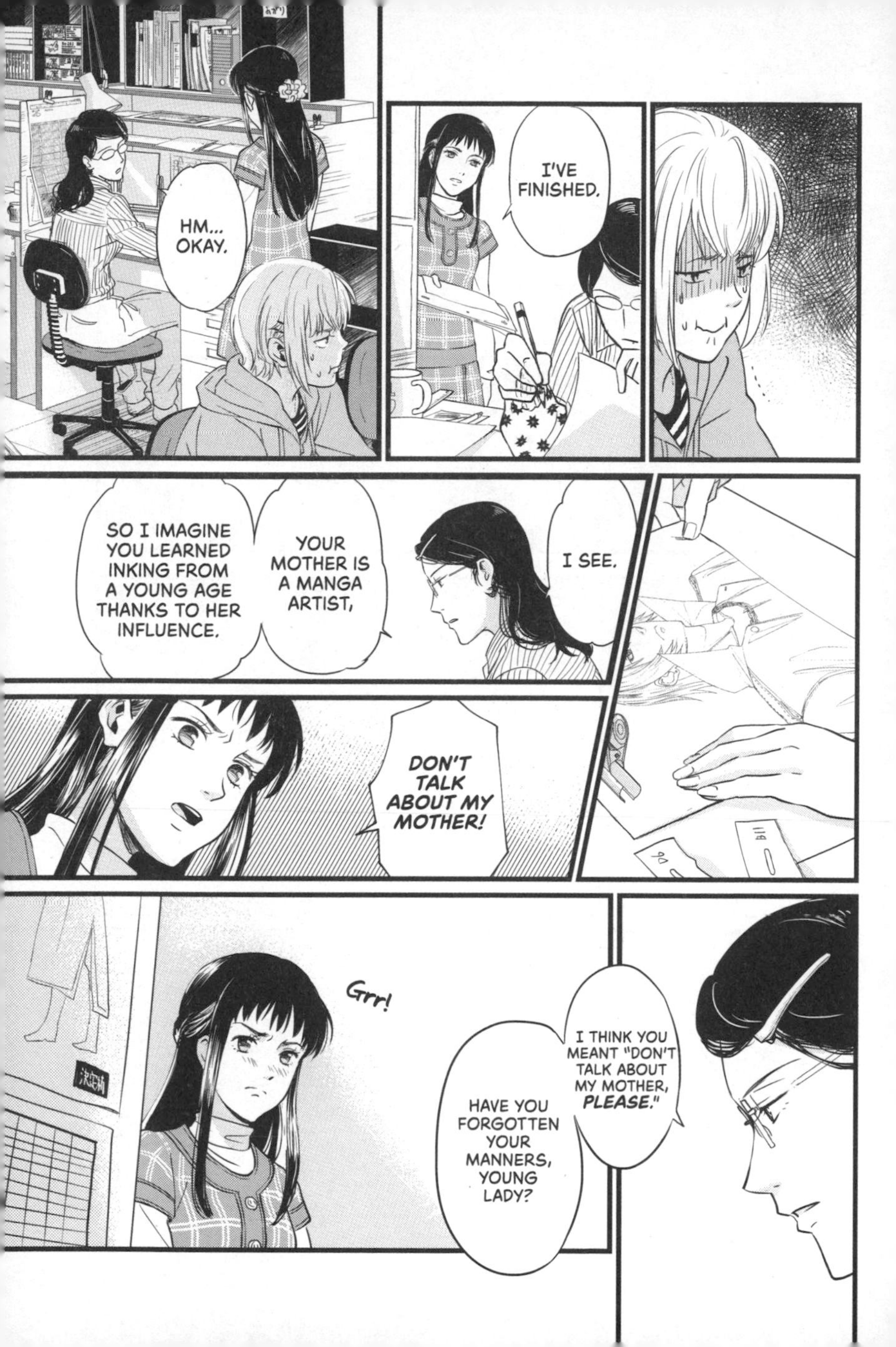
I'VE FINISHED.
HM... OKAY.
I SEE.
YOUR MOTHER IS A MANGA ARTIST,
SO I IMAGINE YOU LEARNED INKING FROM A YOUNG AGE THANKS TO HER INFLUENCE.
DON'T TALK ABOUT MY MOTHER!
I THINK YOU MEANT "DON'T TALK ABOUT MY MOTHER, *PLEASE.*"
HAVE YOU FORGOTTEN YOUR MANNERS, YOUNG LADY?
Grr!

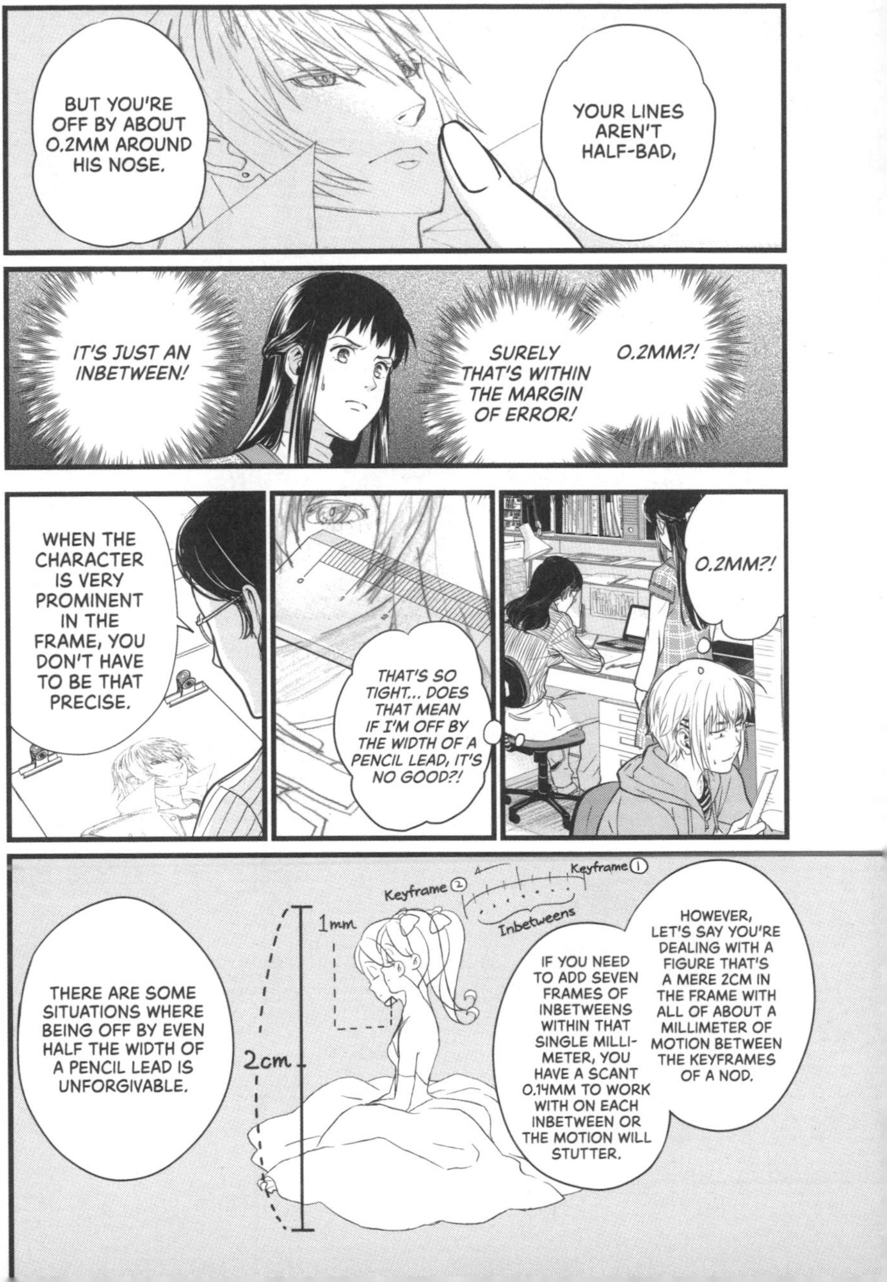
YOUR LINES AREN'T HALF-BAD,
BUT YOU'RE OFF BY ABOUT 0.2MM AROUND HIS NOSE.
0.2MM?!
SURELY THAT'S WITHIN THE MARGIN OF ERROR!
IT'S JUST AN INBETWEEN!
0.2MM?!
THAT'S SO TIGHT... DOES THAT MEAN IF I'M OFF BY THE WIDTH OF A PENCIL LEAD, IT'S NO GOOD?!
WHEN THE CHARACTER IS VERY PROMINENT IN THE FRAME, YOU DON'T HAVE TO BE THAT PRECISE.
HOWEVER, LET'S SAY YOU'RE DEALING WITH A FIGURE THAT'S A MERE 2CM IN THE FRAME WITH ALL OF ABOUT A MILLIMETER OF MOTION BETWEEN THE KEYFRAMES OF A NOD,
IF YOU NEED TO ADD SEVEN FRAMES OF INBETWEENS WITHIN THAT SINGLE MILLIMETER, YOU HAVE A SCANT 0.14MM TO WORK WITH ON EACH INBETWEEN OR THE MOTION WILL STUTTER.
Keyframe ①
Keyframe ②
Inbetweens
1mm
2cm
THERE ARE SOME SITUATIONS WHERE BEING OFF BY EVEN HALF THE WIDTH OF A PENCIL LEAD IS UNFORGIVABLE.

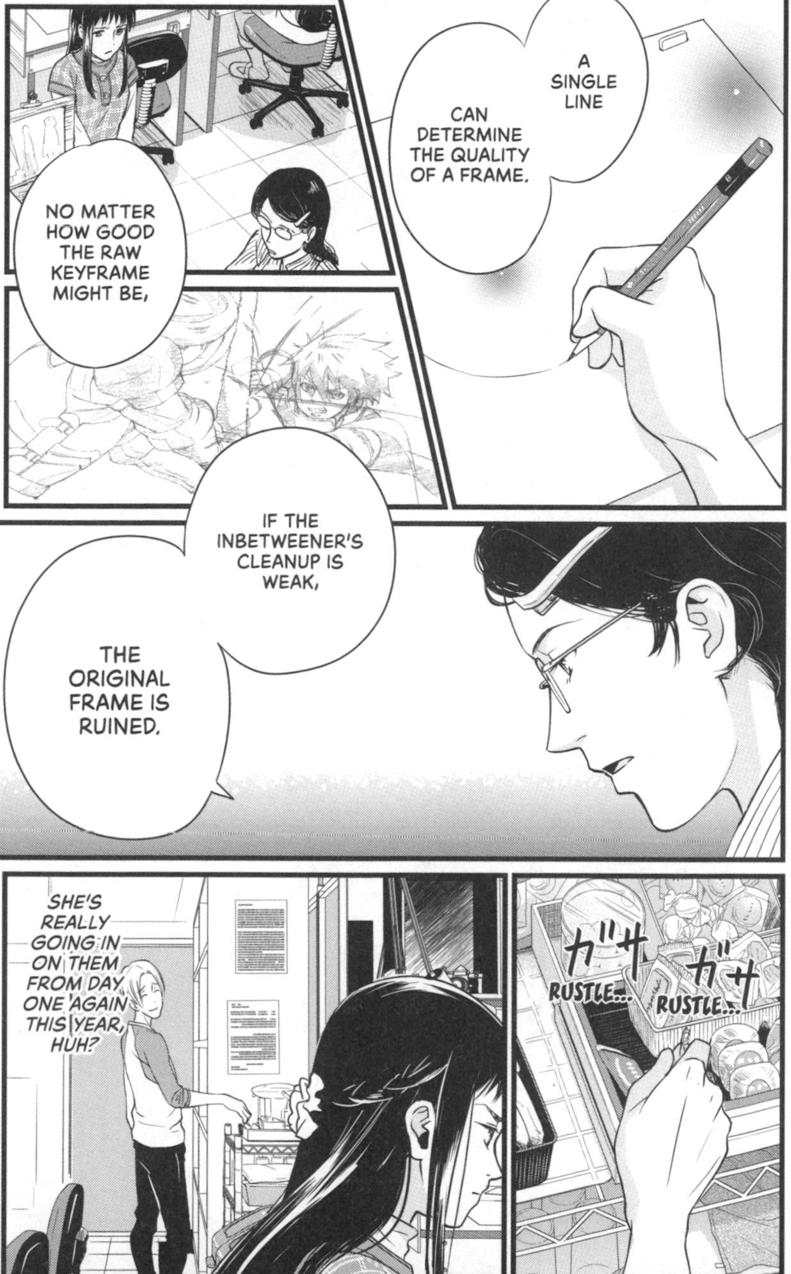
A SINGLE LINE
CAN DETERMINE THE QUALITY OF A FRAME.
NO MATTER HOW GOOD THE RAW KEYFRAME MIGHT BE,
IF THE INBETWEENER'S CLEANUP IS WEAK,
THE ORIGINAL FRAME IS RUINED.
ガサ
RUSTLE...
ガサ
RUSTLE...
SHE'S REALLY GOING IN ON THEM FROM DAY ONE AGAIN THIS YEAR, HUH?

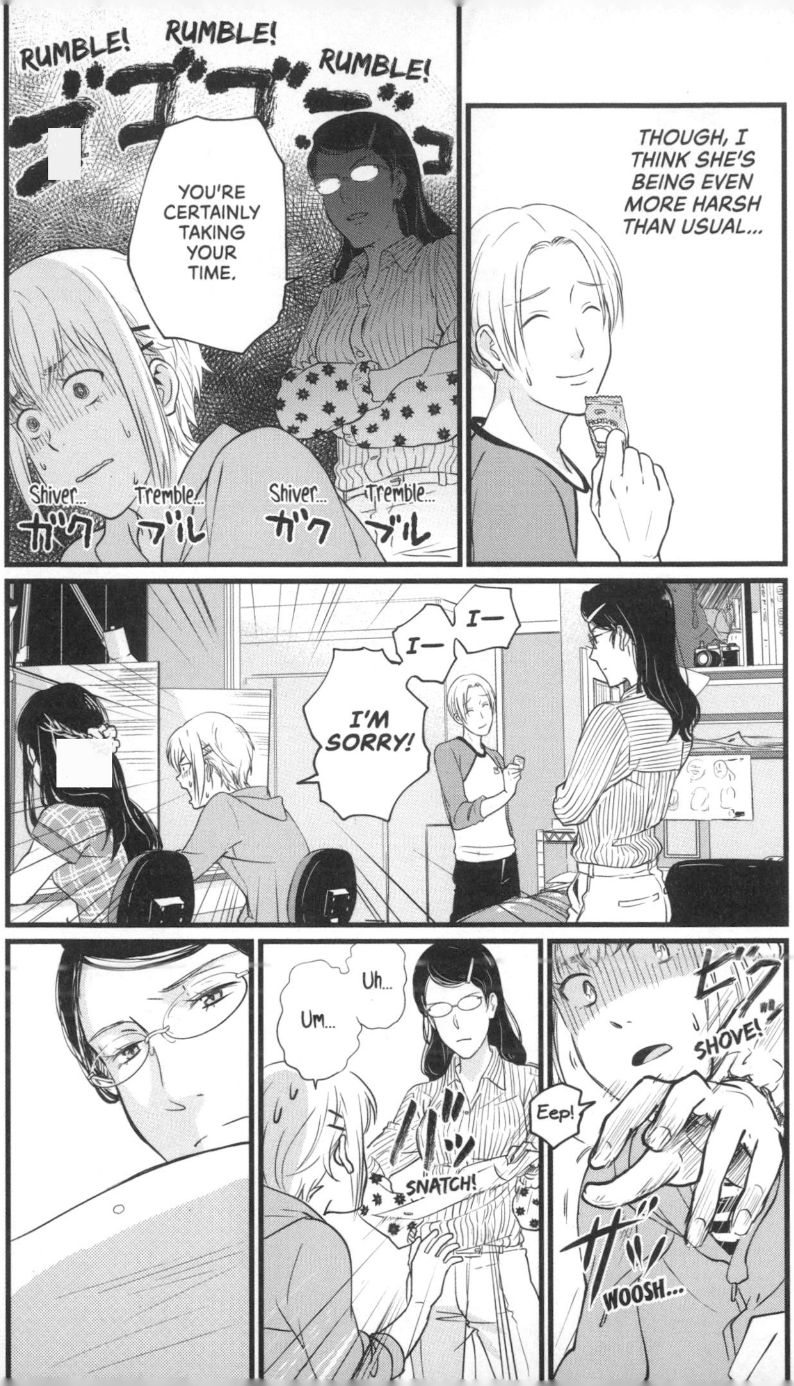

THOUGH, I THINK SHE'S BEING EVEN MORE HARSH THAN USUAL...
RUMBLE!
RUMBLE!
RUMBLE!
YOU'RE CERTAINLY TAKING YOUR TIME.
Tremble...
ブル
Shiver...
ガク
Tremble...
ブル
Shiver...
ガク
I—
I—
I'M SORRY!
SHOVE!
Eep!
WOOSH...
Uh...
Um...
SNATCH!

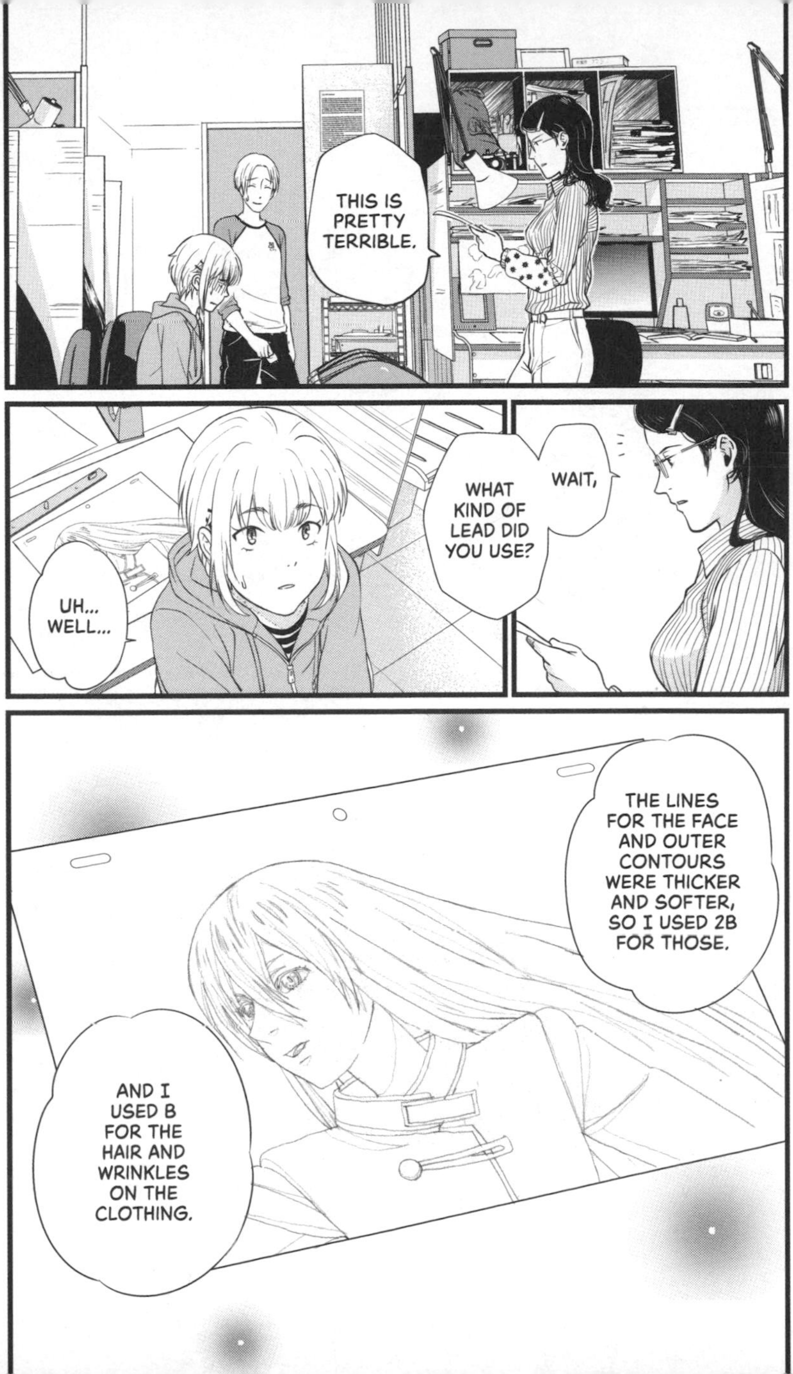
THIS IS PRETTY TERRIBLE.
WAIT,
WHAT KIND OF LEAD DID YOU USE?
UH... WELL...
THE LINES FOR THE FACE AND OUTER CONTOURS WERE THICKER AND SOFTER, SO I USED 2B FOR THOSE.
AND I USED B FOR THE HAIR AND WRINKLES ON THE CLOTHING.

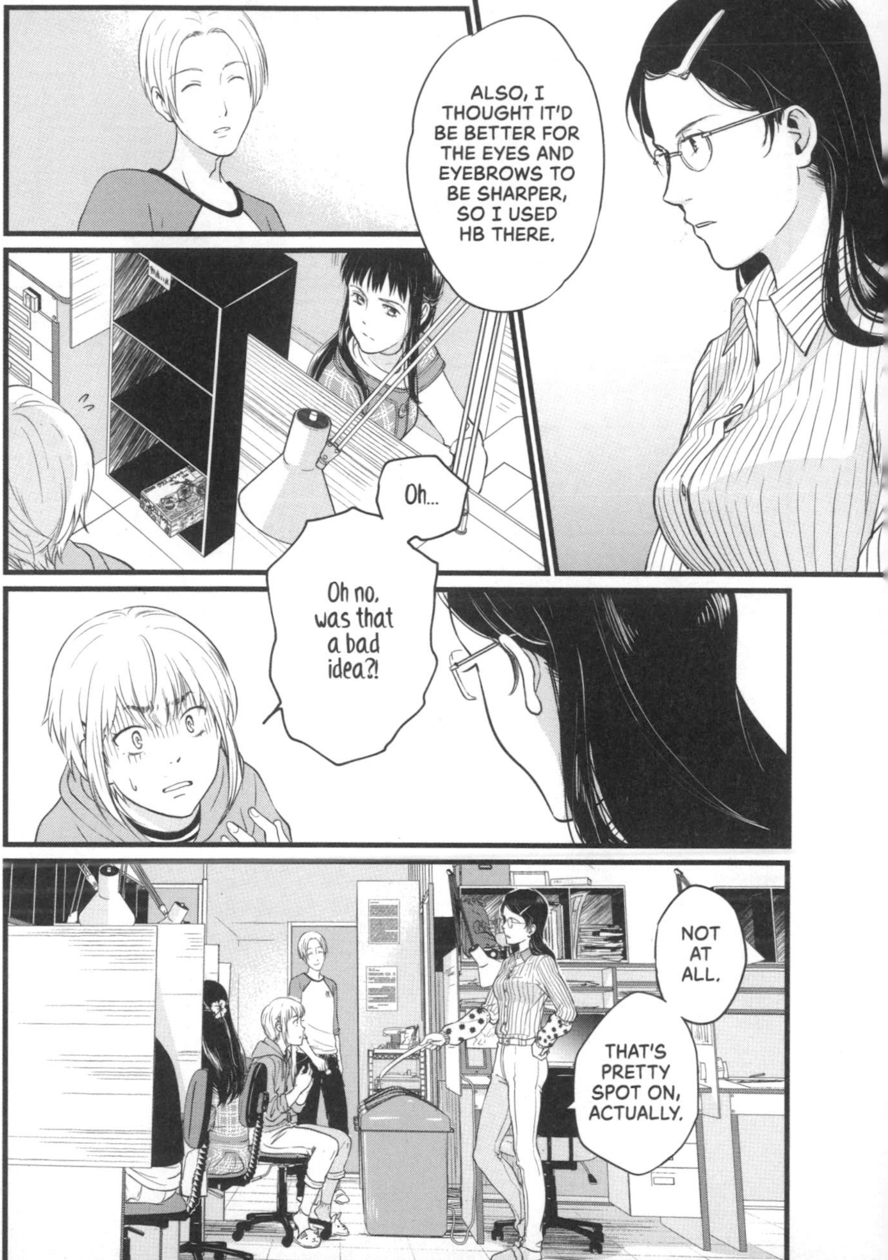
ALSO, I THOUGHT IT'D BE BETTER FOR THE EYES AND EYEBROWS TO BE SHARPER, SO I USED HB THERE.
Oh...
Oh no, was that a bad idea?!
NOT AT ALL.
THAT'S PRETTY SPOT ON, ACTUALLY.

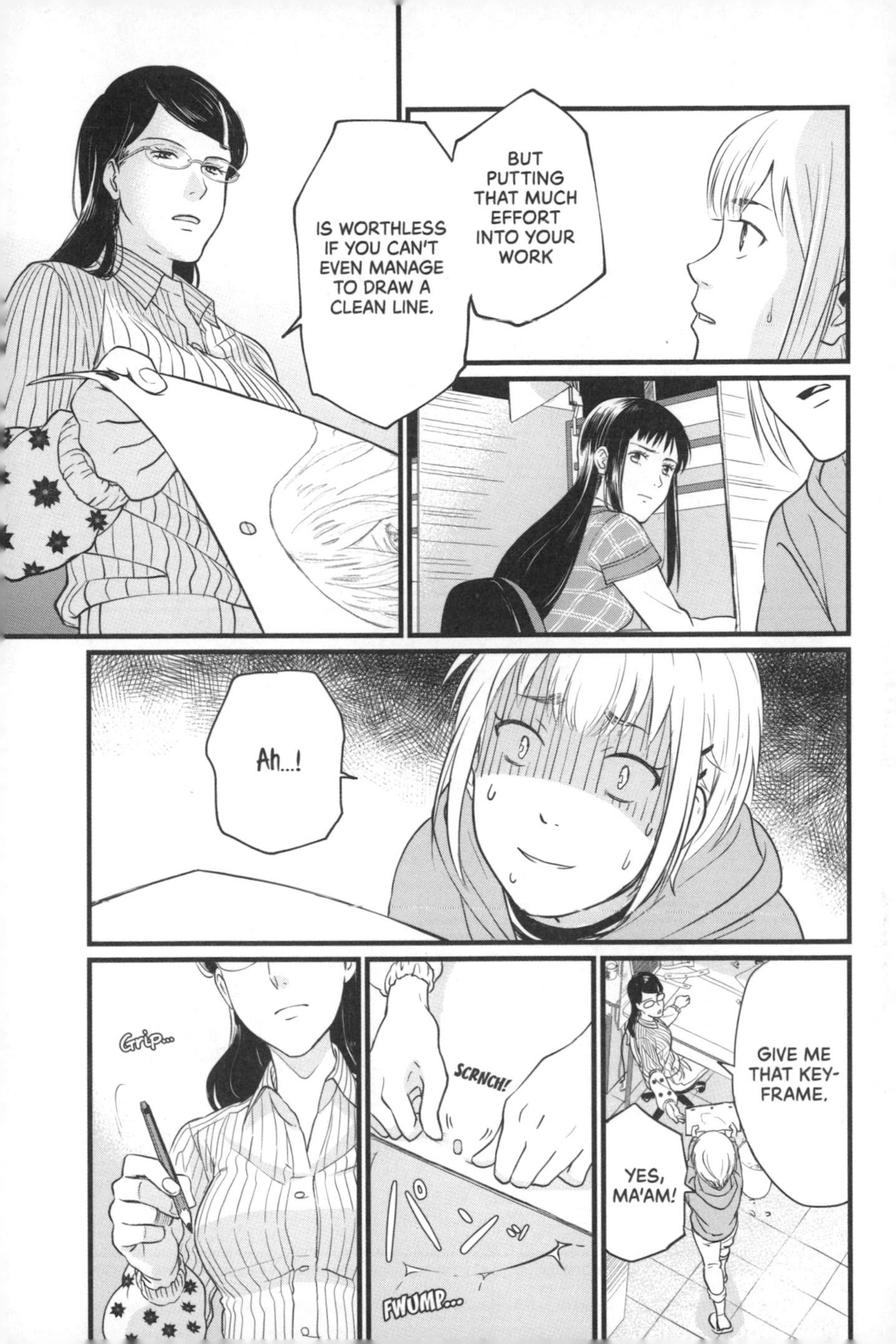
BUT PUTTING THAT MUCH EFFORT INTO YOUR WORK
IS WORTHLESS IF YOU CAN'T EVEN MANAGE TO DRAW A CLEAN LINE.
Ah...!
GIVE ME THAT KEY-FRAME.
YES, MA'AM!
SCRNCH!
FWUMP...
Grip...

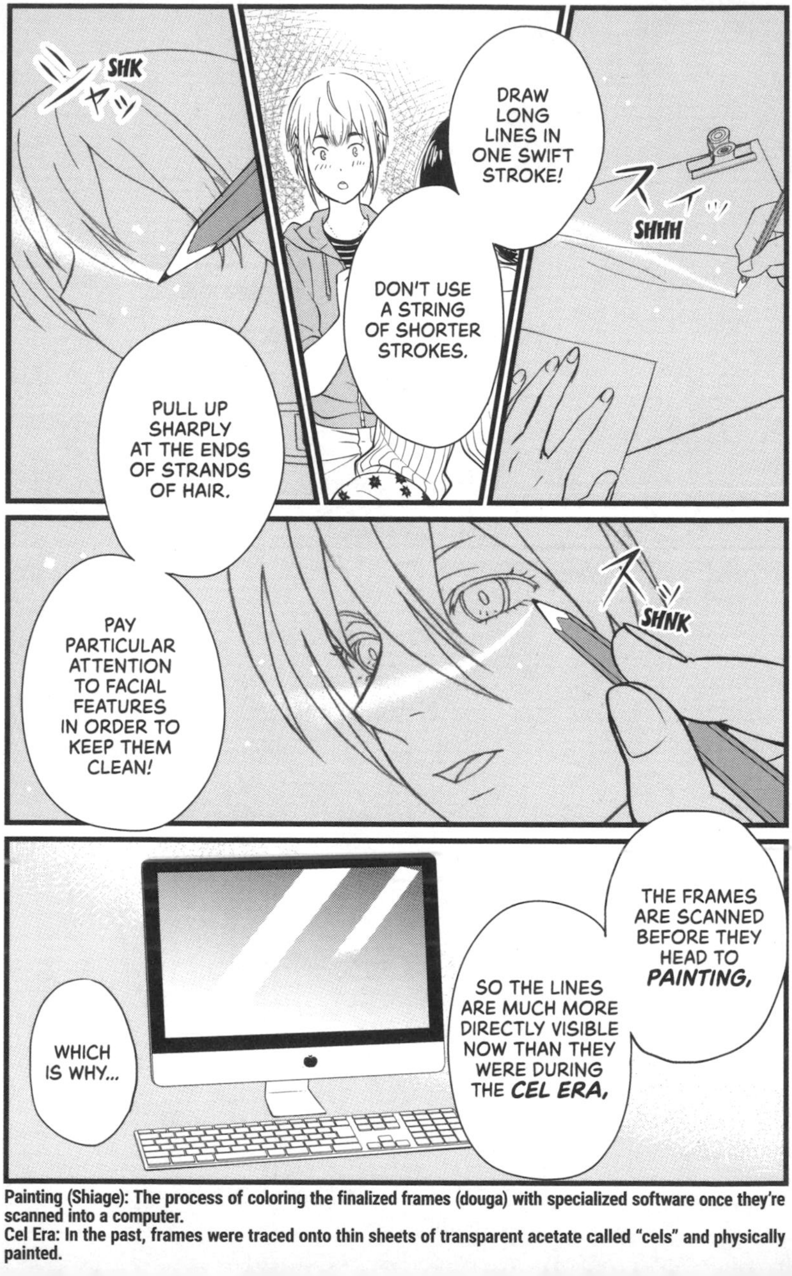
DRAW LONG LINES IN ONE SWIFT STROKE!
スイッ
SHHH
DON'T USE A STRING OF SHORTER STROKES.
シャッ
SHK
PULL UP SHARPLY AT THE ENDS OF STRANDS OF HAIR.
スッ
SHNK
PAY PARTICULAR ATTENTION TO FACIAL FEATURES IN ORDER TO KEEP THEM CLEAN!
THE FRAMES ARE SCANNED BEFORE THEY HEAD TO ***PAINTING,***
SO THE LINES ARE MUCH MORE DIRECTLY VISIBLE NOW THAN THEY WERE DURING THE ***CEL ERA,***
WHICH IS WHY...

Painting (Shiage): The process of coloring the finalized frames (douga) with specialized software once they're scanned into a computer.

Cel Era: In the past, frames were traced onto thin sheets of transparent acetate called "cels" and physically painted.

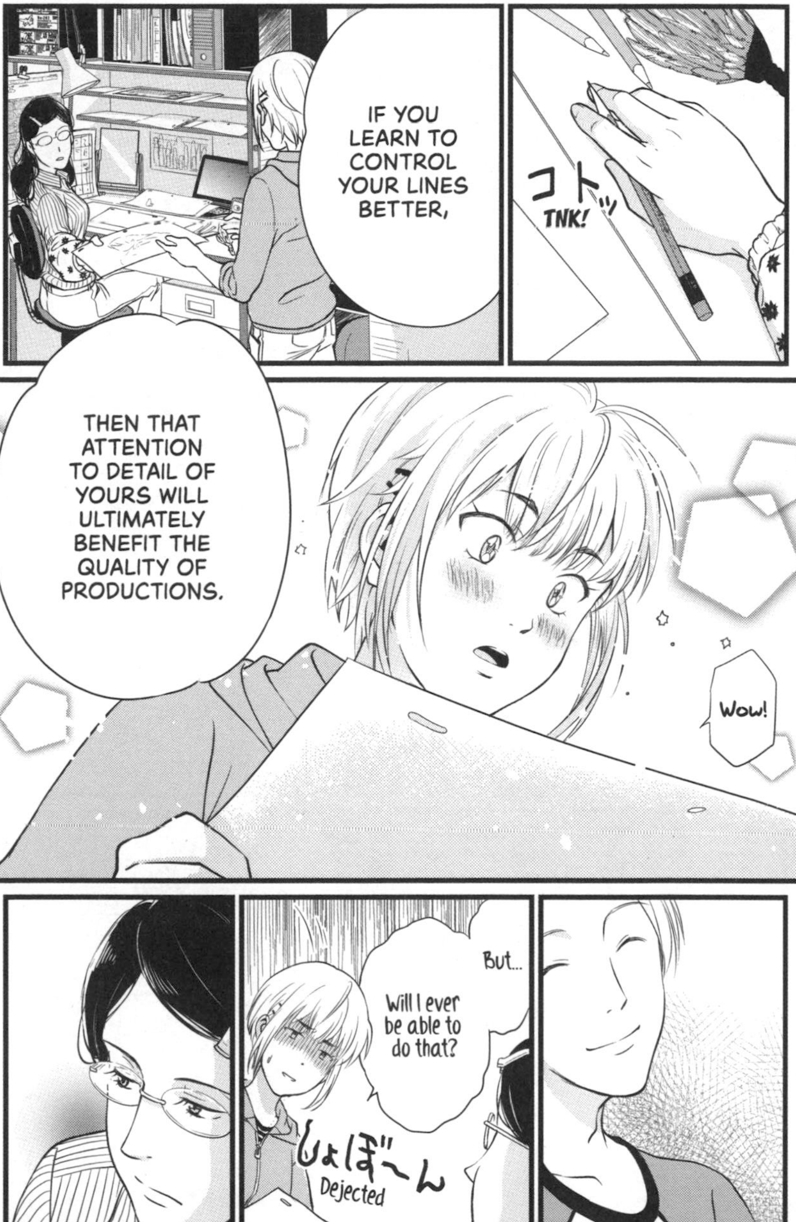
コトッ
TNK!
IF YOU LEARN TO CONTROL YOUR LINES BETTER,
THEN THAT ATTENTION TO DETAIL OF YOURS WILL ULTIMATELY BENEFIT THE QUALITY OF PRODUCTIONS.
Wow!
But...
Will I ever be able to do that?
しょぼ〜ん
Dejected

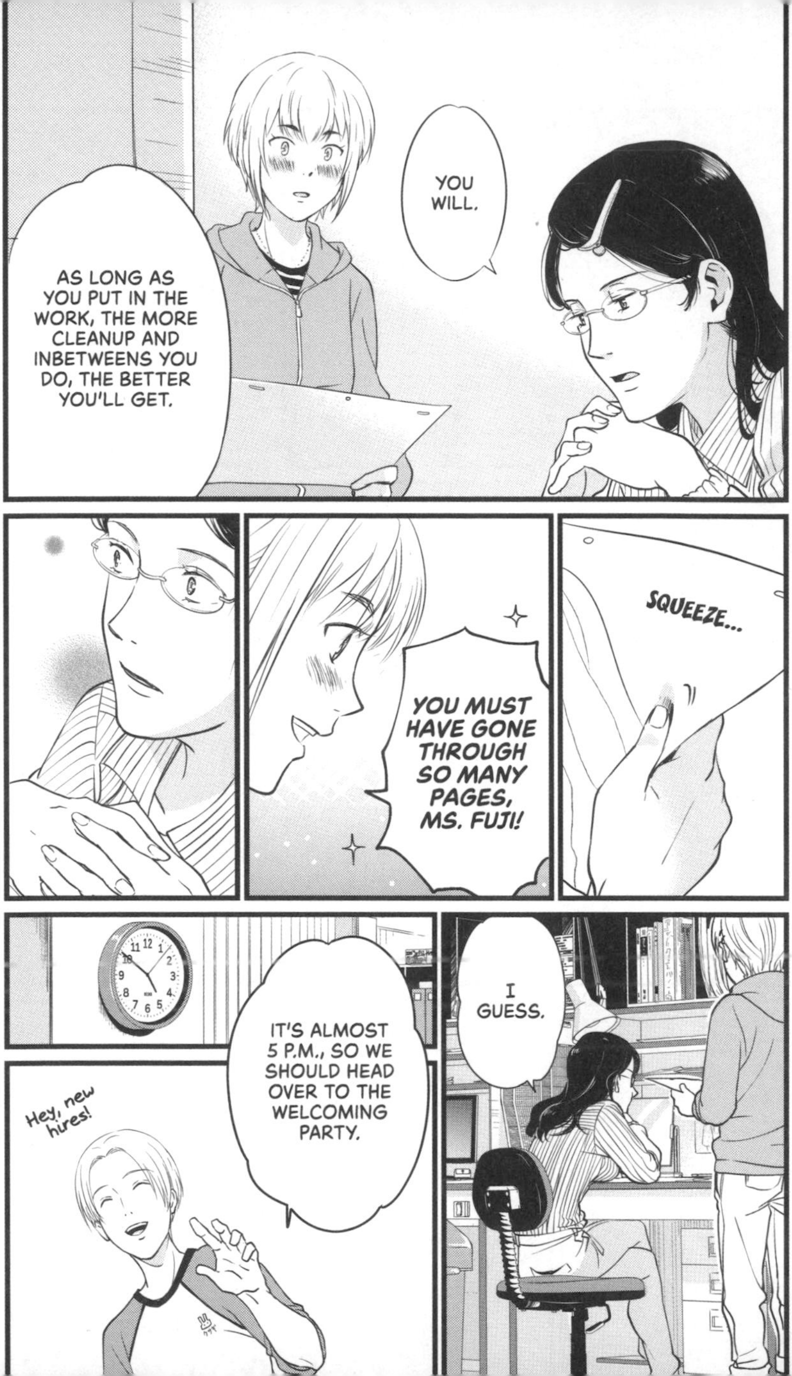
YOU WILL.
AS LONG AS YOU PUT IN THE WORK, THE MORE CLEANUP AND INBETWEENS YOU DO, THE BETTER YOU'LL GET.
SQUEEZE...
YOU MUST HAVE GONE THROUGH SO MANY PAGES, MS. FUJI!
I GUESS.
IT'S ALMOST 5 P.M., SO WE SHOULD HEAD OVER TO THE WELCOMING PARTY.
Hey, new hires!

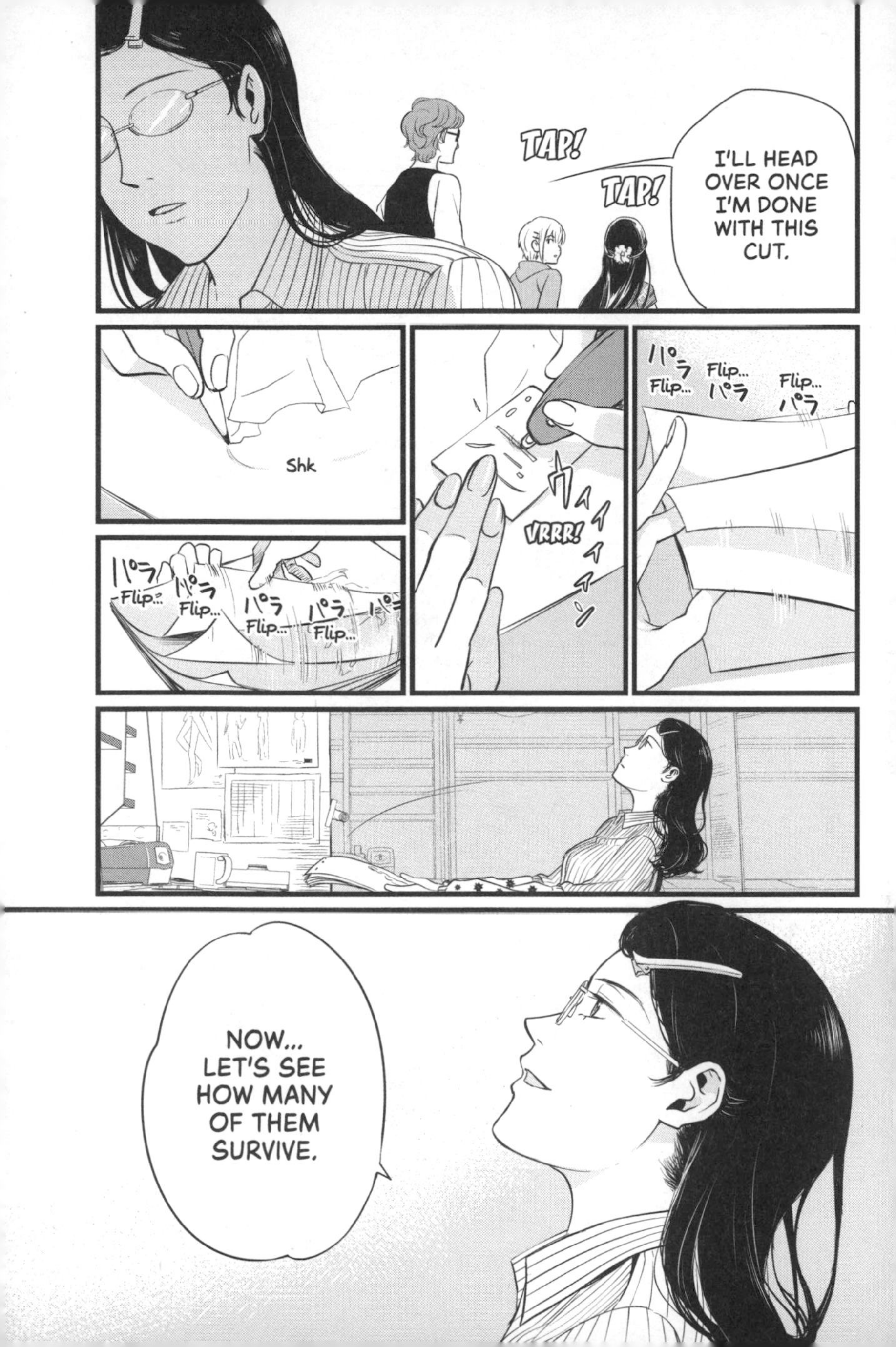

I'LL HEAD OVER ONCE I'M DONE WITH THIS CUT.
TAP!
TAP!
パラ
Flip...
Flip...
パラ
Flip...
パラ
ウィイイイン
VRRR!
Shk
パラ
Flip...
パラ
Flip...
パラ
Flip...
パラ
Flip...
NOW... LET'S SEE HOW MANY OF THEM SURVIVE.

Color of Paper Used in Animation

Make sure you check who's using what color!

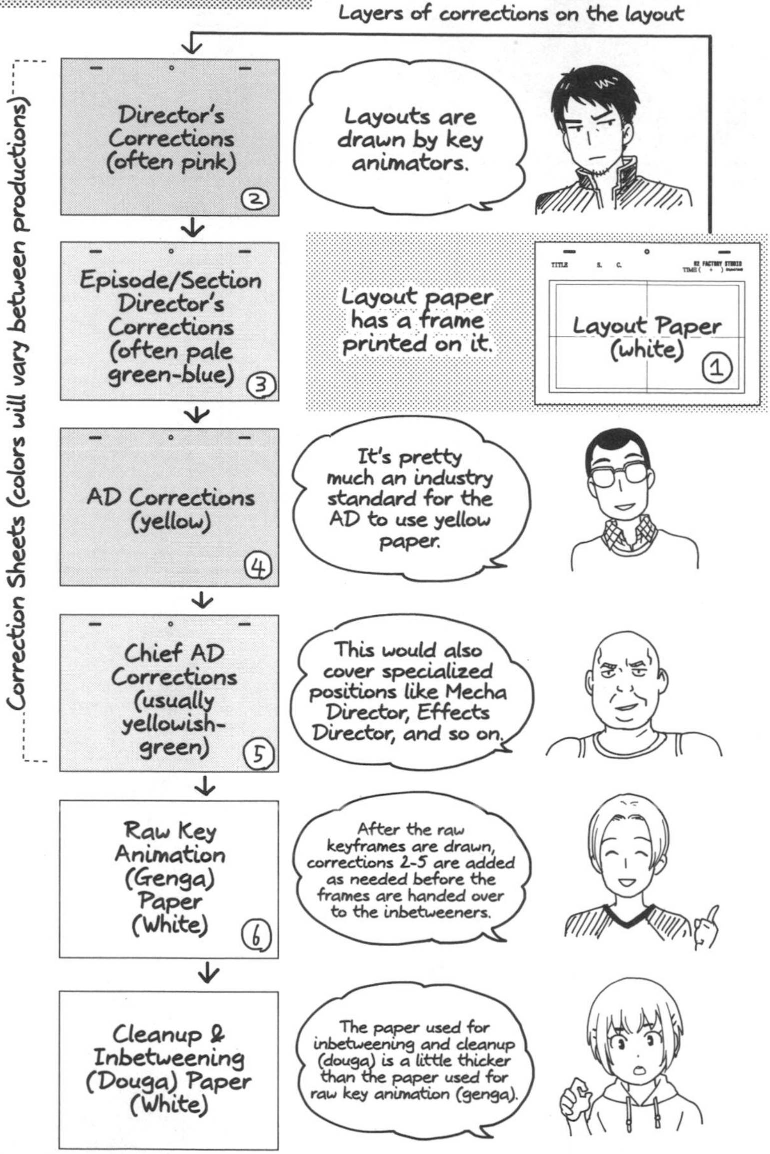
Layers of corrections on the layout
Correction Sheets (colors will vary between productions)
Director's Corrections (often pink) 2
Layouts are drawn by key animators.
Episode/Section Director's Corrections (often pale green-blue) 3
Layout paper has a frame printed on it.
TITLE S. C.
TIME (+)
Layout Paper (white) 1
AD Corrections (yellow) 4
It's pretty much an industry standard for the AD to use yellow paper.
Chief AD Corrections (usually yellowish-green) 5
This would also cover specialized positions like Mecha Director, Effects Director, and so on.
Raw Key Animation (Genga) Paper (White) 6
After the raw keyframes are drawn, corrections 2-5 are added as needed before the frames are handed over to the inbetweeners.
Cleanup & Inbetweening (Douga) Paper (White)
The paper used for inbetweening and cleanup (douga) is a little thicker than the paper used for raw key animation (genga).

CHAPTER 3: FALLING BEHIND

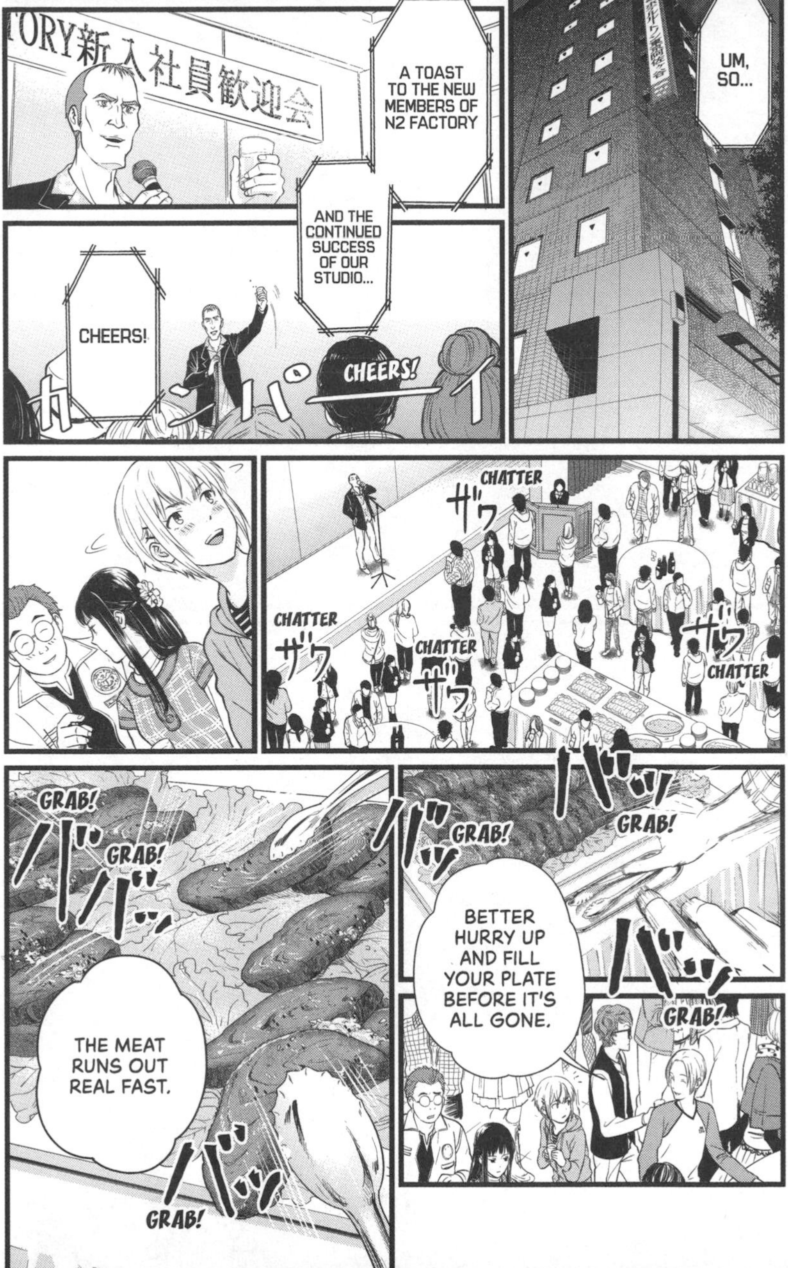
UM, SO...
TORY新入社員歓迎会
A TOAST TO THE NEW MEMBERS OF N2 FACTORY
AND THE CONTINUED SUCCESS OF OUR STUDIO...
CHEERS!
CHEERS!
CHATTER
CHATTER
CHATTER
CHATTER
GRAB!
GRAB!
BETTER HURRY UP AND FILL YOUR PLATE BEFORE IT'S ALL GONE.
GRAB!
GRAB!
GRAB!
THE MEAT RUNS OUT REAL FAST.
GRAB!

SIGN: N2 FACTORY NEW EMPLOYEE WELCOMING PARTY

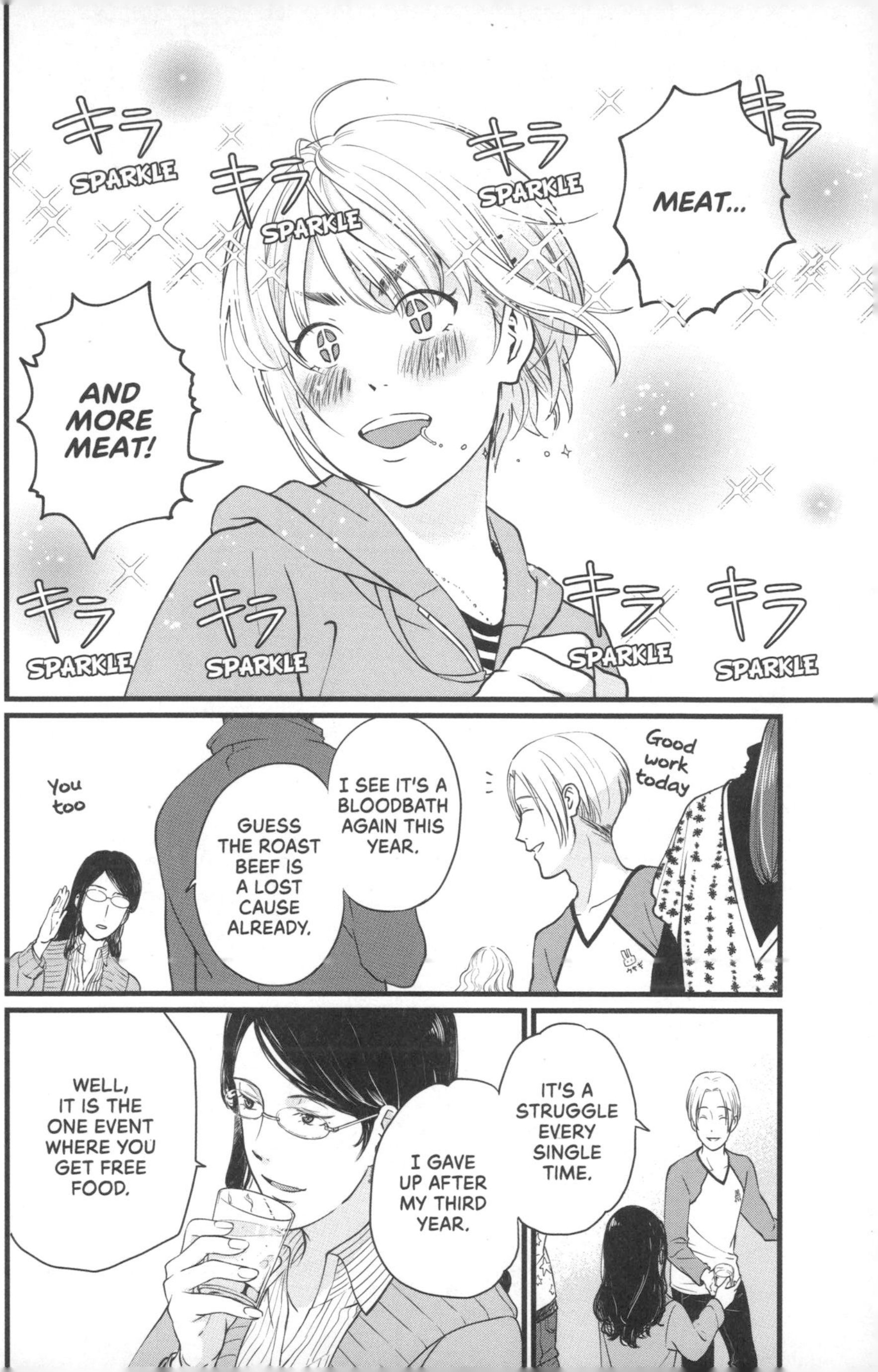
キラ
SPARKLE
MEAT...
キラ
SPARKLE
キラ
SPARKLE
キラ
SPARKLE
AND MORE MEAT!
キラ
SPARKLE
キラ
SPARKLE
キラ
SPARKLE
キラ
SPARKLE
Good work today
I SEE IT'S A BLOODBATH AGAIN THIS YEAR.
GUESS THE ROAST BEEF IS A LOST CAUSE ALREADY.
You too
IT'S A STRUGGLE EVERY SINGLE TIME.
WELL, IT IS THE ONE EVENT WHERE YOU GET FREE FOOD.
I GAVE UP AFTER MY THIRD YEAR.

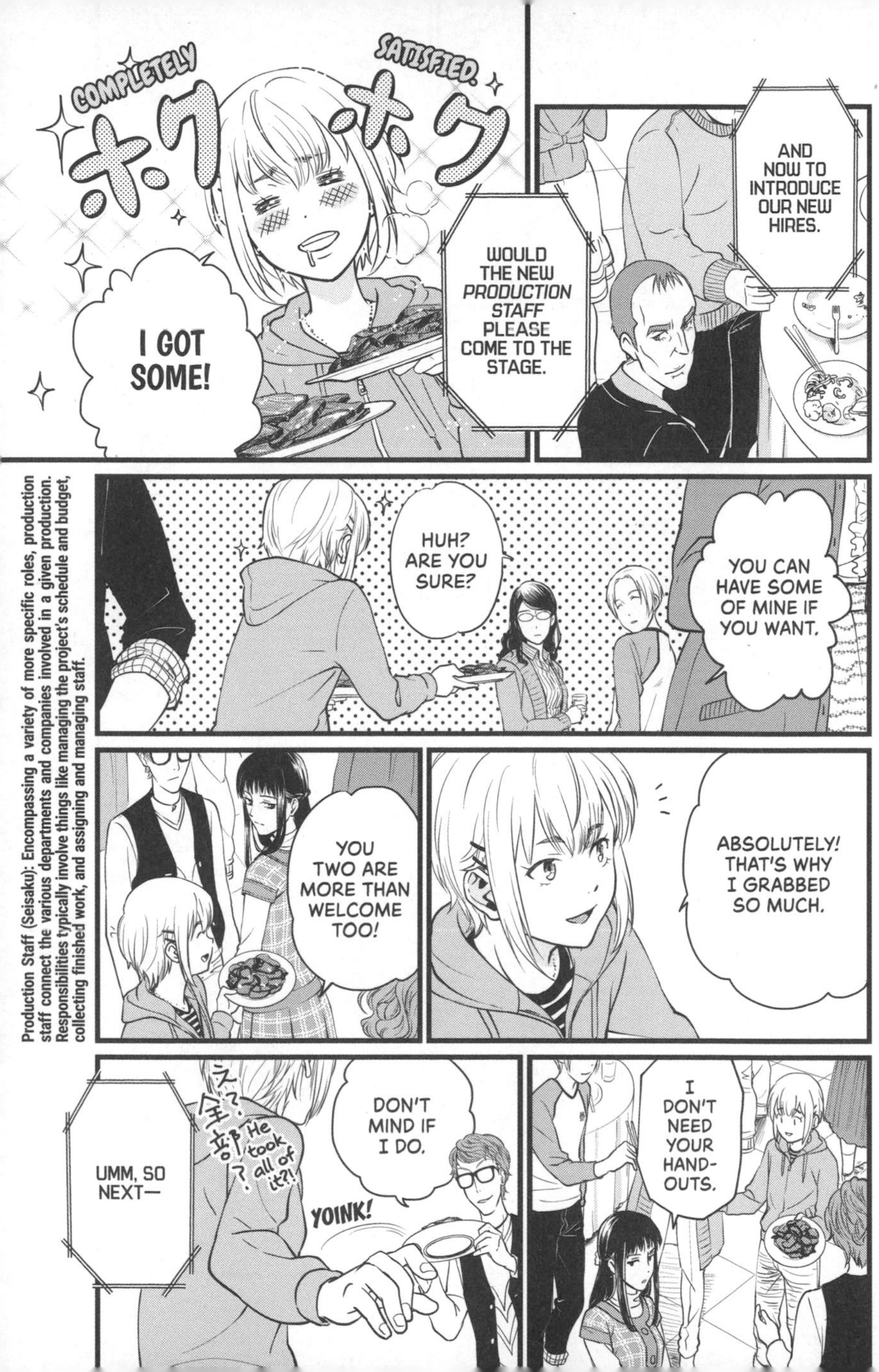
AND NOW TO INTRODUCE OUR NEW HIRES.
WOULD THE NEW *PRODUCTION STAFF* PLEASE COME TO THE STAGE.
COMPLETELY
ホク ホク
SATISFIED.
I GOT SOME!
YOU CAN HAVE SOME OF MINE IF YOU WANT.
HUH? ARE YOU SURE?
ABSOLUTELY! THAT'S WHY I GRABBED SO MUCH.
YOU TWO ARE MORE THAN WELCOME TOO!
I DON'T NEED YOUR HAND-OUTS.
DON'T MIND IF I DO.
YOINK!
え？全部？
He took all of it?!
UMM, SO NEXT—

Production Staff (Seisaku): Encompassing a variety of more specific roles, production staff connect the various departments and companies involved in a given production. Responsibilities typically involve things like managing the project's schedule and budget, collecting finished work, and assigning and managing staff.

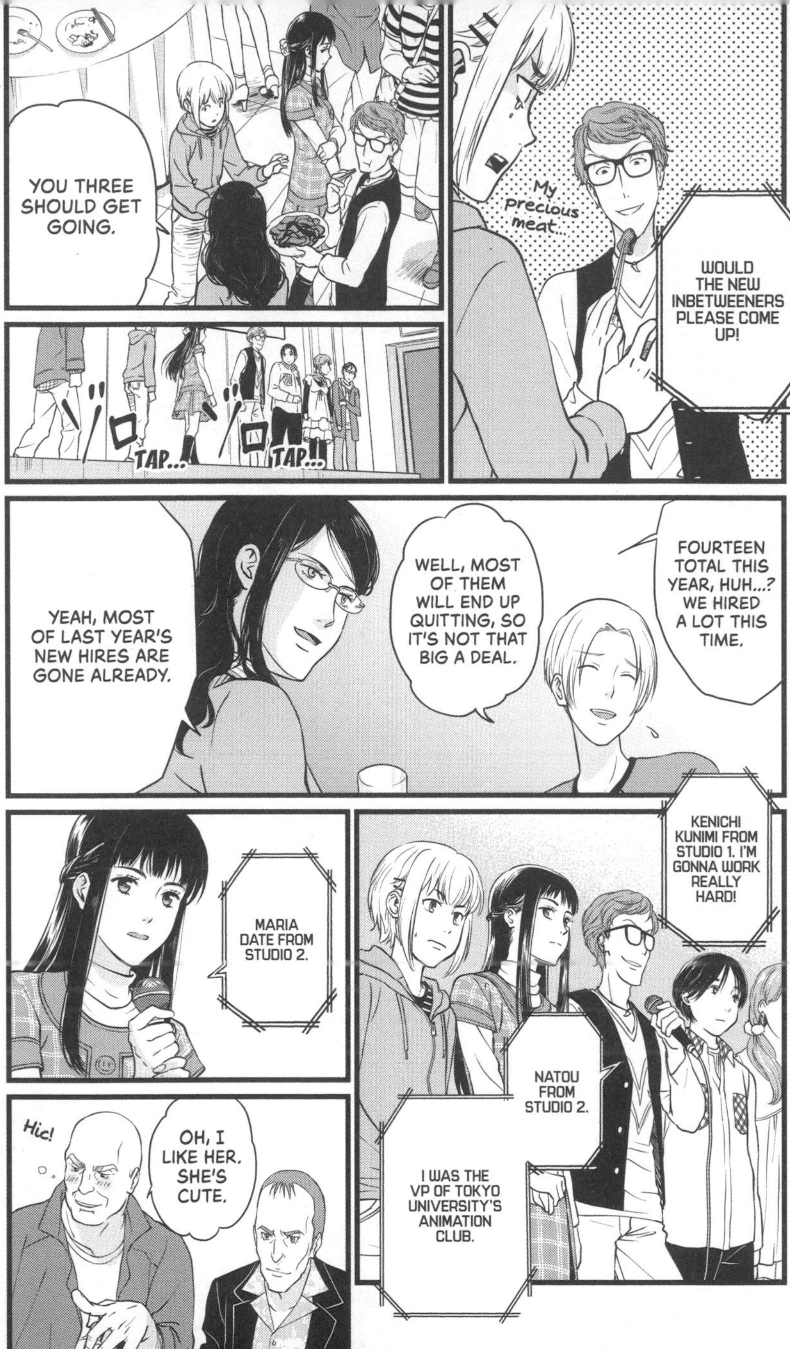
WOULD THE NEW INBETWEENERS PLEASE COME UP!
My precious meat...
YOU THREE SHOULD GET GOING.
TAP...
TAP...
FOURTEEN TOTAL THIS YEAR, HUH...? WE HIRED A LOT THIS TIME.
WELL, MOST OF THEM WILL END UP QUITTING, SO IT'S NOT THAT BIG A DEAL.
YEAH, MOST OF LAST YEAR'S NEW HIRES ARE GONE ALREADY.
KENICHI KUNIMI FROM STUDIO 1. I'M GONNA WORK REALLY HARD!
NATOU FROM STUDIO 2.
I WAS THE VP OF TOKYO UNIVERSITY'S ANIMATION CLUB.
MARIA DATE FROM STUDIO 2.
OH, I LIKE HER. SHE'S CUTE.
Hic!

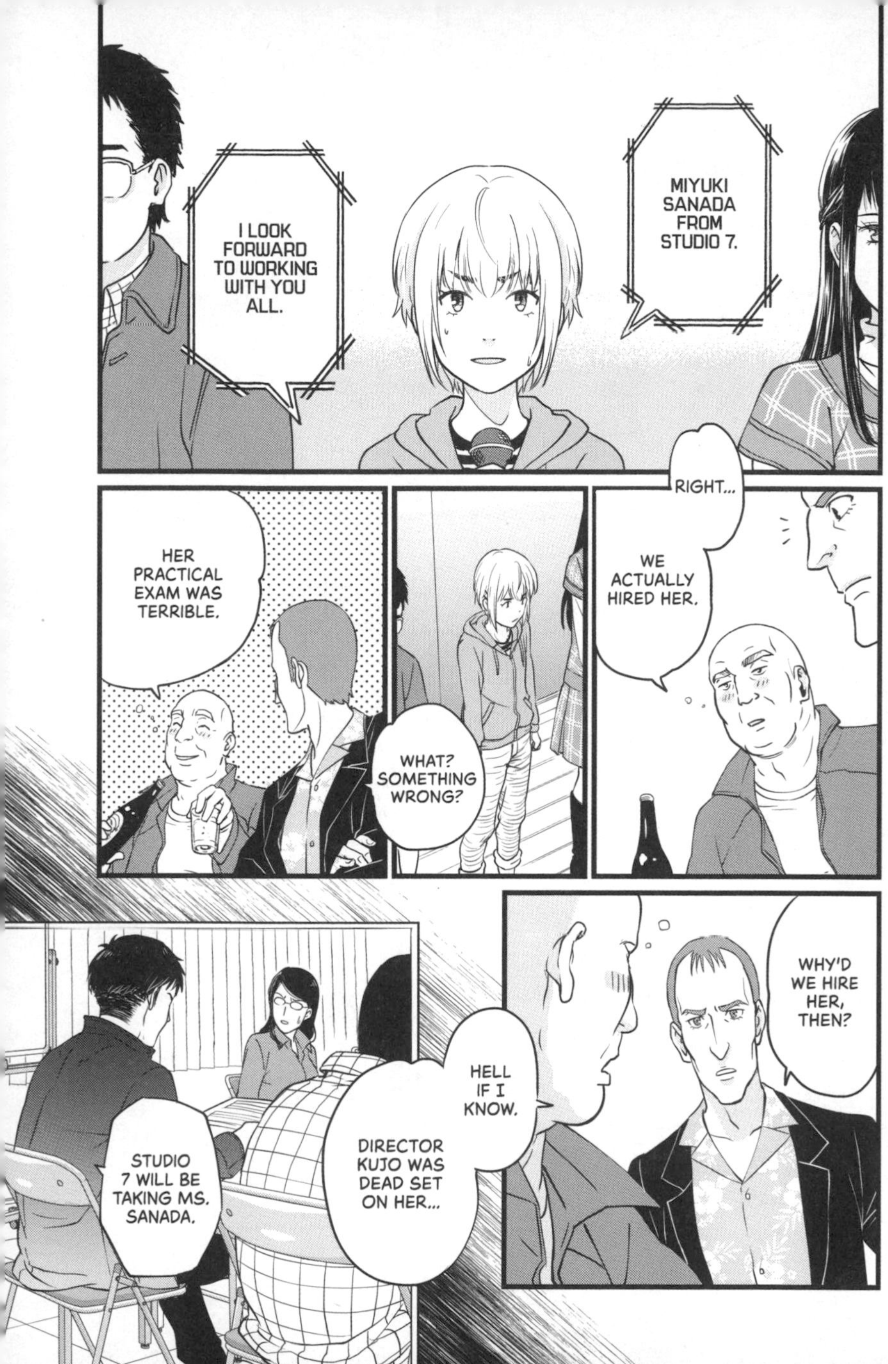
MIYUKI SANADA FROM STUDIO 7.
I LOOK FORWARD TO WORKING WITH YOU ALL.
RIGHT...
WE ACTUALLY HIRED HER.
WHAT? SOMETHING WRONG?
HER PRACTICAL EXAM WAS TERRIBLE.
WHY'D WE HIRE HER, THEN?
HELL IF I KNOW.
DIRECTOR KUJO WAS DEAD SET ON HER...
STUDIO 7 WILL BE TAKING MS. SANADA.

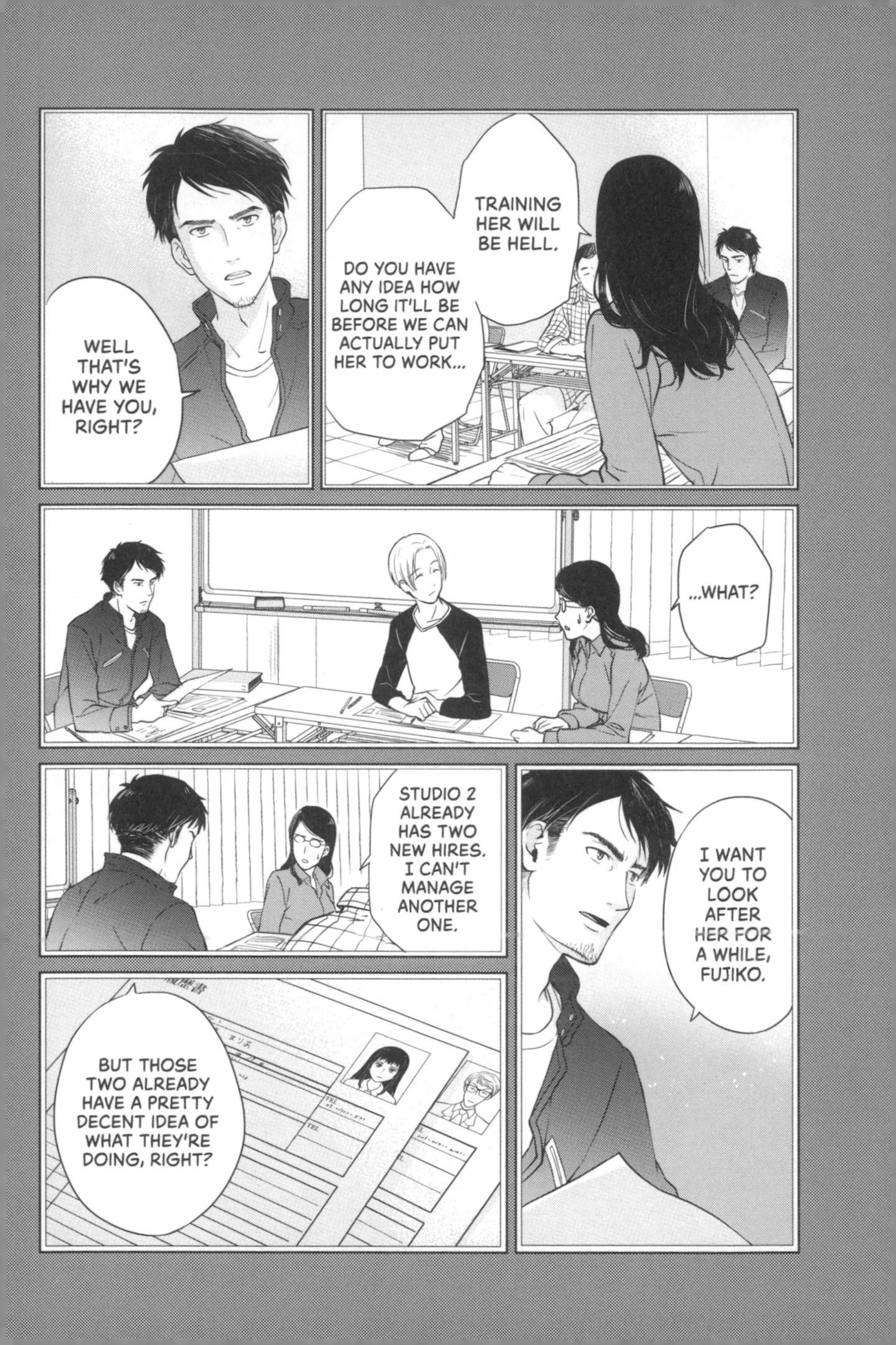
TRAINING HER WILL BE HELL.
DO YOU HAVE ANY IDEA HOW LONG IT'LL BE BEFORE WE CAN ACTUALLY PUT HER TO WORK...
WELL THAT'S WHY WE HAVE YOU, RIGHT?
...WHAT?
I WANT YOU TO LOOK AFTER HER FOR A WHILE, FUJIKO.
STUDIO 2 ALREADY HAS TWO NEW HIRES. I CAN'T MANAGE ANOTHER ONE.
BUT THOSE TWO ALREADY HAVE A PRETTY DECENT IDEA OF WHAT THEY'RE DOING, RIGHT?

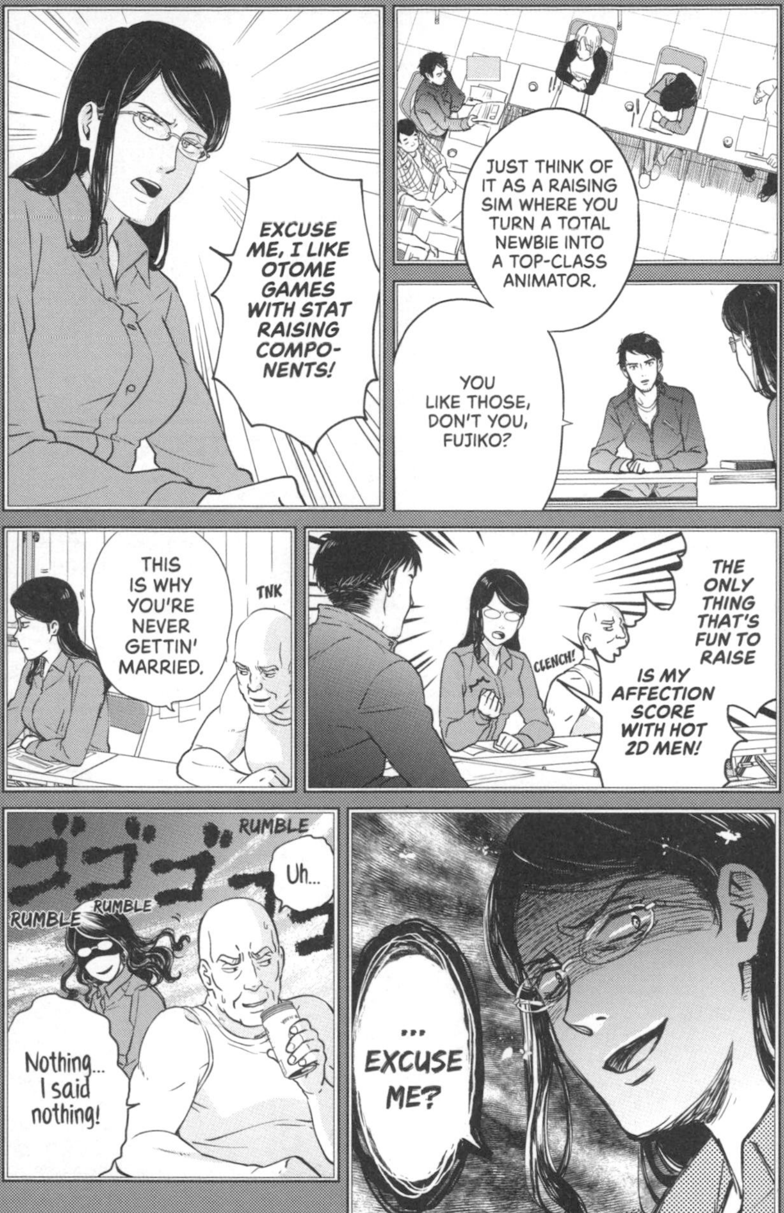

JUST THINK OF IT AS A RAISING SIM WHERE YOU TURN A TOTAL NEWBIE INTO A TOP-CLASS ANIMATOR.
YOU LIKE THOSE, DON'T YOU, FUJIKO?
EXCUSE ME, I LIKE OTOME GAMES WITH STAT RAISING COMPO- NENTS!
THE ONLY THING THAT'S FUN TO RAISE
IS MY AFFECTION SCORE WITH HOT 2D MEN!
CLENCH!
THIS IS WHY YOU'RE NEVER GETTIN' MARRIED.
TNK
...EXCUSE ME?
RUMBLE
Uh...
RUMBLE
RUMBLE
Nothing... I said nothing!

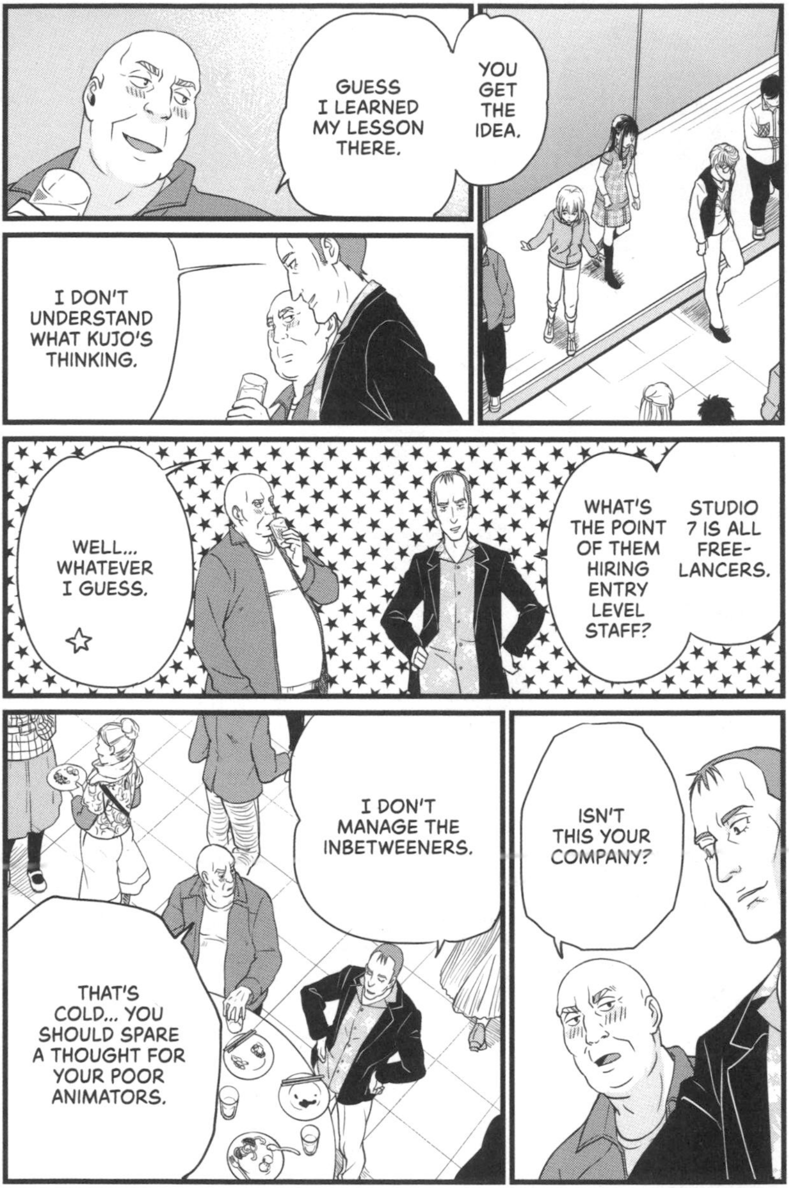
YOU GET THE IDEA.
GUESS I LEARNED MY LESSON THERE.
I DON'T UNDERSTAND WHAT KUJO'S THINKING.
STUDIO 7 IS ALL FREE-LANCERS.
WHAT'S THE POINT OF THEM HIRING ENTRY LEVEL STAFF?
WELL... WHATEVER I GUESS. ☆
ISN'T THIS YOUR COMPANY?
I DON'T MANAGE THE INBETWEENERS.
THAT'S COLD... YOU SHOULD SPARE A THOUGHT FOR YOUR POOR ANIMATORS.

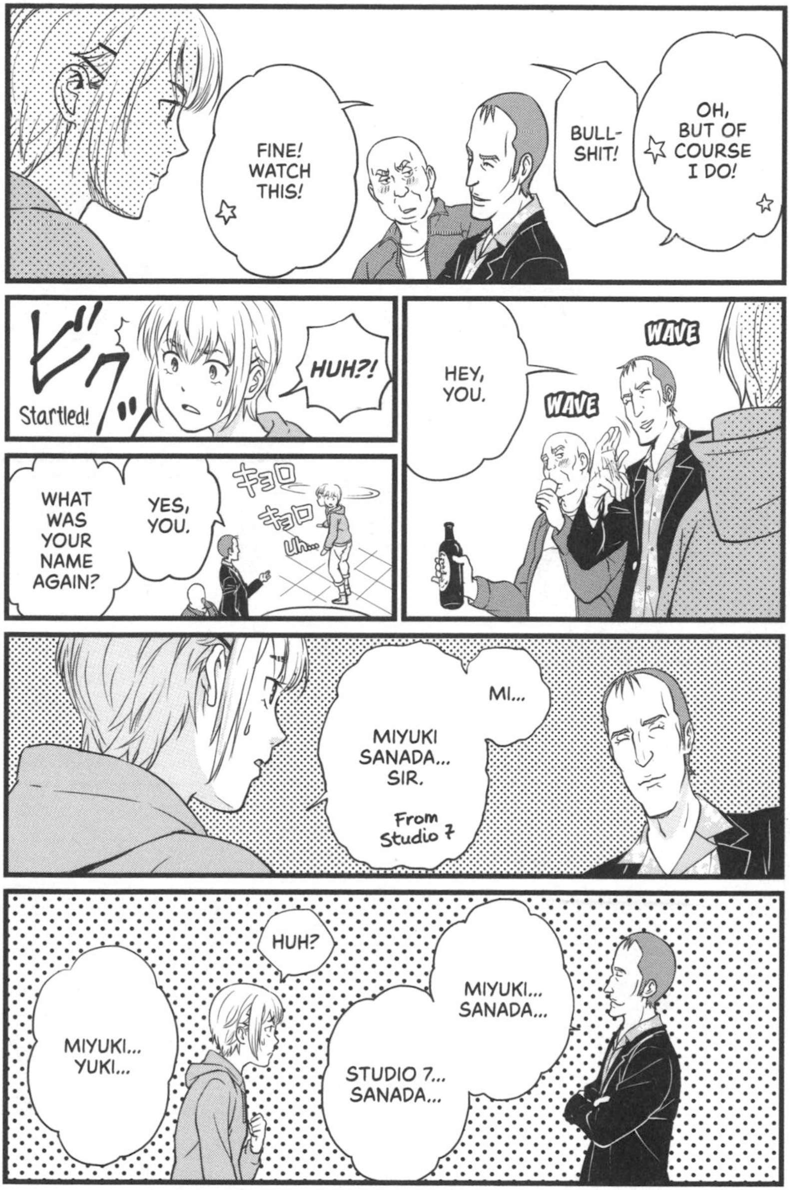
OH, BUT OF COURSE I DO!
BULL-SHIT!
FINE! WATCH THIS!
WAVE
HEY, YOU.
WAVE
HUH?!
ビクッ
Startled!
キョロ
キョロ
YES, YOU.
Uh...
WHAT WAS YOUR NAME AGAIN?
MI...
MIYUKI SANADA... SIR.
From Studio 7
MIYUKI... SANADA...
HUH?
STUDIO 7... SANADA...
MIYUKI... YUKI...

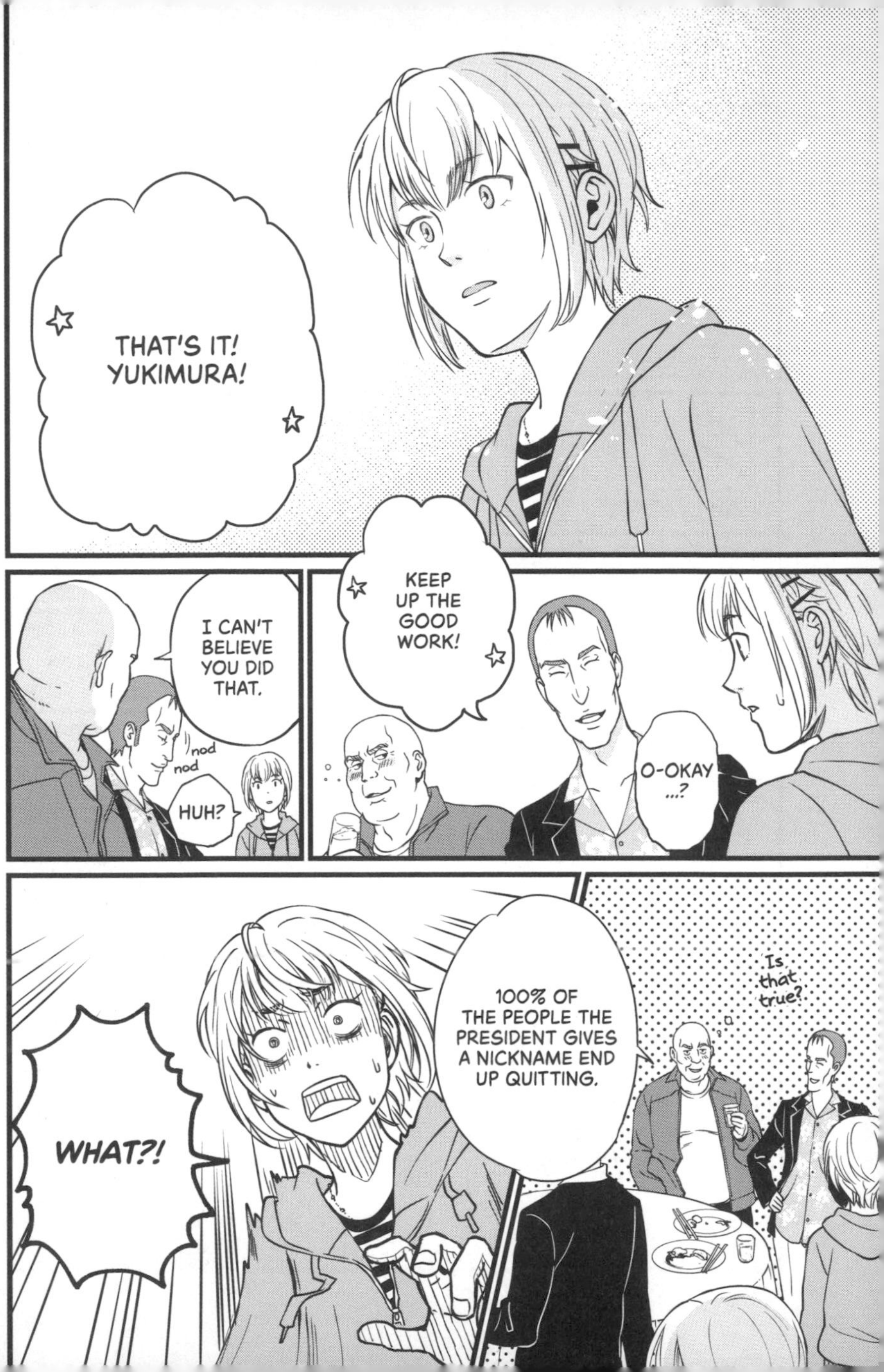
THAT'S IT! YUKIMURA!
KEEP UP THE GOOD WORK!
O-OKAY ...?
I CAN'T BELIEVE YOU DID THAT.
nod nod
HUH?
100% OF THE PEOPLE THE PRESIDENT GIVES A NICKNAME END UP QUITTING.
Is that true?
WHAT?!

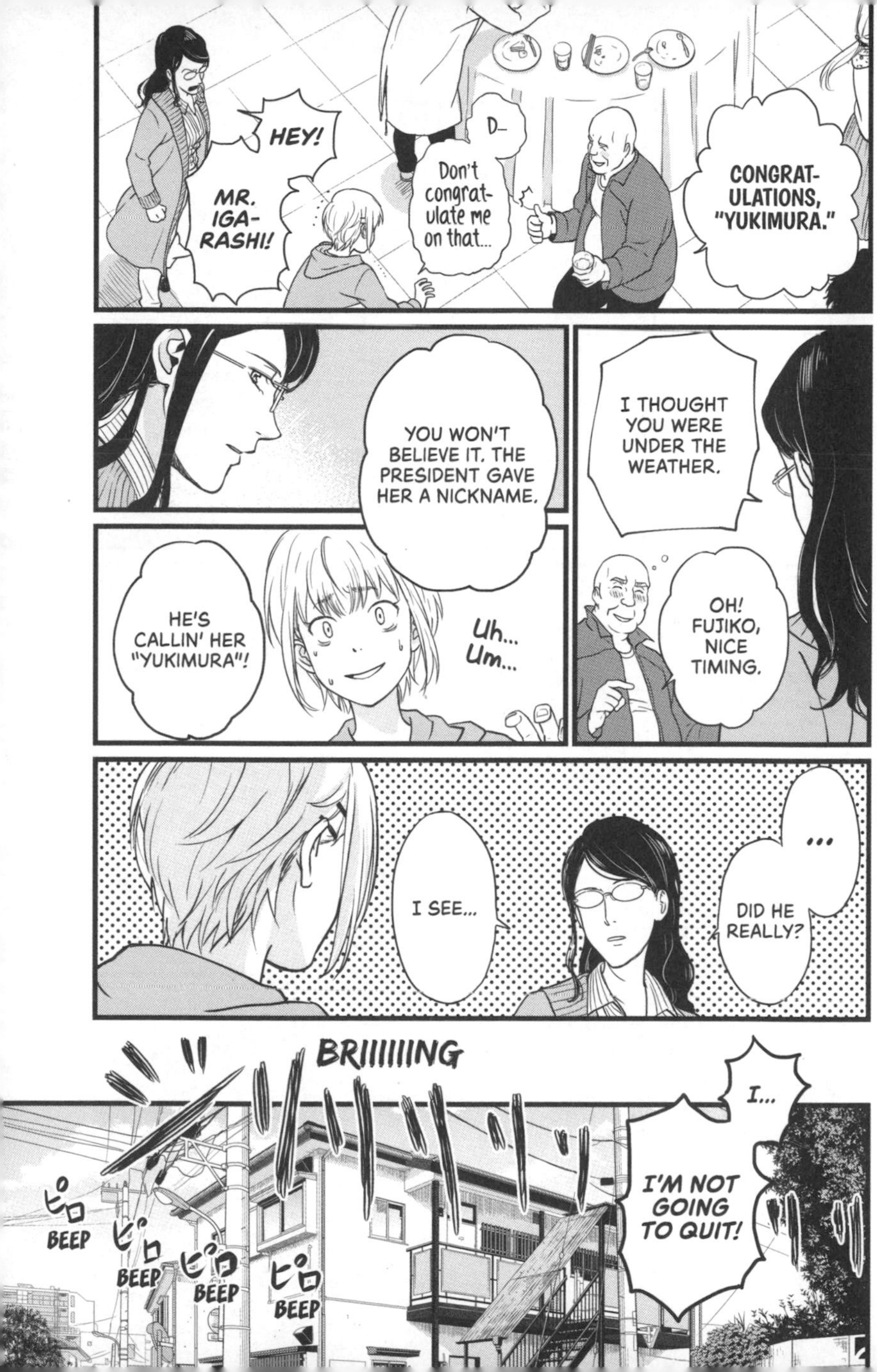
CONGRAT-
ULATIONS,
"YUKIMURA."
D–
Don't congrat-ulate me on that...
HEY!
MR. IGA-RASHI!
I THOUGHT YOU WERE UNDER THE WEATHER.
OH! FUJIKO, NICE TIMING.
YOU WON'T BELIEVE IT. THE PRESIDENT GAVE HER A NICKNAME.
Uh... Um...
HE'S CALLIN' HER "YUKIMURA"!
...
DID HE REALLY?
I SEE...
I...
I'M NOT GOING TO QUIT!
BRIIIIIING
ピロ
BEEP
ピロ
BEEP
ピロ
BEEP
ピロ
BEEP

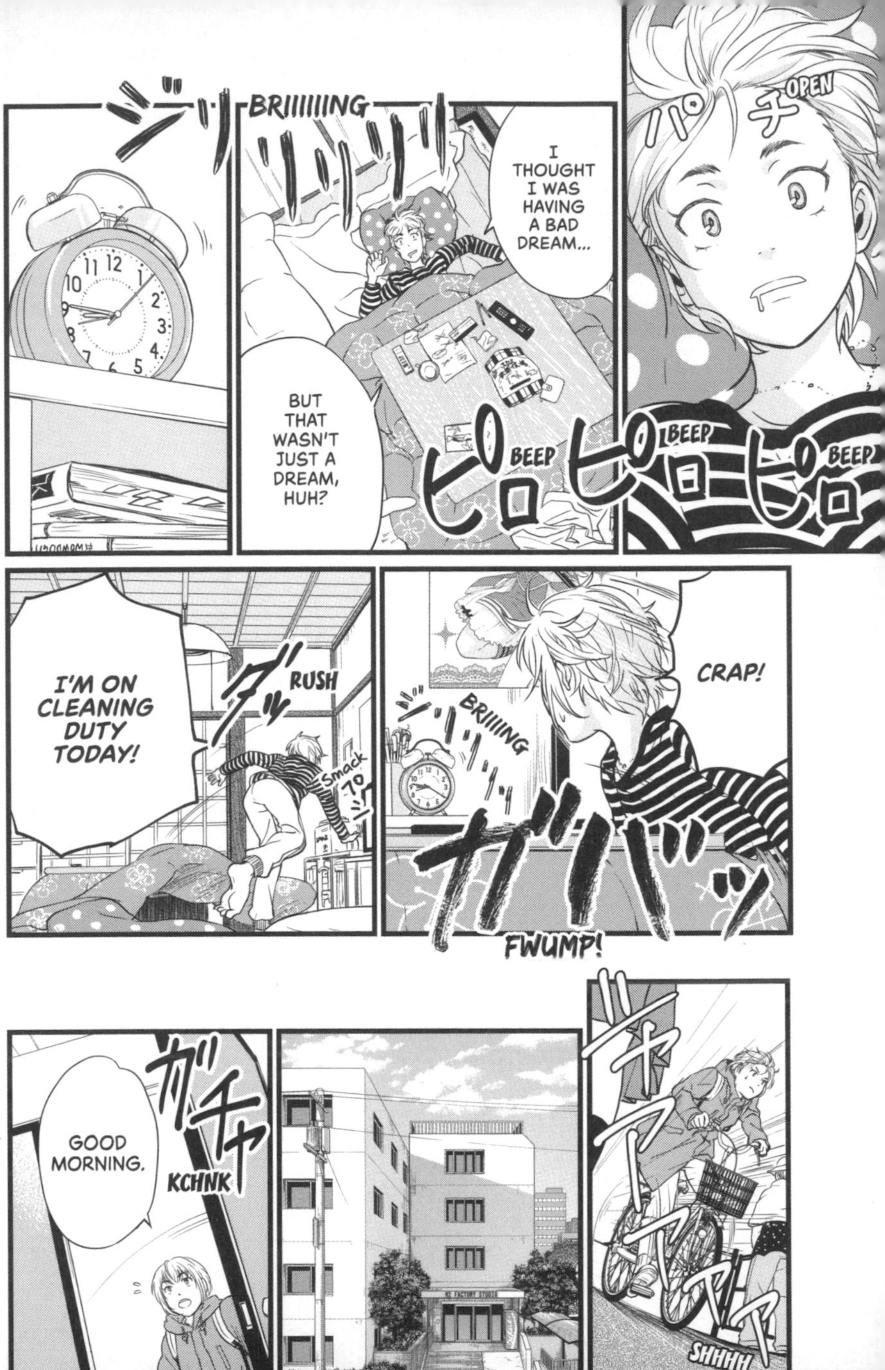
OPEN
BEEP
BEEP
BEEP
BRIIIIIIING
I THOUGHT I WAS HAVING A BAD DREAM...
BUT THAT WASN'T JUST A DREAM, HUH?
CRAP!
BRIIING
FWUMP!
RUSH
Smack
I'M ON CLEANING DUTY TODAY!
SHHHH
KCHNK
GOOD MORNING.

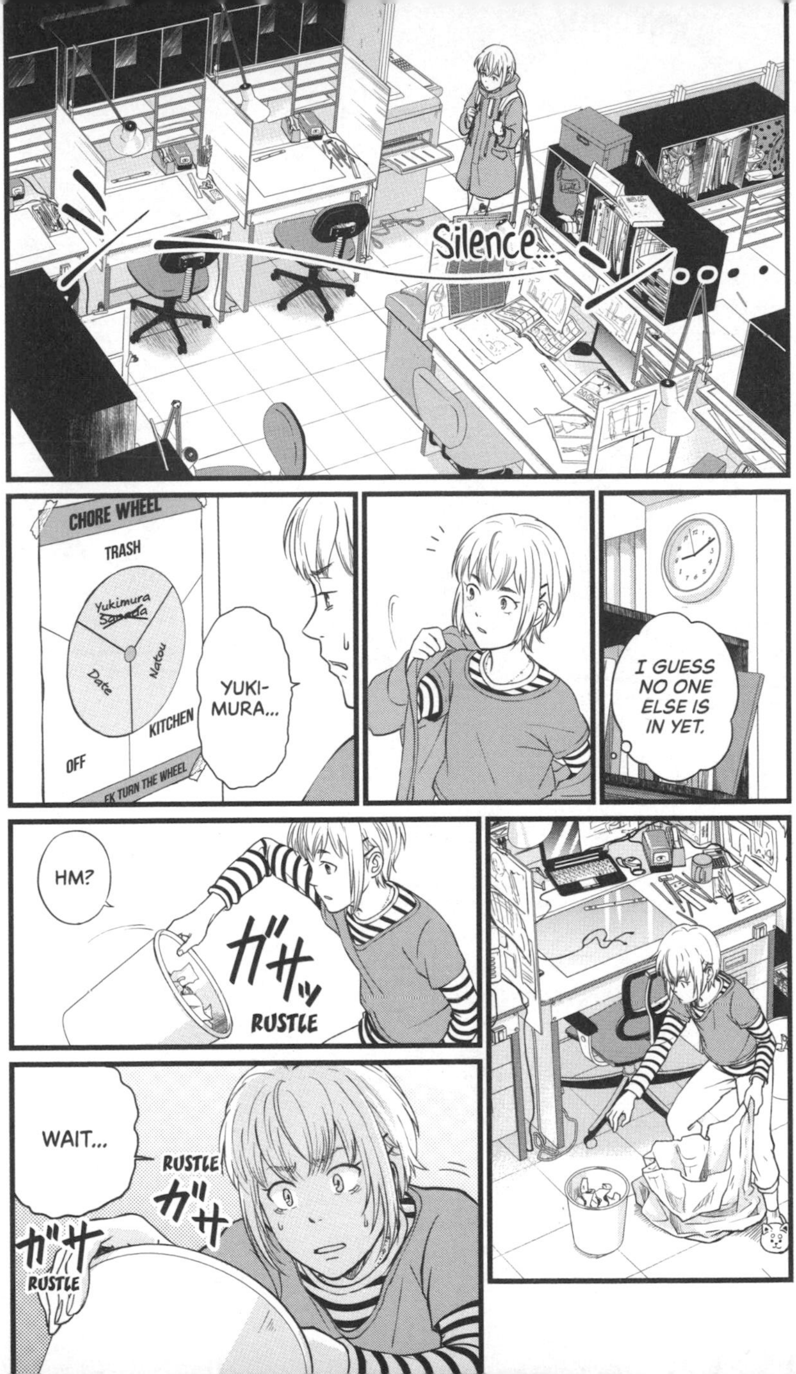

Silence...
...
I GUESS NO ONE ELSE IS IN YET.
CHORE WHEEL
TRASH
Yukimura
Sanada
Natou
Date
KITCHEN
OFF
YUKI-MURA...
HM?
ガサッ
RUSTLE
WAIT...
RUSTLE
ガサ
ガサ
RUSTLE

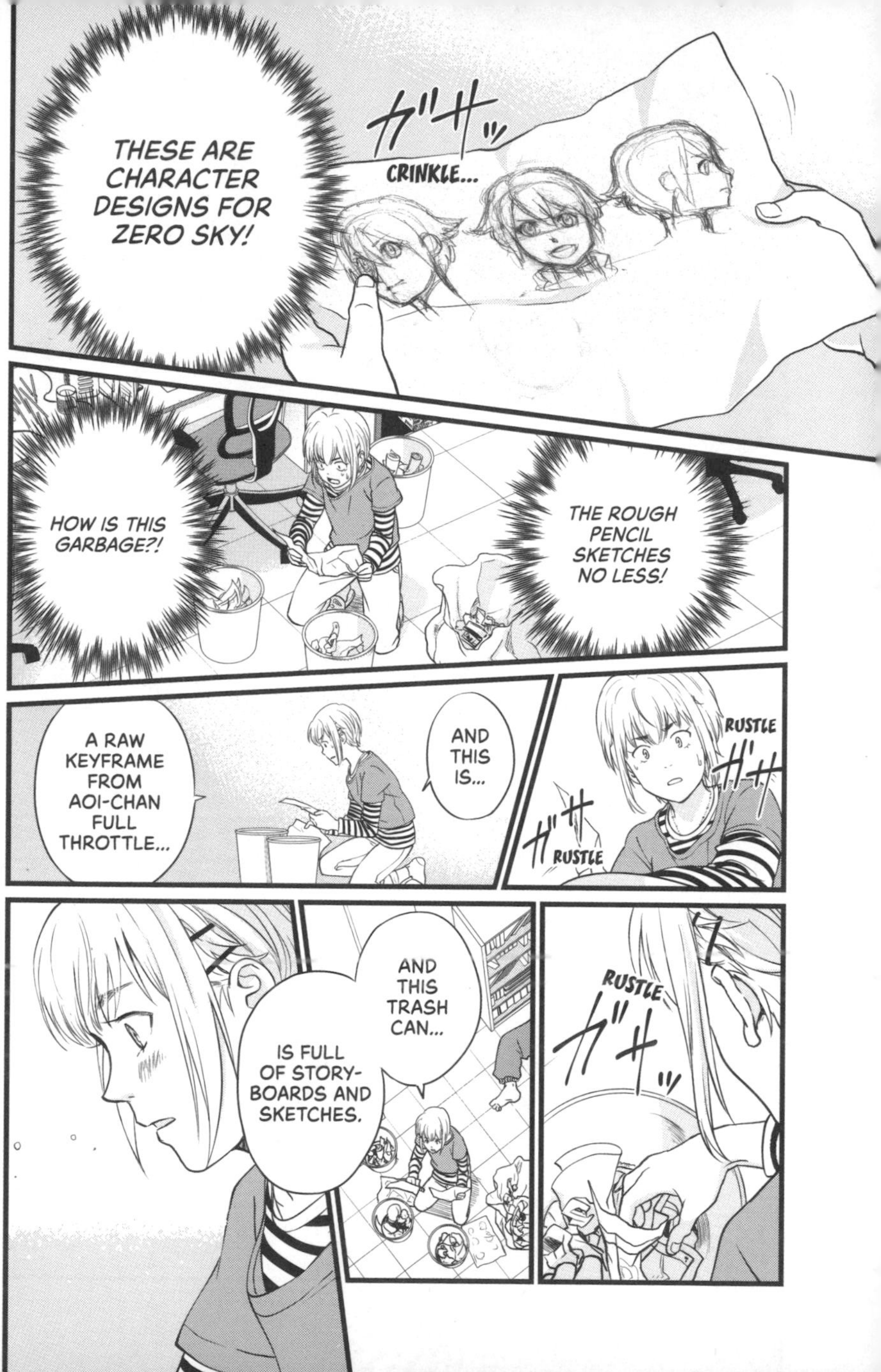
ガサッ
CRINKLE...
THESE ARE CHARACTER DESIGNS FOR ZERO SKY!
THE ROUGH PENCIL SKETCHES NO LESS!
HOW IS THIS GARBAGE?!
RUSTLE
ガサ
ガサ
RUSTLE
AND THIS IS...
A RAW KEYFRAME FROM AOI-CHAN FULL THROTTLE...
RUSTLE
ガサッ
AND THIS TRASH CAN...
IS FULL OF STORY-BOARDS AND SKETCHES.

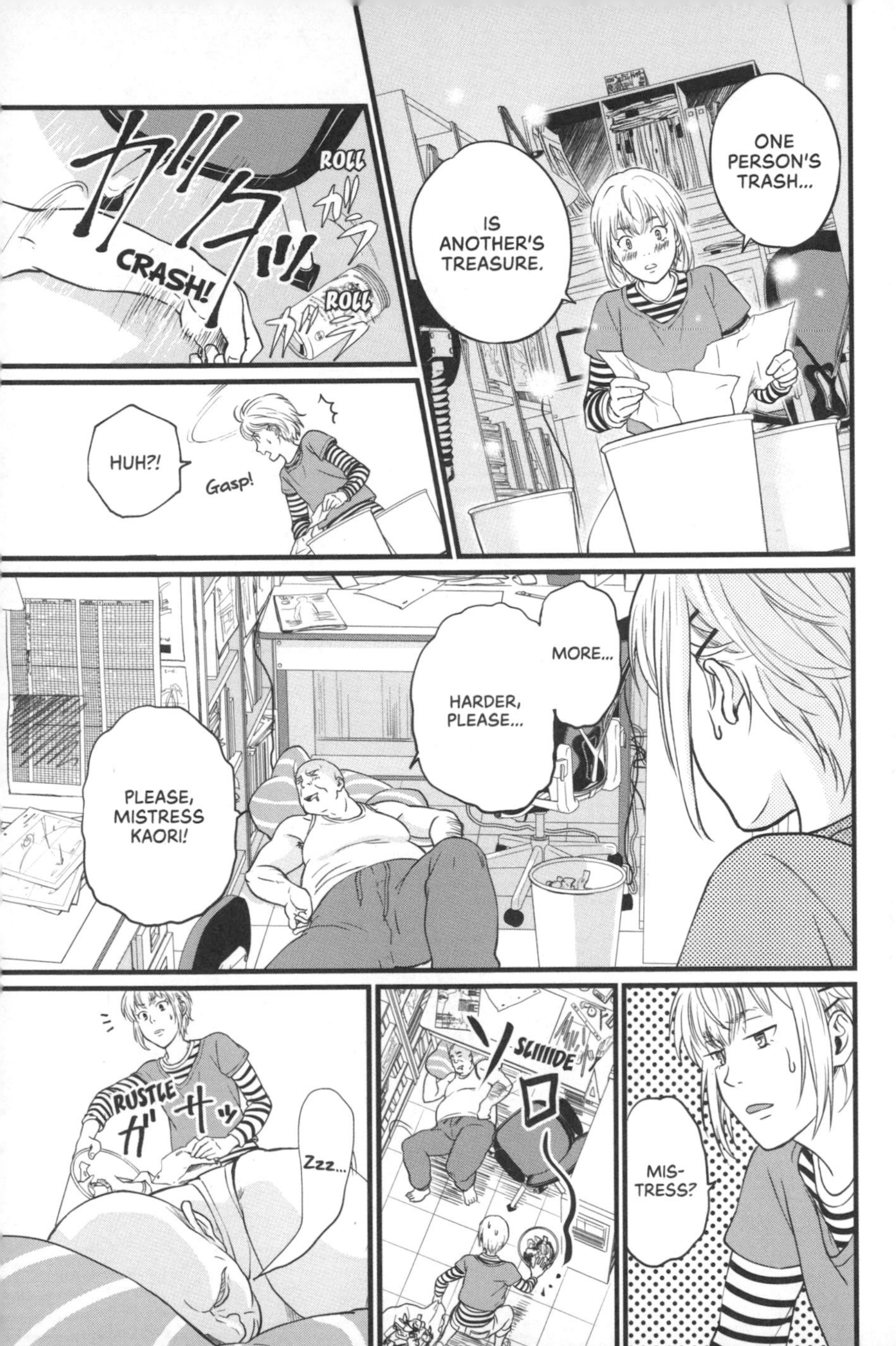
ONE PERSON'S TRASH...
IS ANOTHER'S TREASURE.
ROLL
CRASH!
ROLL
HUH?!
Gasp!
MORE...
HARDER, PLEASE...
PLEASE, MISTRESS KAORI!
MIS-TRESS?
SLIIIDE
RUSTLE
Zzz...

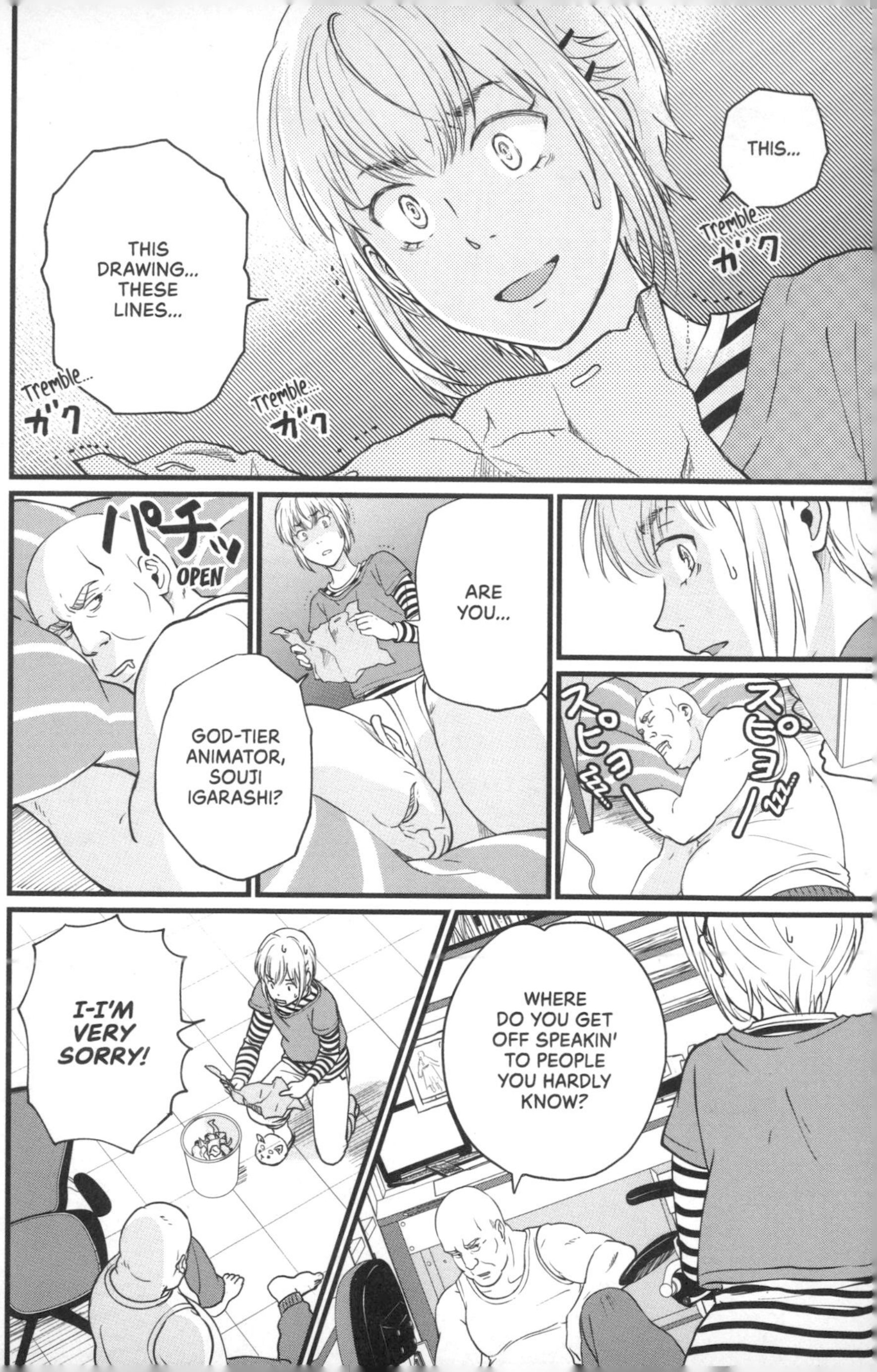
THIS...
Tremble... ガク
THIS DRAWING... THESE LINES...
Tremble... ガク
Tremble... ガク
スピョー zzz...
スピョー zzz...
ARE YOU...
GOD-TIER ANIMATOR, SOUJI IGARASHI?
パチッ OPEN
WHERE DO YOU GET OFF SPEAKIN' TO PEOPLE YOU HARDLY KNOW?
I-I'M VERY SORRY!

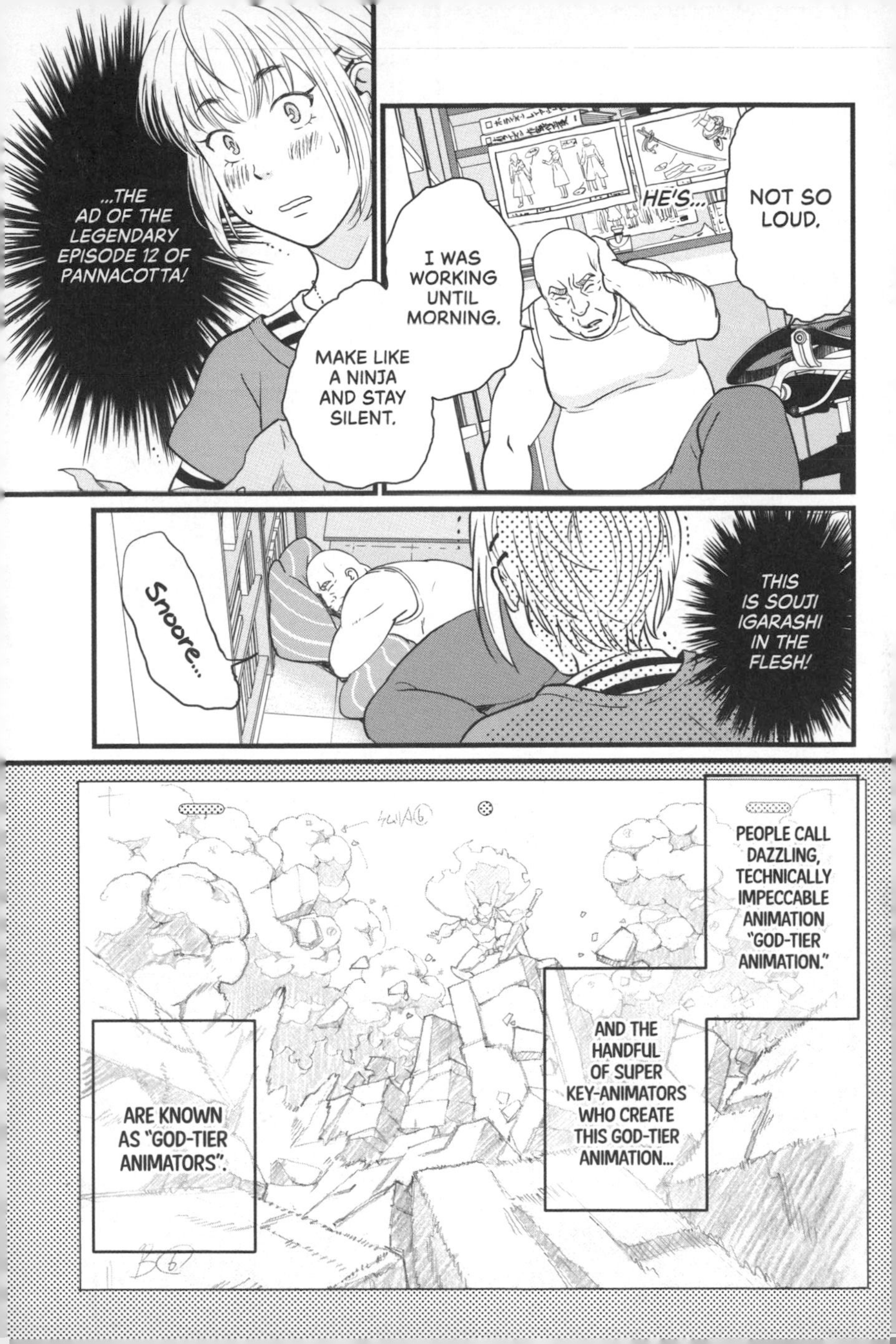
NOT SO LOUD.
I WAS WORKING UNTIL MORNING.
MAKE LIKE A NINJA AND STAY SILENT.
HE'S...
...THE AD OF THE LEGENDARY EPISODE 12 OF PANNACOTTA!
THIS IS SOUJI IGARASHI IN THE FLESH!
Snoore...
PEOPLE CALL DAZZLING, TECHNICALLY IMPECCABLE ANIMATION "GOD-TIER ANIMATION."
AND THE HANDFUL OF SUPER KEY-ANIMATORS WHO CREATE THIS GOD-TIER ANIMATION...
ARE KNOWN AS "GOD-TIER ANIMATORS".

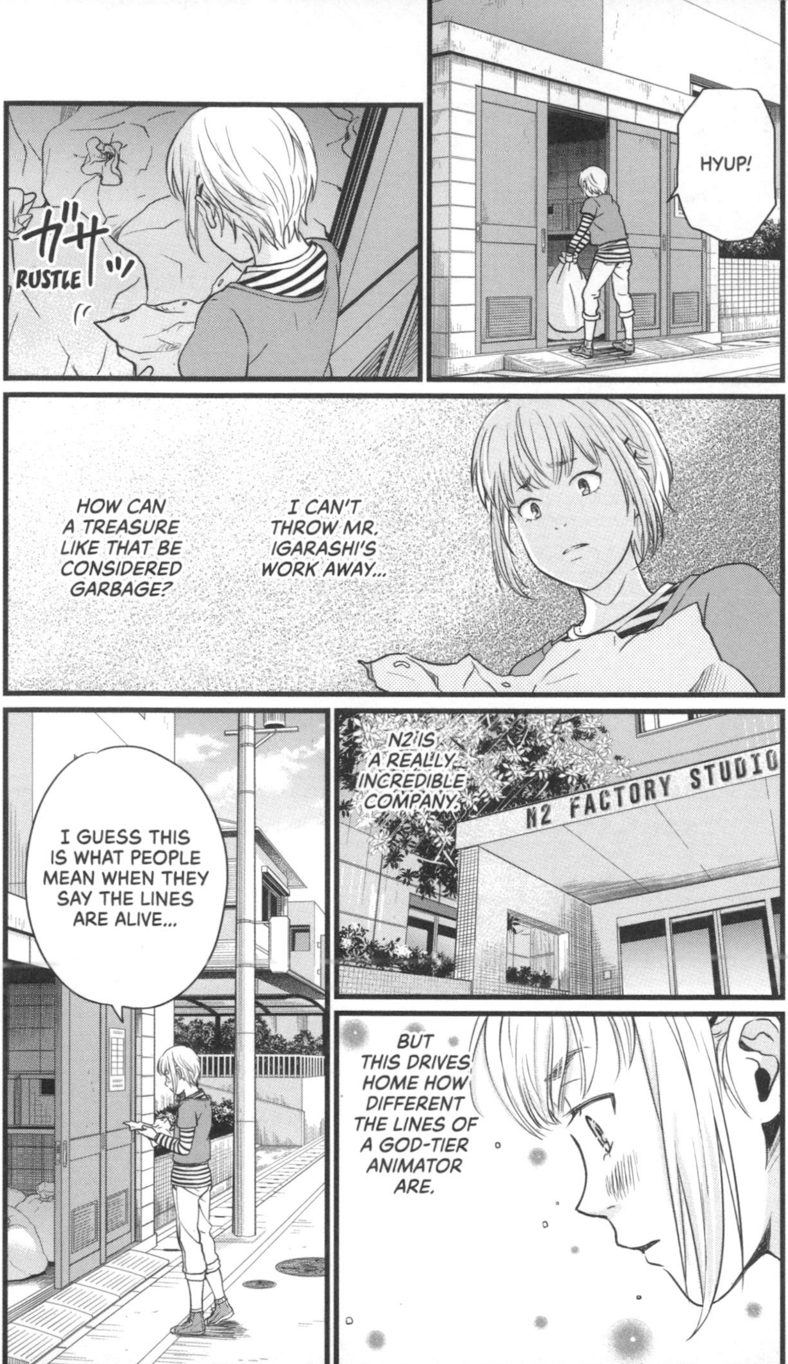
HYUP!
ガサッ
RUSTLE
I CAN'T THROW MR. IGARASHI'S WORK AWAY...
HOW CAN A TREASURE LIKE THAT BE CONSIDERED GARBAGE?
N2 IS A REALLY INCREDIBLE COMPANY.
N2 FACTORY STUDIO
BUT THIS DRIVES HOME HOW DIFFERENT THE LINES OF A GOD-TIER ANIMATOR ARE.
I GUESS THIS IS WHAT PEOPLE MEAN WHEN THEY SAY THE LINES ARE ALIVE...

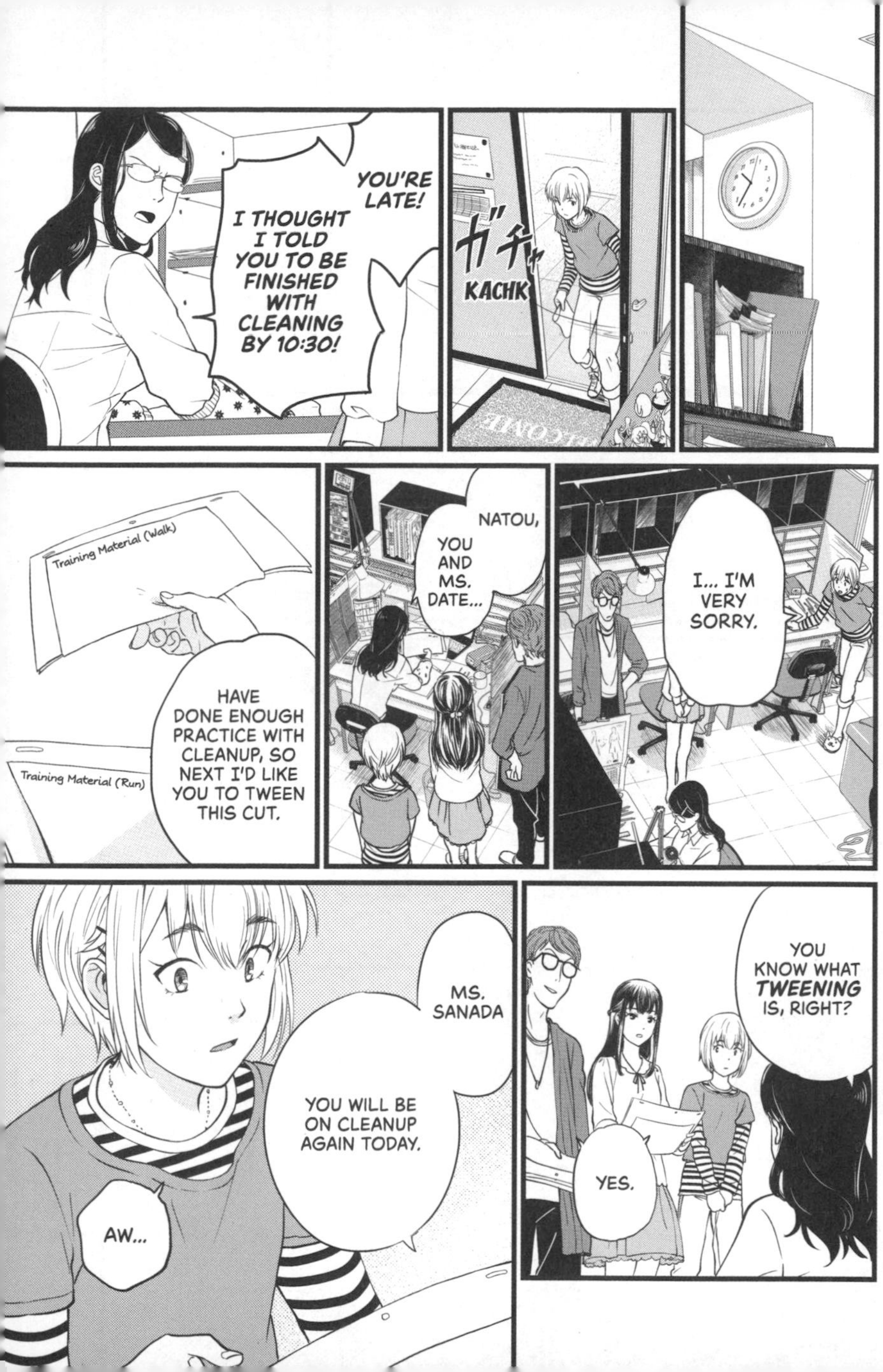
ガチャ
KACHK
YOU'RE LATE!
I THOUGHT I TOLD YOU TO BE FINISHED WITH CLEANING BY 10:30!
I... I'M VERY SORRY.
NATOU, YOU AND MS. DATE...
Training Material (Walk)
Training Material (Run)
HAVE DONE ENOUGH PRACTICE WITH CLEANUP, SO NEXT I'D LIKE YOU TO TWEEN THIS CUT.
YOU KNOW WHAT TWEENING IS, RIGHT?
YES.
MS. SANADA
YOU WILL BE ON CLEANUP AGAIN TODAY.
AW...

inbetweening are largely interchangeable in English, for clarity we'll be using "tweening" to describe only the actual process of drawing the inbetween frames (nakawari).

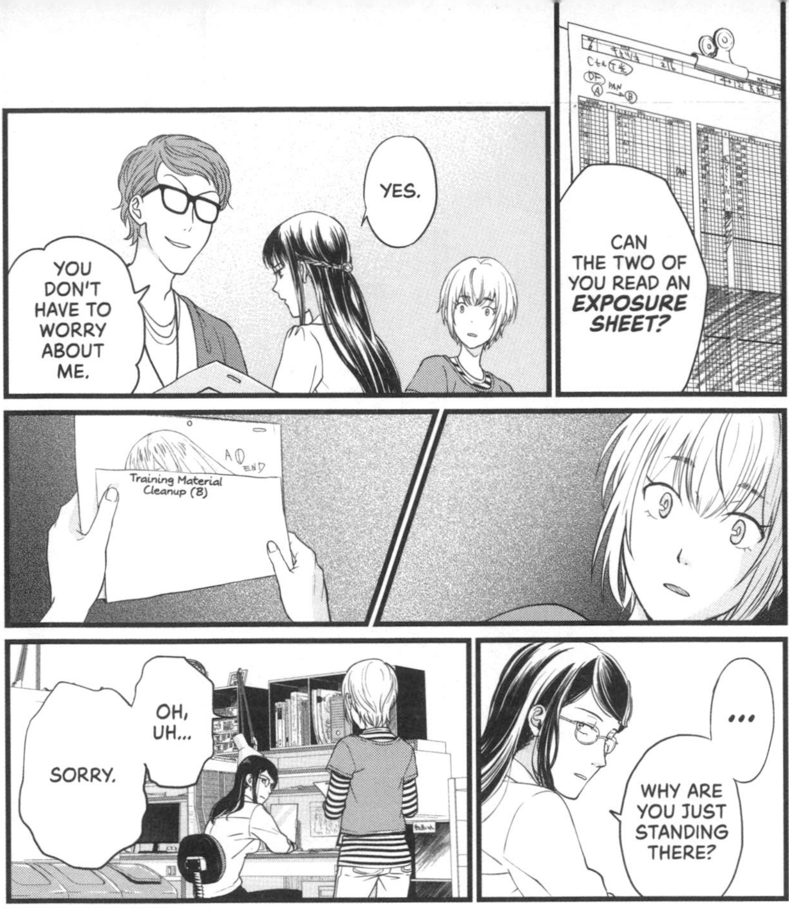
CAN THE TWO OF YOU READ AN **EXPOSURE SHEET?**
YES.
YOU DON'T HAVE TO WORRY ABOUT ME.
A① END
Training Material Cleanup (B)
...
WHY ARE YOU JUST STANDING THERE?
OH, UH...
SORRY.

Exposure Sheet (Time Sheet): A very important piece of paper that details the timing of movements, camera work, post-processing, etc. in a cut.

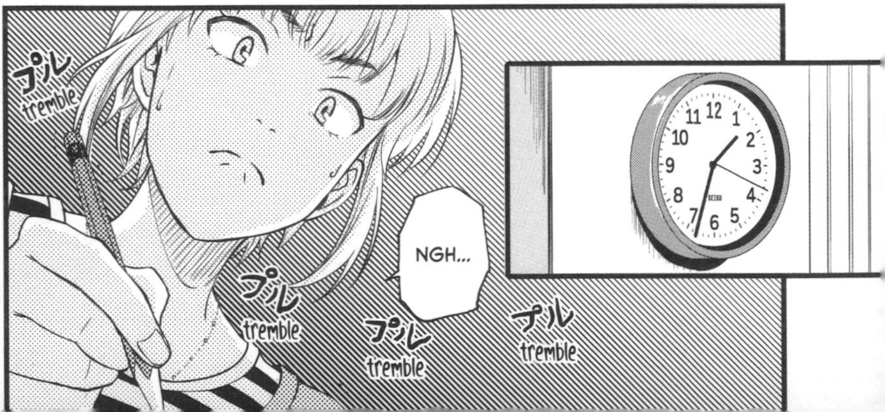
プル
tremble
NGH...
プル
tremble
プル
tremble
プル
tremble

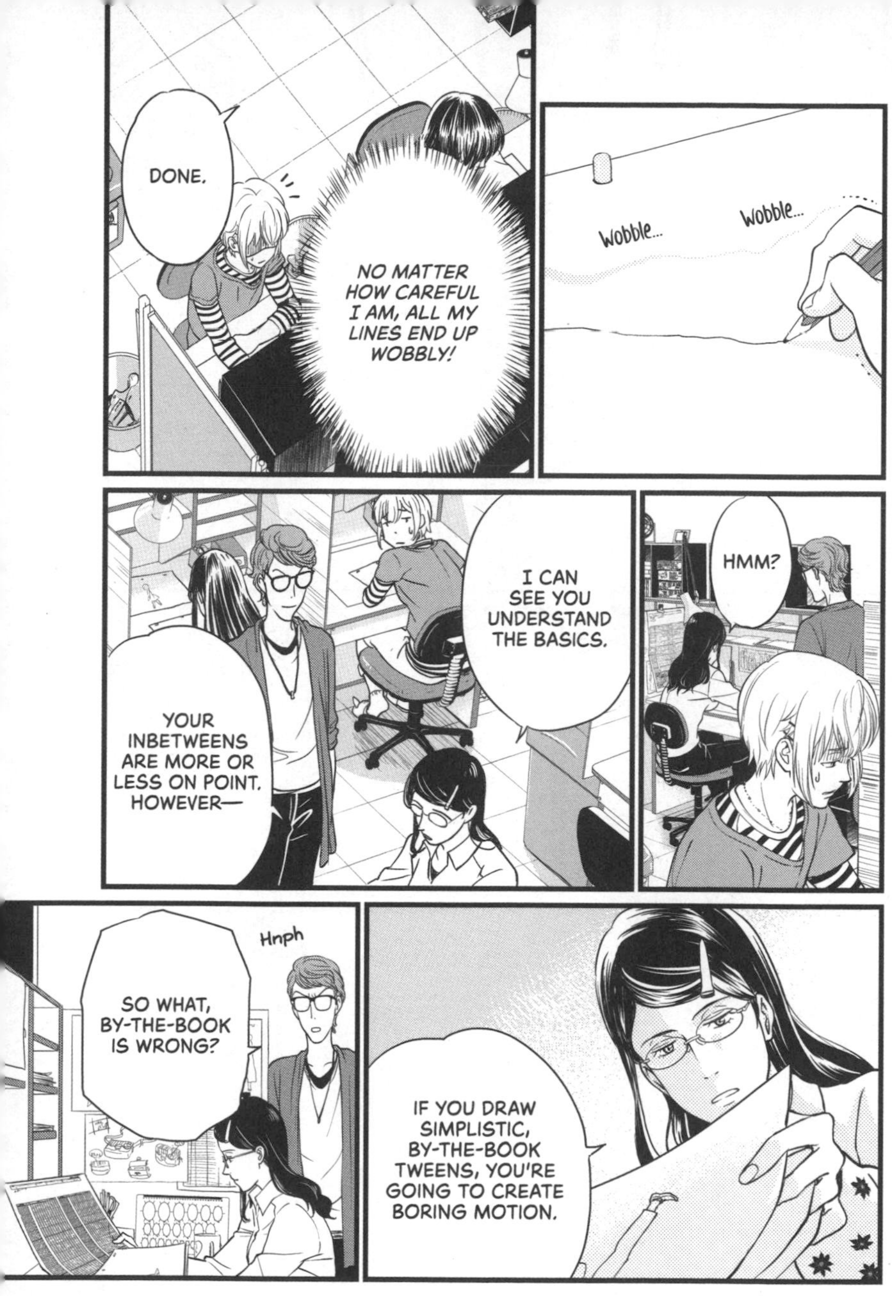
Wobble...
Wobble...
NO MATTER HOW CAREFUL I AM, ALL MY LINES END UP WOBBLY!
DONE.
HMM?
I CAN SEE YOU UNDERSTAND THE BASICS.
YOUR INBETWEENS ARE MORE OR LESS ON POINT. HOWEVER—
IF YOU DRAW SIMPLISTIC, BY-THE-BOOK TWEENS, YOU'RE GOING TO CREATE BORING MOTION.
Hnph
SO WHAT, BY-THE-BOOK IS WRONG?

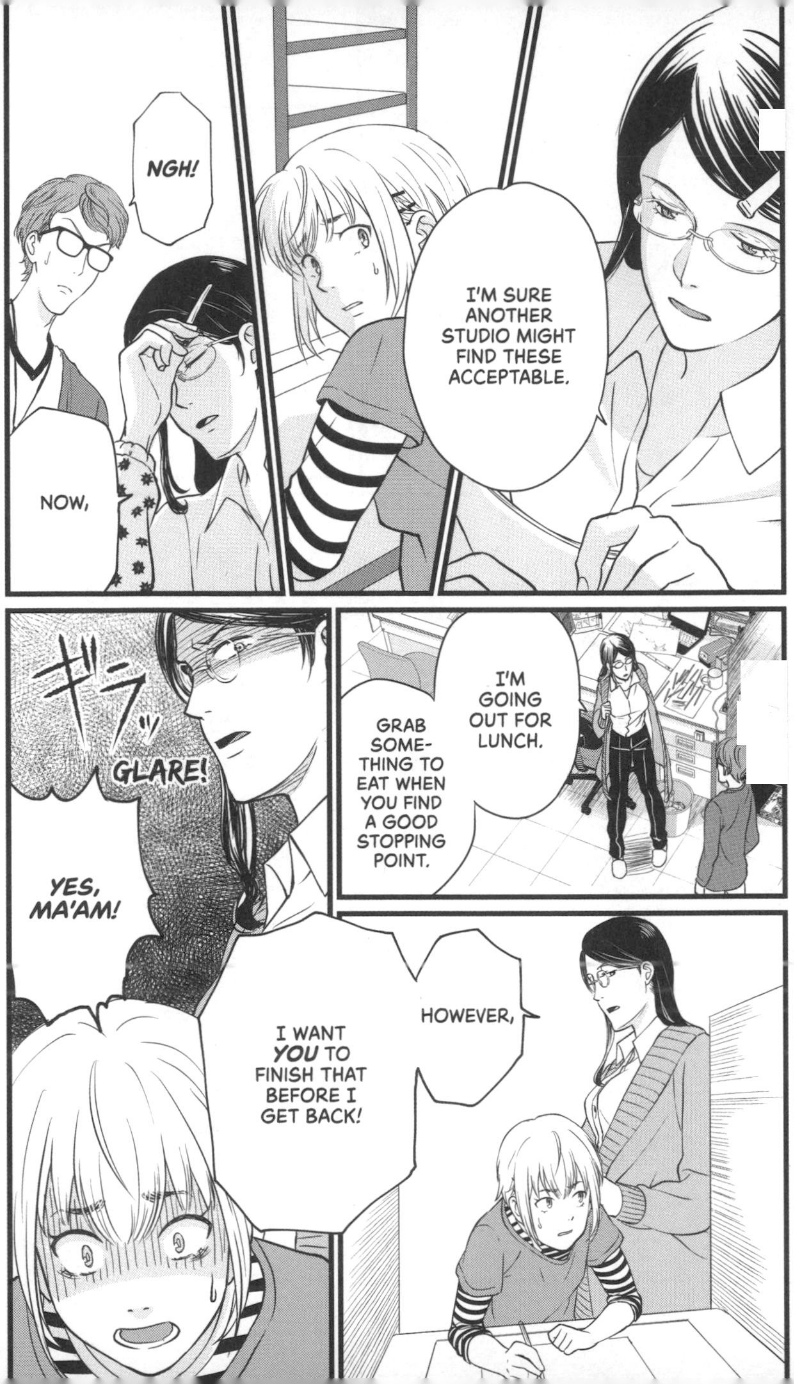
I'M SURE ANOTHER STUDIO MIGHT FIND THESE ACCEPTABLE.
NGH!
NOW,
I'M GOING OUT FOR LUNCH.
GRAB SOME-THING TO EAT WHEN YOU FIND A GOOD STOPPING POINT.
HOWEVER,
I WANT YOU TO FINISH THAT BEFORE I GET BACK!
ギラッ
GLARE!
YES, MA'AM!

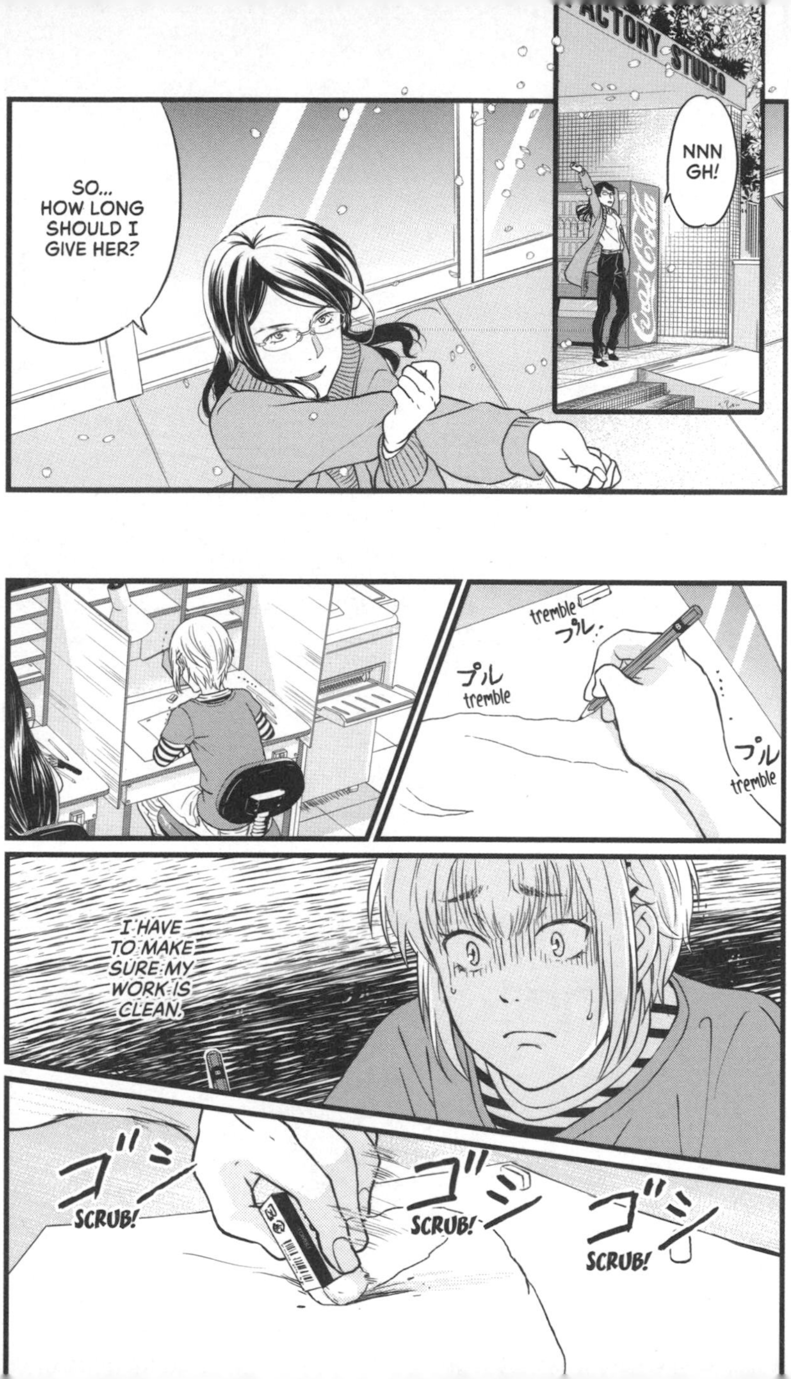

FACTORY STUDIO
NNN GH!
SO... HOW LONG SHOULD I GIVE HER?
tremble プル
プル tremble
プル tremble
I HAVE TO MAKE SURE MY WORK IS CLEAN.
ゴシ SCRUB!
ゴシ SCRUB!
ゴシ SCRUB!

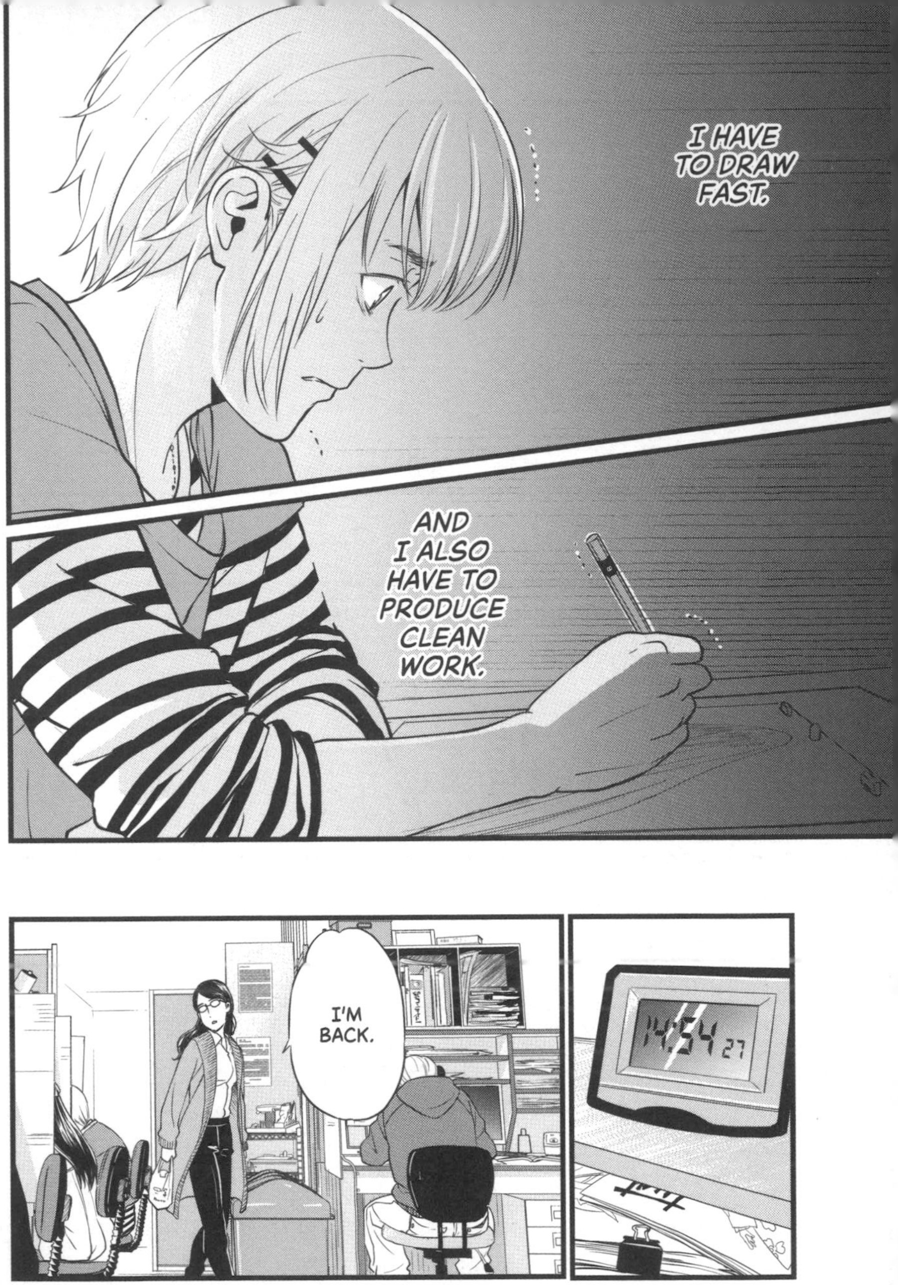
I HAVE TO DRAW FAST.
AND I ALSO HAVE TO PRODUCE CLEAN WORK.
14:54 27
I'M BACK.

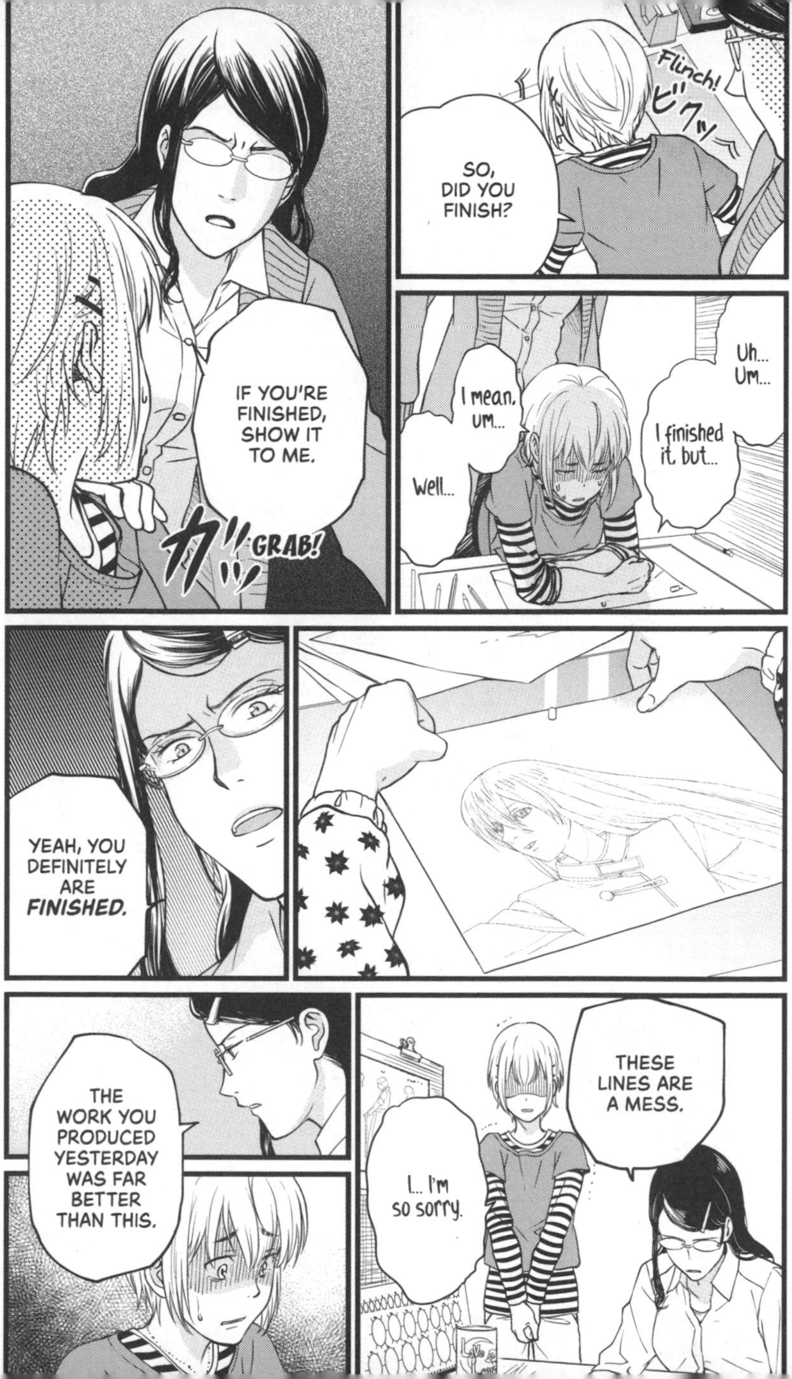
Flinch!
ビクッ
SO, DID YOU FINISH?
Uh... Um...
I finished it, but...
I mean, um...
Well...
IF YOU'RE FINISHED, SHOW IT TO ME.
カッ
GRAB!
YEAH, YOU DEFINITELY ARE FINISHED.
THESE LINES ARE A MESS.
I... I'm so sorry.
THE WORK YOU PRODUCED YESTERDAY WAS FAR BETTER THAN THIS.

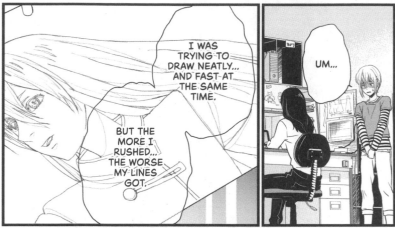

I WAS TRYING TO DRAW NEATLY... AND FAST AT THE SAME TIME.

BUT THE MORE I RUSHED... THE WORSE MY LINES GOT.

UM...

OH, SHUT UP.

LISTEN,

PROFESSIONALS NEVER MAKE EXCUSES.

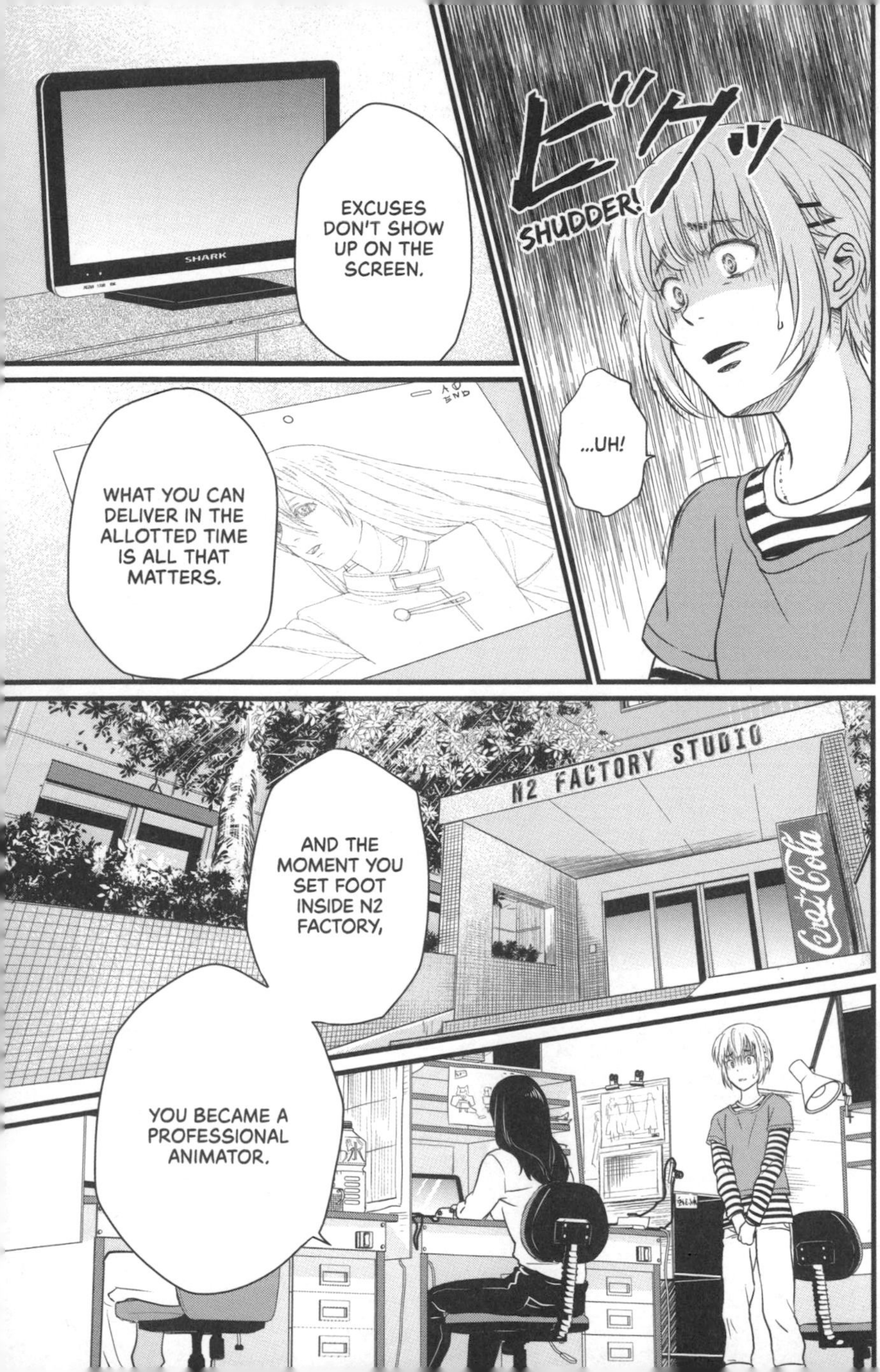
ビクッ
SHUDDER!
...UH!
SHARK
EXCUSES DON'T SHOW UP ON THE SCREEN.
WHAT YOU CAN DELIVER IN THE ALLOTTED TIME IS ALL THAT MATTERS.
N2 FACTORY STUDIO
AND THE MOMENT YOU SET FOOT INSIDE N2 FACTORY,
YOU BECAME A PROFESSIONAL ANIMATOR.

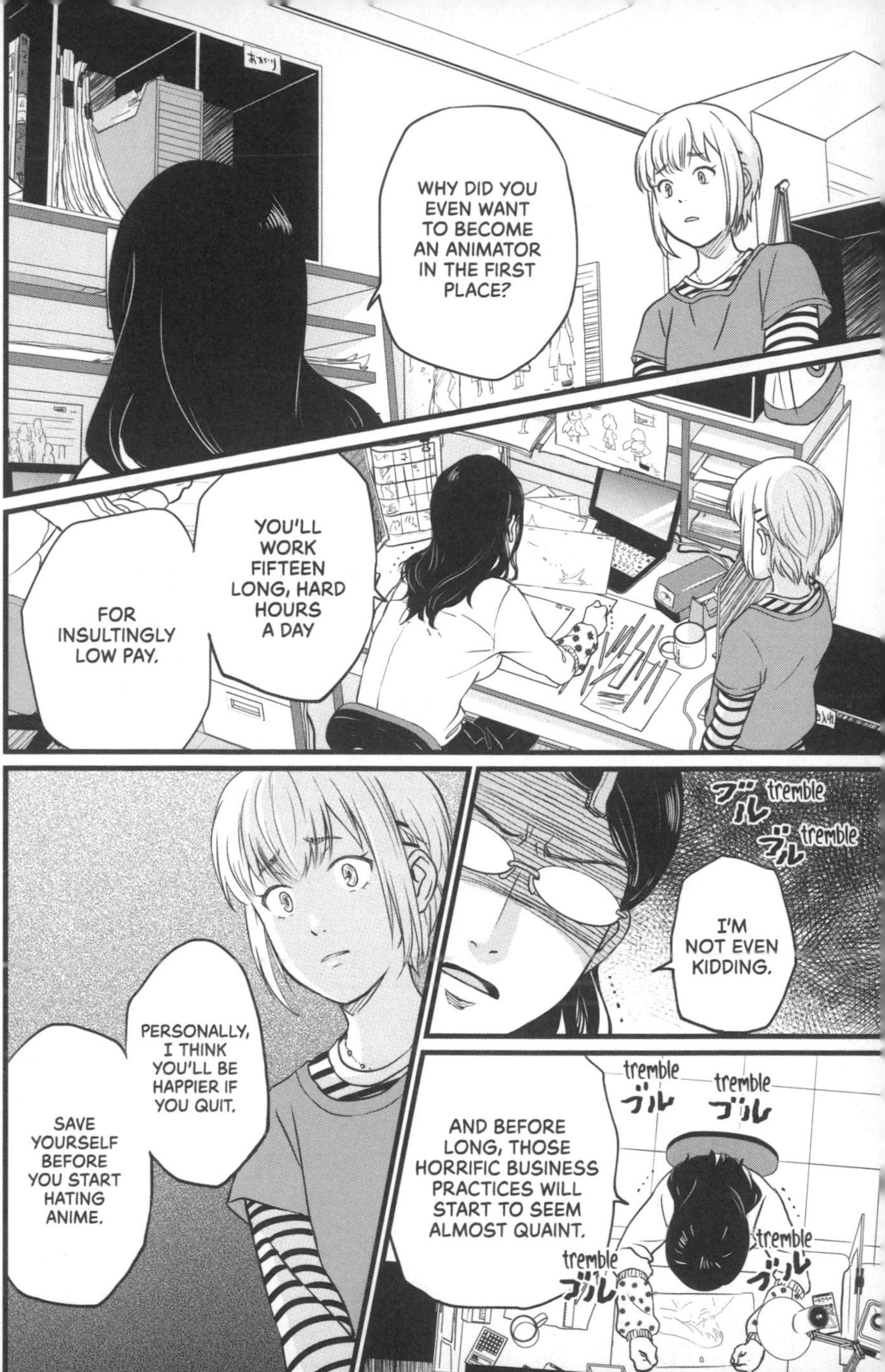
WHY DID YOU EVEN WANT TO BECOME AN ANIMATOR IN THE FIRST PLACE?
YOU'LL WORK FIFTEEN LONG, HARD HOURS A DAY
FOR INSULTINGLY LOW PAY.
ブル tremble
ブル tremble
I'M NOT EVEN KIDDING.
ブル tremble
ブル tremble
AND BEFORE LONG, THOSE HORRIFIC BUSINESS PRACTICES WILL START TO SEEM ALMOST QUAINT.
ブル tremble
ブル tremble
PERSONALLY, I THINK YOU'LL BE HAPPIER IF YOU QUIT.
SAVE YOURSELF BEFORE YOU START HATING ANIME.

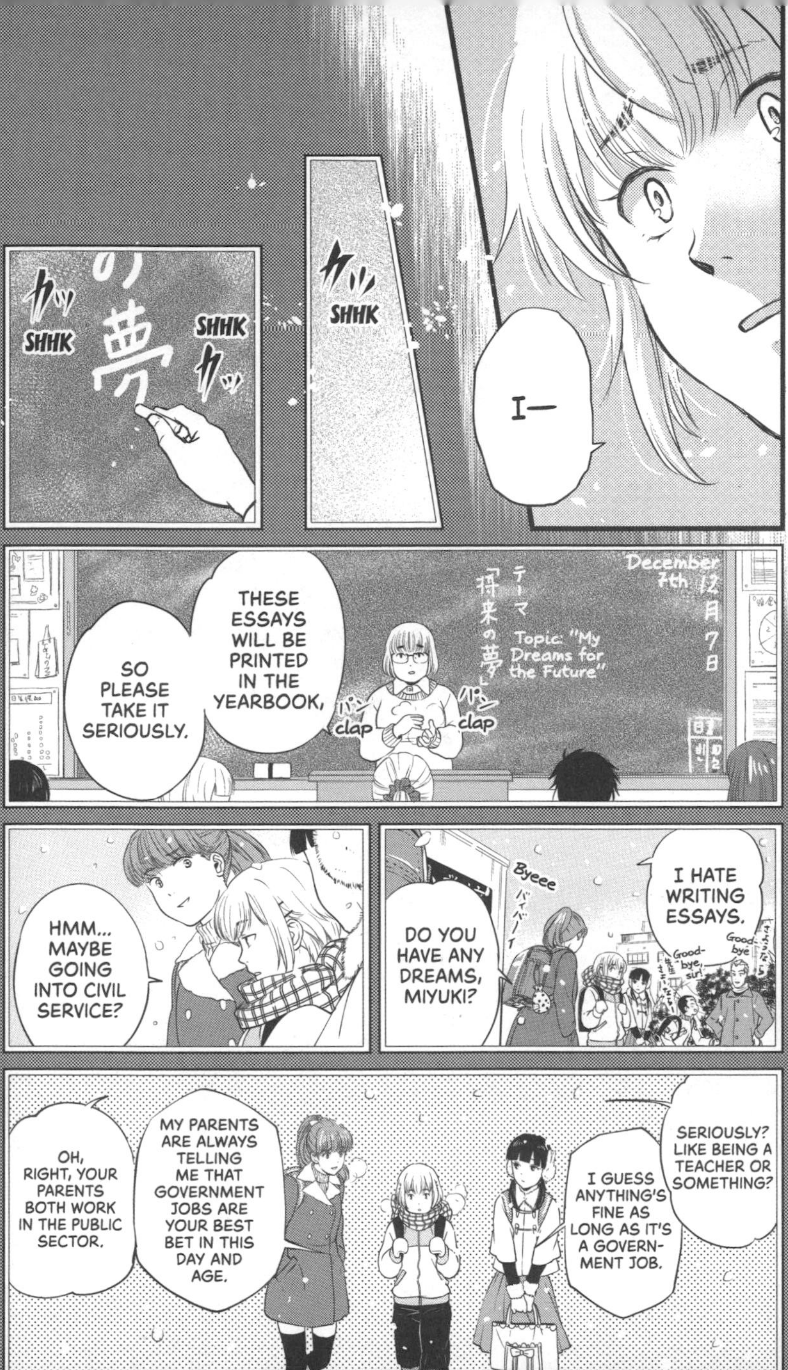
I—
SHHK
SHHK
夢
SHHK
December 7th
12月7日
テーマ「将来の夢」
Topic: "My Dreams for the Future"
THESE ESSAYS WILL BE PRINTED IN THE YEARBOOK,
SO PLEASE TAKE IT SERIOUSLY.
clap
clap
I HATE WRITING ESSAYS.
Byeee
DO YOU HAVE ANY DREAMS, MIYUKI?
Good-bye
Good-bye, sir!
HMM... MAYBE GOING INTO CIVIL SERVICE?
SERIOUSLY? LIKE BEING A TEACHER OR SOMETHING?
I GUESS ANYTHING'S FINE AS LONG AS IT'S A GOVERNMENT JOB.
MY PARENTS ARE ALWAYS TELLING ME THAT GOVERNMENT JOBS ARE YOUR BEST BET IN THIS DAY AND AGE.
OH, RIGHT, YOUR PARENTS BOTH WORK IN THE PUBLIC SECTOR.

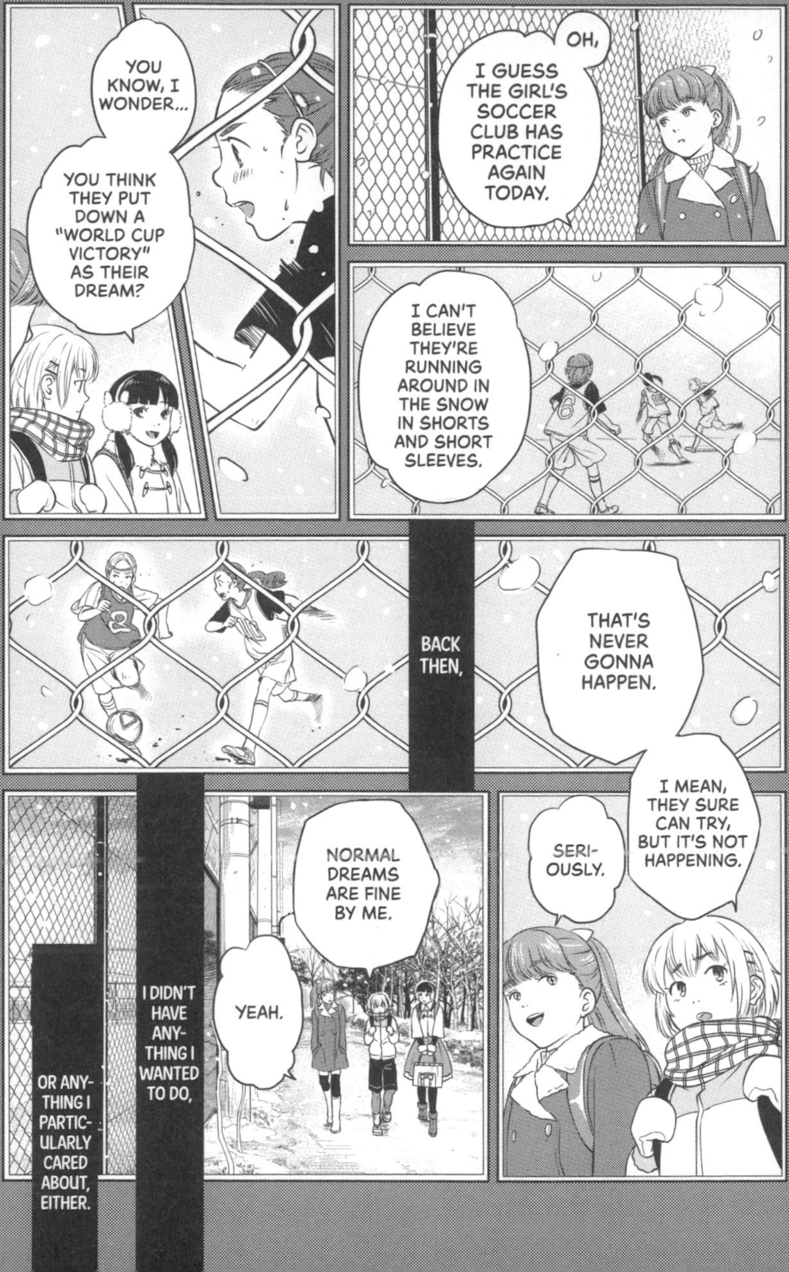
OH,
I GUESS THE GIRL'S SOCCER CLUB HAS PRACTICE AGAIN TODAY.
I CAN'T BELIEVE THEY'RE RUNNING AROUND IN THE SNOW IN SHORTS AND SHORT SLEEVES.
YOU KNOW, I WONDER...
YOU THINK THEY PUT DOWN A "WORLD CUP VICTORY" AS THEIR DREAM?
THAT'S NEVER GONNA HAPPEN.
BACK THEN,
I MEAN, THEY SURE CAN TRY, BUT IT'S NOT HAPPENING.
SERI-OUSLY.
NORMAL DREAMS ARE FINE BY ME.
YEAH.
I DIDN'T HAVE ANY-THING I WANTED TO DO,
OR ANY-THING I PARTIC-ULARLY CARED ABOUT, EITHER.

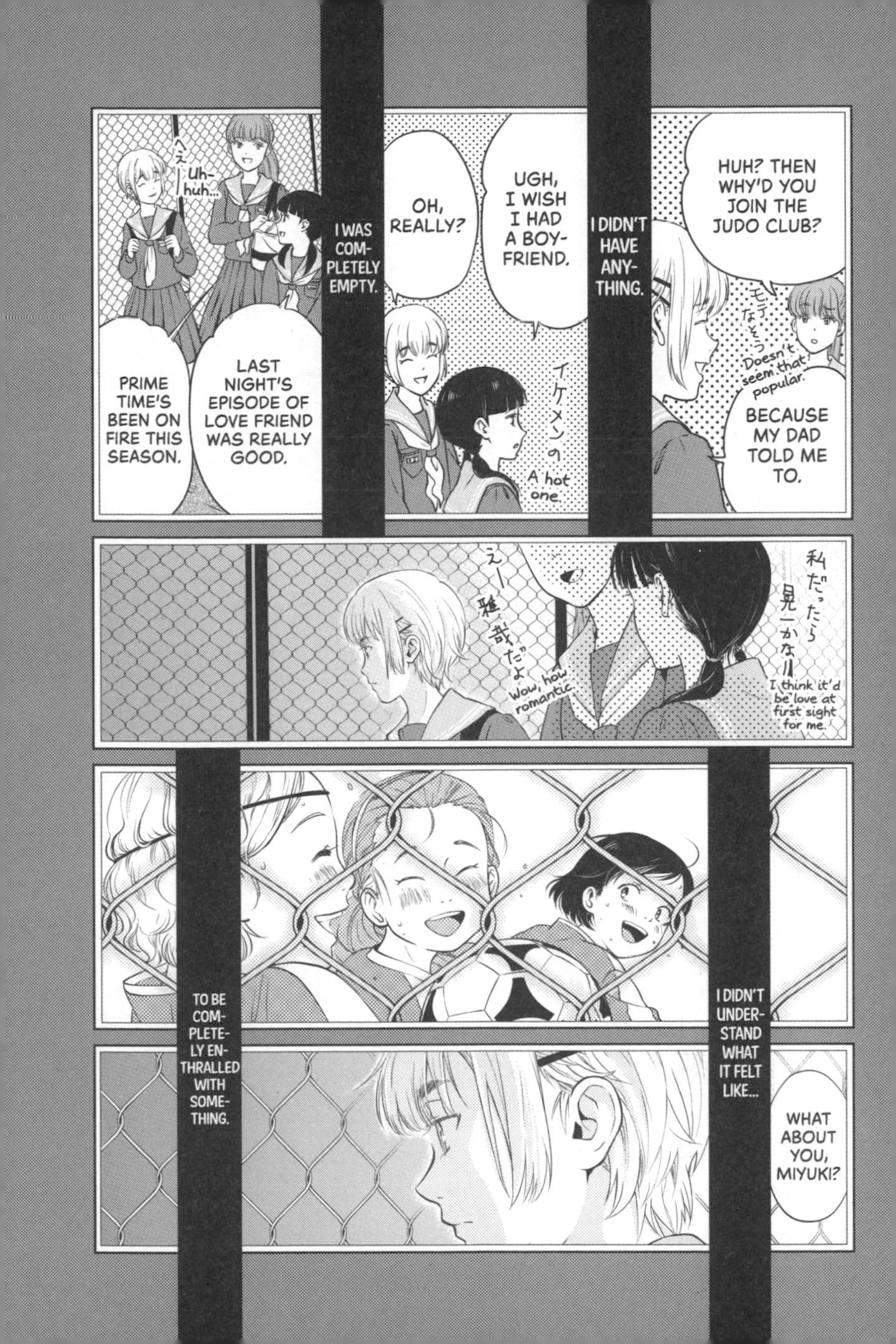
HUH? THEN WHY'D YOU JOIN THE JUDO CLUB?
モテなそう
Doesn't seem that popular.
BECAUSE MY DAD TOLD ME TO.
I DIDN'T HAVE ANYTHING.
UGH, I WISH I HAD A BOY-FRIEND.
イケメンの
A hot one.
OH, REALLY?
I WAS COM-PLETELY EMPTY.
へぇー
Uh-huh...
LAST NIGHT'S EPISODE OF LOVE FRIEND WAS REALLY GOOD.
PRIME TIME'S BEEN ON FIRE THIS SEASON.
私だったら
I think it'd be love at first sight for me.
えー
Wow, how romantic.
I DIDN'T UNDER-STAND WHAT IT FELT LIKE...
TO BE COM-PLETE-LY EN-THRALLED WITH SOME-THING.
WHAT ABOUT YOU, MIYUKI?

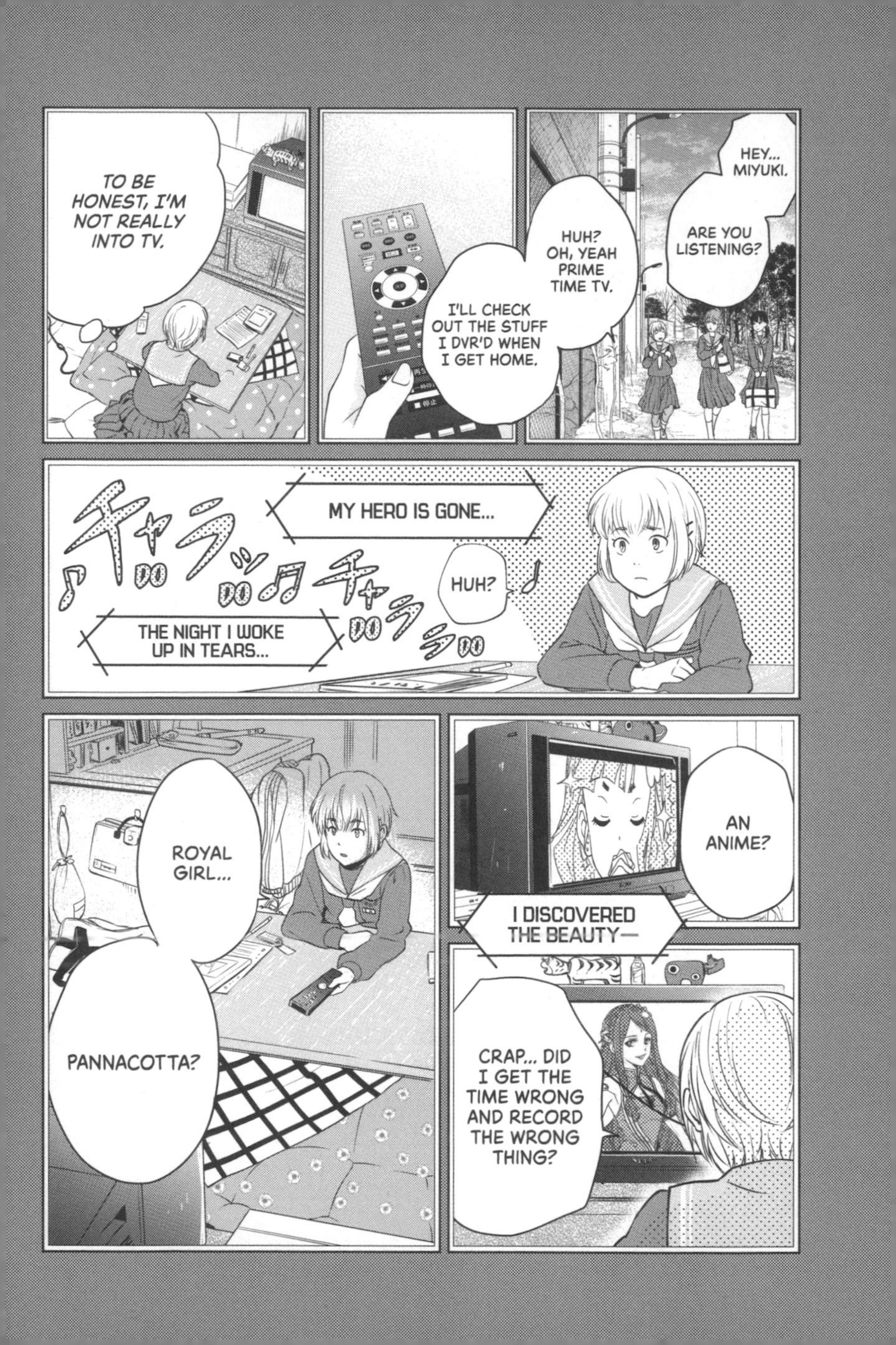
HEY... MIYUKI.
ARE YOU LISTENING?
HUH? OH, YEAH PRIME TIME TV.
I'LL CHECK OUT THE STUFF I DVR'D WHEN I GET HOME.
TO BE HONEST, I'M NOT REALLY INTO TV.
MY HERO IS GONE...
HUH?
THE NIGHT I WOKE UP IN TEARS...
AN ANIME?
I DISCOVERED THE BEAUTY—
CRAP... DID I GET THE TIME WRONG AND RECORD THE WRONG THING?
ROYAL GIRL...
PANNACOTTA?

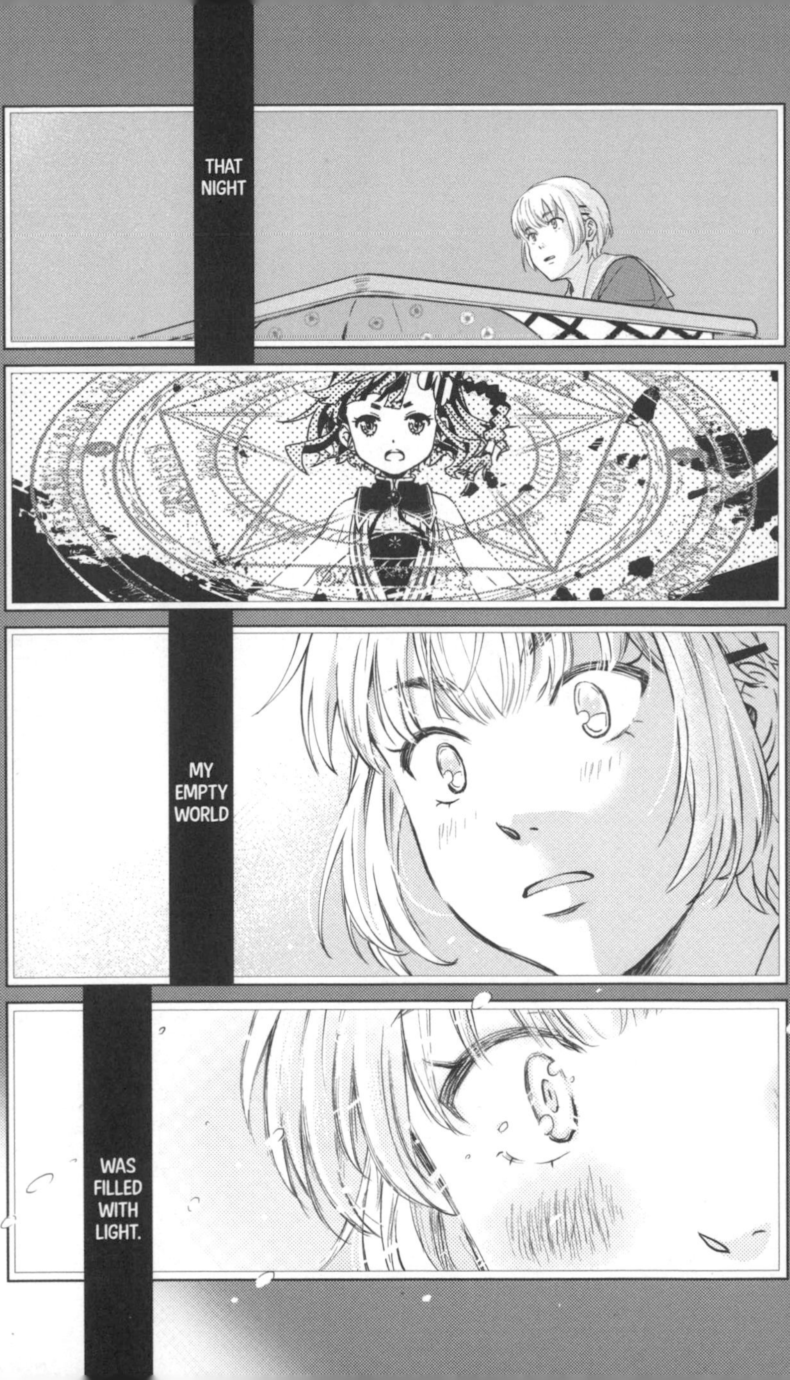
THAT NIGHT
MY EMPTY WORLD
WAS FILLED WITH LIGHT.

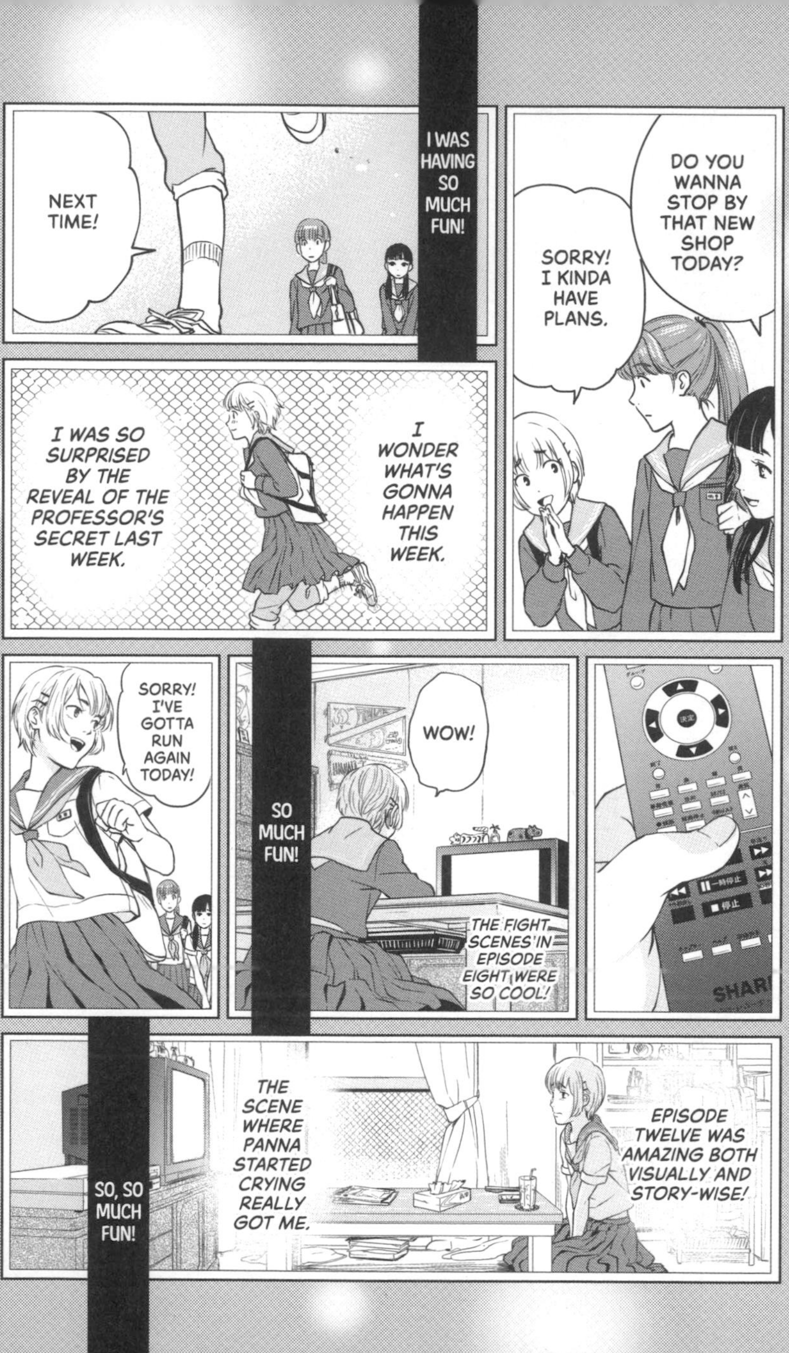
DO YOU WANNA STOP BY THAT NEW SHOP TODAY?
SORRY! I KINDA HAVE PLANS.
I WAS HAVING SO MUCH FUN!
NEXT TIME!
I WONDER WHAT'S GONNA HAPPEN THIS WEEK.
I WAS SO SURPRISED BY THE REVEAL OF THE PROFESSOR'S SECRET LAST WEEK.
WOW!
THE FIGHT SCENES IN EPISODE EIGHT WERE SO COOL!
SO MUCH FUN!
SORRY! I'VE GOTTA RUN AGAIN TODAY!
EPISODE TWELVE WAS AMAZING BOTH VISUALLY AND STORY-WISE!
THE SCENE WHERE PANNA STARTED CRYING REALLY GOT ME.
SO, SO MUCH FUN!

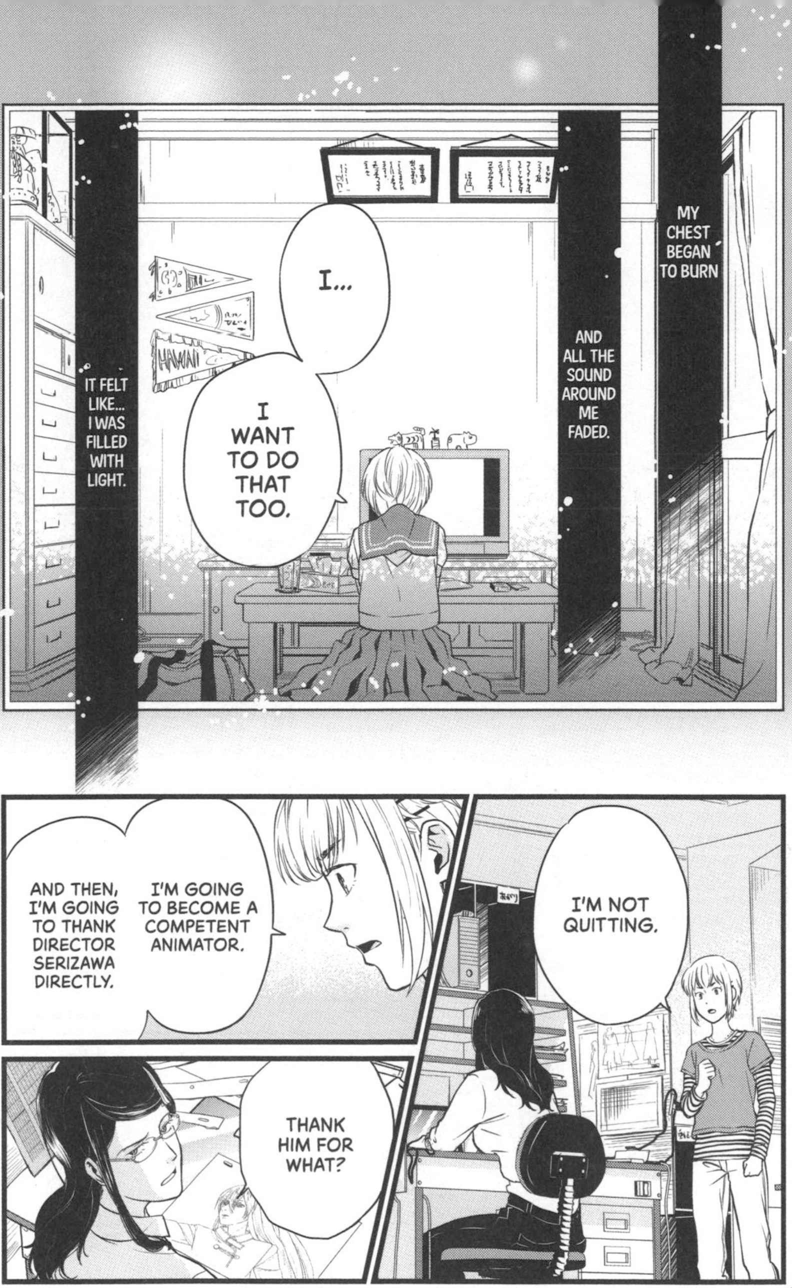
MY CHEST BEGAN TO BURN
AND ALL THE SOUND AROUND ME FADED.
I...
I WANT TO DO THAT TOO.
IT FELT LIKE... I WAS FILLED WITH LIGHT.
HAWAII
I'M NOT QUITTING.
I'M GOING TO BECOME A COMPETENT ANIMATOR.
AND THEN, I'M GOING TO THANK DIRECTOR SERIZAWA DIRECTLY.
THANK HIM FOR WHAT?

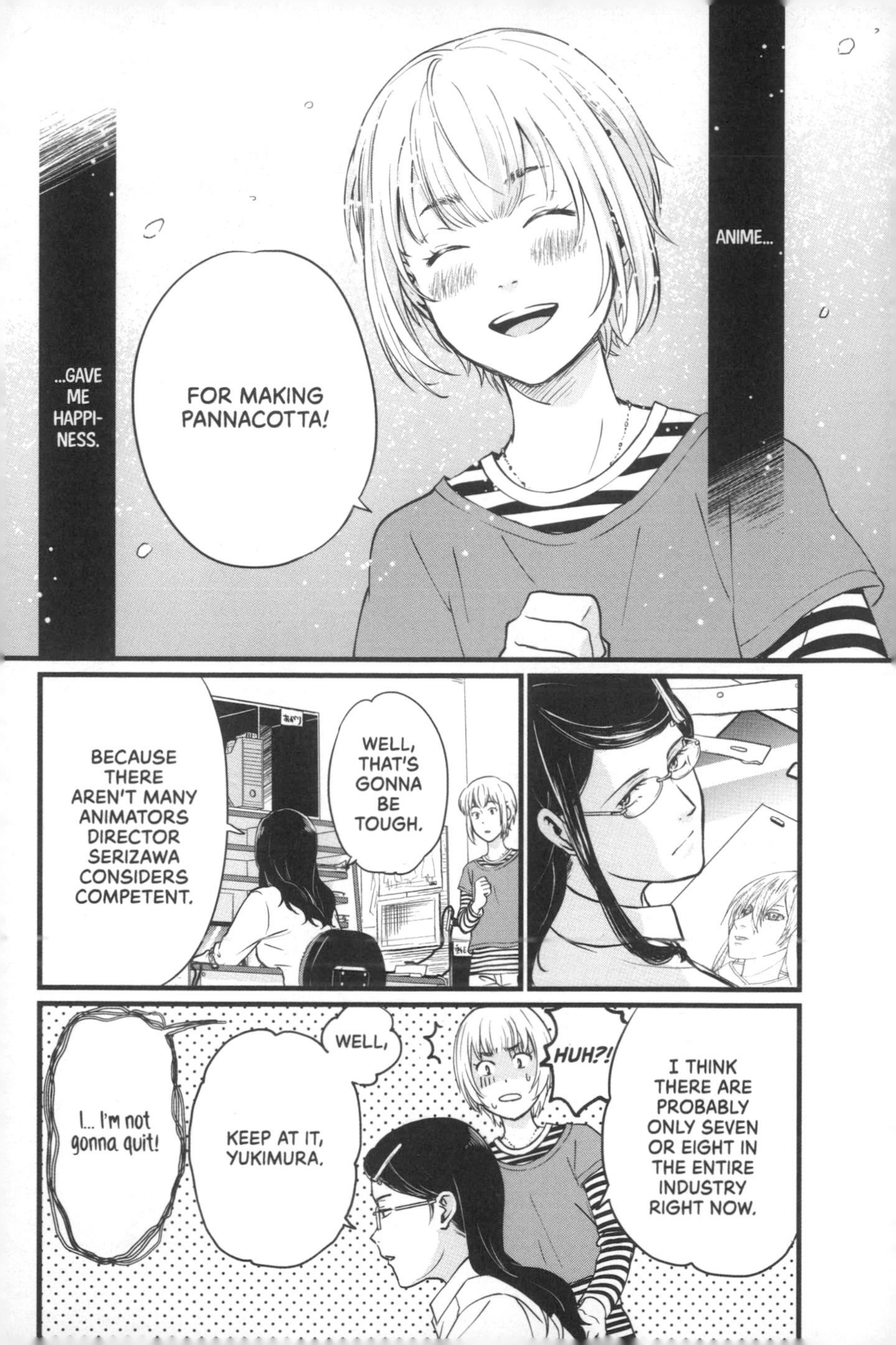
ANIME...
FOR MAKING PANNACOTTA!
...GAVE ME HAPPI-NESS.
WELL, THAT'S GONNA BE TOUGH.
BECAUSE THERE AREN'T MANY ANIMATORS DIRECTOR SERIZAWA CONSIDERS COMPETENT.
I THINK THERE ARE PROBABLY ONLY SEVEN OR EIGHT IN THE ENTIRE INDUSTRY RIGHT NOW.
HUH?!
WELL,
KEEP AT IT, YUKIMURA.
I... I'm not gonna quit!

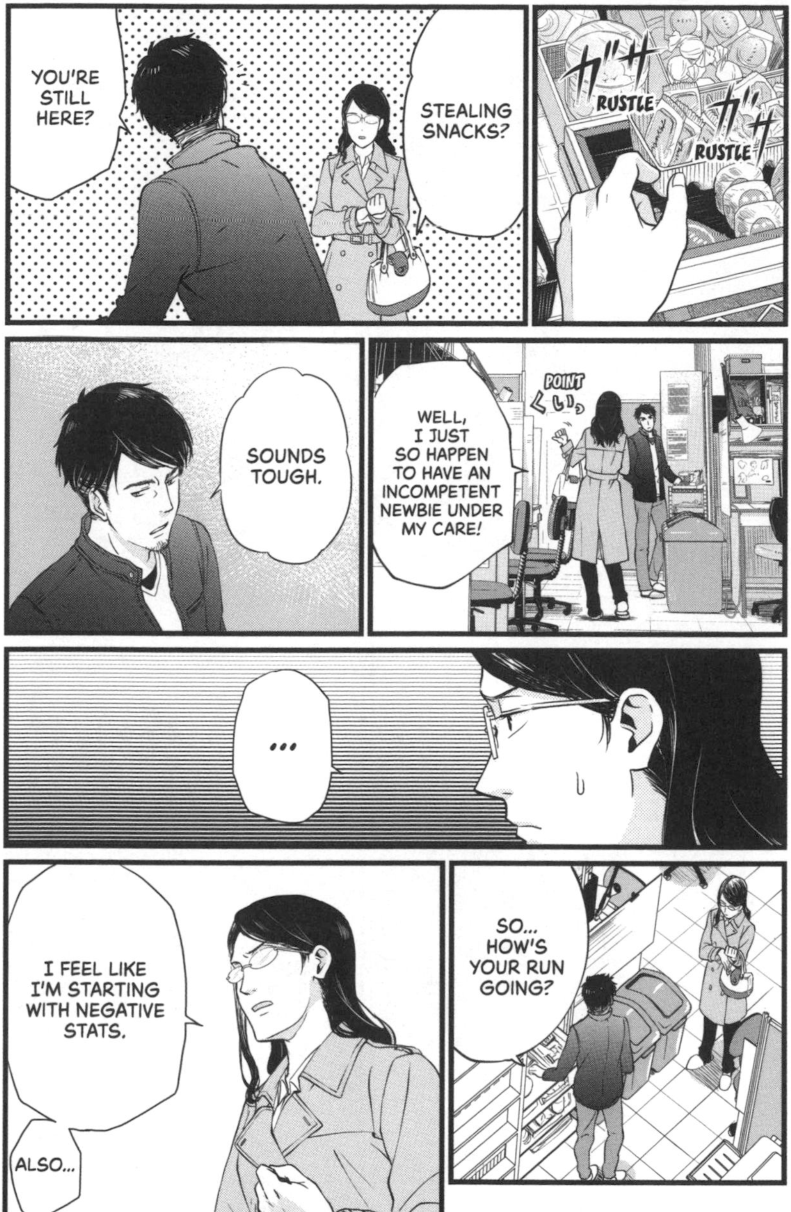
RUSTLE
RUSTLE
STEALING SNACKS?
YOU'RE STILL HERE?
POINT
WELL, I JUST SO HAPPEN TO HAVE AN INCOMPETENT NEWBIE UNDER MY CARE!
SOUNDS TOUGH.
...
SO... HOW'S YOUR RUN GOING?
I FEEL LIKE I'M STARTING WITH NEGATIVE STATS.
ALSO...

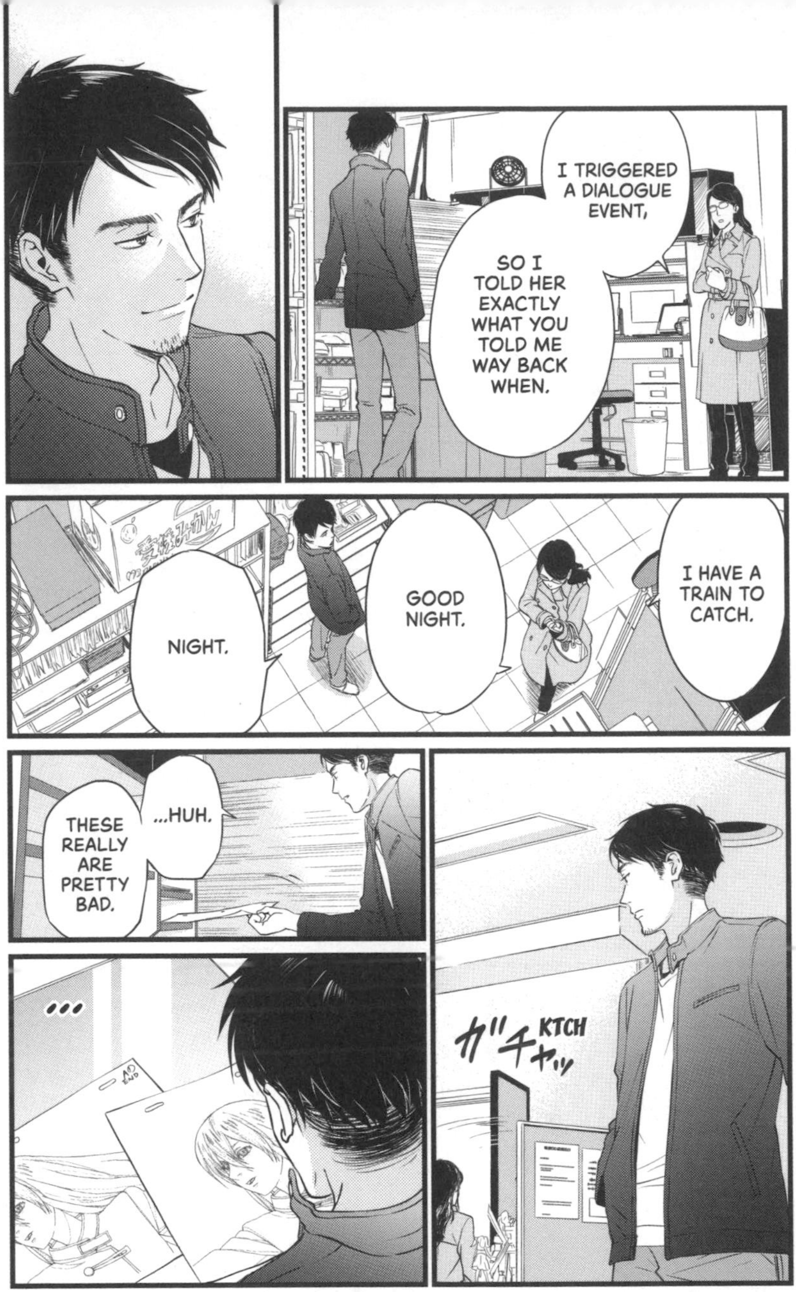
I TRIGGERED A DIALOGUE EVENT,
SO I TOLD HER EXACTLY WHAT YOU TOLD ME WAY BACK WHEN.
I HAVE A TRAIN TO CATCH.
GOOD NIGHT.
NIGHT.
ガチャッ
KTCH
...HUH.
THESE REALLY ARE PRETTY BAD.
...

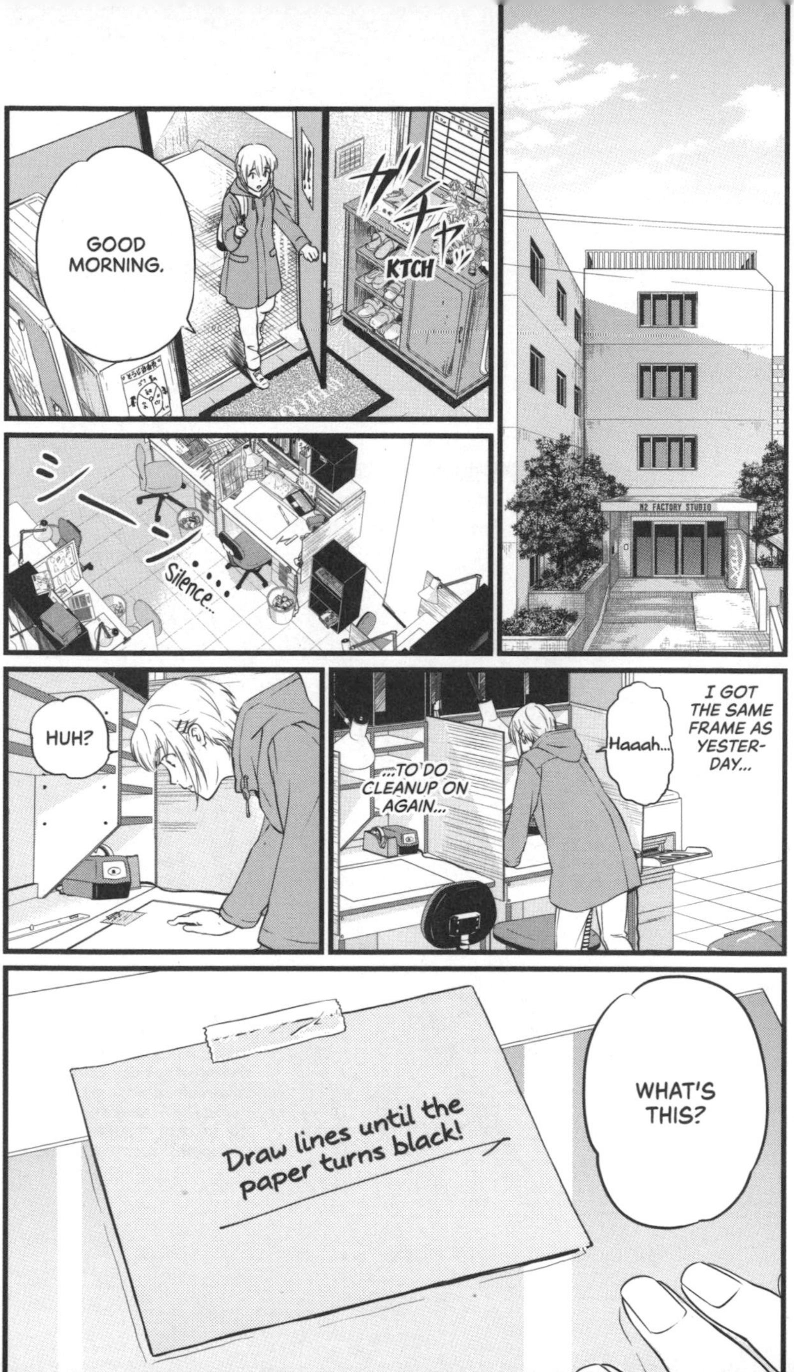
N2 FACTORY STUDIO
KTCH
GOOD MORNING.
Silence...
I GOT THE SAME FRAME AS YESTER-DAY...
Haaah...
...TO DO CLEANUP ON AGAIN...
HUH?
WHAT'S THIS?
Draw lines until the paper turns black!

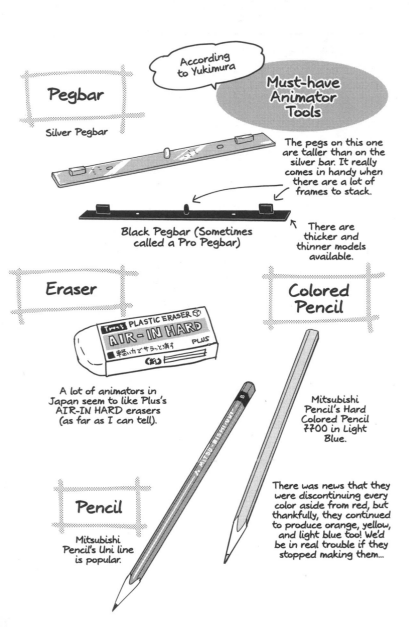

According to Yukimura

Must-have Animator Tools

Pegbar

Silver Pegbar

The pegs on this one are taller than on the silver bar. It really comes in handy when there are a lot of frames to stack.

Black Pegbar (Sometimes called a Pro Pegbar)

There are thicker and thinner models available.

Eraser

PLASTIC ERASER
AIR-IN HARD
■ 軽い力でサラッと消す
PLUS
〈新〉

A lot of animators in Japan seem to like Plus's AIR-IN HARD erasers (as far as I can tell).

Colored Pencil

Mitsubishi Pencil's Hard Colored Pencil 7700 in Light Blue.

There was news that they were discontinuing every color aside from red, but thankfully, they continued to produce orange, yellow, and light blue too! We'd be in real trouble if they stopped making them...

Pencil

Mitsubishi Pencil's Uni line is popular.

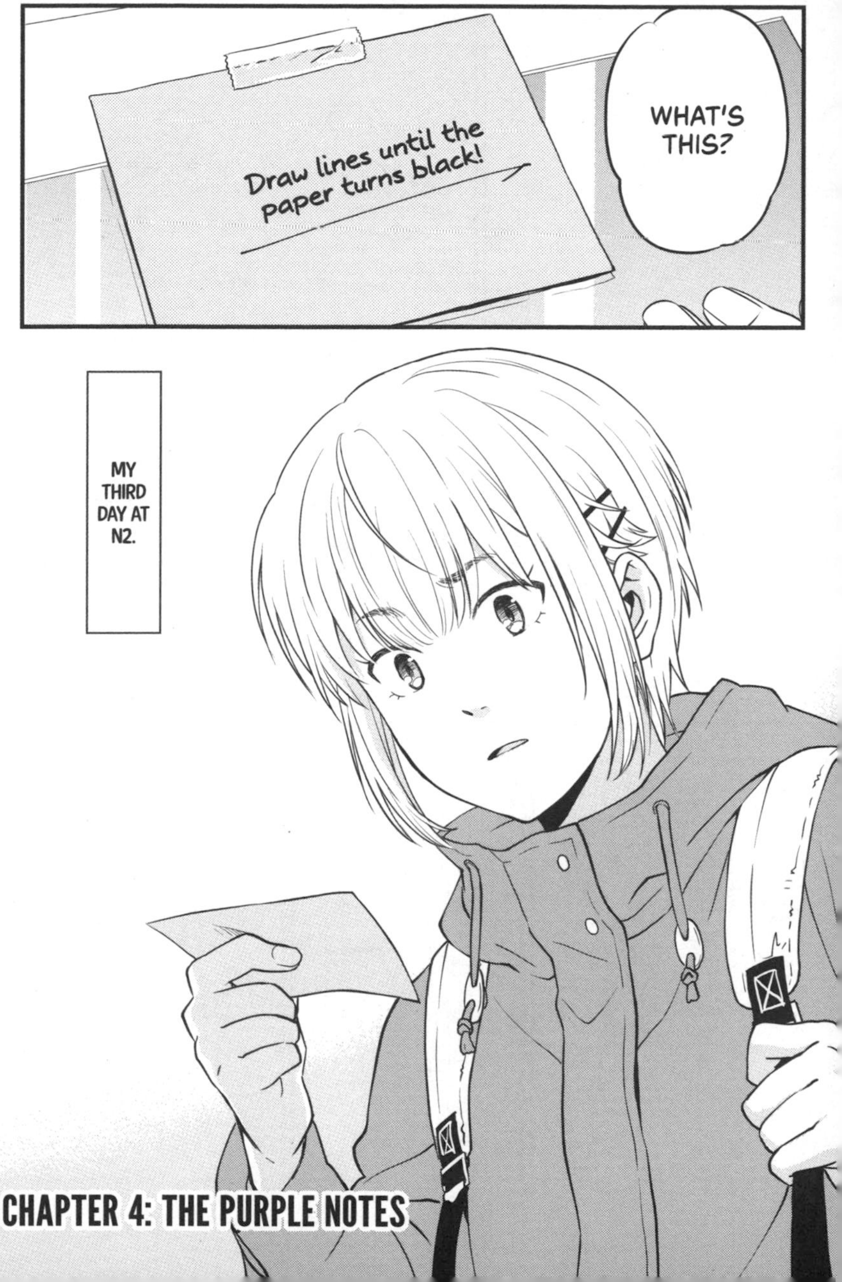
WHAT'S THIS?
Draw lines until the paper turns black!
MY THIRD DAY AT N2.

CHAPTER 4: THE PURPLE NOTES

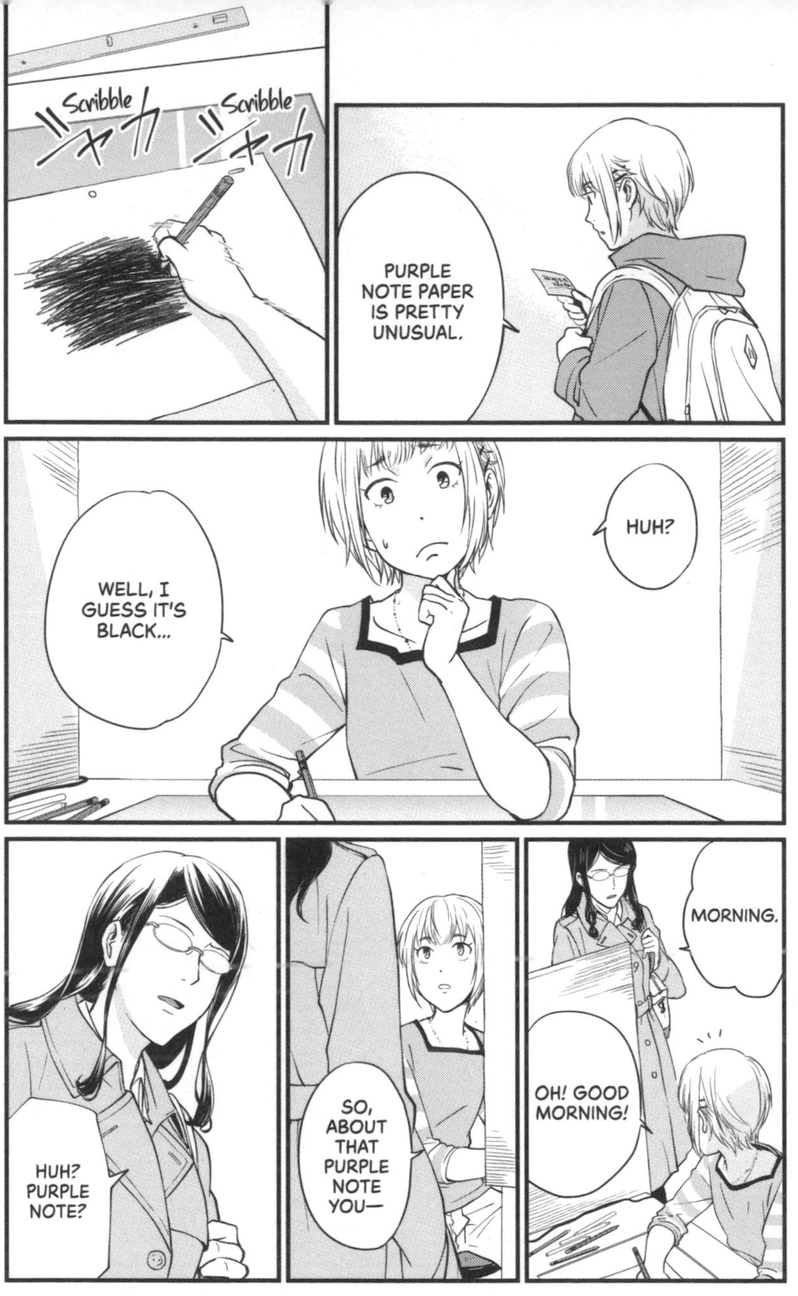
PURPLE NOTE PAPER IS PRETTY UNUSUAL.
Scribble ジャカ
Scribble ジャカ
HUH?
WELL, I GUESS IT'S BLACK...
MORNING.
OH! GOOD MORNING!
SO, ABOUT THAT PURPLE NOTE YOU—
HUH? PURPLE NOTE?

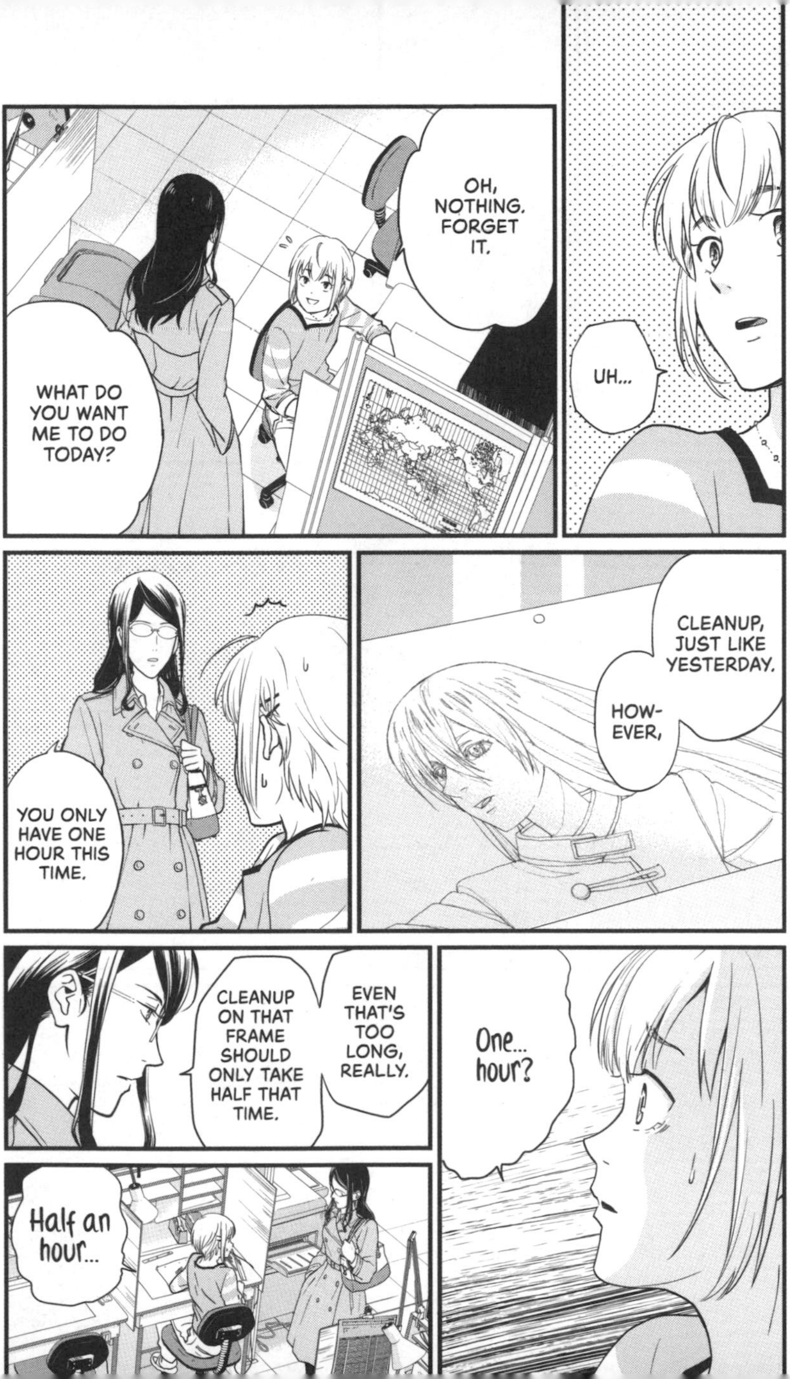
UH...
OH, NOTHING. FORGET IT.
WHAT DO YOU WANT ME TO DO TODAY?
CLEANUP, JUST LIKE YESTERDAY.
HOW-EVER,
YOU ONLY HAVE ONE HOUR THIS TIME.
One... hour?
EVEN THAT'S TOO LONG, REALLY.
CLEANUP ON THAT FRAME SHOULD ONLY TAKE HALF THAT TIME.
Half an hour...

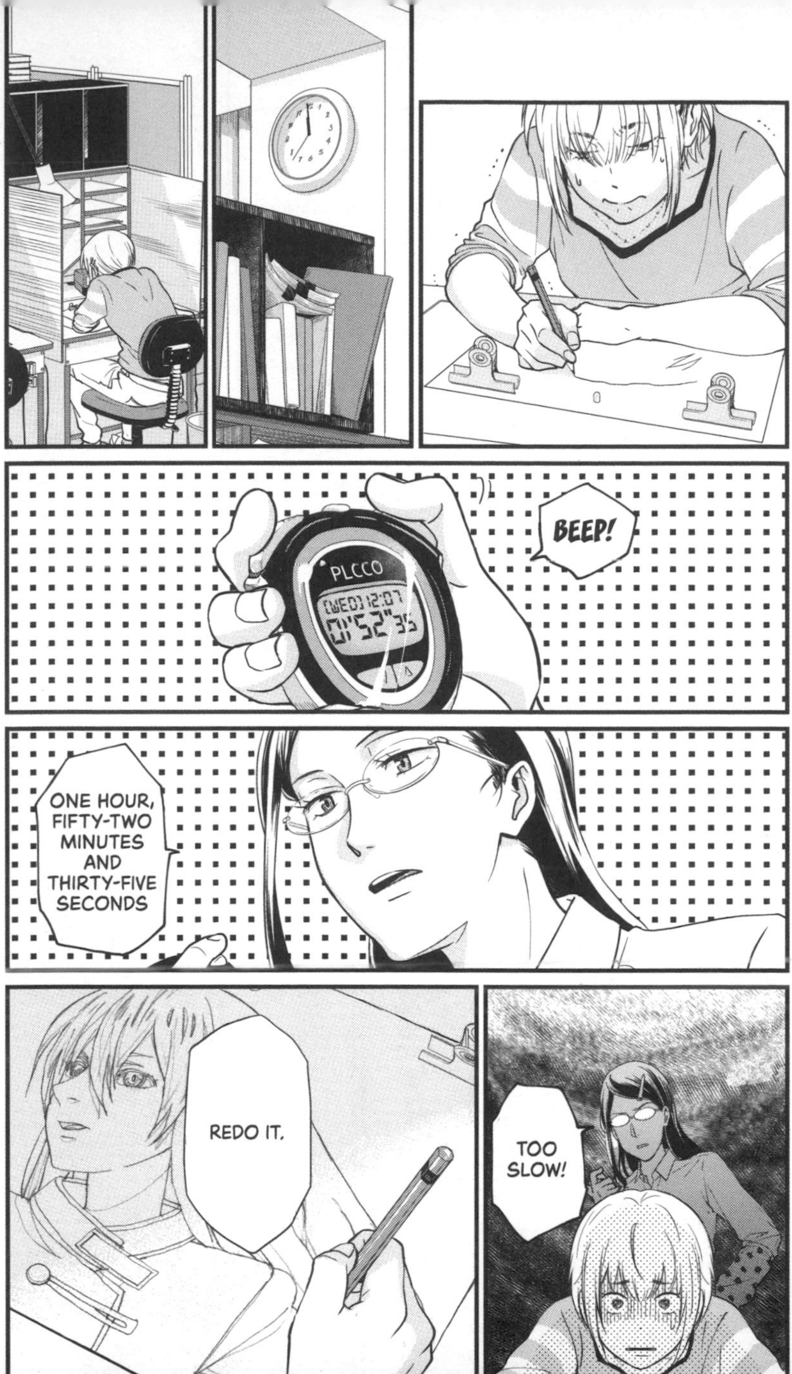
BEEP!
ONE HOUR, FIFTY-TWO MINUTES AND THIRTY-FIVE SECONDS
TOO SLOW!
REDO IT.

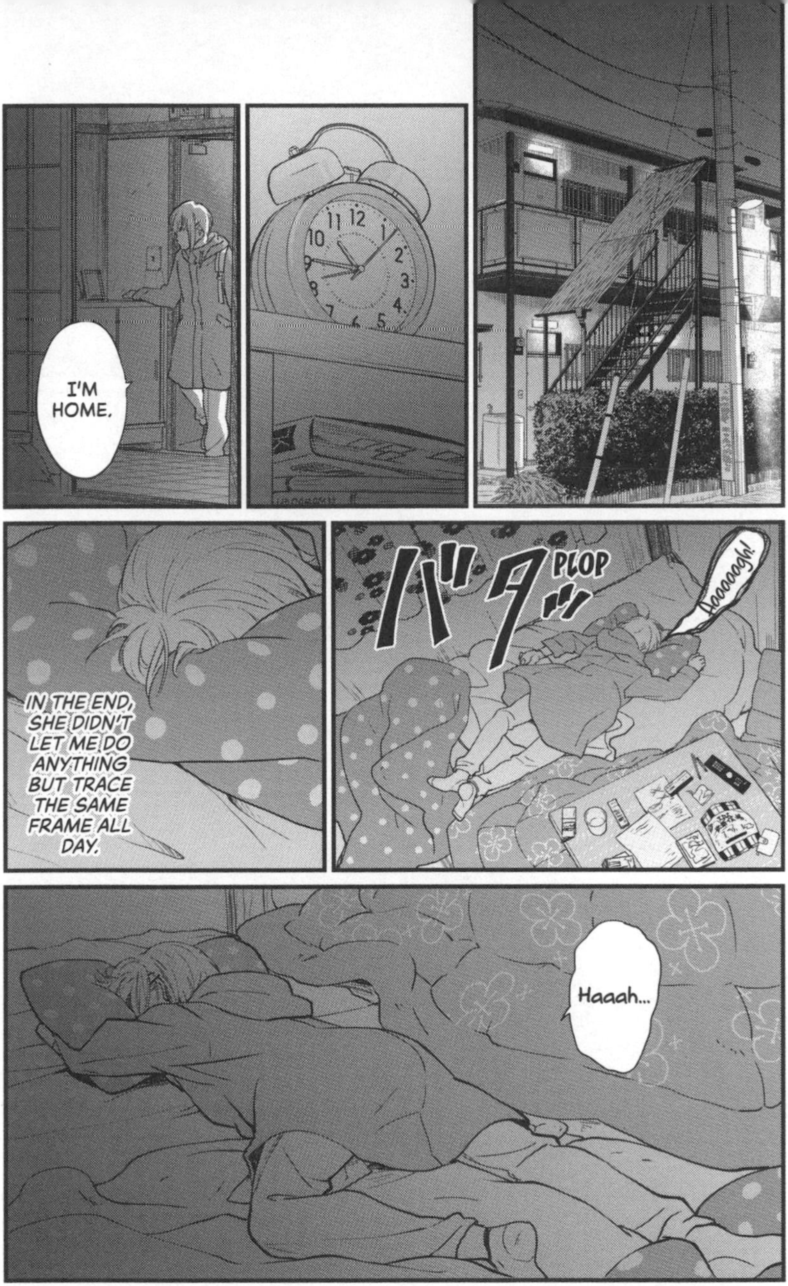
I'M HOME.
バタッ
PLOP
Aaaaaagh!
IN THE END, SHE DIDN'T LET ME DO ANYTHING BUT TRACE THE SAME FRAME ALL DAY.
Haaah...

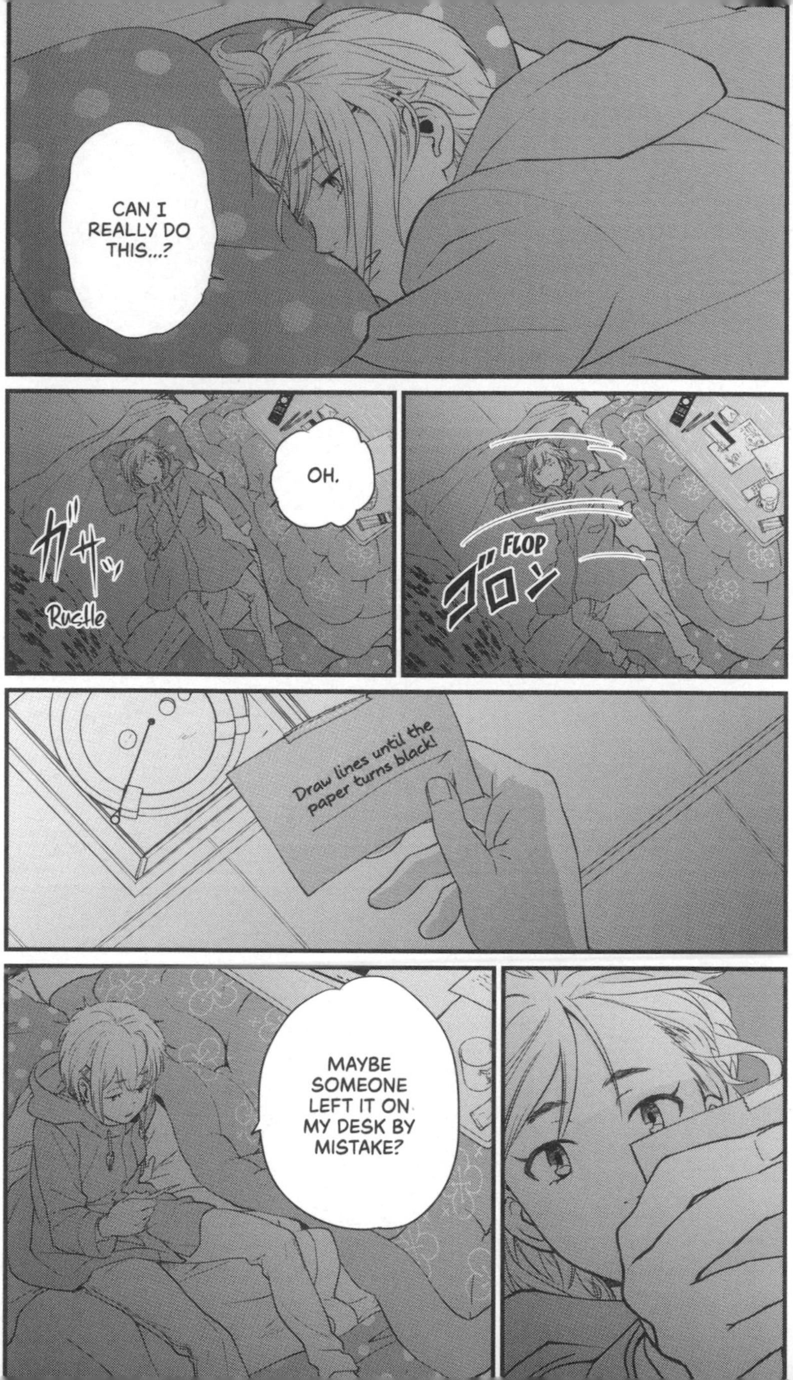
CAN I REALLY DO THIS...?
ゴロン
FLOP
OH.
ガサッ
Rustle
Draw lines until the paper turns black!
MAYBE SOMEONE LEFT IT ON MY DESK BY MISTAKE?

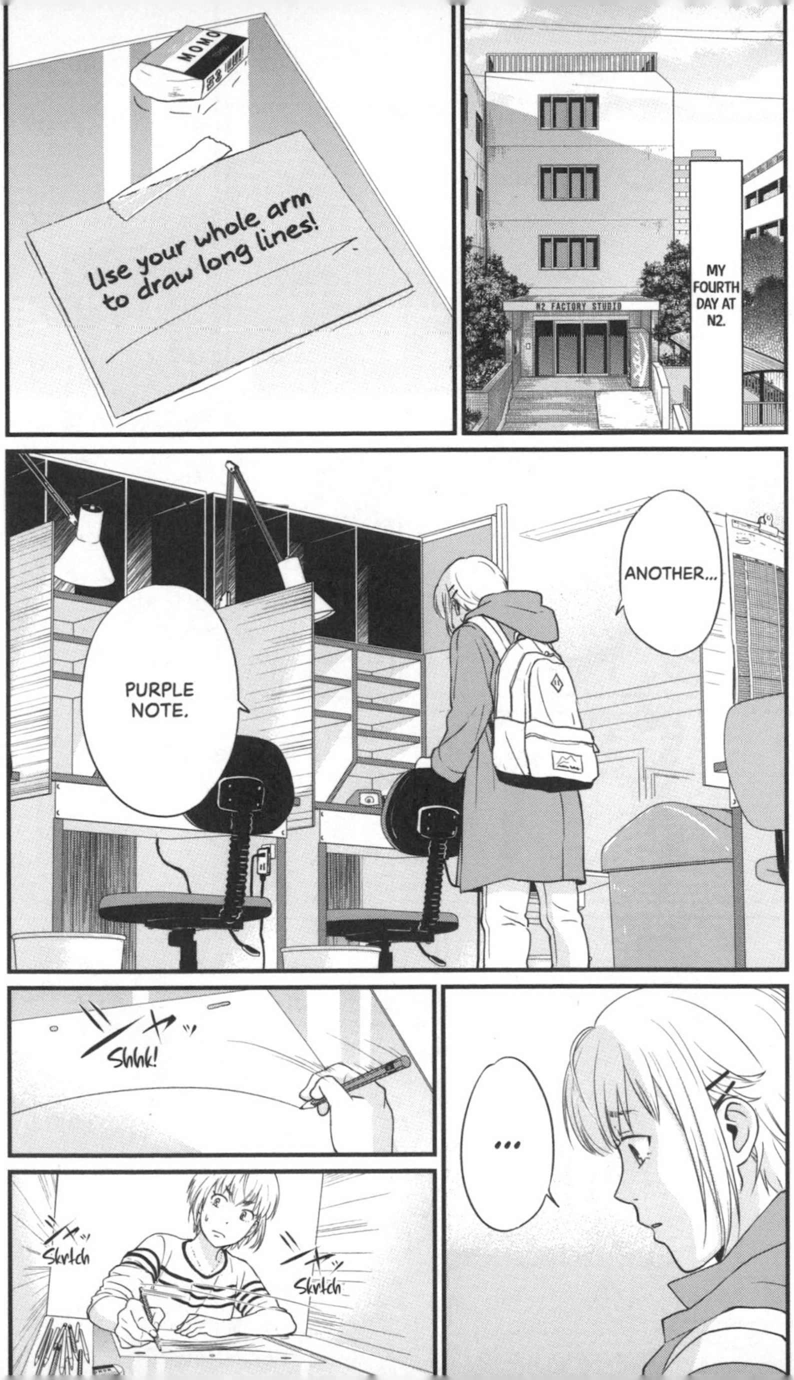
N2 FACTORY STUDIO
MY FOURTH DAY AT N2.
MOMO
Use your whole arm to draw long lines!
ANOTHER...
PURPLE NOTE.
...
Shhk!
Skrtch
Skrtch

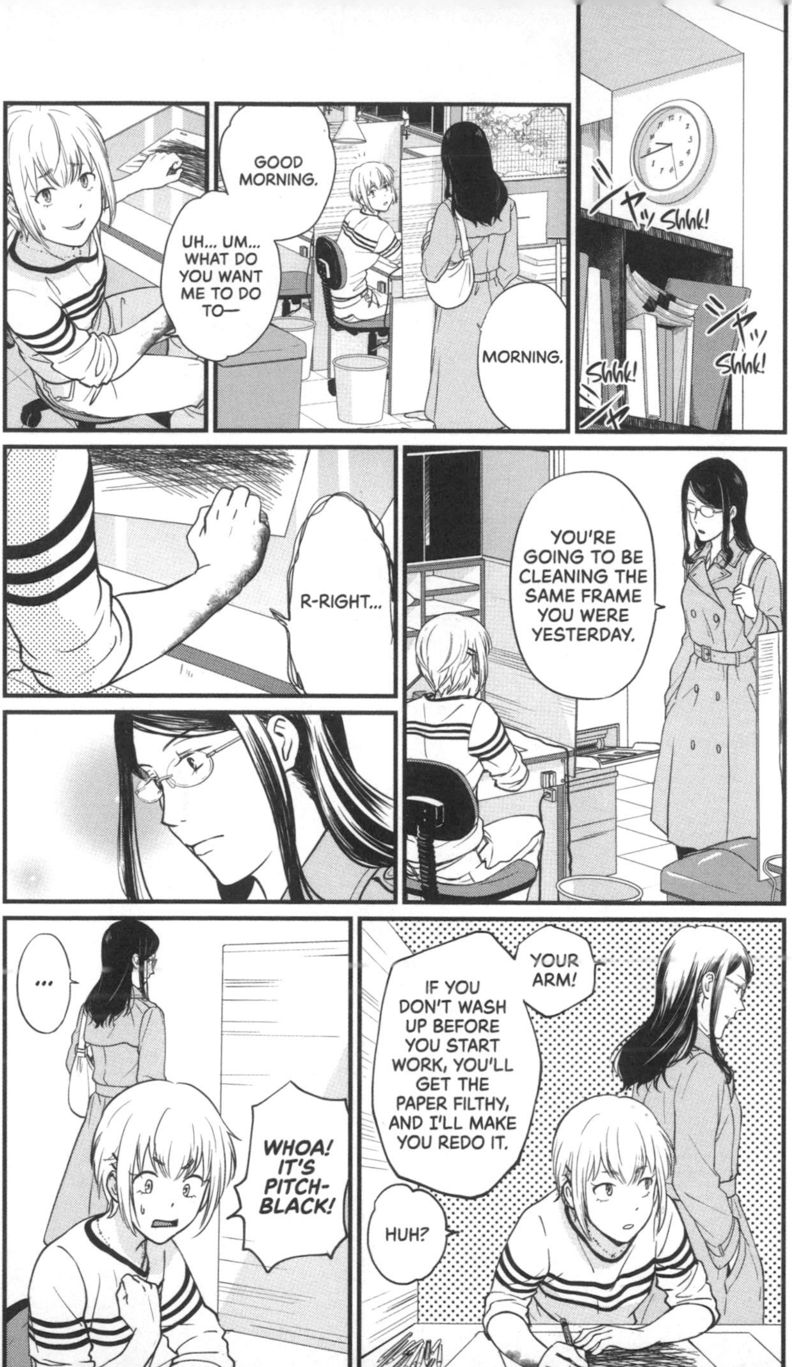

Shhk!
Shhk!
Shhk!
GOOD MORNING.
MORNING.
UH... UM... WHAT DO YOU WANT ME TO DO TO—
YOU'RE GOING TO BE CLEANING THE SAME FRAME YOU WERE YESTERDAY.
R-RIGHT...
YOUR ARM!
IF YOU DON'T WASH UP BEFORE YOU START WORK, YOU'LL GET THE PAPER FILTHY, AND I'LL MAKE YOU REDO IT.
HUH?
...
WHOA! IT'S PITCH-BLACK!

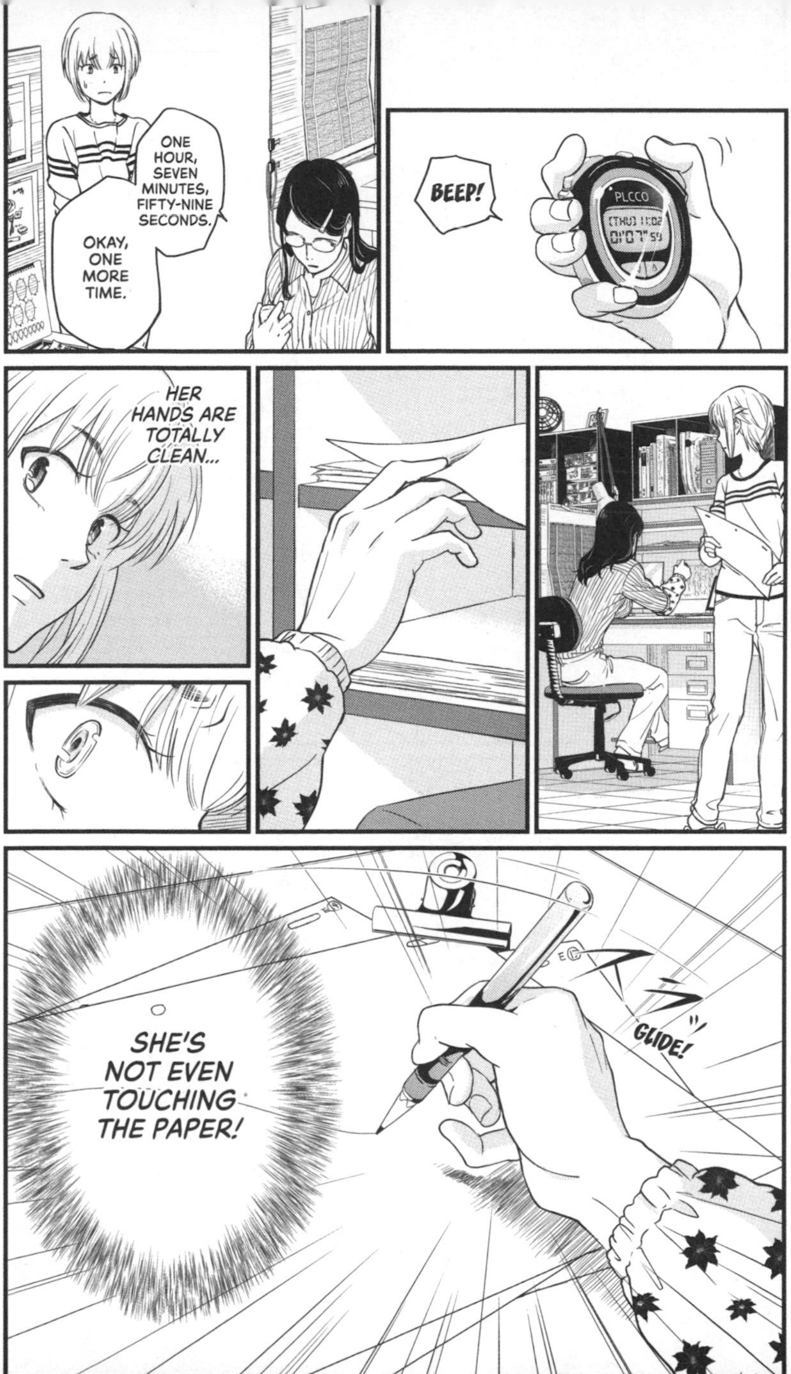
BEEP!
PLCCO
ONE HOUR, SEVEN MINUTES, FIFTY-NINE SECONDS.
OKAY, ONE MORE TIME.
HER HANDS ARE TOTALLY CLEAN...
SHE'S NOT EVEN TOUCHING THE PAPER!
GLIDE!

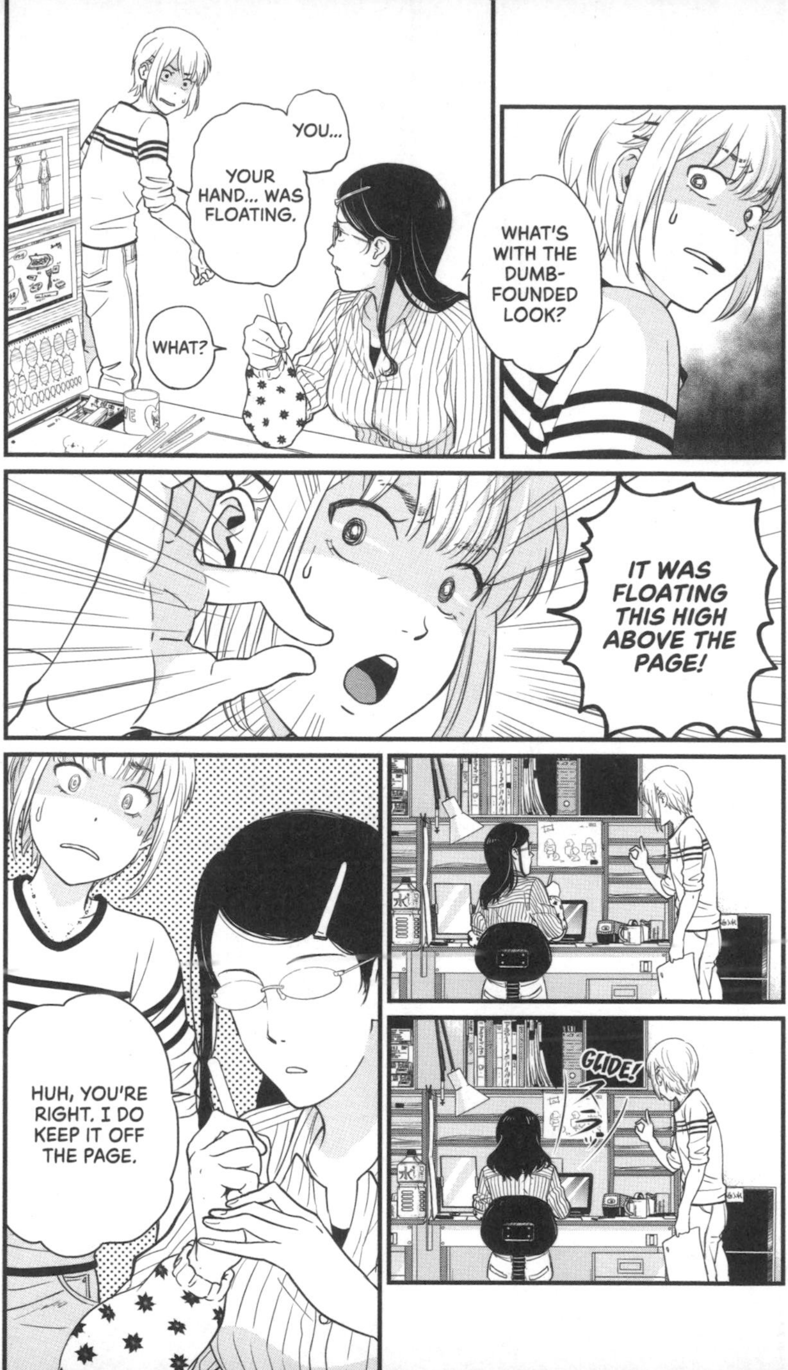
WHAT'S WITH THE DUMB-FOUNDED LOOK?
YOU...
YOUR HAND... WAS FLOATING.
WHAT?
IT WAS FLOATING THIS HIGH ABOVE THE PAGE!
GLIDE!
HUH, YOU'RE RIGHT. I DO KEEP IT OFF THE PAGE.

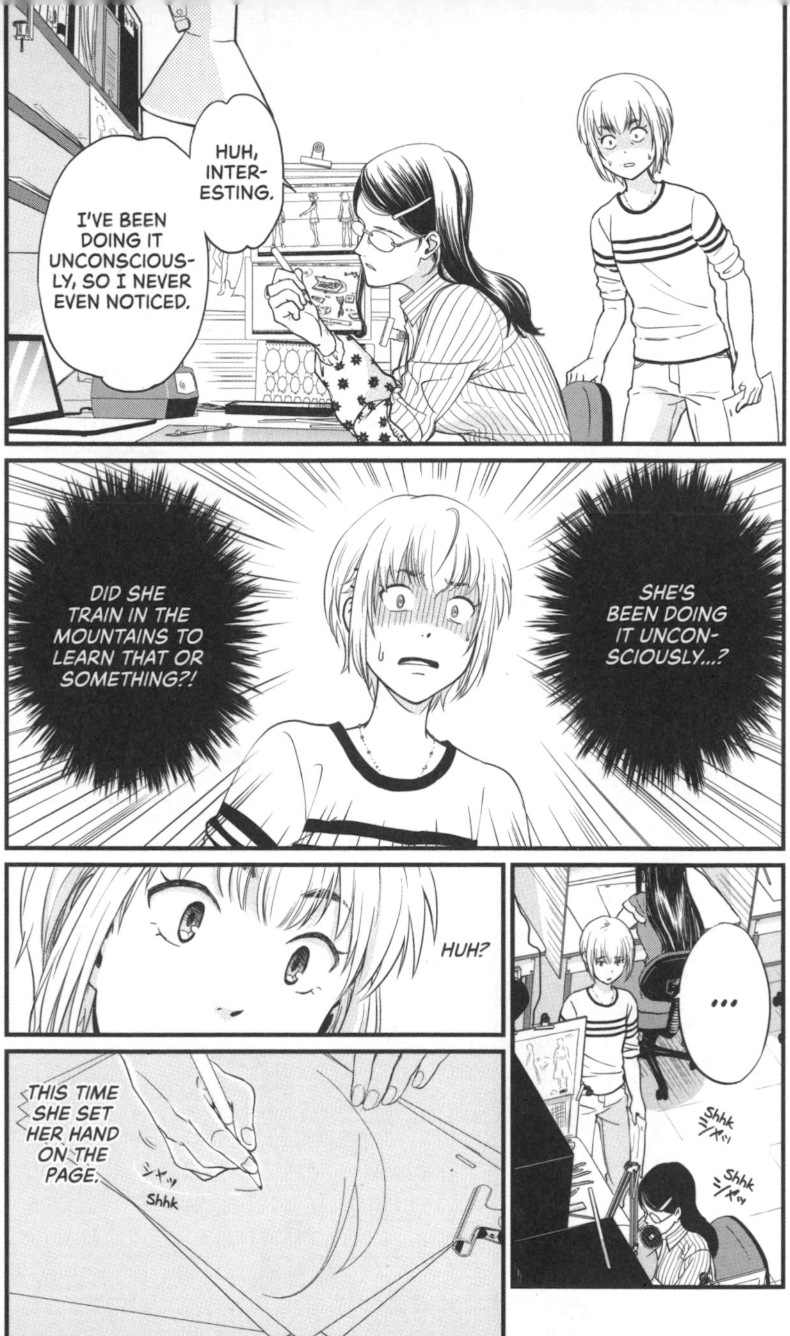
HUH, INTERESTING.
I'VE BEEN DOING IT UNCONSCIOUSLY, SO I NEVER EVEN NOTICED.
SHE'S BEEN DOING IT UNCONSCIOUSLY...?
DID SHE TRAIN IN THE MOUNTAINS TO LEARN THAT OR SOMETHING?!
...
Shhk シャッ
Shhk シャッ
HUH?
THIS TIME SHE SET HER HAND ON THE PAGE.
シャッ Shhk

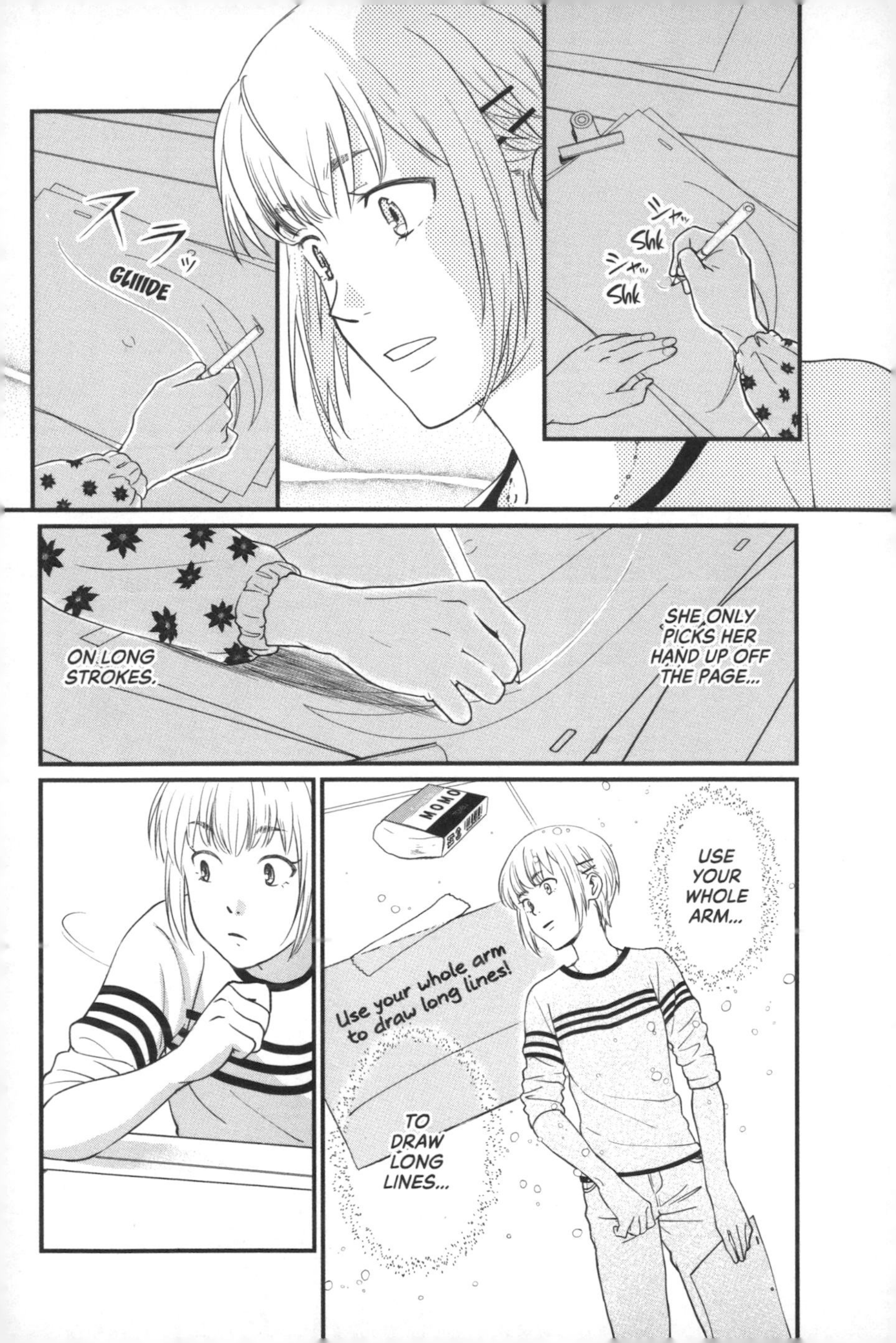
シャッ
Shk
シャッ
Shk
スラッ
GLIIIDE
SHE ONLY PICKS HER HAND UP OFF THE PAGE...
ON LONG STROKES.
MOMO
USE YOUR WHOLE ARM...
Use your whole arm to draw long lines!
TO DRAW LONG LINES...

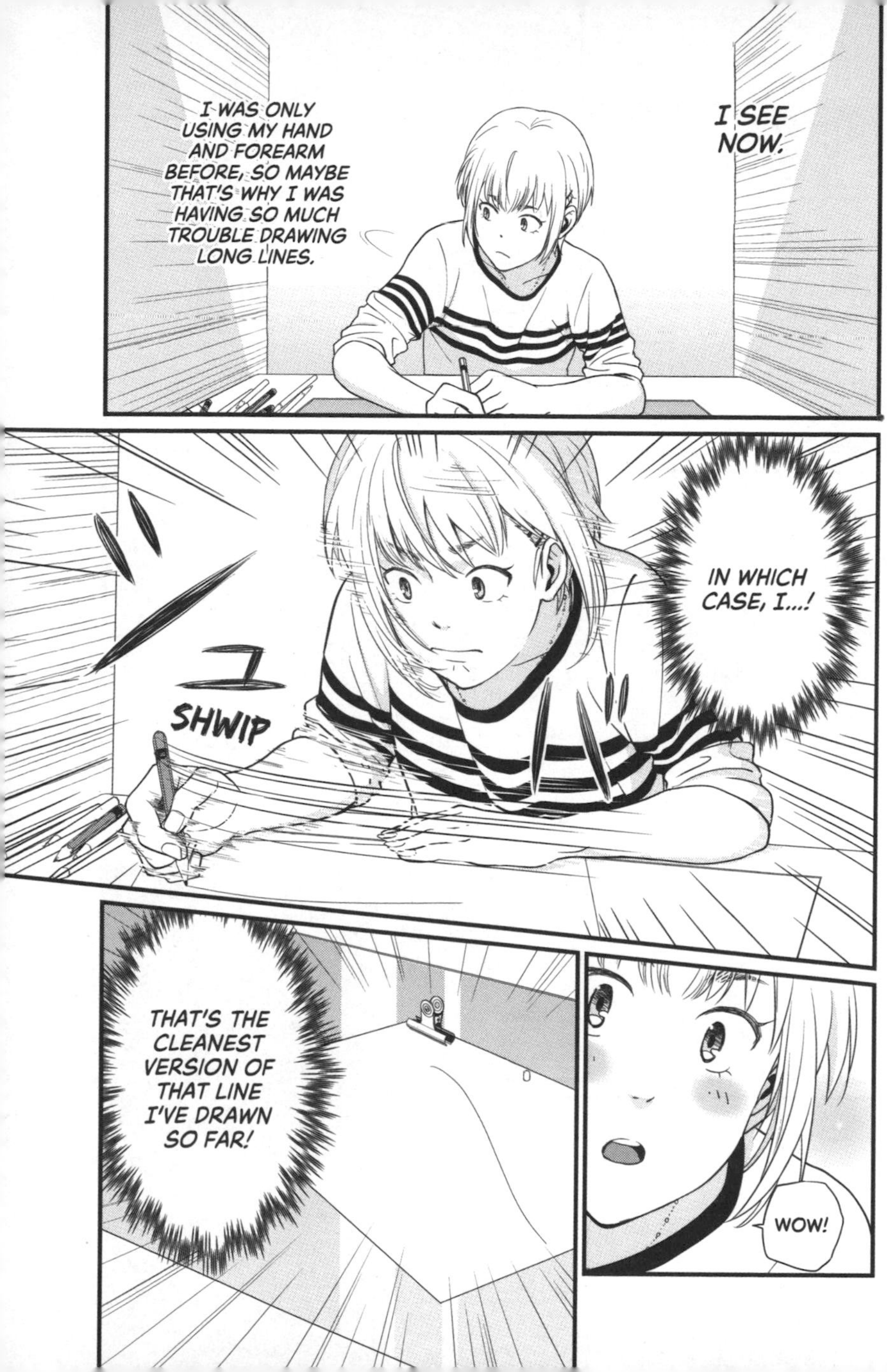
I SEE NOW.
I WAS ONLY USING MY HAND AND FOREARM BEFORE, SO MAYBE THAT'S WHY I WAS HAVING SO MUCH TROUBLE DRAWING LONG LINES.
IN WHICH CASE, I...!
SHWIP
WOW!
THAT'S THE CLEANEST VERSION OF THAT LINE I'VE DRAWN SO FAR!

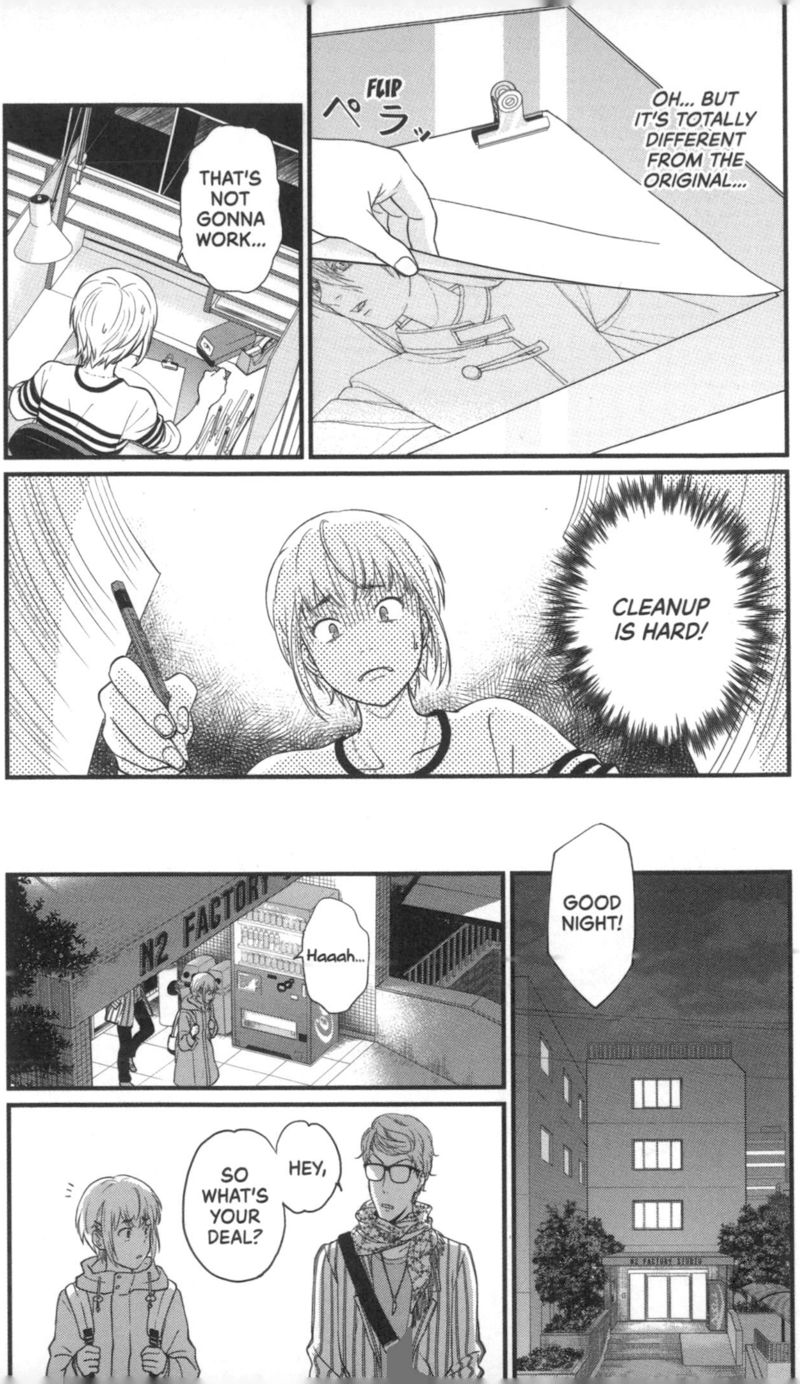
FLIP
ペラッ
OH... BUT IT'S TOTALLY DIFFERENT FROM THE ORIGINAL...
THAT'S NOT GONNA WORK...
CLEANUP IS HARD!
GOOD NIGHT!
Haaah...
N2 FACTORY
HEY,
SO WHAT'S YOUR DEAL?

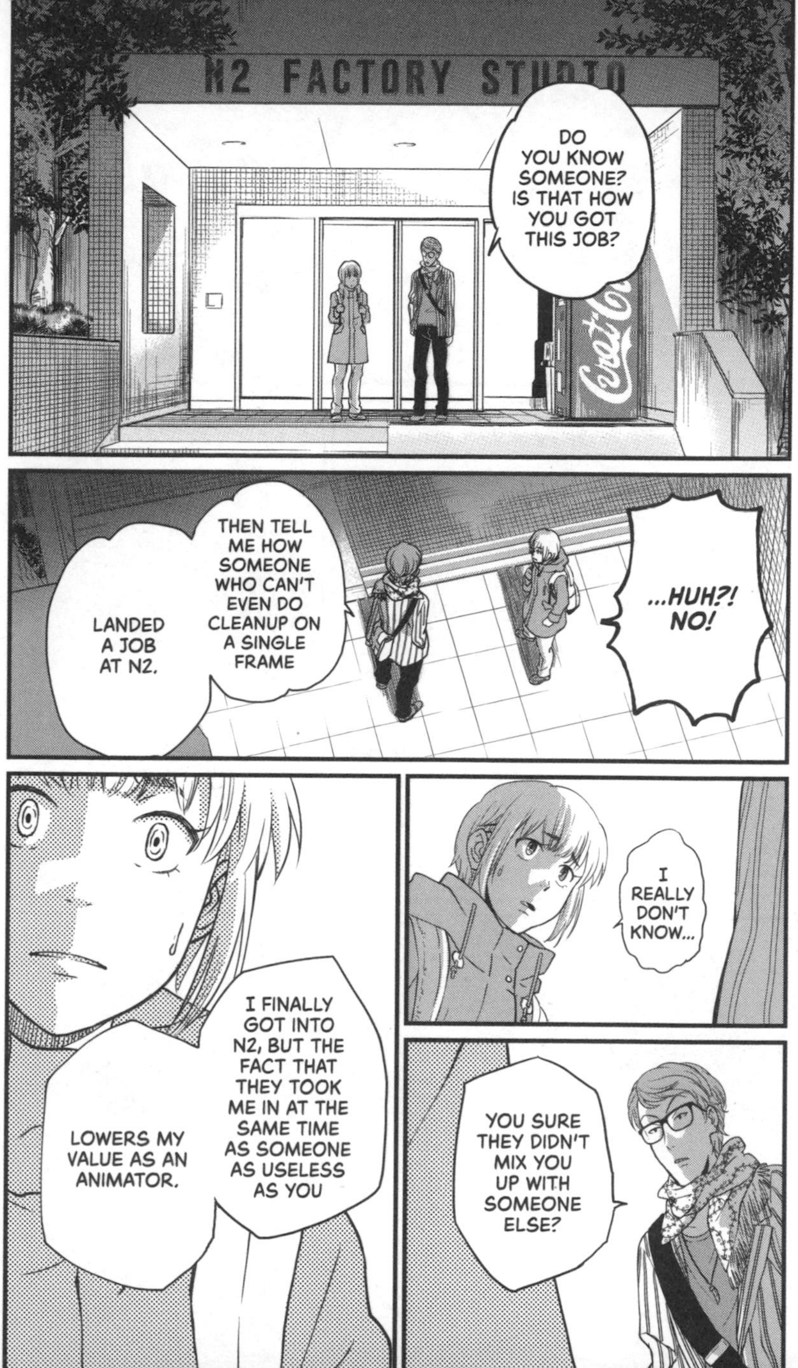
N2 FACTORY STUDIO
DO YOU KNOW SOMEONE? IS THAT HOW YOU GOT THIS JOB?
...HUH?! NO!
THEN TELL ME HOW SOMEONE WHO CAN'T EVEN DO CLEANUP ON A SINGLE FRAME
LANDED A JOB AT N2.
I REALLY DON'T KNOW...
YOU SURE THEY DIDN'T MIX YOU UP WITH SOMEONE ELSE?
I FINALLY GOT INTO N2, BUT THE FACT THAT THEY TOOK ME IN AT THE SAME TIME AS SOMEONE AS USELESS AS YOU
LOWERS MY VALUE AS AN ANIMATOR.

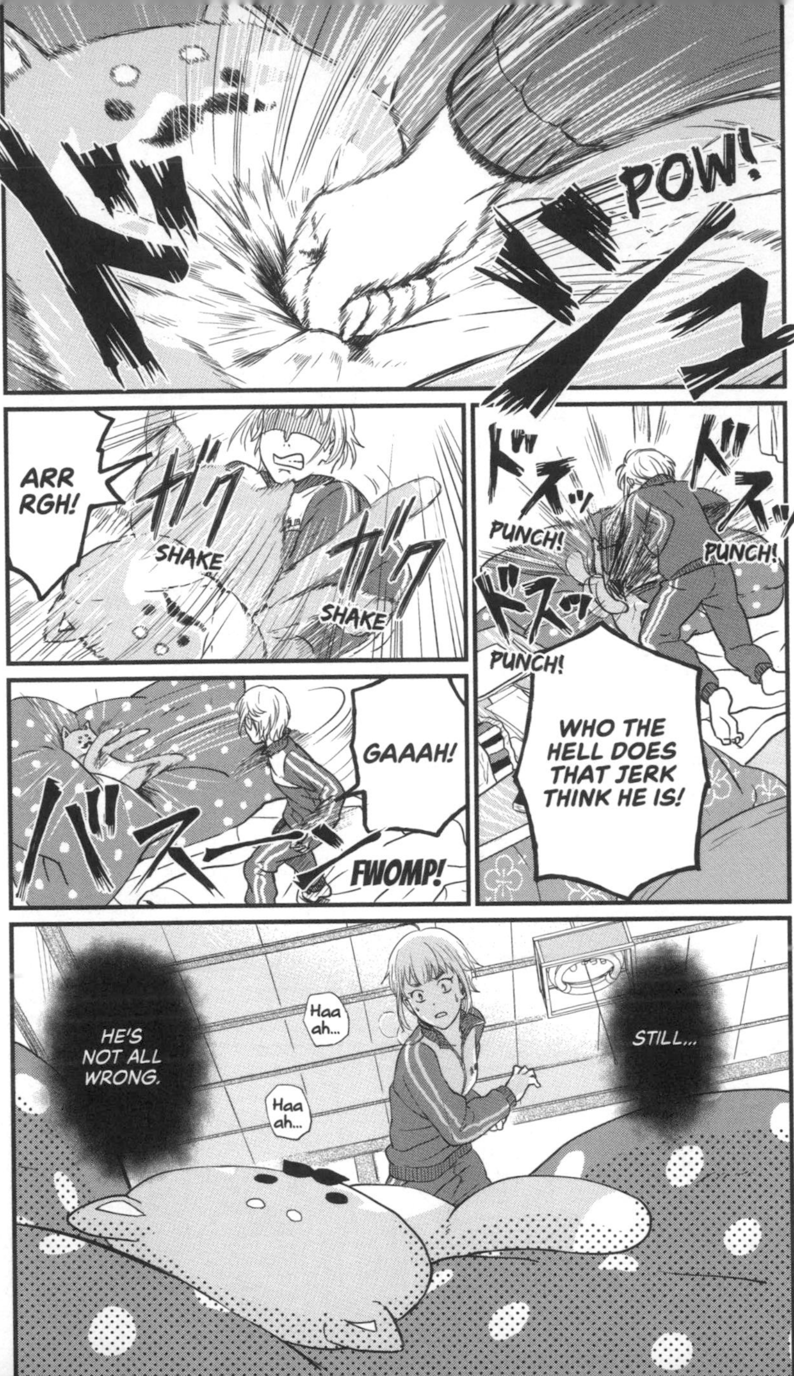
POW!
ドスッ
PUNCH!
ドスッ
PUNCH!
ドスッ
PUNCH!
WHO THE HELL DOES THAT JERK THINK HE IS!
ARR RGH!
ガク
SHAKE
ガク
SHAKE
GAAAH!
バス
FWOMP!
STILL...
Haa ah...
Haa ah...
HE'S NOT ALL WRONG.

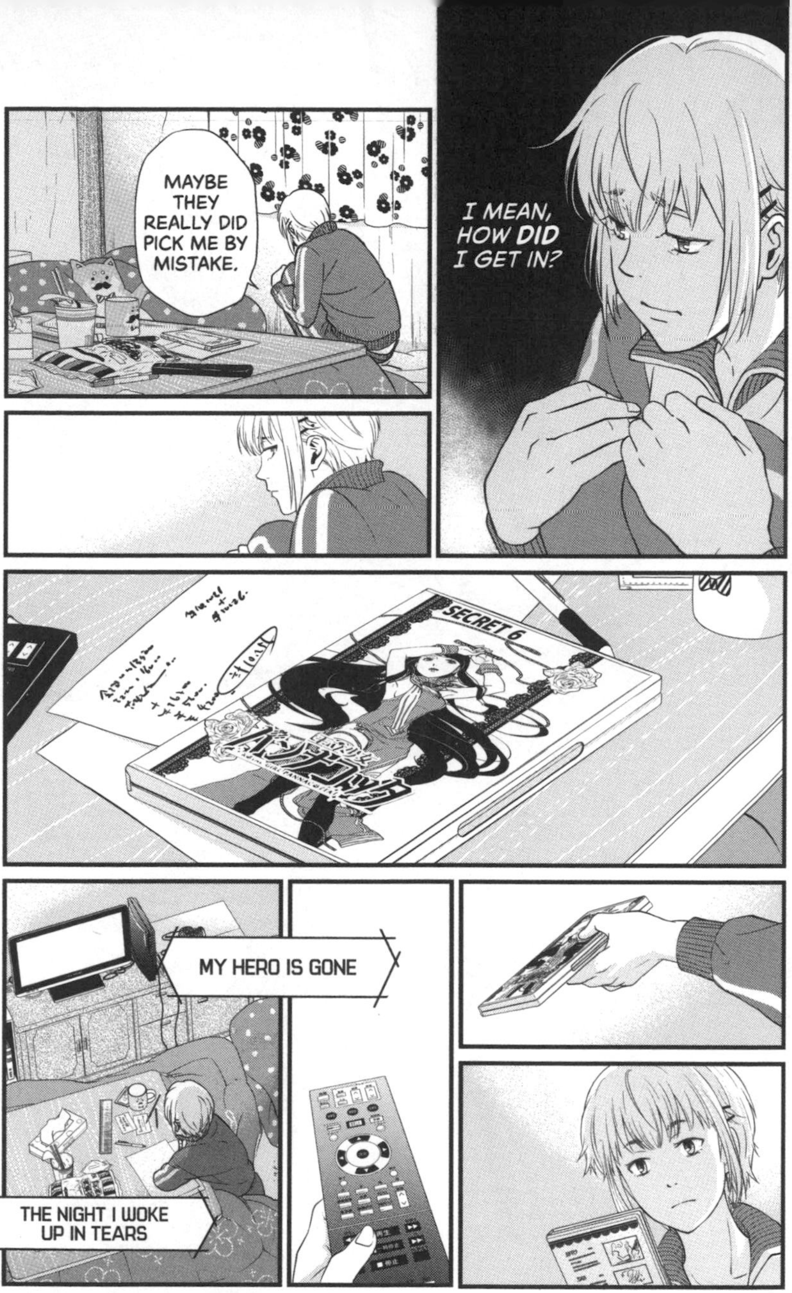

I MEAN, HOW DID I GET IN?
MAYBE THEY REALLY DID PICK ME BY MISTAKE.
SECRET 6
MY HERO IS GONE
THE NIGHT I WOKE UP IN TEARS

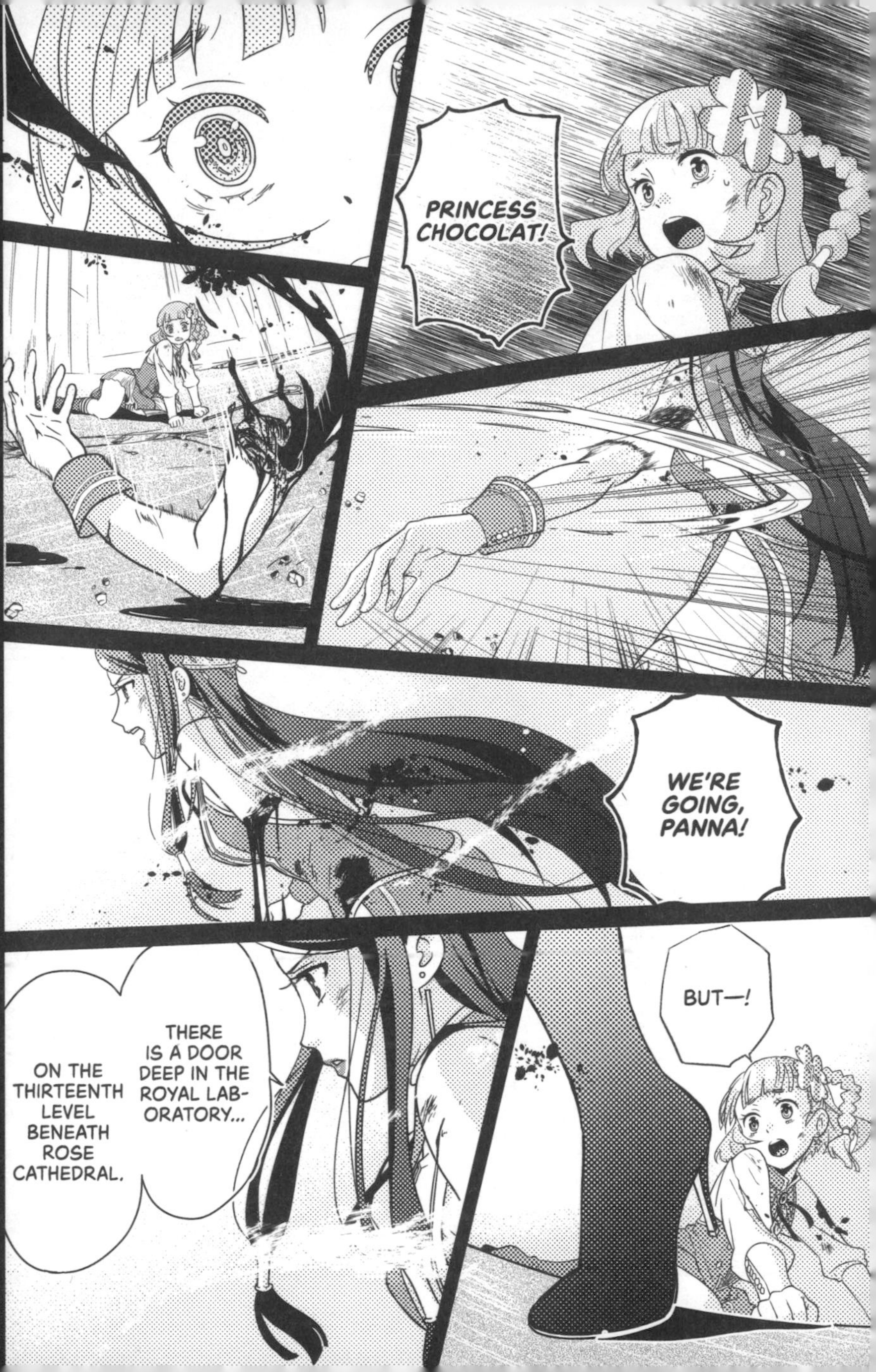
PRINCESS CHOCOLAT!
WE'RE GOING, PANNA!
BUT—!
THERE IS A DOOR DEEP IN THE ROYAL LAB-ORATORY...
ON THE THIRTEENTH LEVEL BENEATH ROSE CATHEDRAL.

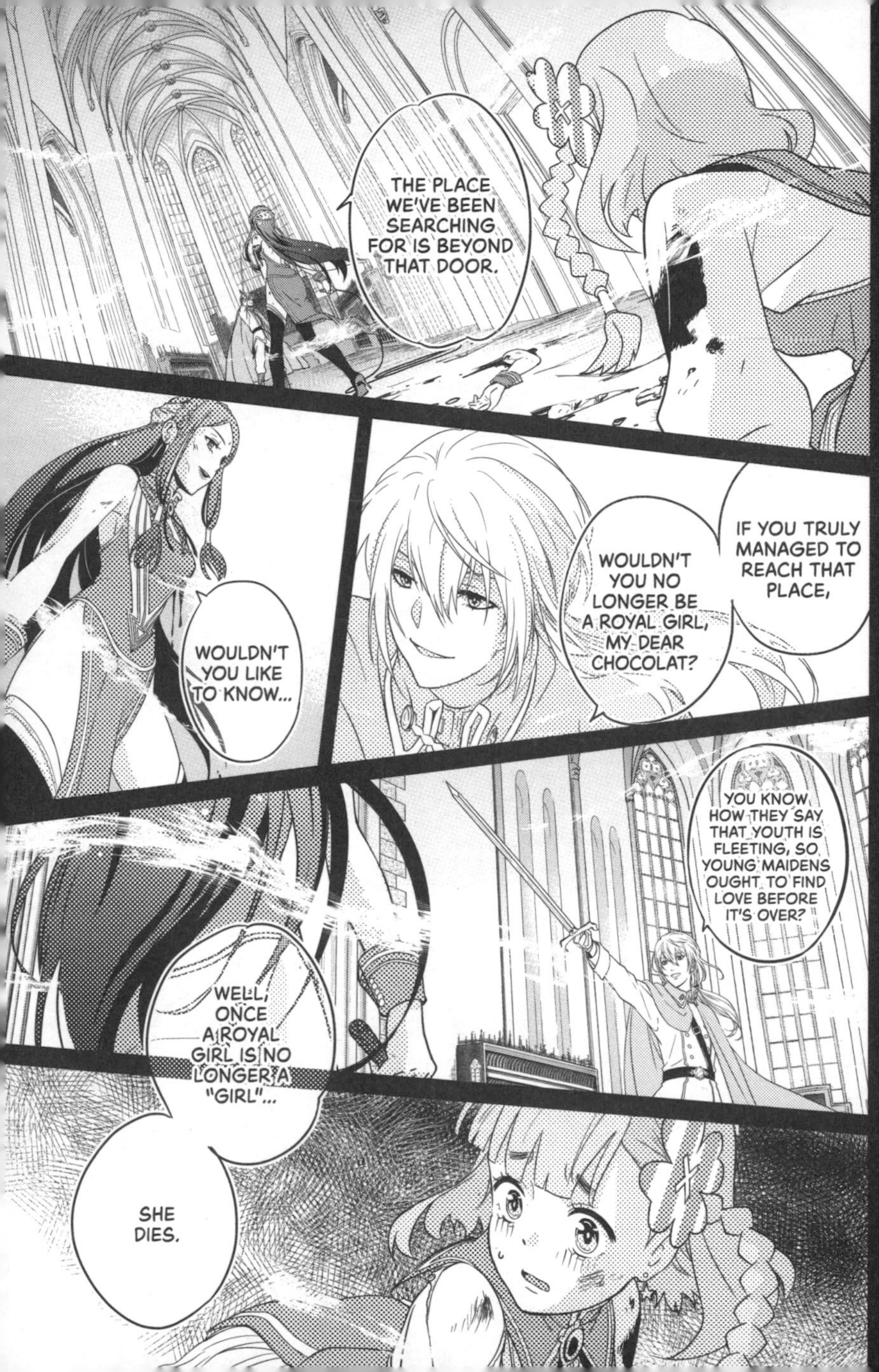
THE PLACE WE'VE BEEN SEARCHING FOR IS BEYOND THAT DOOR.
IF YOU TRULY MANAGED TO REACH THAT PLACE,
WOULDN'T YOU NO LONGER BE A ROYAL GIRL, MY DEAR CHOCOLAT?
WOULDN'T YOU LIKE TO KNOW...
YOU KNOW HOW THEY SAY THAT YOUTH IS FLEETING, SO YOUNG MAIDENS OUGHT TO FIND LOVE BEFORE IT'S OVER?
WELL, ONCE A ROYAL GIRL IS NO LONGER A "GIRL"...
SHE DIES.

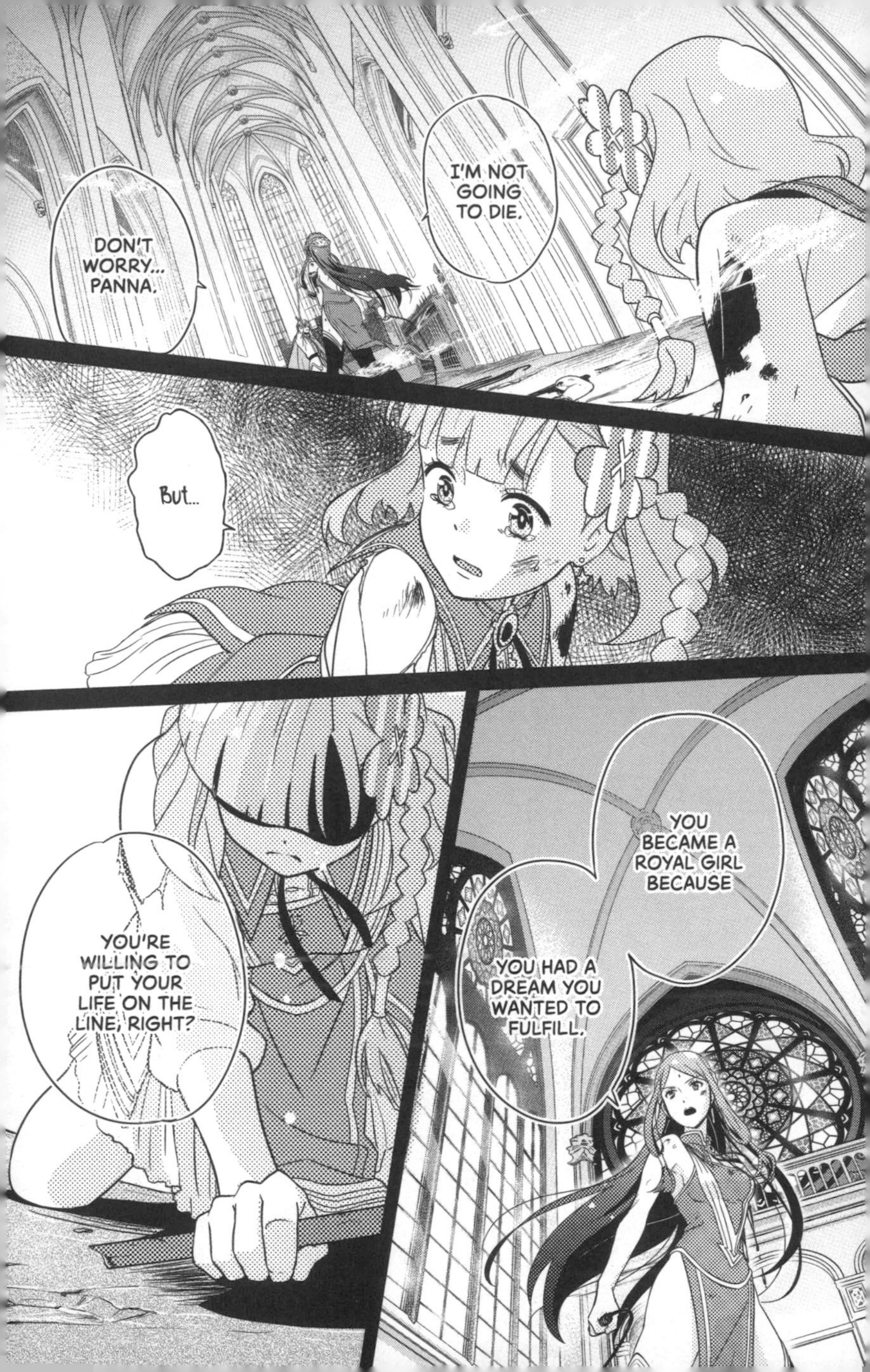
I'M NOT GOING TO DIE.
DON'T WORRY... PANNA.
But...
YOU BECAME A ROYAL GIRL BECAUSE
YOU HAD A DREAM YOU WANTED TO FULFILL.
YOU'RE WILLING TO PUT YOUR LIFE ON THE LINE, RIGHT?

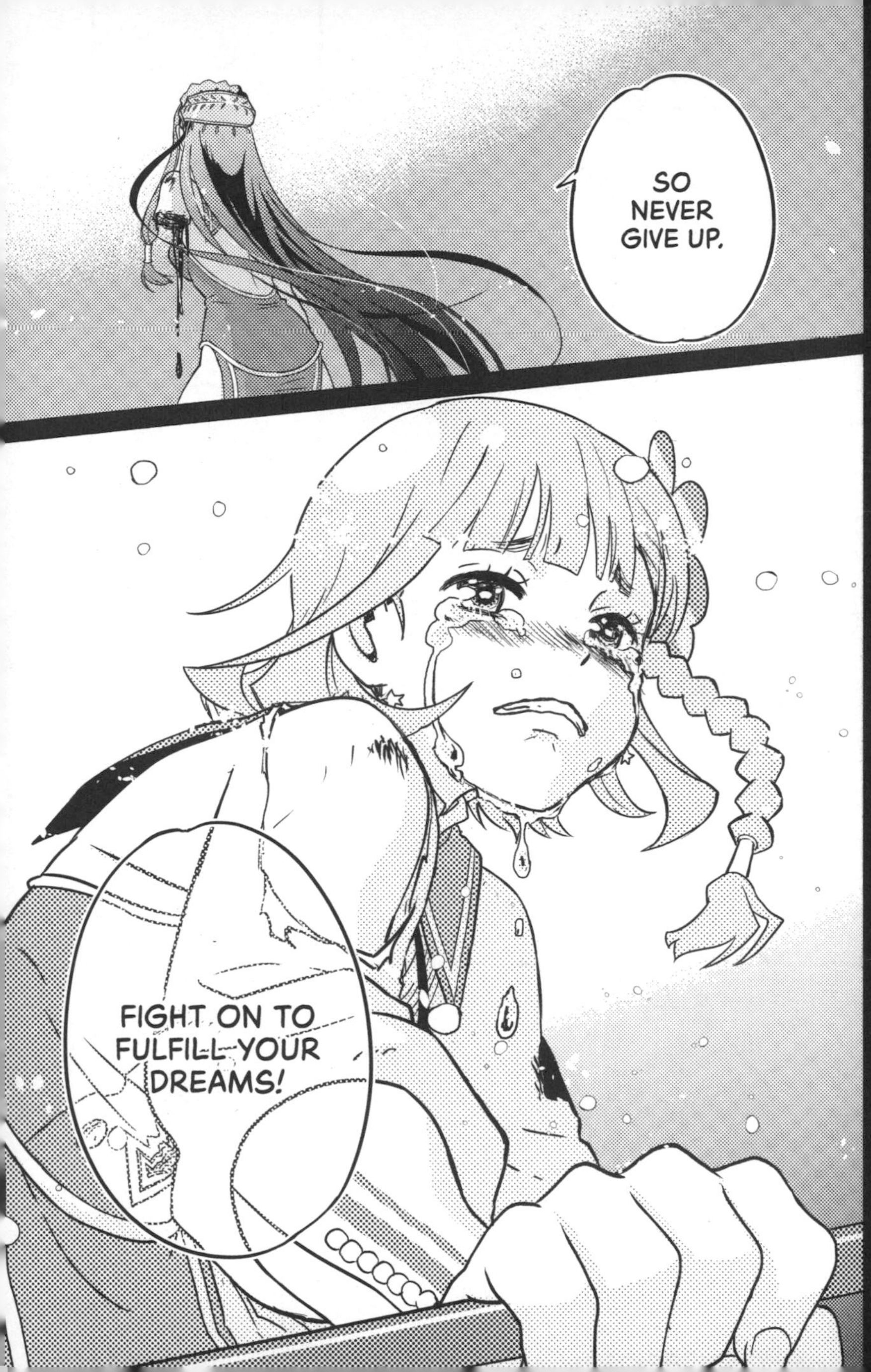
SO NEVER GIVE UP.
FIGHT ON TO FULFILL YOUR DREAMS!

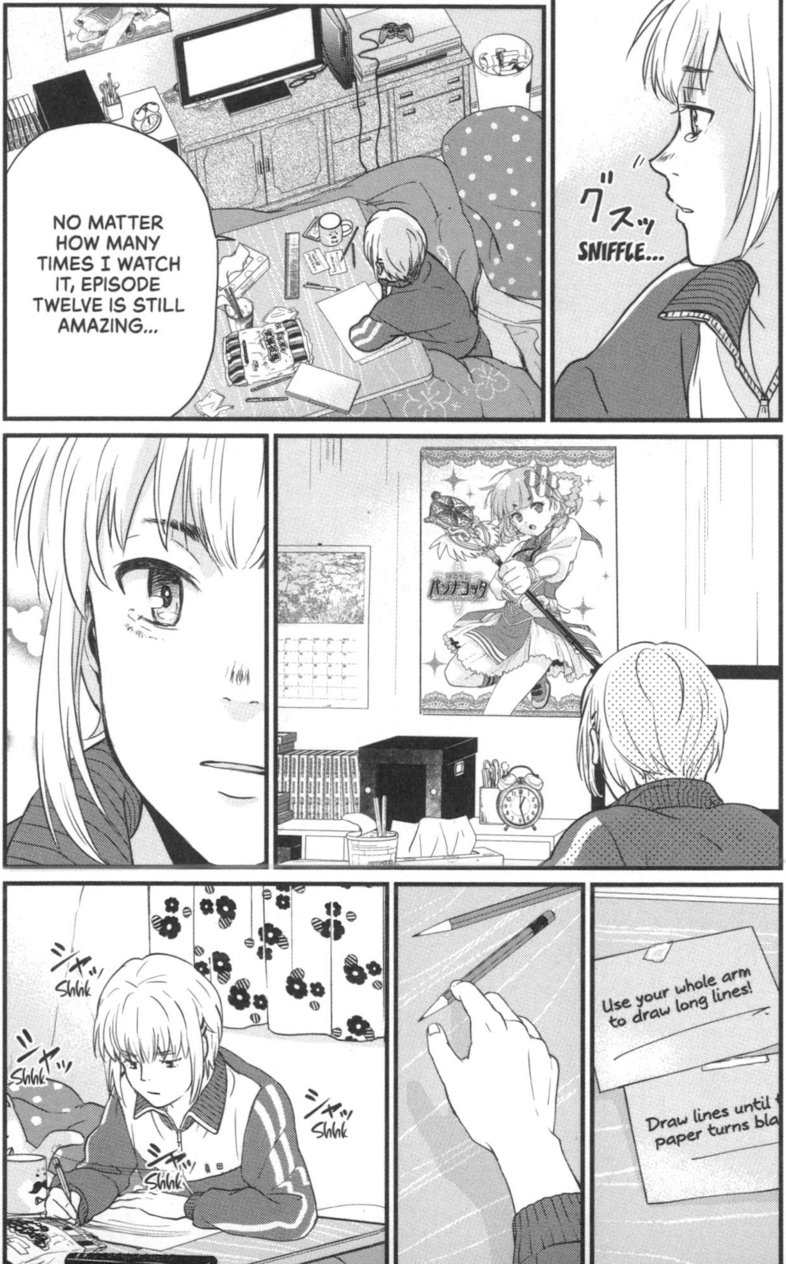

グスッ
SNIFFLE...
NO MATTER HOW MANY TIMES I WATCH IT, EPISODE TWELVE IS STILL AMAZING...
パンナコッタ
Use your whole arm to draw long lines!
Draw lines until
paper turns bla
シャッ
Shhk
シャッ
Shhk
シャッ
Shhk
シャッ
Shhk

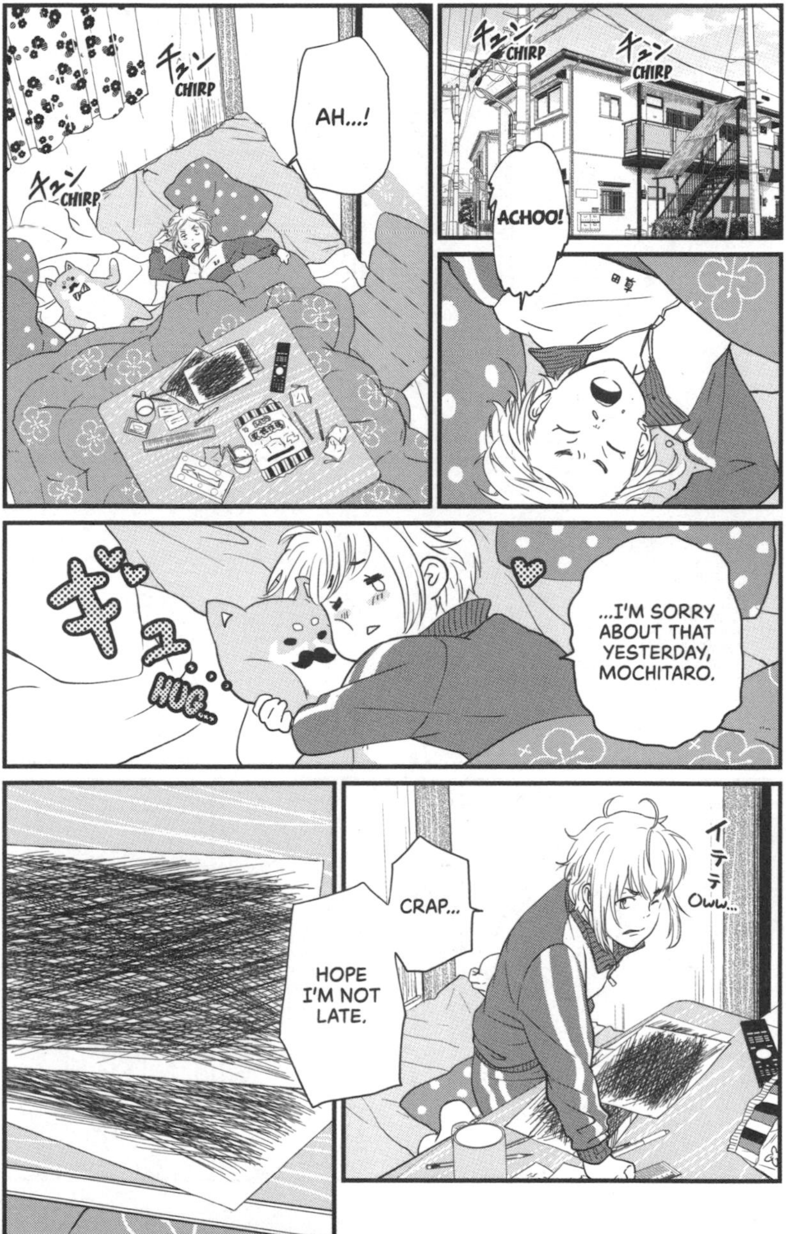

チュン
CHIRP
チュン
CHIRP
ACHOO!
チュン
CHIRP
AH...!
チュン
CHIRP
...I'M SORRY ABOUT THAT YESTERDAY, MOCHITARO.
ギュ
HUG...
イテテ
Oww...
CRAP...
HOPE I'M NOT LATE.

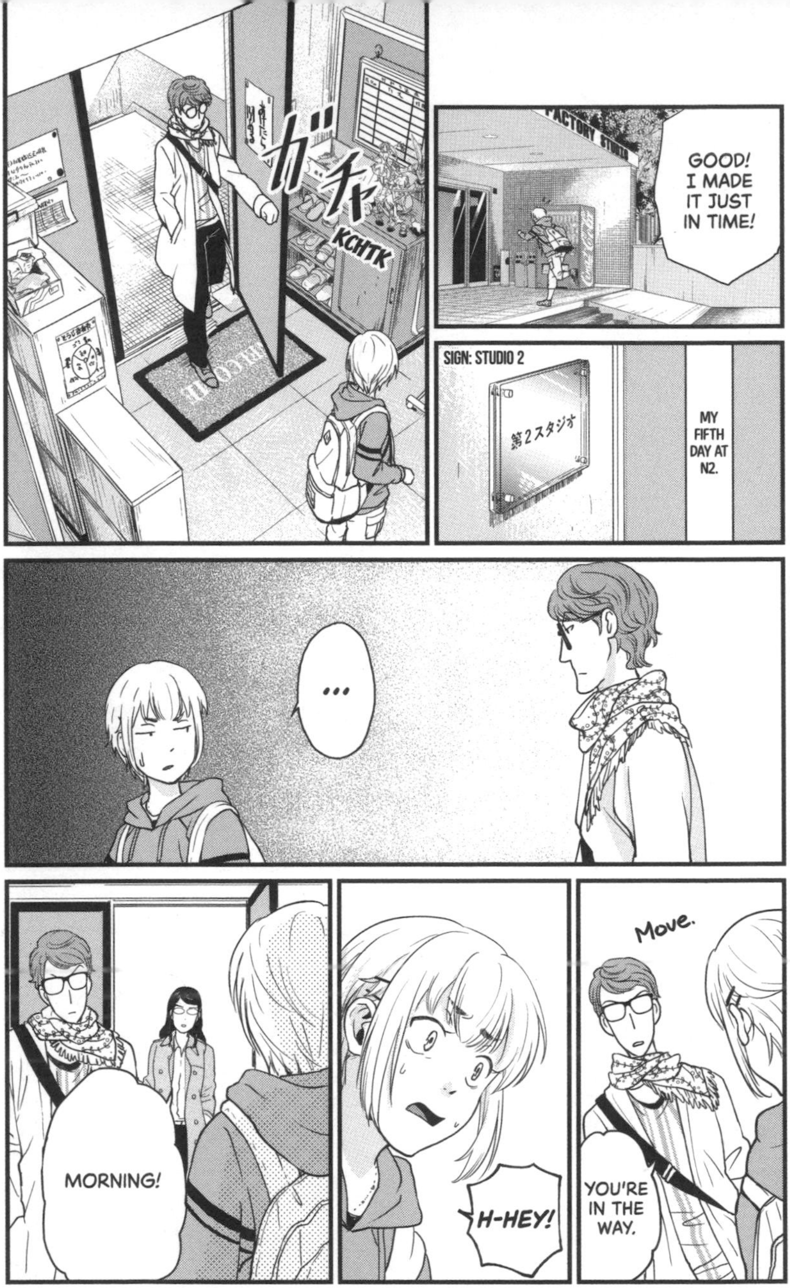
FACTORY STUDIO
GOOD! I MADE IT JUST IN TIME!
SIGN: STUDIO 2
第2スタジオ
MY FIFTH DAY AT N2.
ガチャ
KCHTK
...
Move.
YOU'RE IN THE WAY.
H-HEY!
MORNING!

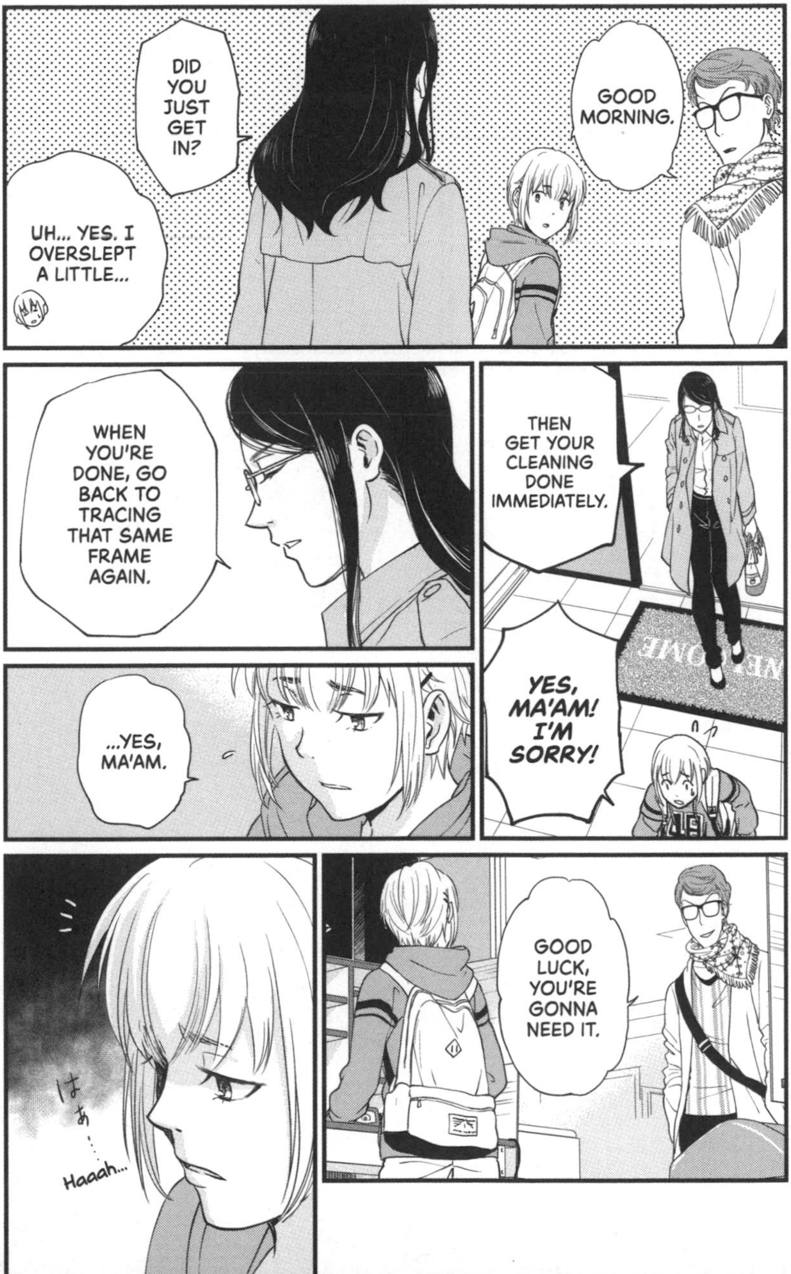
GOOD MORNING.
DID YOU JUST GET IN?
UH... YES. I OVERSLEPT A LITTLE...
THEN GET YOUR CLEANING DONE IMMEDIATELY.
YES, MA'AM! I'M SORRY!
WHEN YOU'RE DONE, GO BACK TO TRACING THAT SAME FRAME AGAIN.
...YES, MA'AM.
GOOD LUCK, YOU'RE GONNA NEED IT.
はあ…
Haaah...

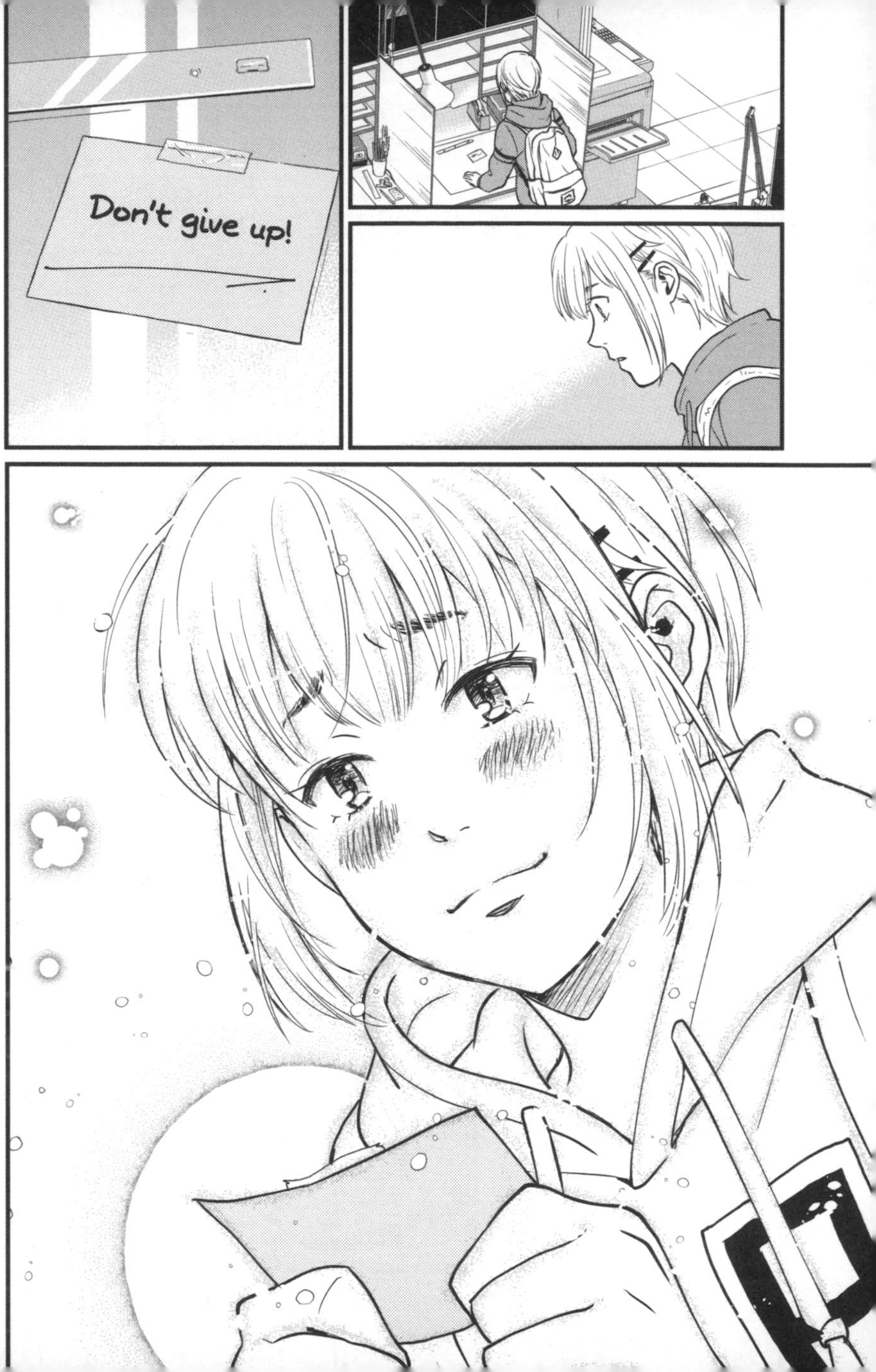
Don't give up!

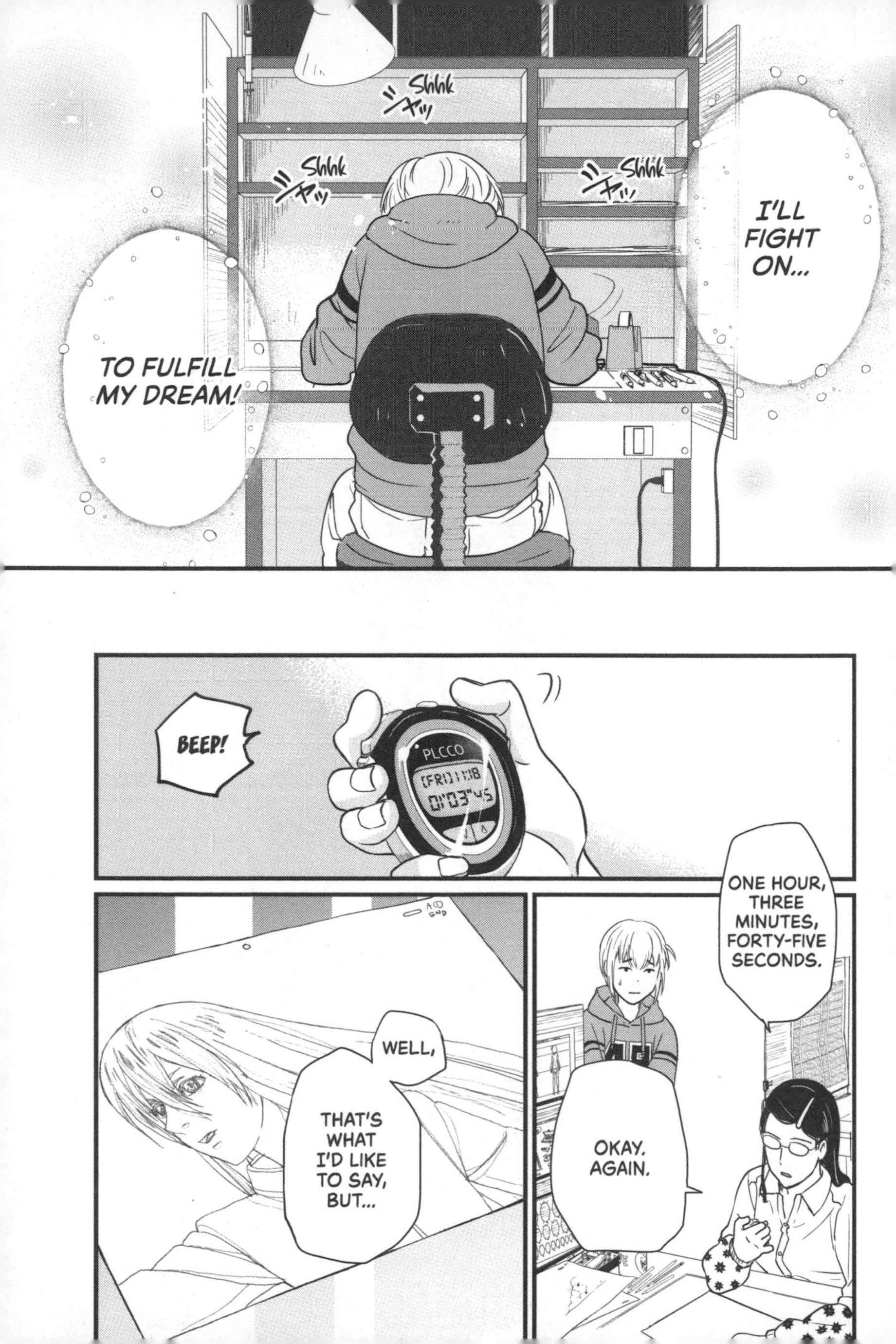
Shhk
ジャッ
Shhk
ジャッ
Shhk
ジャッ
I'LL FIGHT ON...
TO FULFILL MY DREAM!
BEEP!
PLCCO
[FRI] 11:18
01'03"45
ONE HOUR, THREE MINUTES, FORTY-FIVE SECONDS.
OKAY. AGAIN.
WELL,
THAT'S WHAT I'D LIKE TO SAY, BUT...

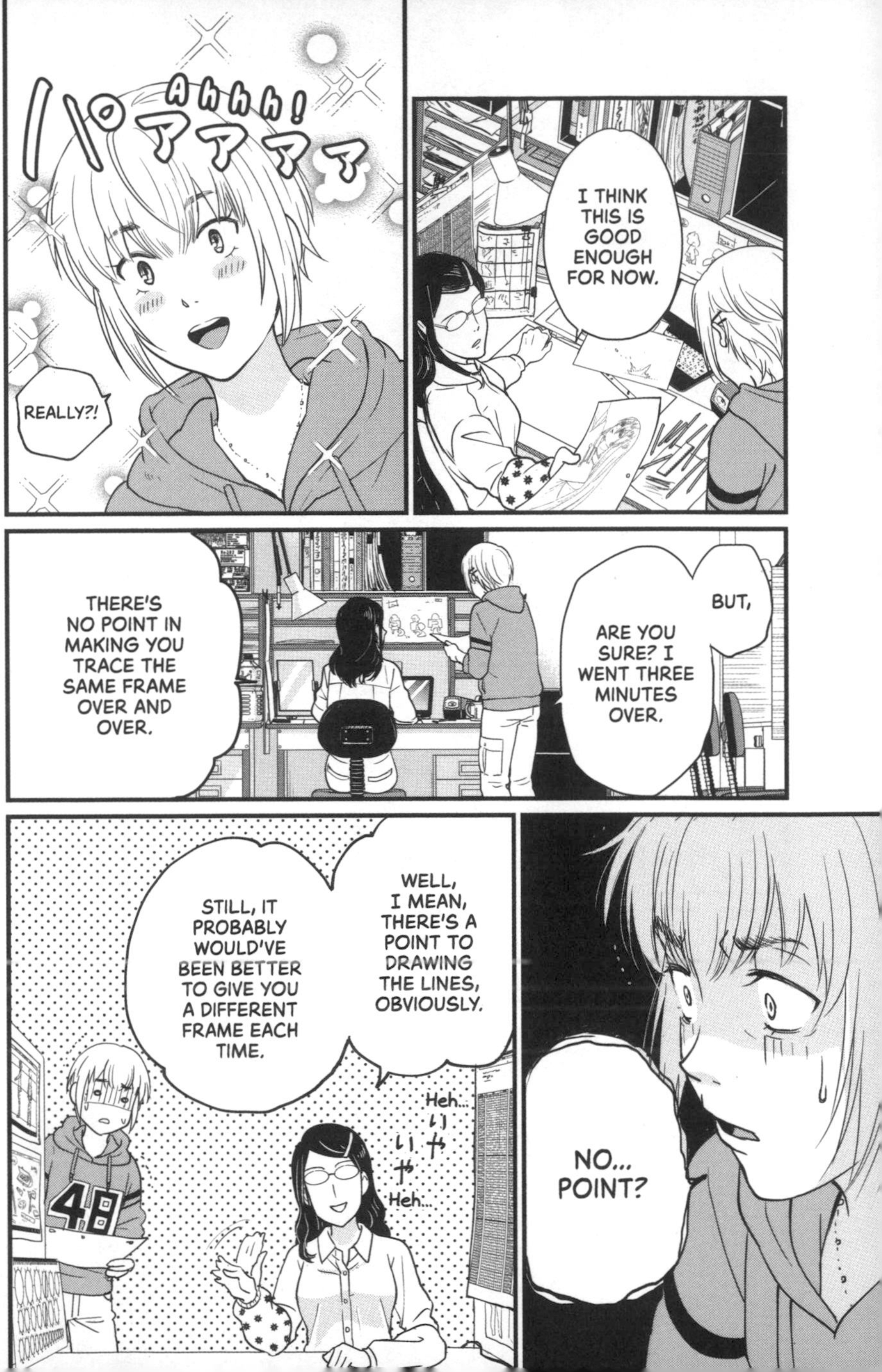
I THINK THIS IS GOOD ENOUGH FOR NOW.
パアアアア
Ahhhh!
REALLY?!
BUT,
ARE YOU SURE? I WENT THREE MINUTES OVER.
THERE'S NO POINT IN MAKING YOU TRACE THE SAME FRAME OVER AND OVER.
NO... POINT?
WELL, I MEAN, THERE'S A POINT TO DRAWING THE LINES, OBVIOUSLY.
STILL, IT PROBABLY WOULD'VE BEEN BETTER TO GIVE YOU A DIFFERENT FRAME EACH TIME.
Heh... いや
いや Heh...

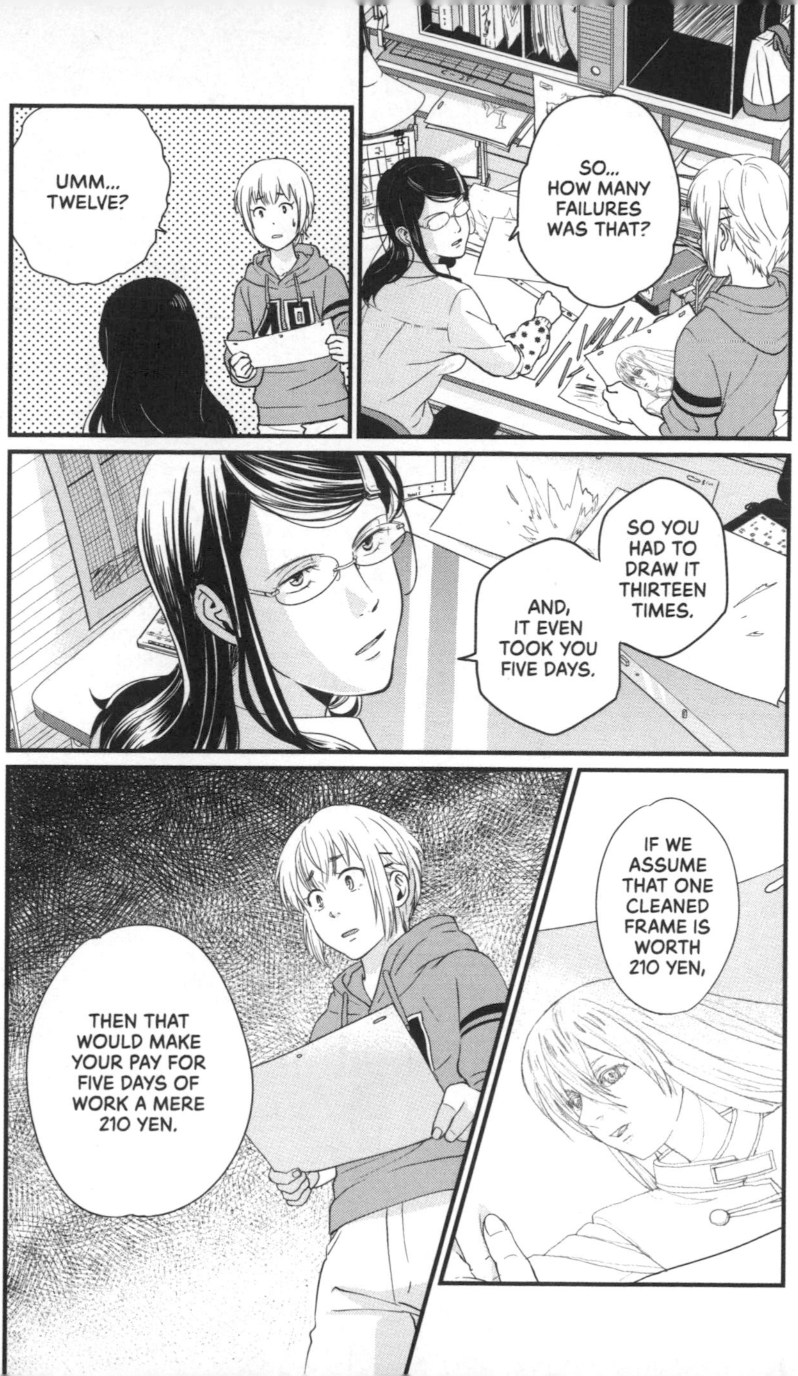
SO... HOW MANY FAILURES WAS THAT?
UMM... TWELVE?
SO YOU HAD TO DRAW IT THIRTEEN TIMES.
AND, IT EVEN TOOK YOU FIVE DAYS.
IF WE ASSUME THAT ONE CLEANED FRAME IS WORTH 210 YEN,
THEN THAT WOULD MAKE YOUR PAY FOR FIVE DAYS OF WORK A MERE 210 YEN.

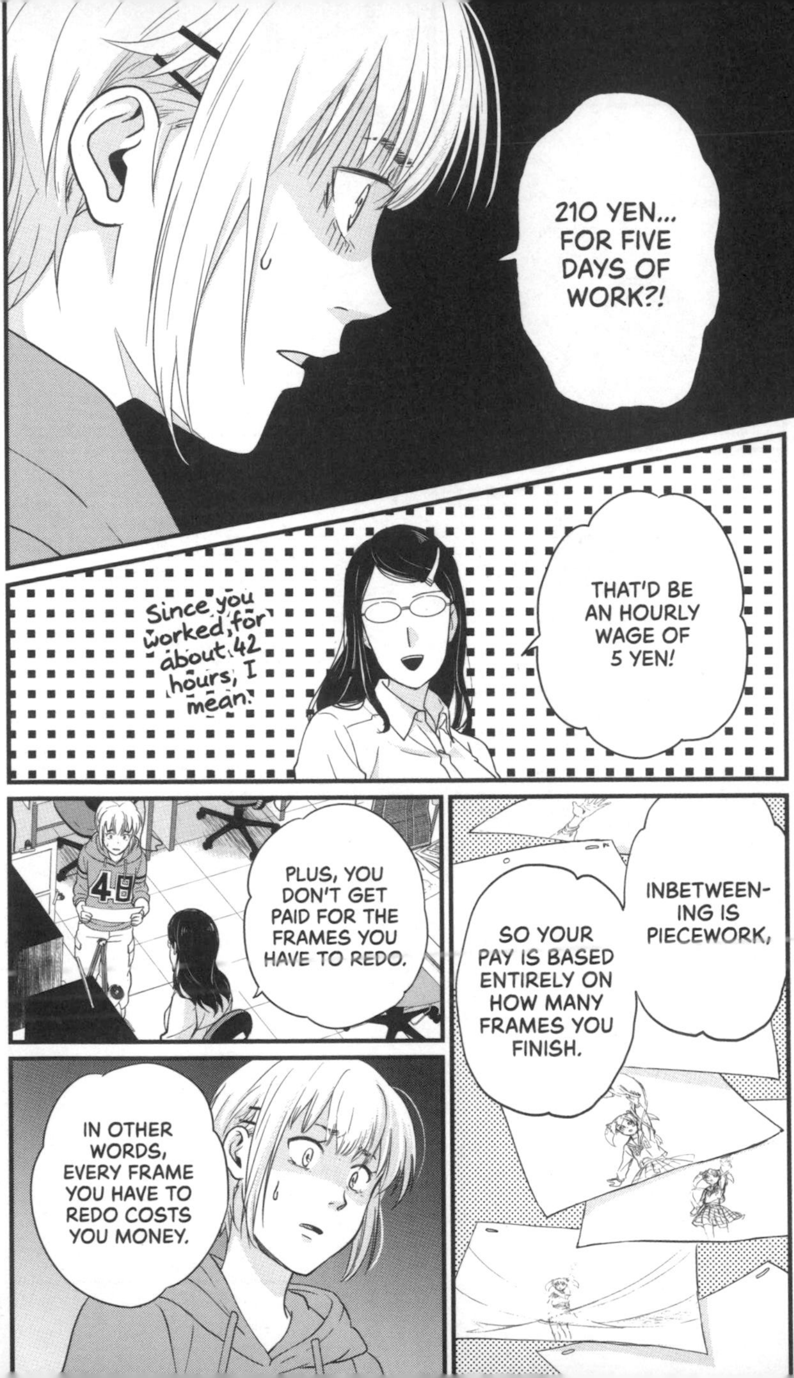
210 YEN... FOR FIVE DAYS OF WORK?!
THAT'D BE AN HOURLY WAGE OF 5 YEN!
Since you worked for about 42 hours, I mean.
INBETWEEN-ING IS PIECEWORK,
SO YOUR PAY IS BASED ENTIRELY ON HOW MANY FRAMES YOU FINISH.
PLUS, YOU DON'T GET PAID FOR THE FRAMES YOU HAVE TO REDO.
IN OTHER WORDS, EVERY FRAME YOU HAVE TO REDO COSTS YOU MONEY.

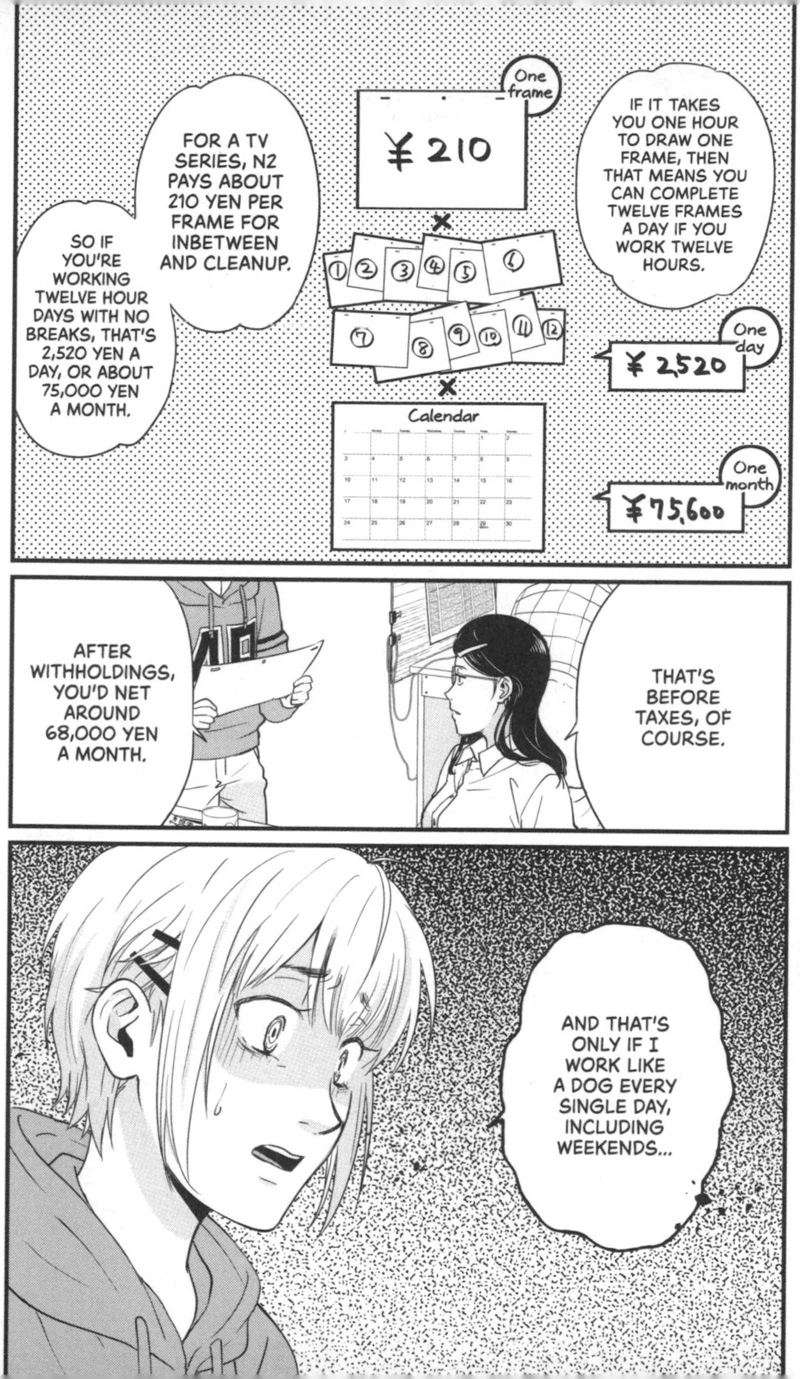
One frame
¥210
IF IT TAKES YOU ONE HOUR TO DRAW ONE FRAME, THEN THAT MEANS YOU CAN COMPLETE TWELVE FRAMES A DAY IF YOU WORK TWELVE HOURS.
FOR A TV SERIES, N2 PAYS ABOUT 210 YEN PER FRAME FOR INBETWEEN AND CLEANUP.
One day
¥2,520
SO IF YOU'RE WORKING TWELVE HOUR DAYS WITH NO BREAKS, THAT'S 2,520 YEN A DAY, OR ABOUT 75,000 YEN A MONTH.
Calendar
One month
¥75,600
THAT'S BEFORE TAXES, OF COURSE.
AFTER WITHHOLDINGS, YOU'D NET AROUND 68,000 YEN A MONTH.
AND THAT'S ONLY IF I WORK LIKE A DOG EVERY SINGLE DAY, INCLUDING WEEKENDS...

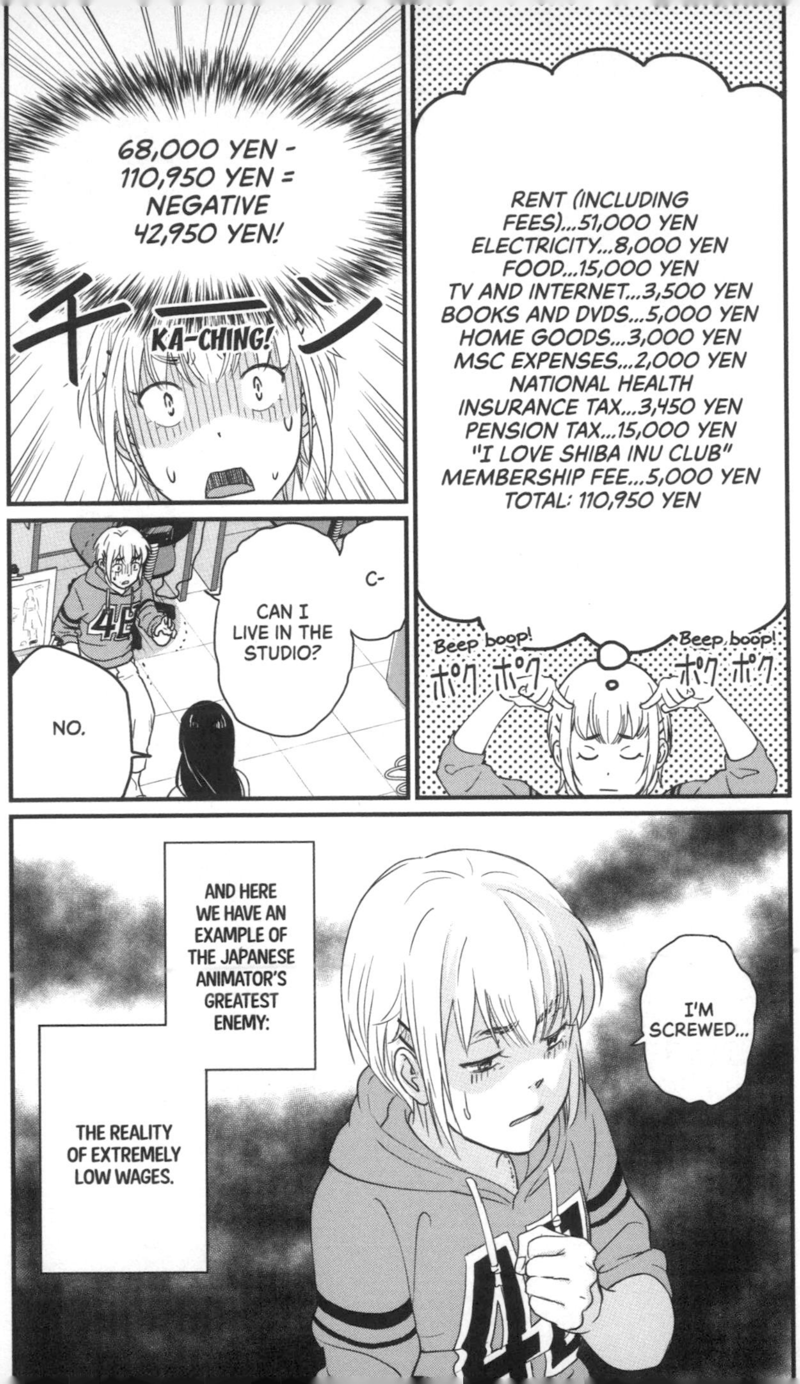
RENT (INCLUDING FEES)...51,000 YEN
ELECTRICITY...8,000 YEN
FOOD...15,000 YEN
TV AND INTERNET...3,500 YEN
BOOKS AND DVDS...5,000 YEN
HOME GOODS...3,000 YEN
MSC EXPENSES...2,000 YEN
NATIONAL HEALTH INSURANCE TAX...3,450 YEN
PENSION TAX...15,000 YEN
"I LOVE SHIBA INU CLUB" MEMBERSHIP FEE...5,000 YEN
TOTAL: 110,950 YEN
Beep boop!
ポク ポク
Beep boop!
ポク ポク
68,000 YEN - 110,950 YEN = NEGATIVE 42,950 YEN!
チーーン
KA-CHING!
C-
CAN I LIVE IN THE STUDIO?
NO.
I'M SCREWED...
AND HERE WE HAVE AN EXAMPLE OF THE JAPANESE ANIMATOR'S GREATEST ENEMY:
THE REALITY OF EXTREMELY LOW WAGES.

The Mascot of the
"I Love Shiba Inu Club"

Baron Shiba

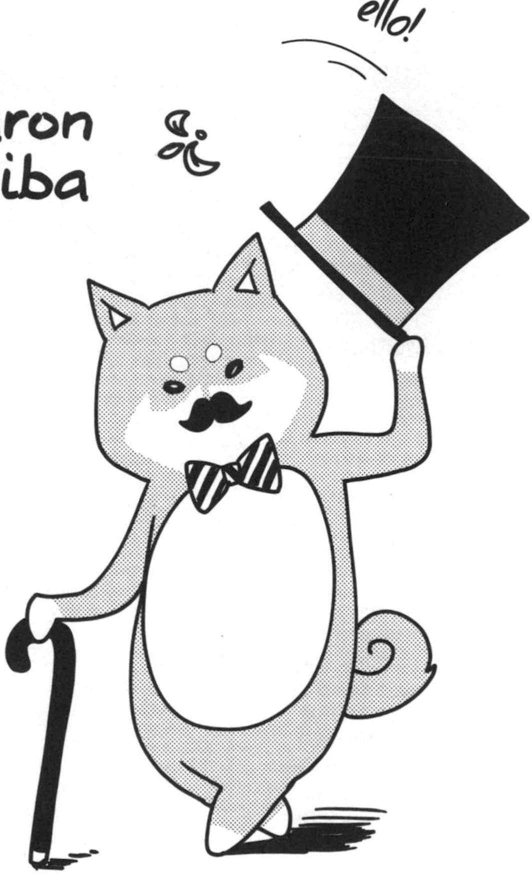
'ello!

*Mochitaro is the name Yukimura gave the stuffed animal version she owns.

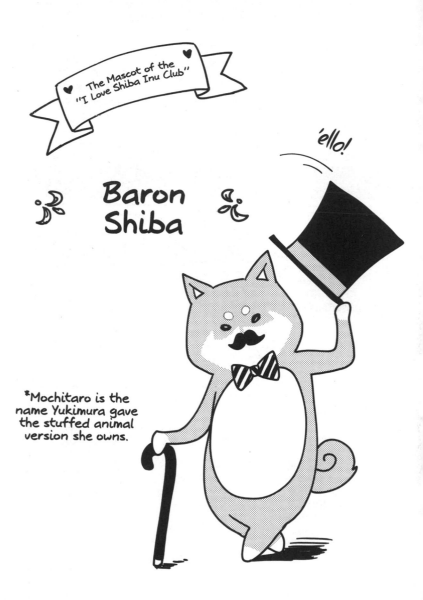

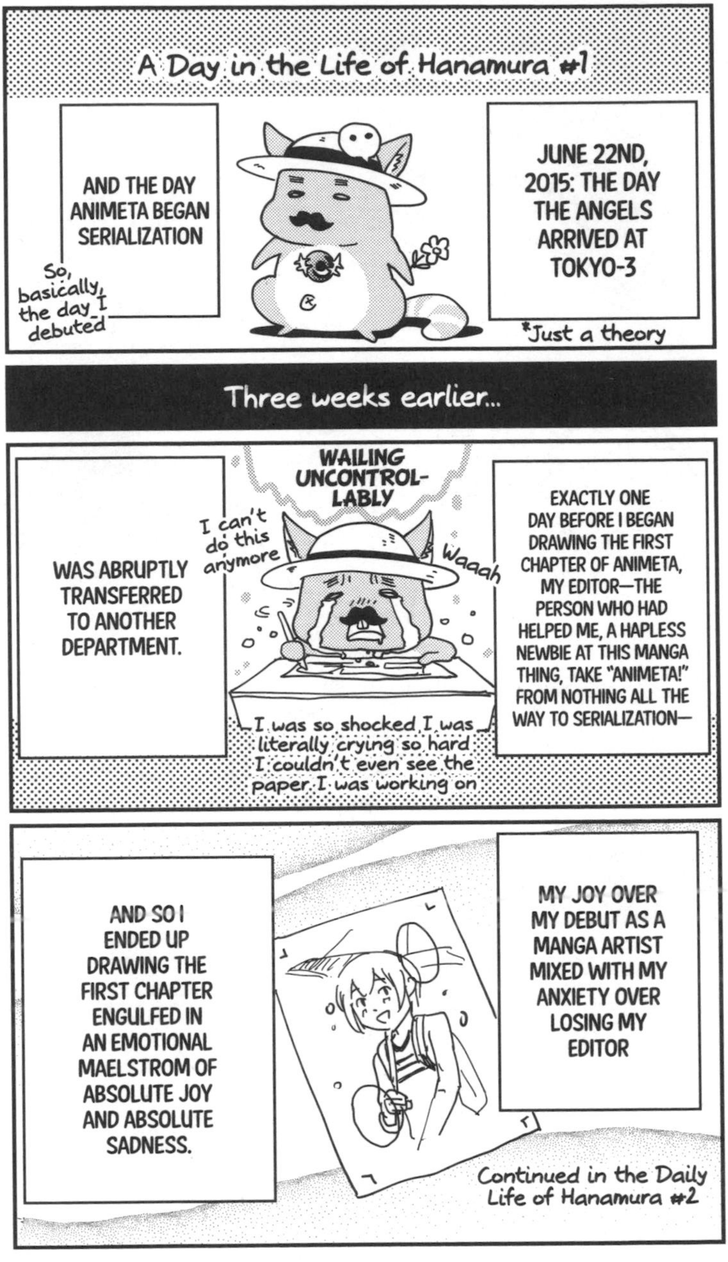
A Day in the Life of Hanamura #1
JUNE 22ND, 2015: THE DAY THE ANGELS ARRIVED AT TOKYO-3
*Just a theory
AND THE DAY ANIMETA BEGAN SERIALIZATION
So, basically, the day I debuted
Three weeks earlier...
EXACTLY ONE DAY BEFORE I BEGAN DRAWING THE FIRST CHAPTER OF ANIMETA, MY EDITOR—THE PERSON WHO HAD HELPED ME, A HAPLESS NEWBIE AT THIS MANGA THING, TAKE "ANIMETA!" FROM NOTHING ALL THE WAY TO SERIALIZATION—
Waaah
WAILING UNCONTROL-LABLY
I can't do this anymore
I was so shocked I was literally crying so hard I couldn't even see the paper I was working on
WAS ABRUPTLY TRANSFERRED TO ANOTHER DEPARTMENT.
MY JOY OVER MY DEBUT AS A MANGA ARTIST MIXED WITH MY ANXIETY OVER LOSING MY EDITOR
Continued in the Daily Life of Hanamura #2
AND SO I ENDED UP DRAWING THE FIRST CHAPTER ENGULFED IN AN EMOTIONAL MAELSTROM OF ABSOLUTE JOY AND ABSOLUTE SADNESS.

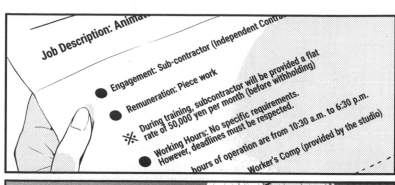

Job Description: Animat...

● Engagement: Sub-contractor (Independent Contra...

● Remuneration: Piece work

※ During training, subcontractor will be provided a flat rate of 50,000 yen per month (before withholding)

● Working Hours: No specific requirements. However, deadlines must be respected.

hours of operation are from 10:30 a.m. to 6:30 p.m.

Worker's Comp (provided by the studio)

I WAS SO EXCITED TO JOIN N2, BUT...

THE MORE I THINK ABOUT IT, THE DETAILS OF THIS CONTRACT ARE PRETTY...

MAN, THIS SUCKS!

CHAPTER 5: STRONG FEELINGS, STRONG LOVE

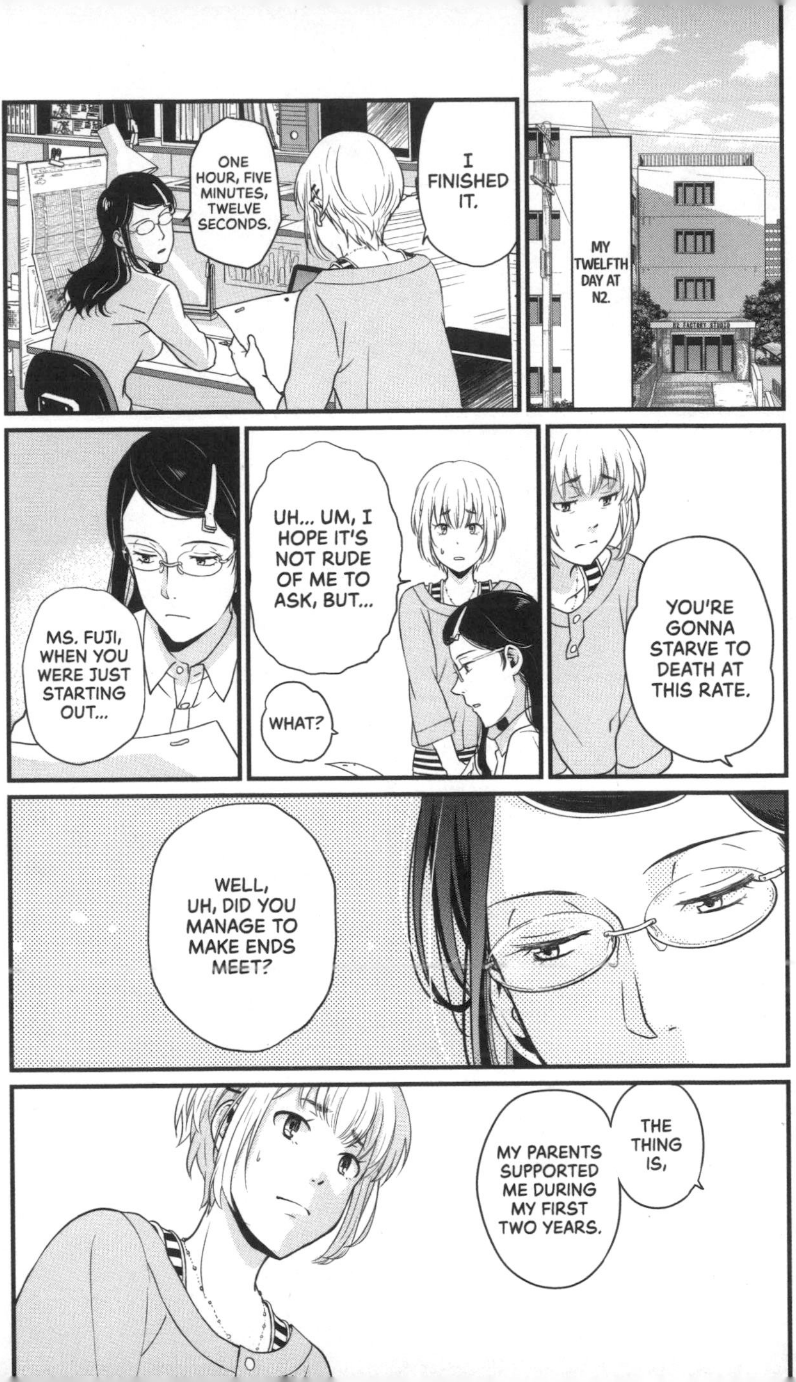
MY TWELFTH DAY AT N2.
I FINISHED IT.
ONE HOUR, FIVE MINUTES, TWELVE SECONDS.
YOU'RE GONNA STARVE TO DEATH AT THIS RATE.
UH... UM, I HOPE IT'S NOT RUDE OF ME TO ASK, BUT...
WHAT?
MS. FUJI, WHEN YOU WERE JUST STARTING OUT...
WELL, UH, DID YOU MANAGE TO MAKE ENDS MEET?
THE THING IS,
MY PARENTS SUPPORTED ME DURING MY FIRST TWO YEARS.

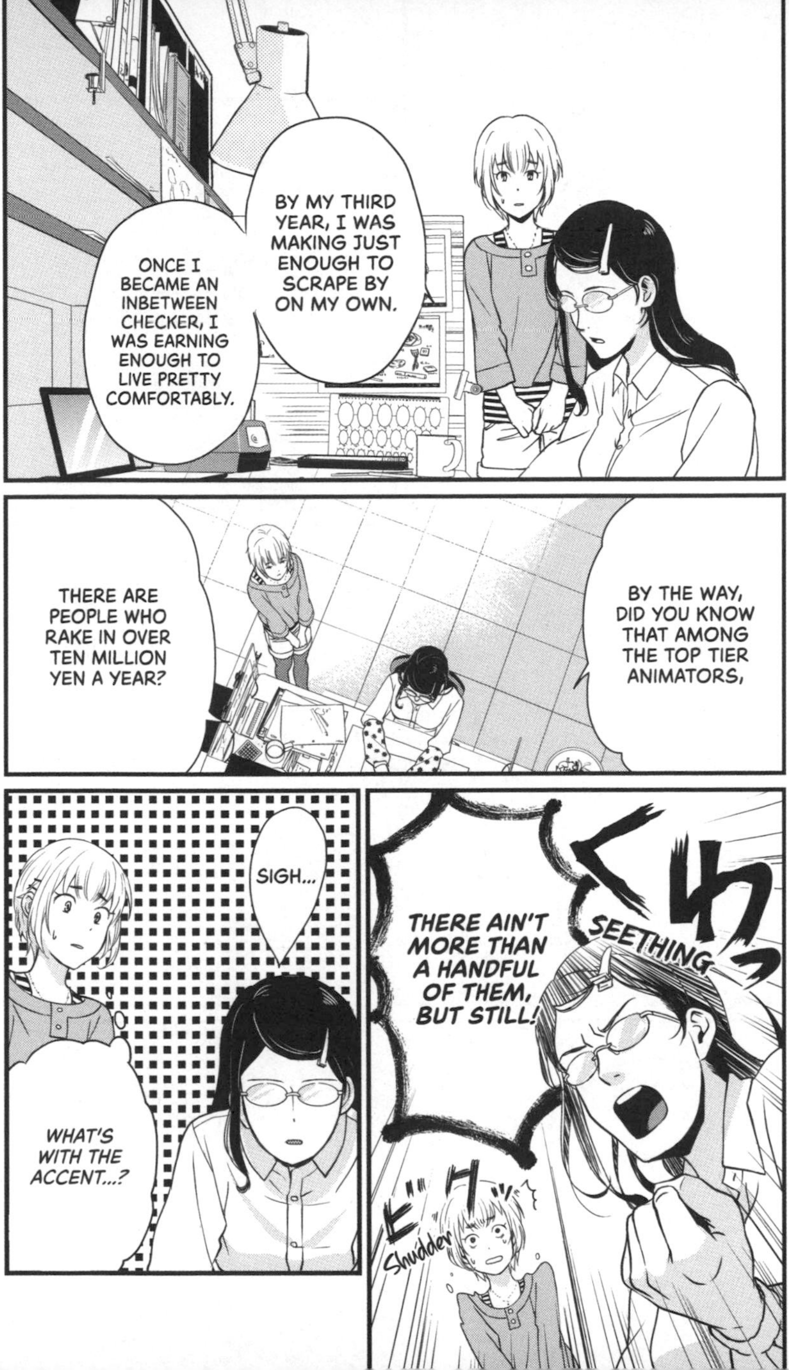
BY MY THIRD YEAR, I WAS MAKING JUST ENOUGH TO SCRAPE BY ON MY OWN.
ONCE I BECAME AN INBETWEEN CHECKER, I WAS EARNING ENOUGH TO LIVE PRETTY COMFORTABLY.
BY THE WAY, DID YOU KNOW THAT AMONG THE TOP TIER ANIMATORS,
THERE ARE PEOPLE WHO RAKE IN OVER TEN MILLION YEN A YEAR?
くわっ
SEETHING
THERE AIN'T MORE THAN A HANDFUL OF THEM, BUT STILL!
ビクッ
Shudder
SIGH...
WHAT'S WITH THE ACCENT...?

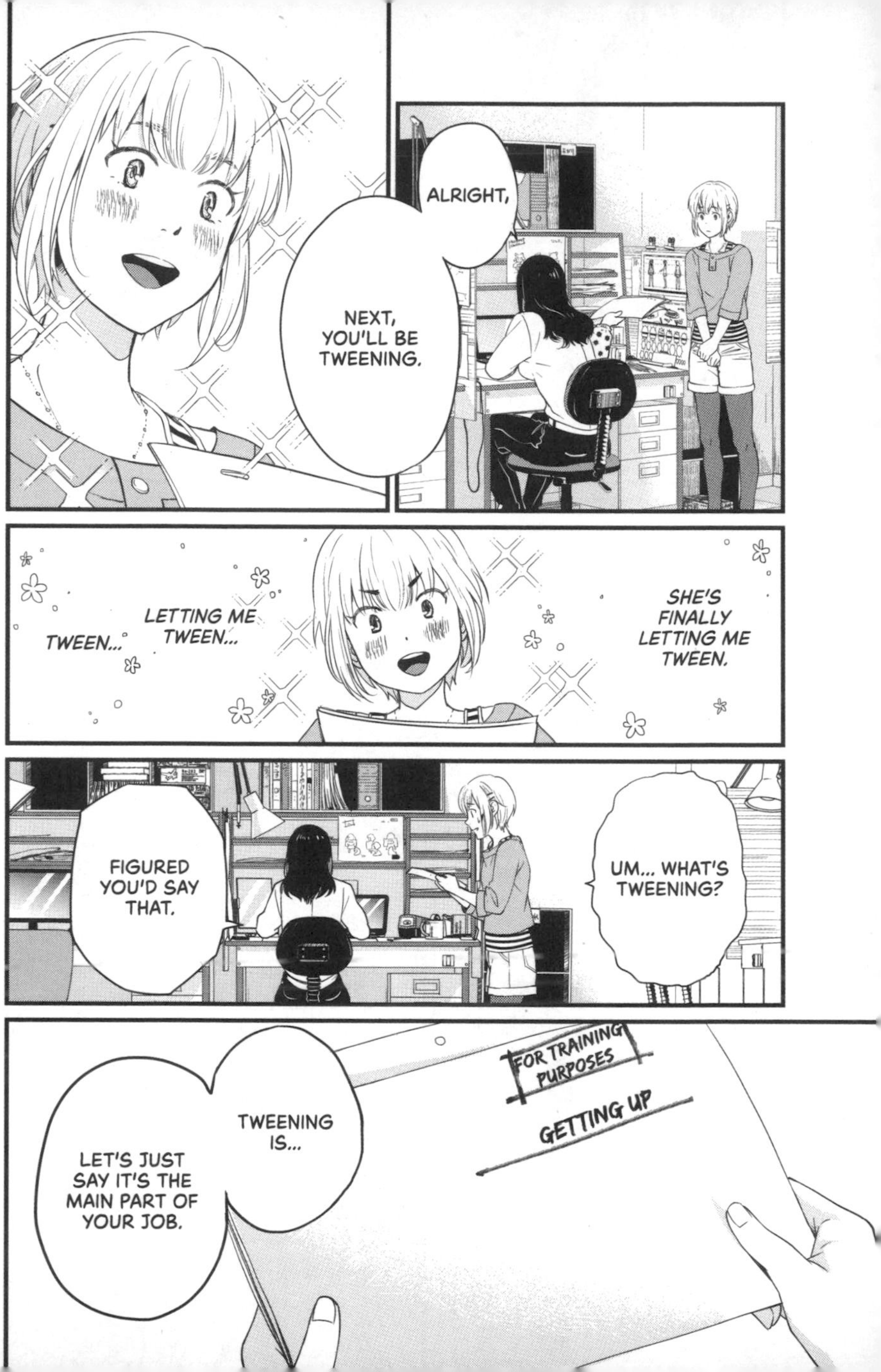
ALRIGHT,
NEXT, YOU'LL BE TWEENING.
SHE'S FINALLY LETTING ME TWEEN.
LETTING ME TWEEN...
TWEEN...
UM... WHAT'S TWEENING?
FIGURED YOU'D SAY THAT.
FOR TRAINING PURPOSES
GETTING UP
TWEENING IS...
LET'S JUST SAY IT'S THE MAIN PART OF YOUR JOB.

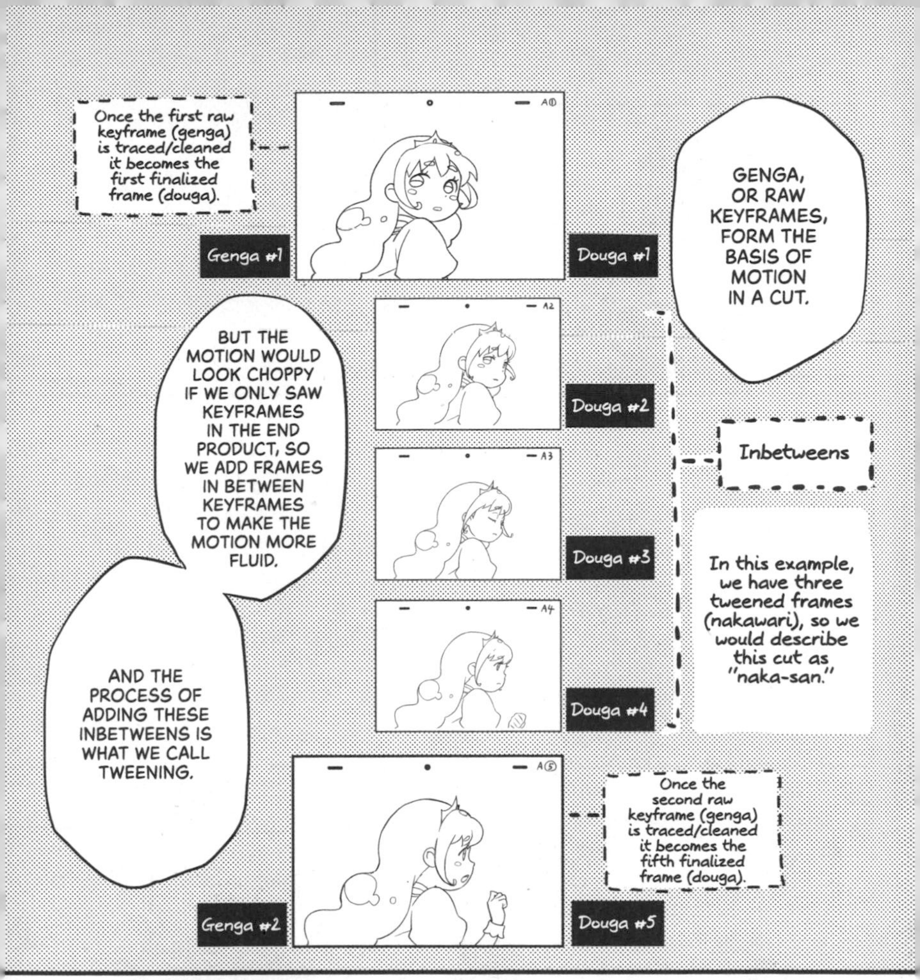
GENGA, OR RAW KEYFRAMES, FORM THE BASIS OF MOTION IN A CUT.
Douga #1
Genga #1
Once the first raw keyframe (genga) is traced/cleaned it becomes the first finalized frame (douga).
Inbetweens
In this example, we have three tweened frames (nakawari), so we would describe this cut as "naka-san."
Douga #2
Douga #3
Douga #4
BUT THE MOTION WOULD LOOK CHOPPY IF WE ONLY SAW KEYFRAMES IN THE END PRODUCT, SO WE ADD FRAMES IN BETWEEN KEYFRAMES TO MAKE THE MOTION MORE FLUID.
AND THE PROCESS OF ADDING THESE INBETWEENS IS WHAT WE CALL TWEENING.
Once the second raw keyframe (genga) is traced/cleaned it becomes the fifth finalized frame (douga).
Douga #5
Genga #2

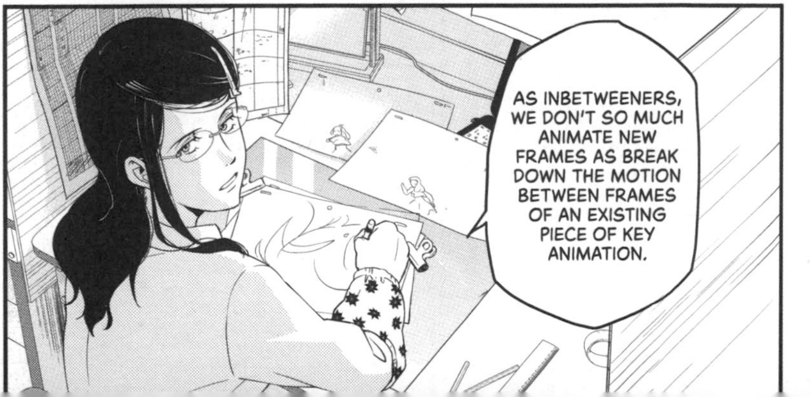
AS INBETWEENERS, WE DON'T SO MUCH ANIMATE NEW FRAMES AS BREAK DOWN THE MOTION BETWEEN FRAMES OF AN EXISTING PIECE OF KEY ANIMATION.

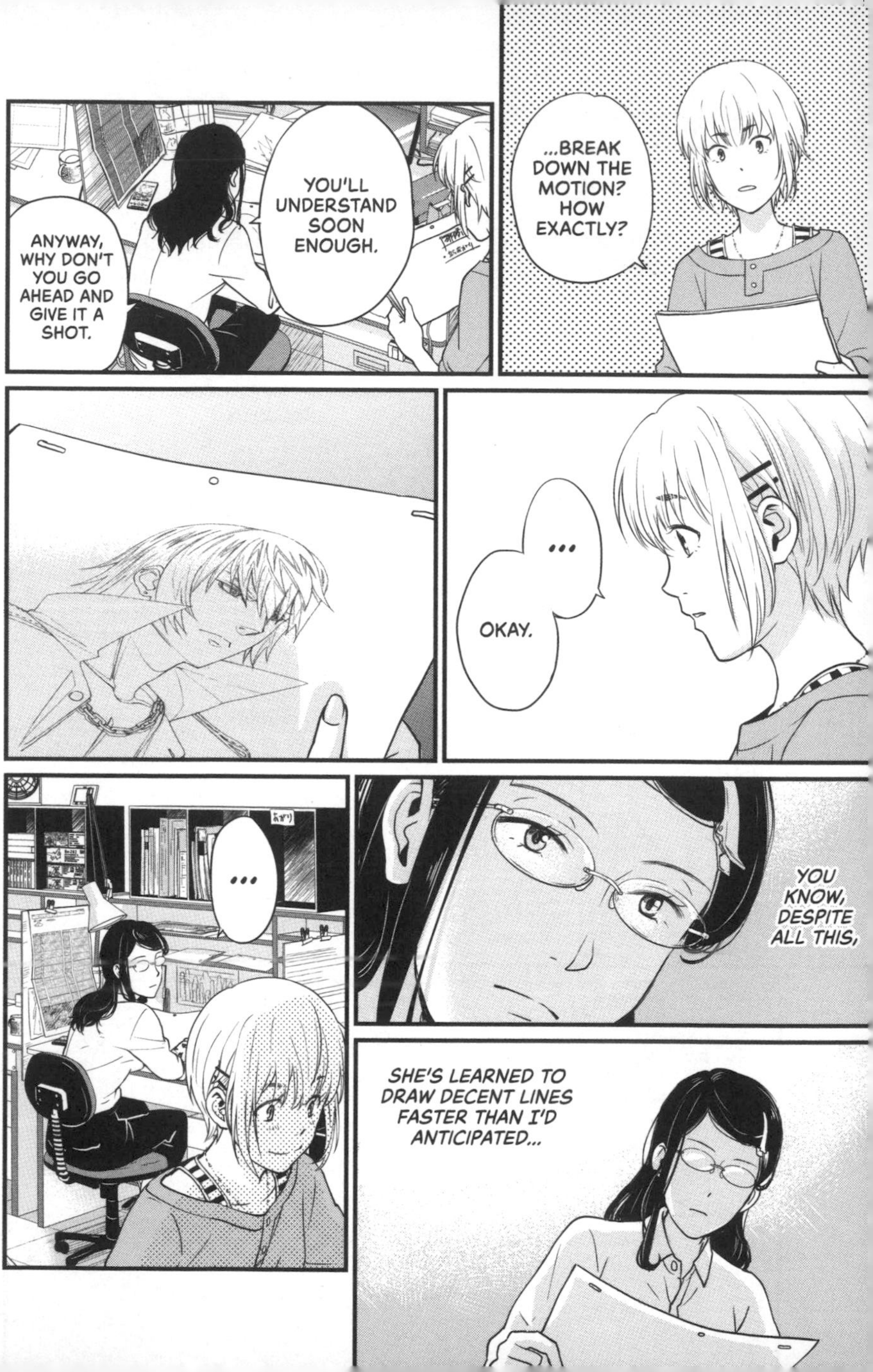
...BREAK DOWN THE MOTION? HOW EXACTLY?
YOU'LL UNDERSTAND SOON ENOUGH.
ANYWAY, WHY DON'T YOU GO AHEAD AND GIVE IT A SHOT.
...
OKAY.
YOU KNOW, DESPITE ALL THIS,
SHE'S LEARNED TO DRAW DECENT LINES FASTER THAN I'D ANTICIPATED...
...

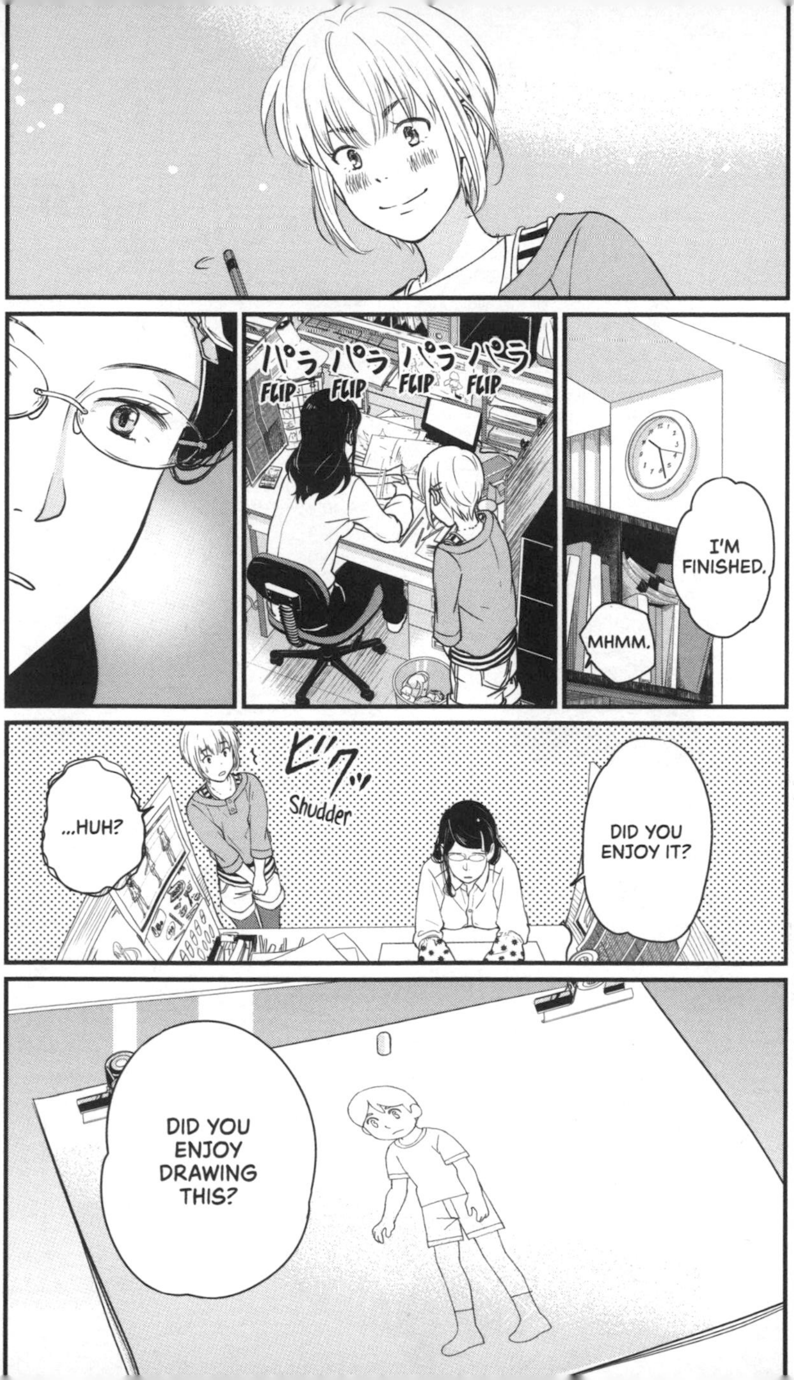
I'M FINISHED.
MHMM.
パラ パラ パラ パラ
FLIP FLIP FLIP FLIP
DID YOU ENJOY IT?
ビクッ
Shudder
...HUH?
DID YOU ENJOY DRAWING THIS?

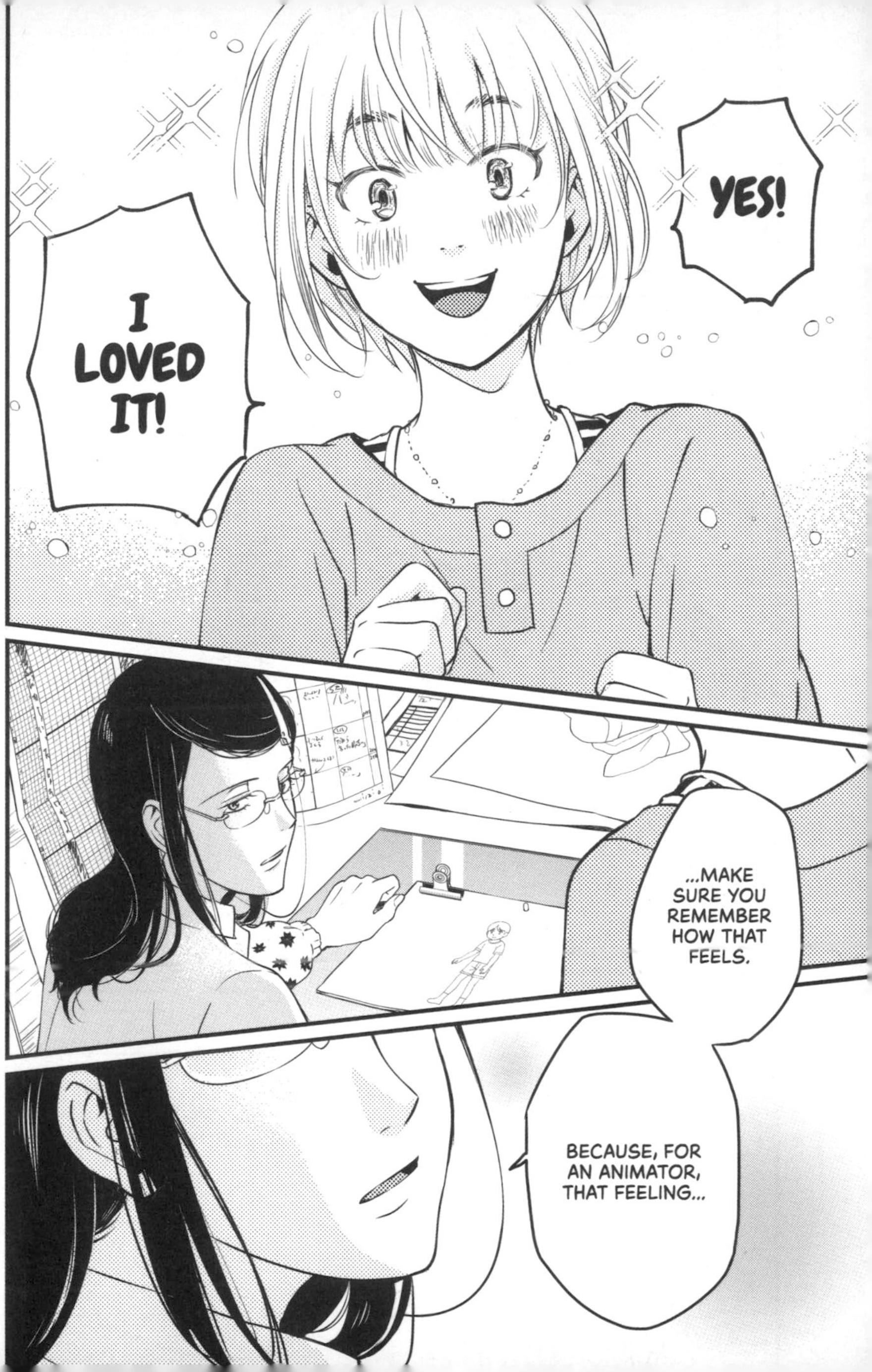
YES!
I LOVED IT!
...MAKE SURE YOU REMEMBER HOW THAT FEELS.
BECAUSE, FOR AN ANIMATOR, THAT FEELING...

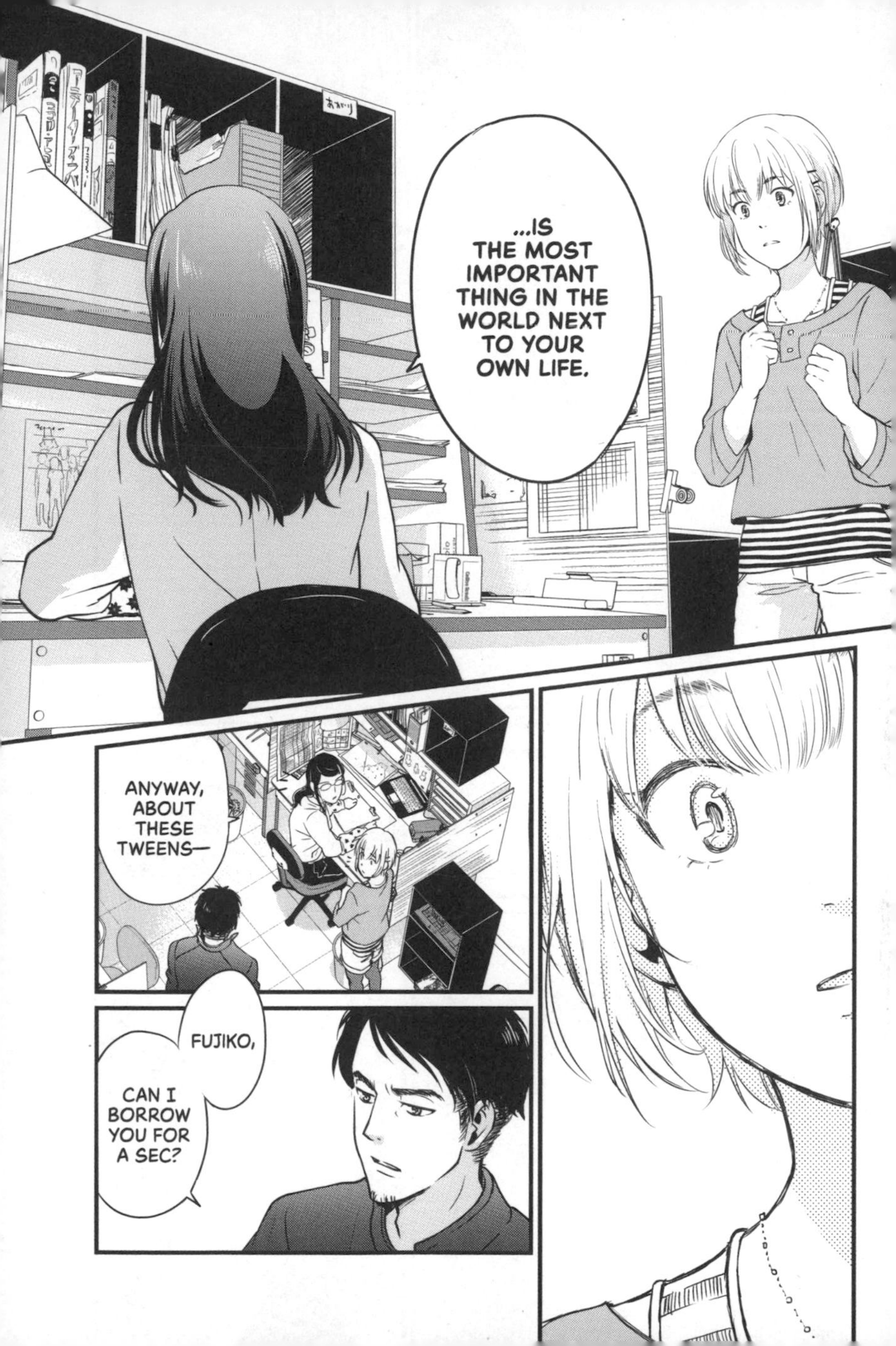
あがり
...IS THE MOST IMPORTANT THING IN THE WORLD NEXT TO YOUR OWN LIFE.
ANYWAY, ABOUT THESE TWEENS—
FUJIKO,
CAN I BORROW YOU FOR A SEC?

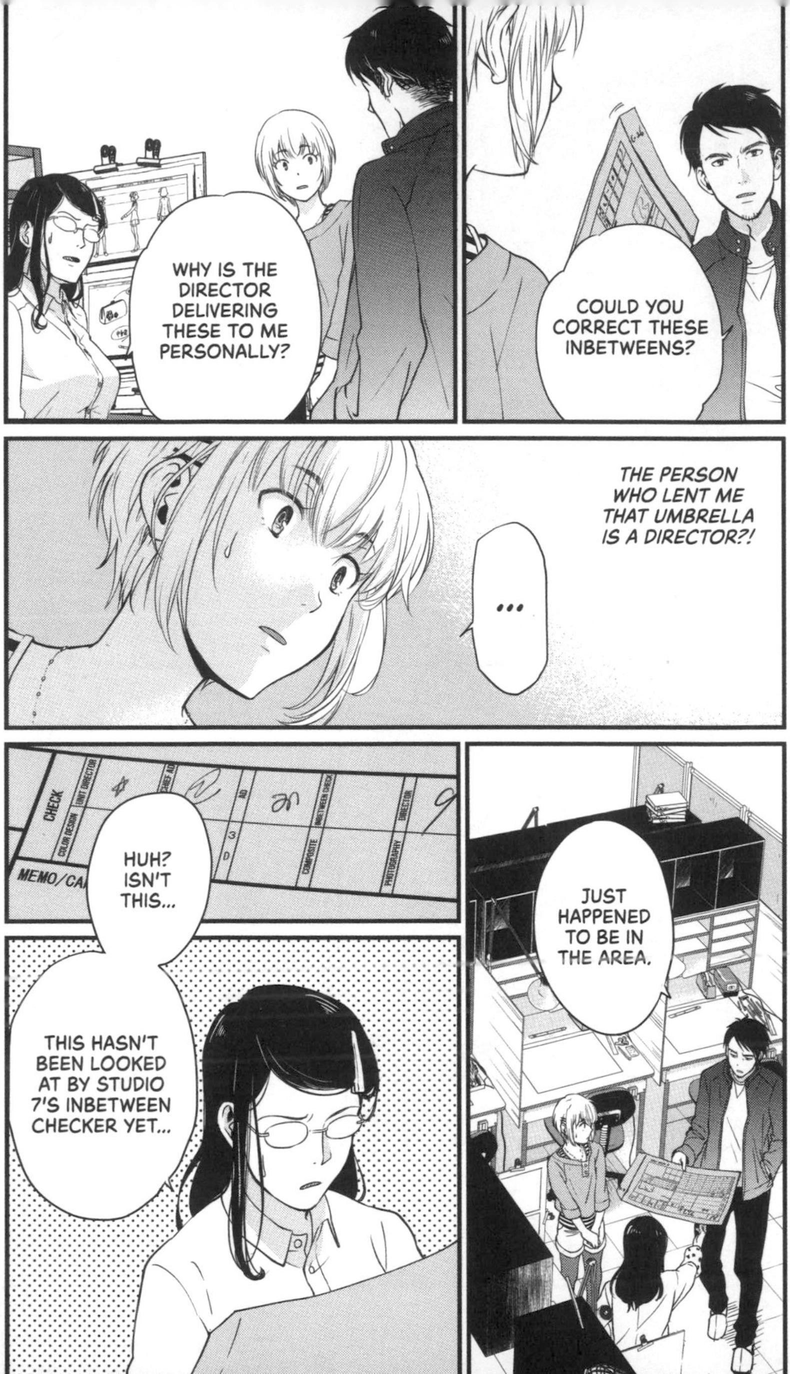
COULD YOU CORRECT THESE INBETWEENS?
WHY IS THE DIRECTOR DELIVERING THESE TO ME PERSONALLY?
THE PERSON WHO LENT ME THAT UMBRELLA IS A DIRECTOR?!
...
JUST HAPPENED TO BE IN THE AREA.
CHECK
UNIT DIRECTOR
COLOR DESIGN
AD
3D
INBETWEEN CHECK
COMPOSITE
DIRECTOR
PHOTOGRAPHY
HUH? ISN'T THIS...
THIS HASN'T BEEN LOOKED AT BY STUDIO 7'S INBETWEEN CHECKER YET...

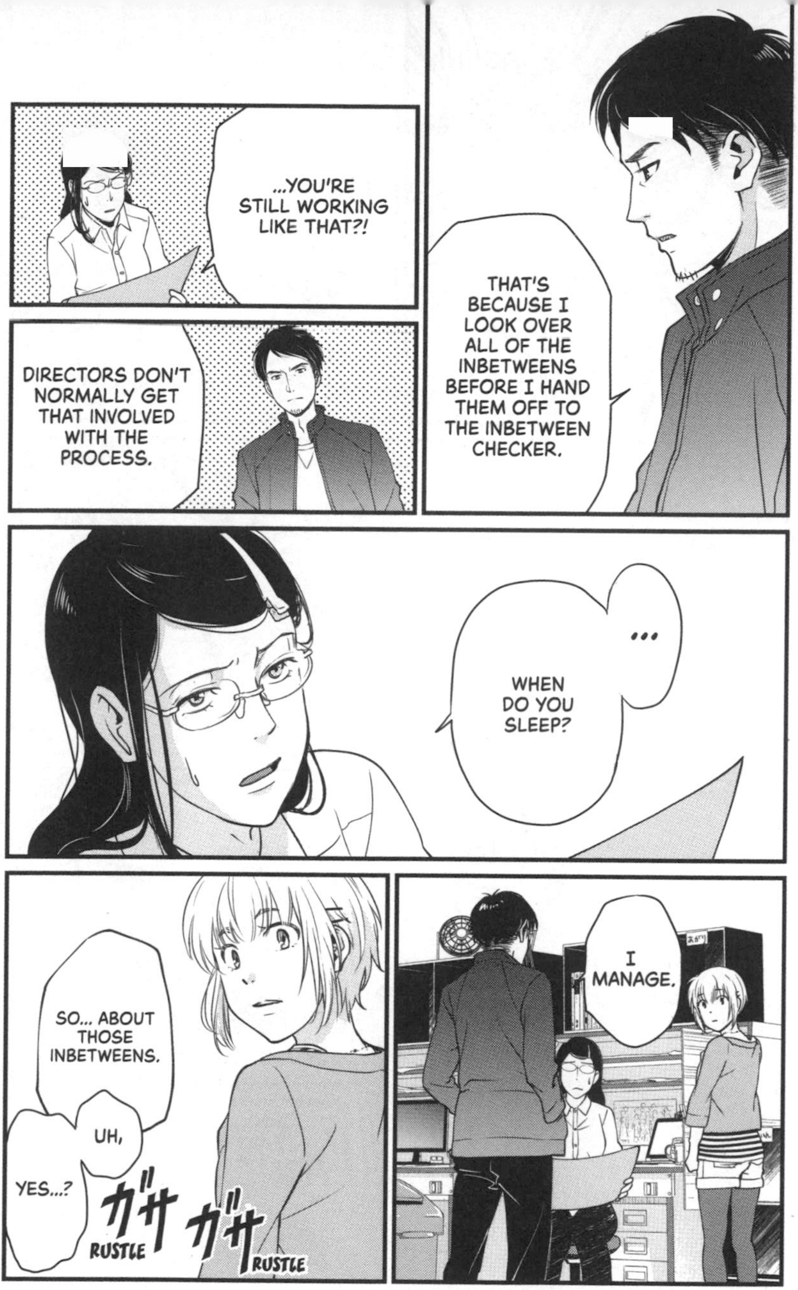
THAT'S BECAUSE I LOOK OVER ALL OF THE INBETWEENS BEFORE I HAND THEM OFF TO THE INBETWEEN CHECKER.
...YOU'RE STILL WORKING LIKE THAT?!
DIRECTORS DON'T NORMALLY GET THAT INVOLVED WITH THE PROCESS.
...
WHEN DO YOU SLEEP?
I MANAGE.
SO... ABOUT THOSE INBETWEENS.
UH,
YES...?
ガサ
RUSTLE
ガサ
RUSTLE

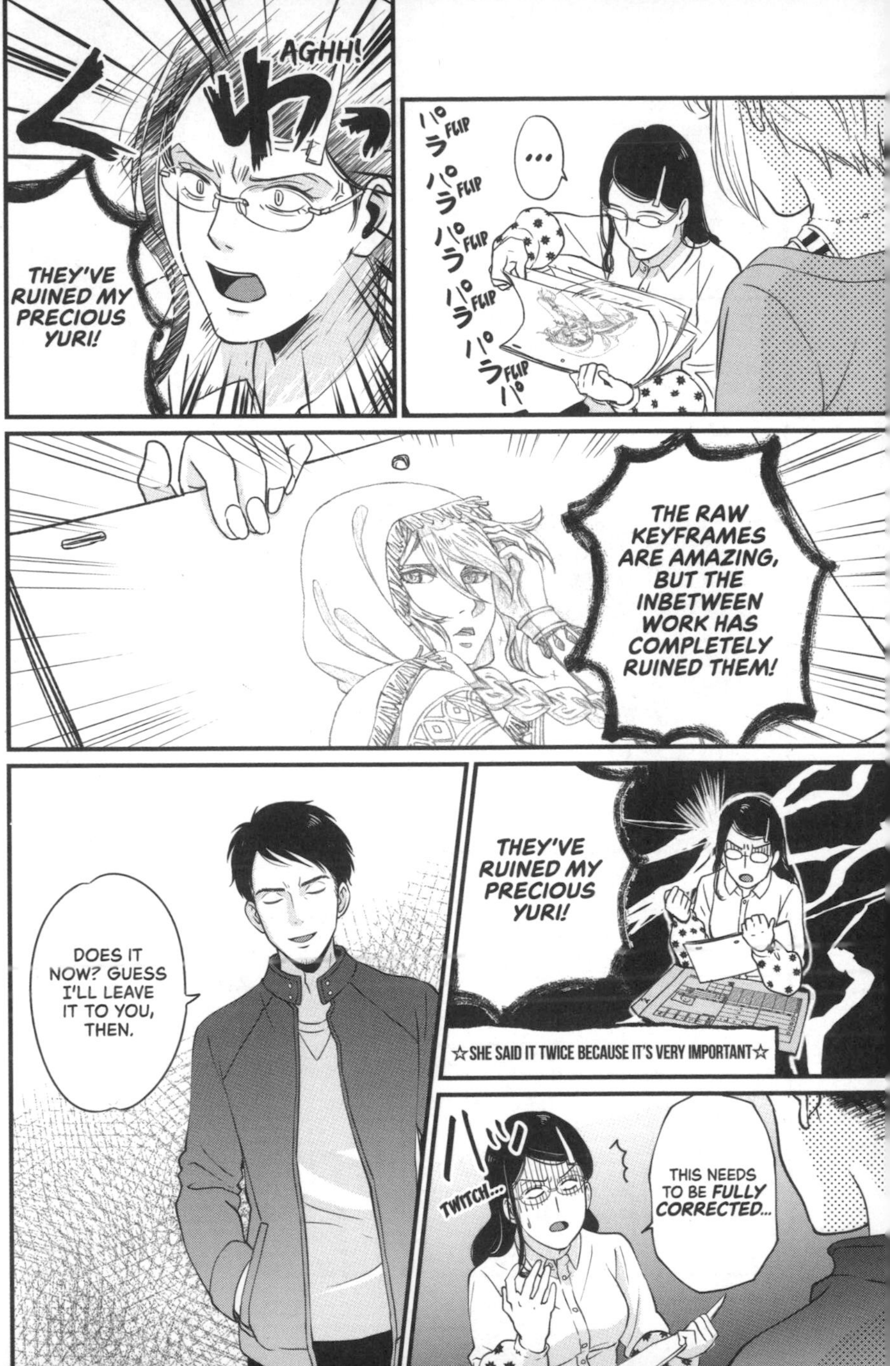

パラ FLIP
パラ FLIP
パラ FLIP
パラ FLIP
パラ FLIP
パ
...
AGHH!
THEY'VE RUINED MY PRECIOUS YURI!
THE RAW KEYFRAMES ARE AMAZING, BUT THE INBETWEEN WORK HAS COMPLETELY RUINED THEM!
THEY'VE RUINED MY PRECIOUS YURI!
☆SHE SAID IT TWICE BECAUSE IT'S VERY IMPORTANT☆
TWITCH...
THIS NEEDS TO BE FULLY CORRECTED...
DOES IT NOW? GUESS I'LL LEAVE IT TO YOU, THEN.

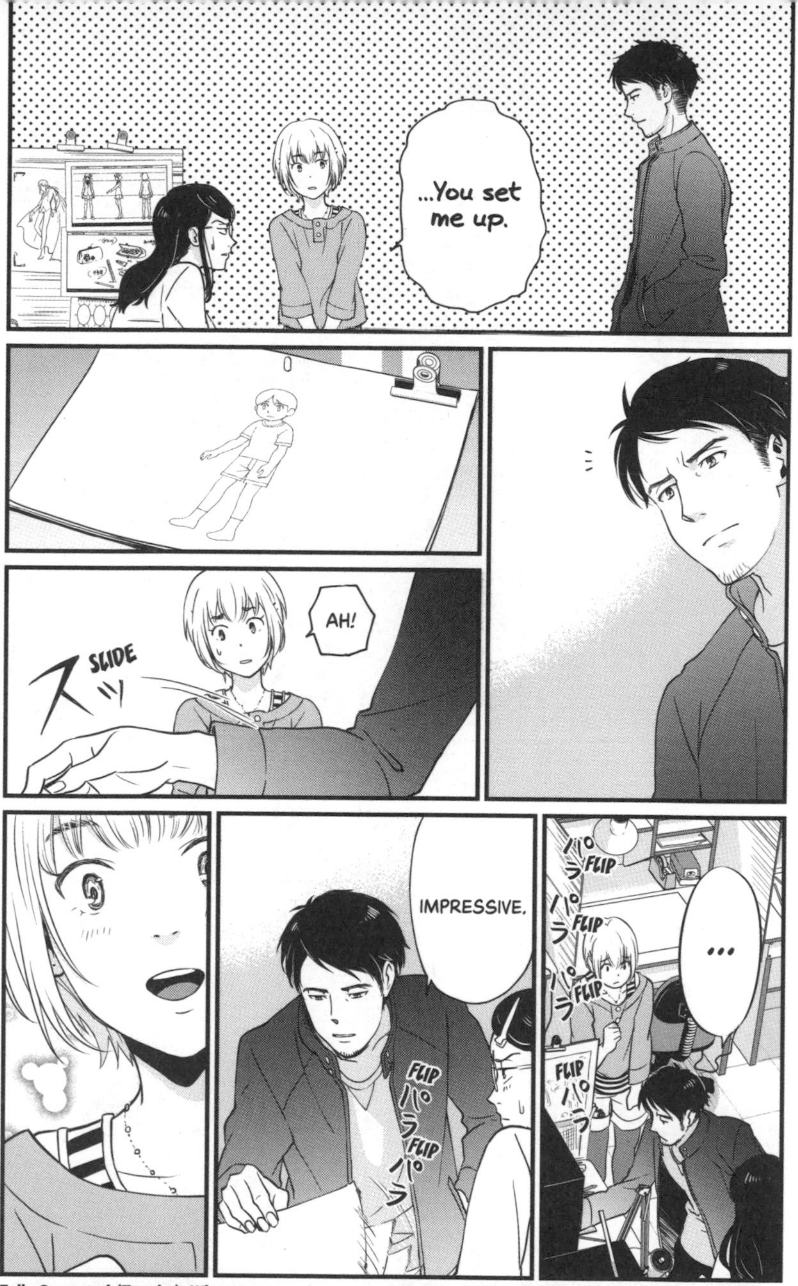
...You set me up.
AH!
SLIDE
FLIP
FLIP
FLIP
...
FLIP
IMPRESSIVE.
FLIP
FLIP

Fully Corrected (Zenshu): When someone in a supervisory role (animation director, inbetween checker, etc) redraws work from scratch rather than correcting portions of individual frames. In this case, Fuji is going to be redrawing all the douga (inbetweens and corrected keyframes), but not the raw keyframes (genga).

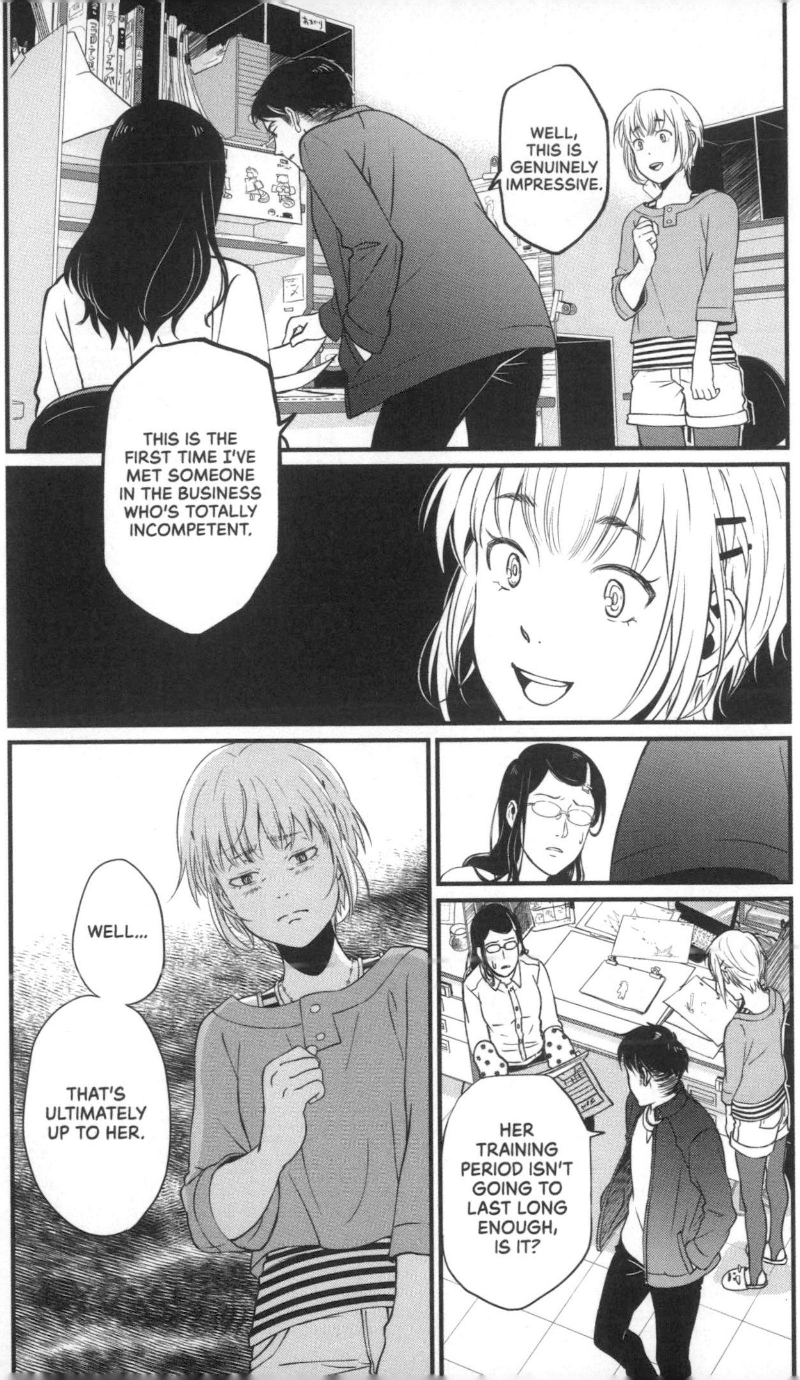
WELL, THIS IS GENUINELY IMPRESSIVE.
THIS IS THE FIRST TIME I'VE MET SOMEONE IN THE BUSINESS WHO'S TOTALLY INCOMPETENT.
HER TRAINING PERIOD ISN'T GOING TO LAST LONG ENOUGH, IS IT?
WELL...
THAT'S ULTIMATELY UP TO HER.

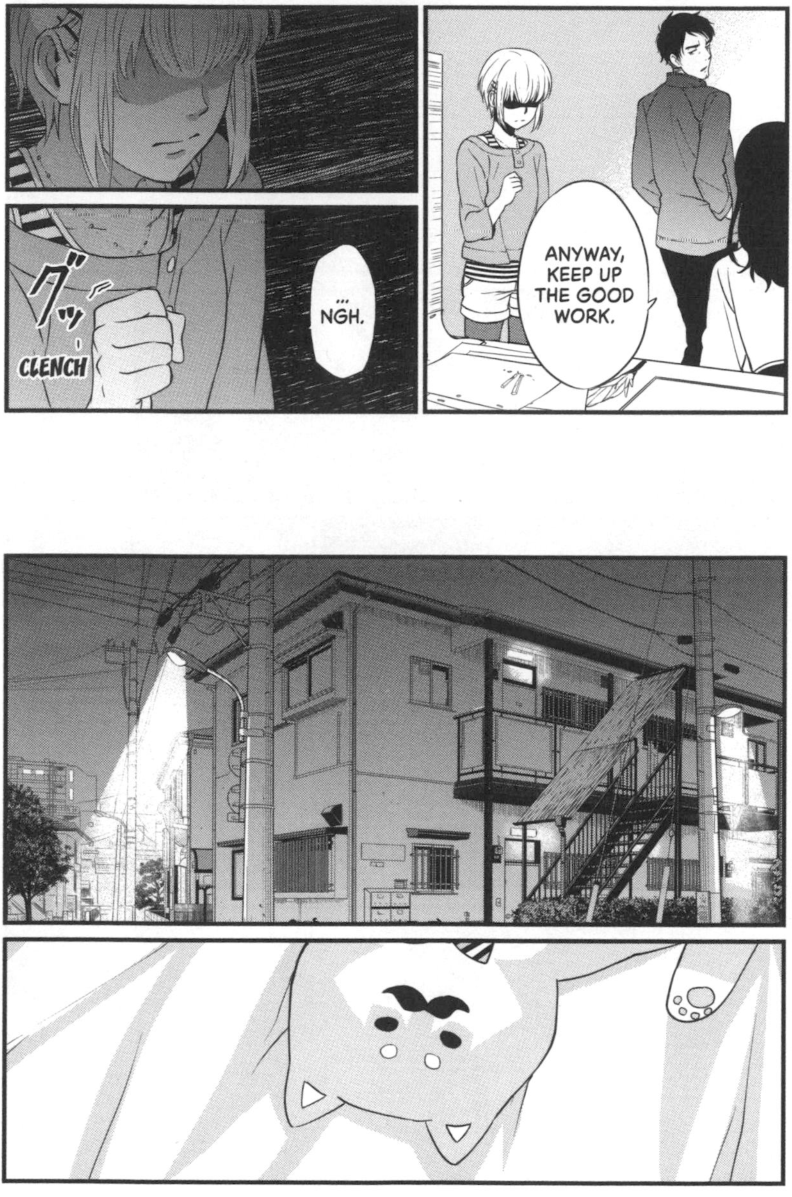
ANYWAY, KEEP UP THE GOOD WORK.
... NGH.
グッ
CLENCH

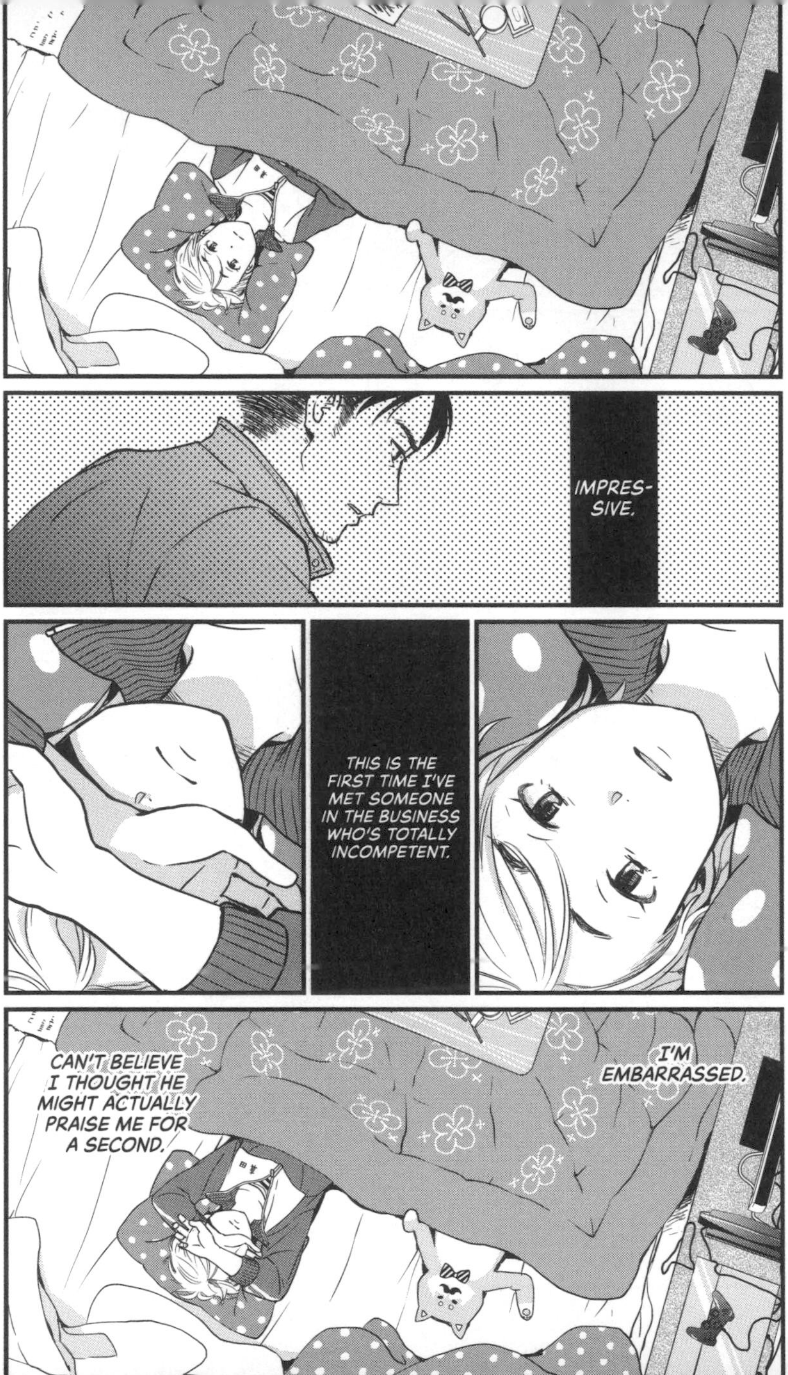
IMPRES-
SIVE.
THIS IS THE FIRST TIME I'VE MET SOMEONE IN THE BUSINESS WHO'S TOTALLY INCOMPETENT.
I'M EMBARRASSED.
CAN'T BELIEVE I THOUGHT HE MIGHT ACTUALLY PRAISE ME FOR A SECOND.

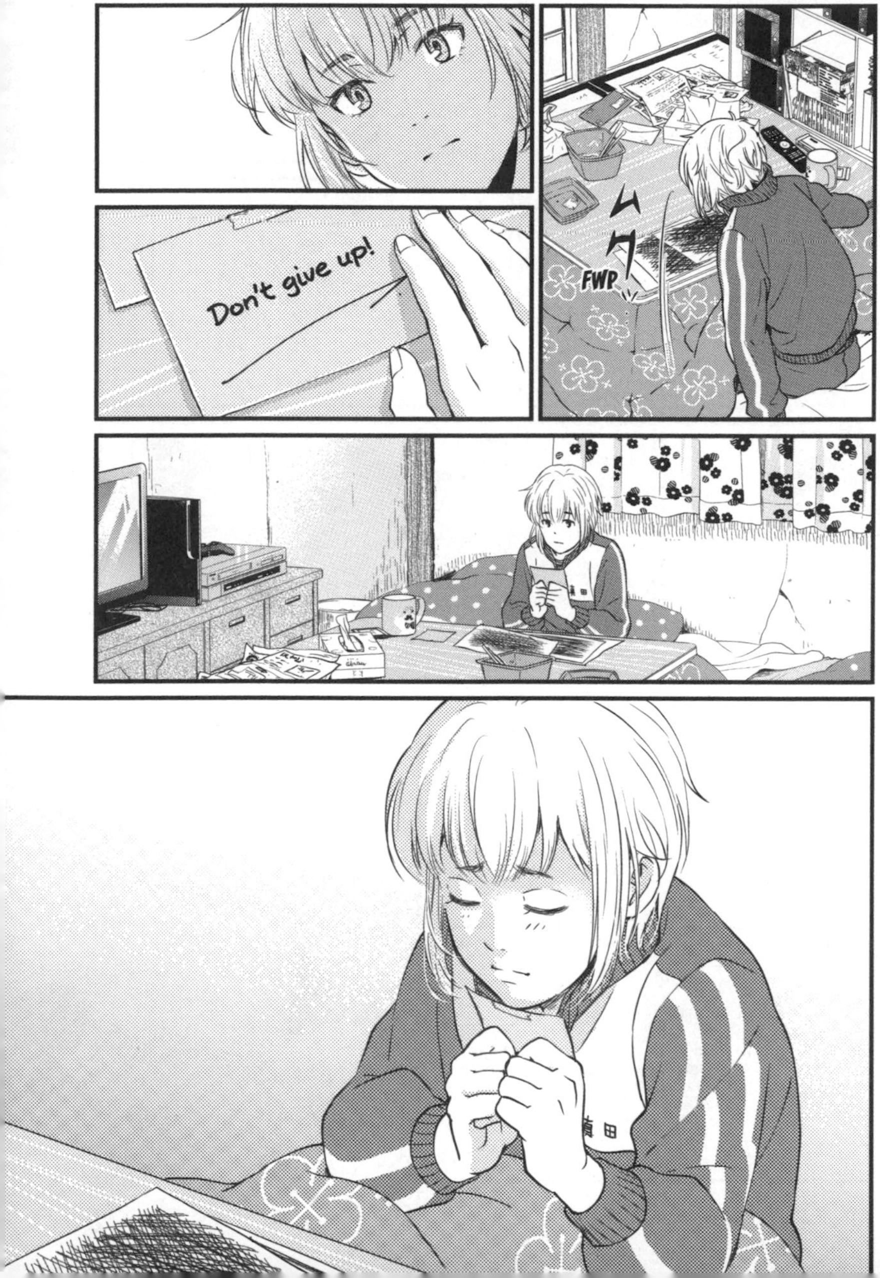
ムク
FWP
Don't give up!

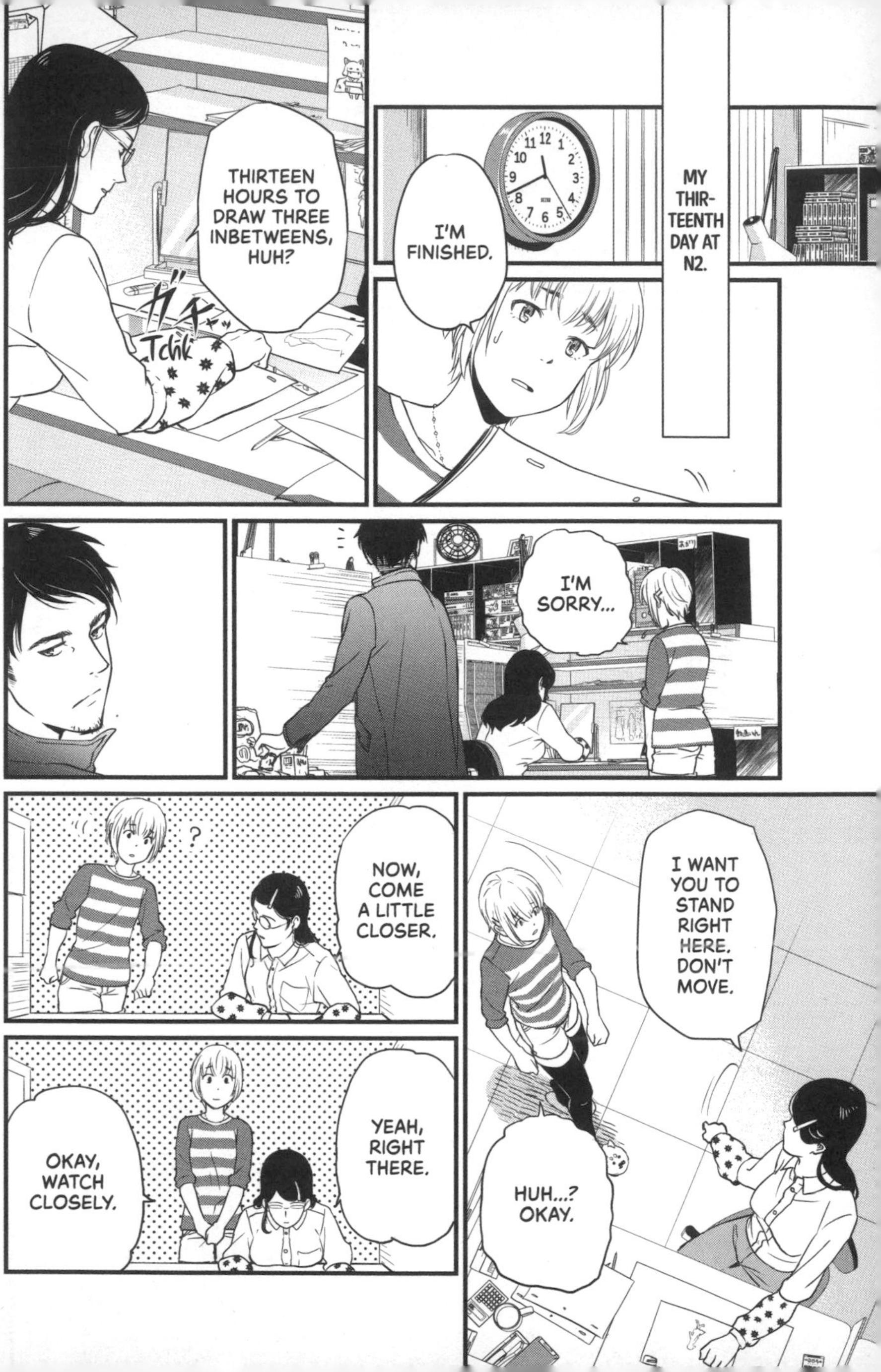
MY THIRTEENTH DAY AT N2.
I'M FINISHED.
THIRTEEN HOURS TO DRAW THREE INBETWEENS, HUH?
ガチャッ
Tchik
I'M SORRY...
I WANT YOU TO STAND RIGHT HERE. DON'T MOVE.
HUH...? OKAY.
NOW, COME A LITTLE CLOSER.
YEAH, RIGHT THERE.
OKAY, WATCH CLOSELY.

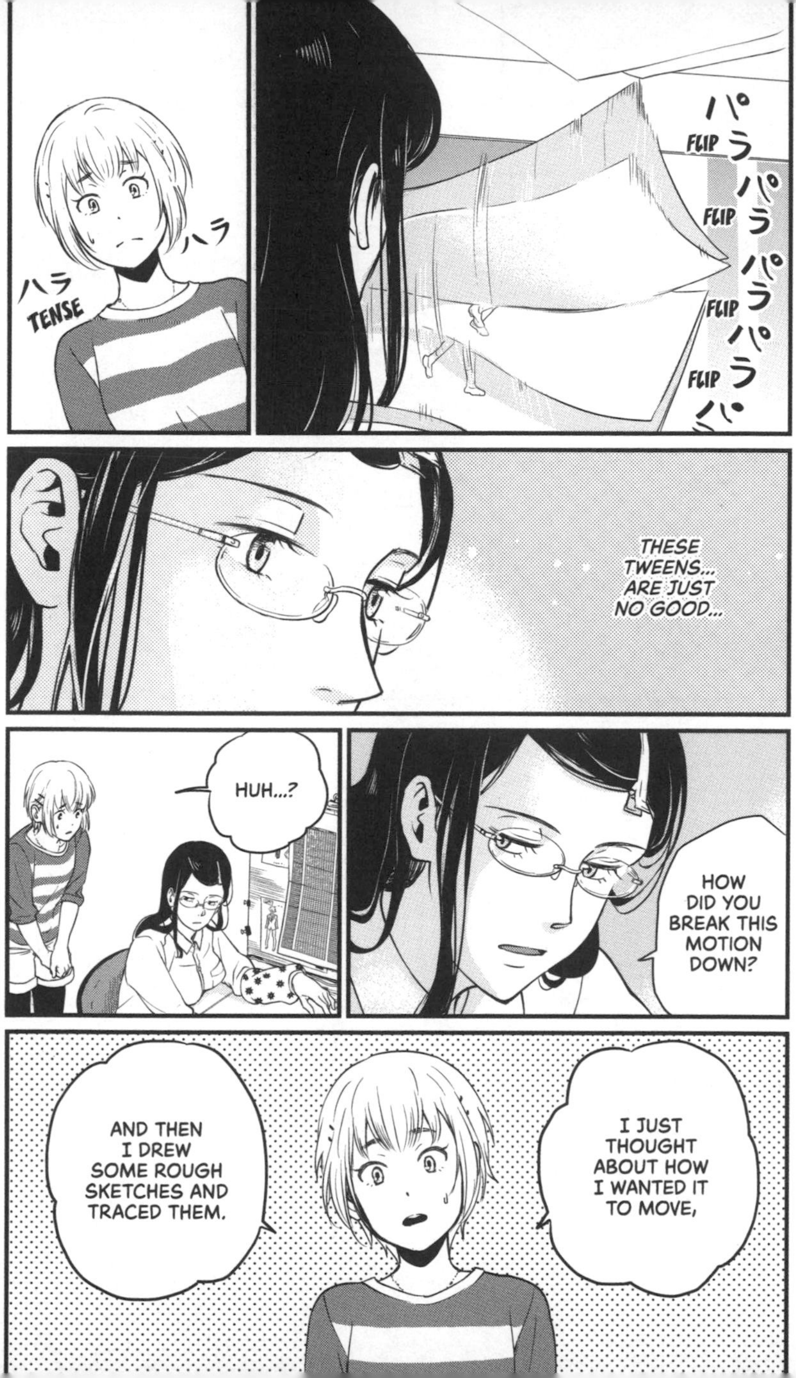
パラ
FLIP
パラ
FLIP
パラ
FLIP
パラ
FLIP
ハラ
ハラ
TENSE
THESE TWEENS... ARE JUST NO GOOD...
HOW DID YOU BREAK THIS MOTION DOWN?
HUH...?
I JUST THOUGHT ABOUT HOW I WANTED IT TO MOVE,
AND THEN I DREW SOME ROUGH SKETCHES AND TRACED THEM.

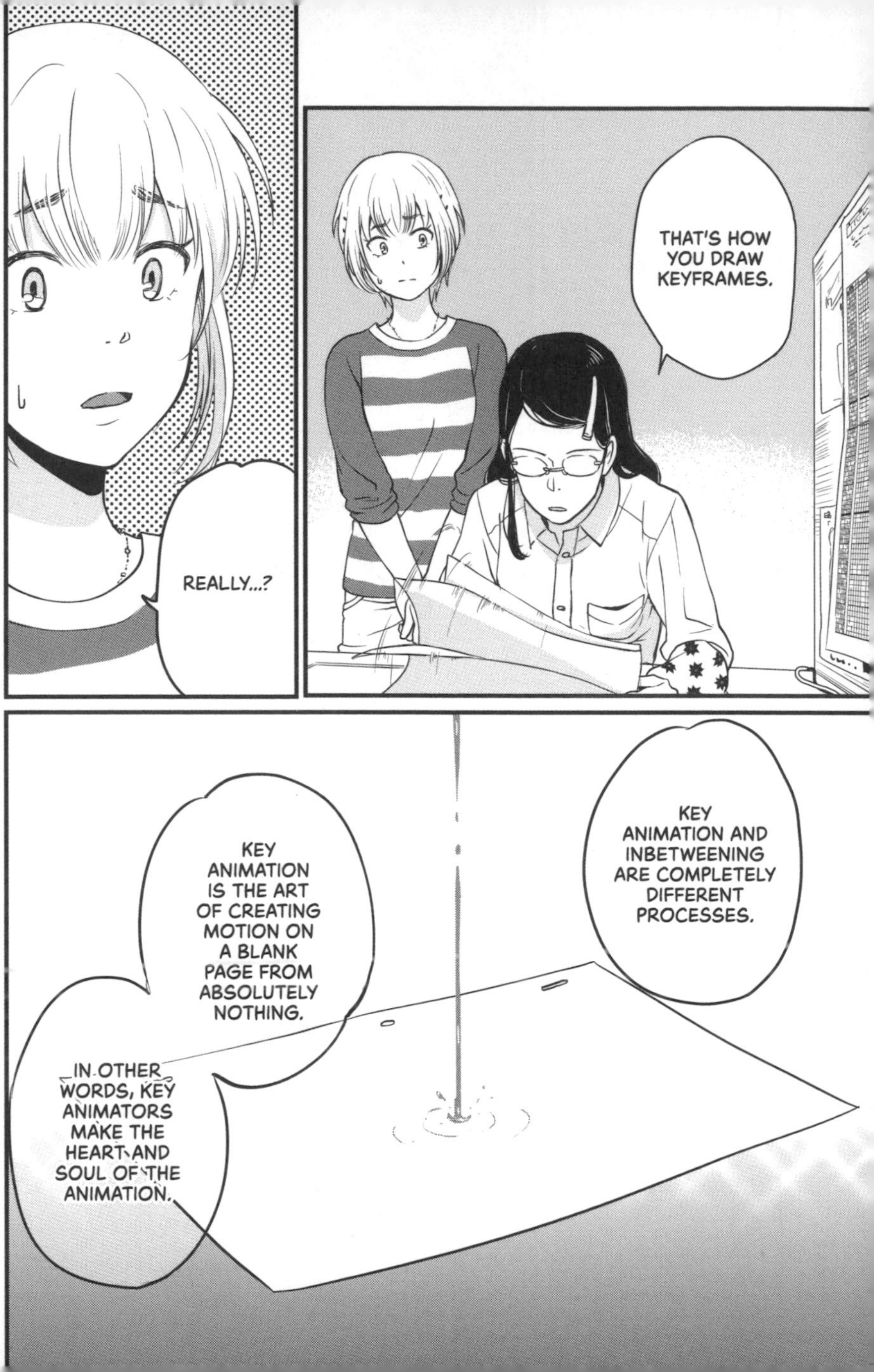
THAT'S HOW YOU DRAW KEYFRAMES.
REALLY...?
KEY ANIMATION AND INBETWEENING ARE COMPLETELY DIFFERENT PROCESSES.
KEY ANIMATION IS THE ART OF CREATING MOTION ON A BLANK PAGE FROM ABSOLUTELY NOTHING.
IN OTHER WORDS, KEY ANIMATORS MAKE THE HEART AND SOUL OF THE ANIMATION.

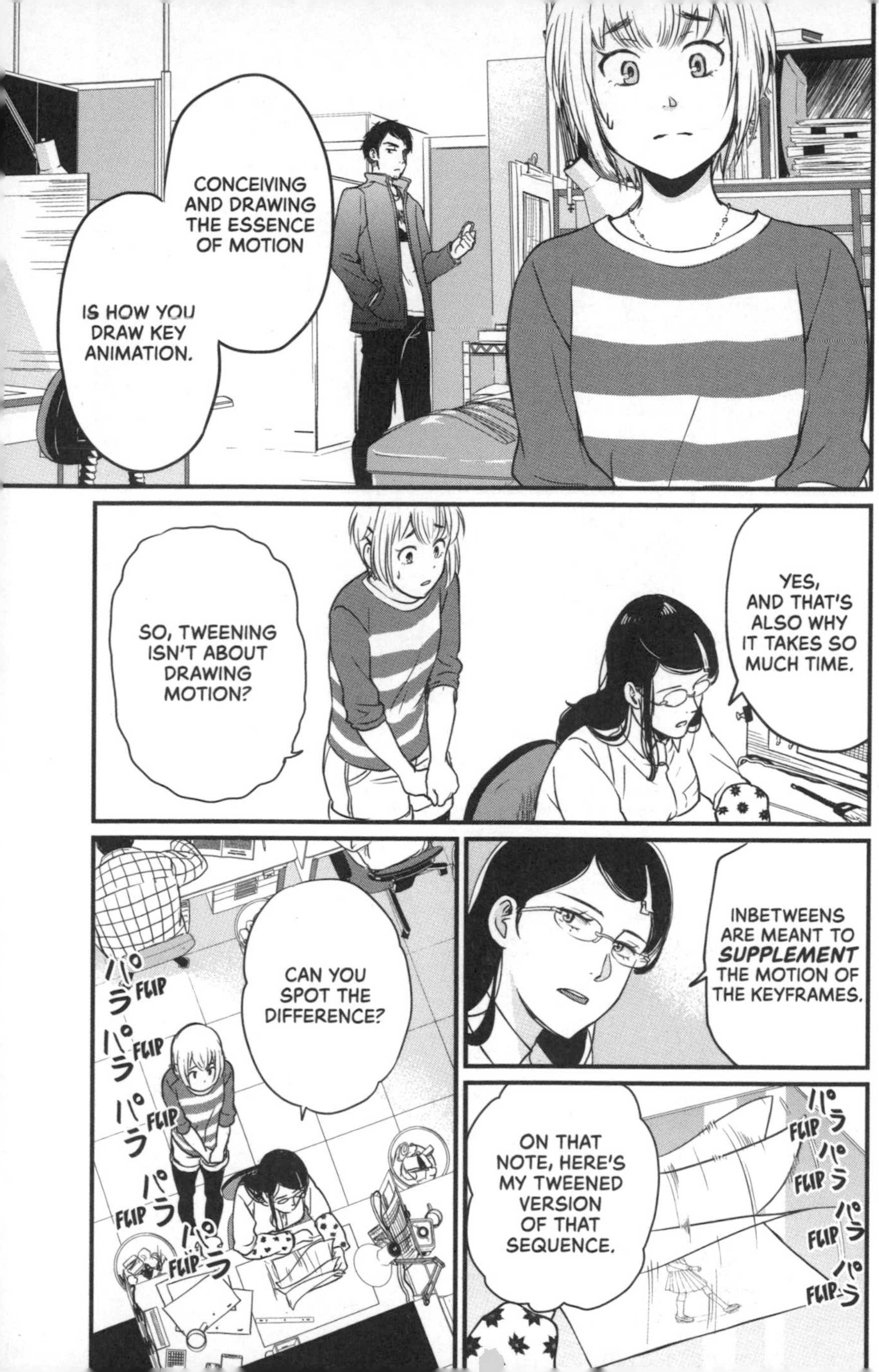

CONCEIVING AND DRAWING THE ESSENCE OF MOTION
IS HOW YOU DRAW KEY ANIMATION.
YES, AND THAT'S ALSO WHY IT TAKES SO MUCH TIME.
SO, TWEENING ISN'T ABOUT DRAWING MOTION?
INBETWEENS ARE MEANT TO ***SUPPLEMENT*** THE MOTION OF THE KEYFRAMES.
パラ FLIP
パラ FLIP
パラ FLIP
パラ FLIP
ON THAT NOTE, HERE'S MY TWEENED VERSION OF THAT SEQUENCE.
CAN YOU SPOT THE DIFFERENCE?
パラ FLIP
パラ FLIP
パラ FLIP
パラ FLIP
パラ FLIP

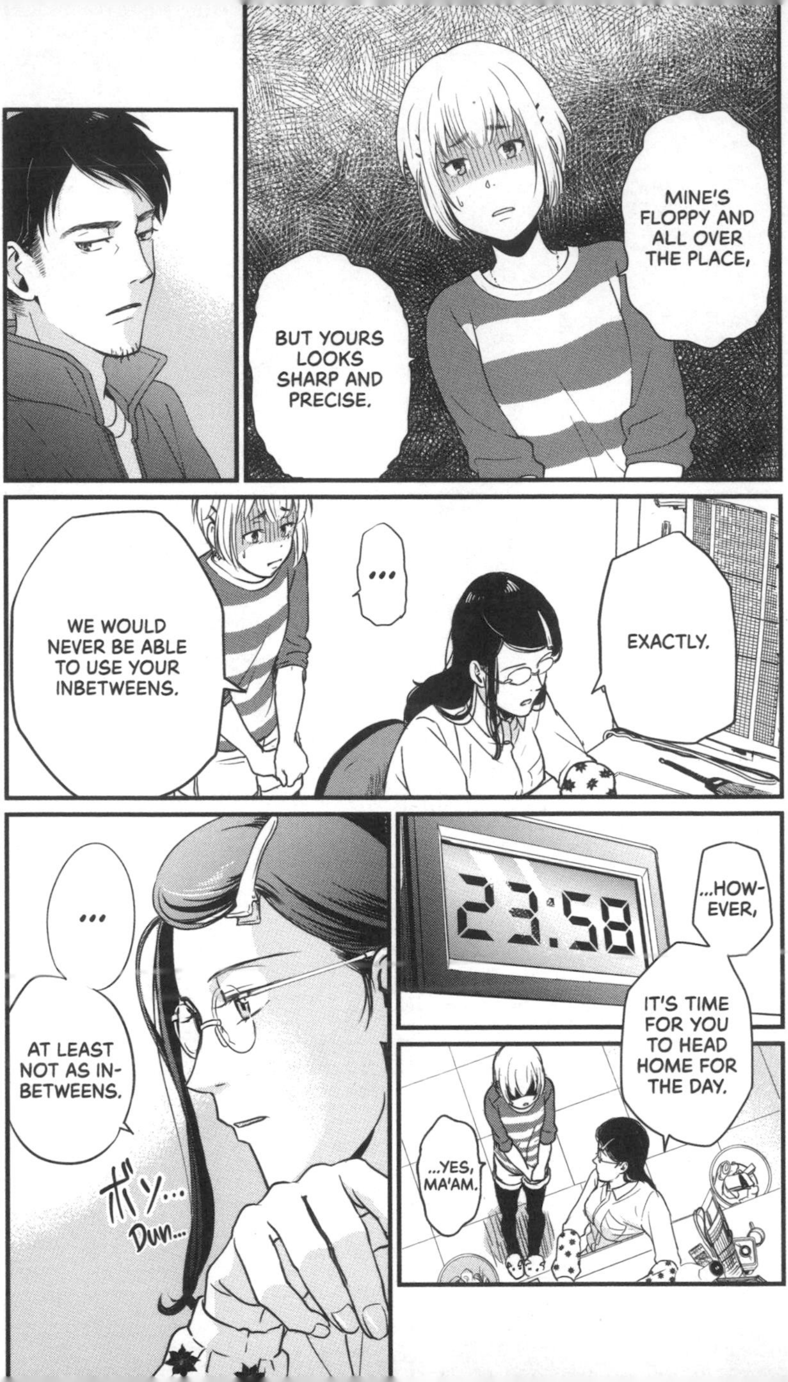
MINE'S FLOPPY AND ALL OVER THE PLACE,
BUT YOURS LOOKS SHARP AND PRECISE.
EXACTLY.
...
WE WOULD NEVER BE ABLE TO USE YOUR INBETWEENS.
23:58
...HOW-EVER,
IT'S TIME FOR YOU TO HEAD HOME FOR THE DAY.
...YES, MA'AM.
...
AT LEAST NOT AS IN-BETWEENS.
ボソ...
Dun...

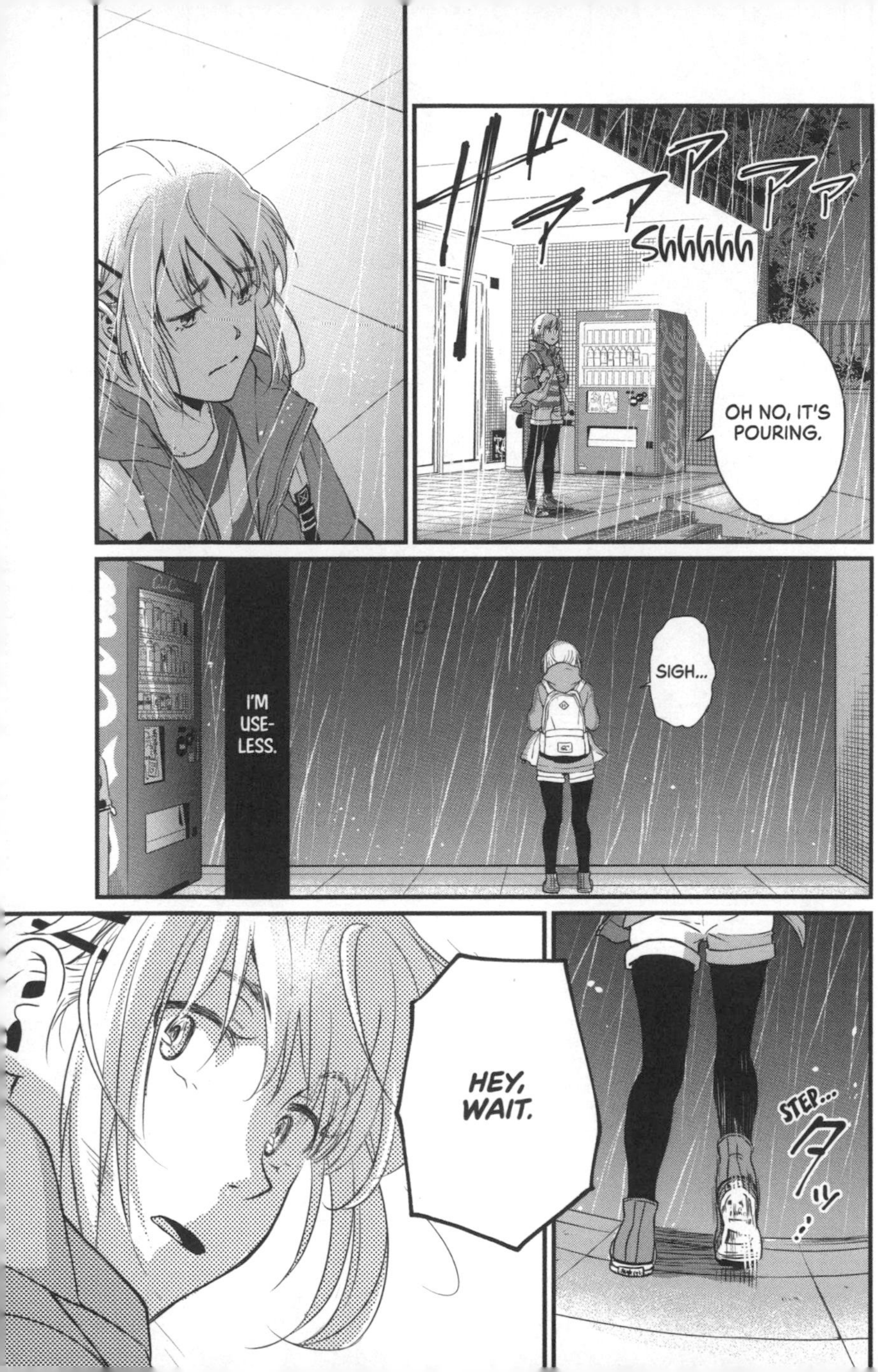
Shhhhh
OH NO, IT'S POURING.
SIGH...
I'M USE-LESS.
STEP...
HEY, WAIT.

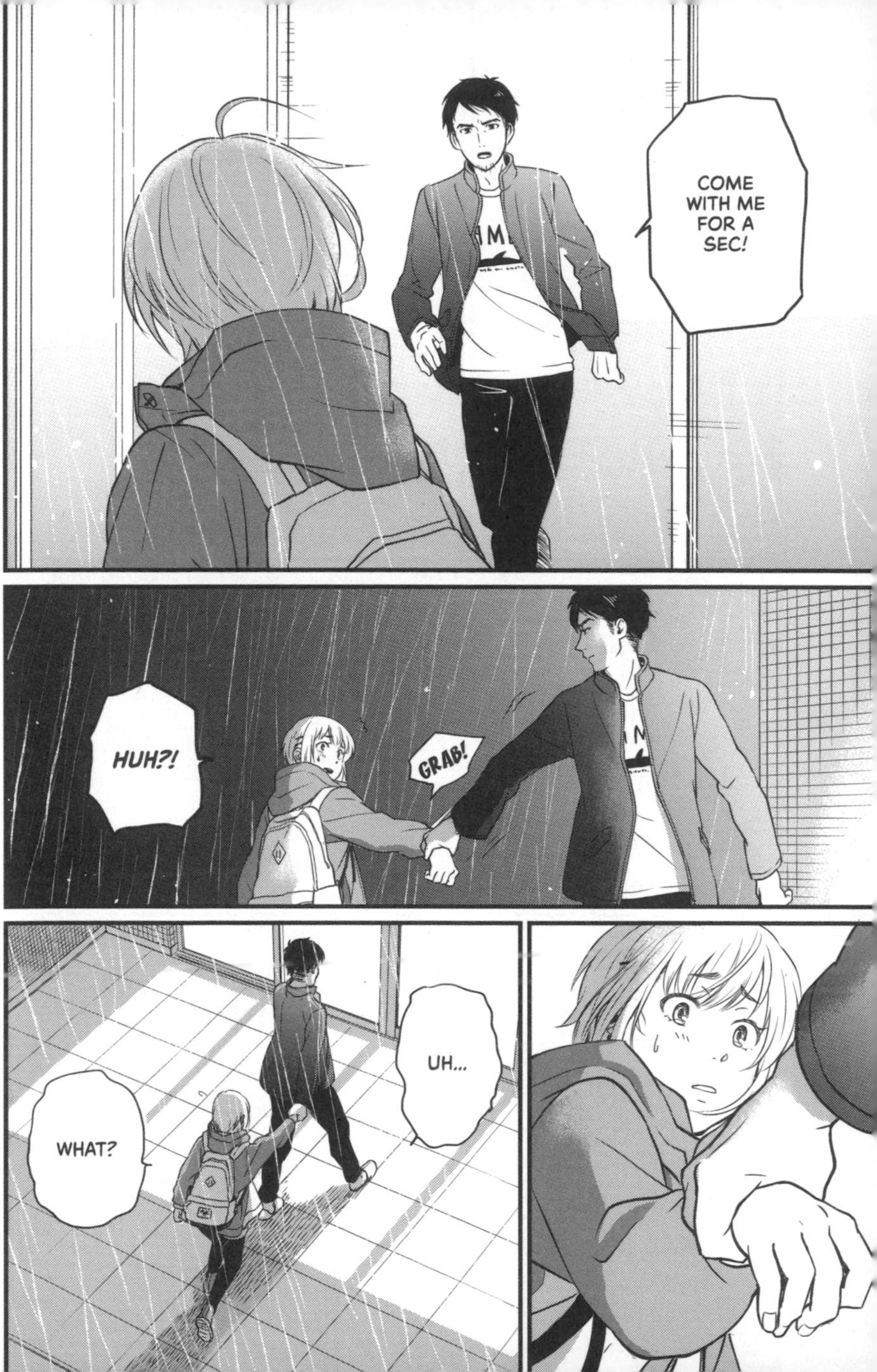
COME WITH ME FOR A SEC!
GRAB!
HUH?!
UH...
WHAT?

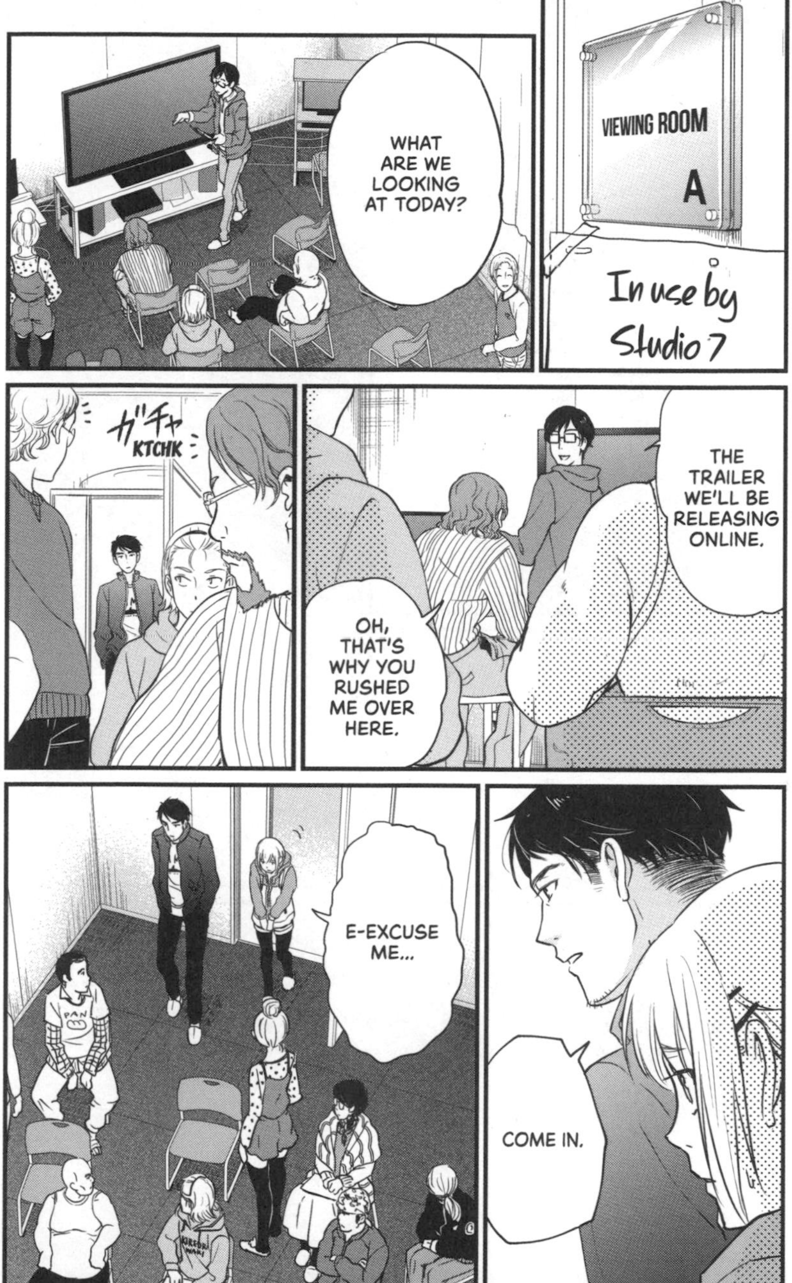
VIEWING ROOM
A
In use by Studio 7
WHAT ARE WE LOOKING AT TODAY?
THE TRAILER WE'LL BE RELEASING ONLINE.
OH, THAT'S WHY YOU RUSHED ME OVER HERE.
ガチャ
KTCHK
COME IN.
E-EXCUSE ME...

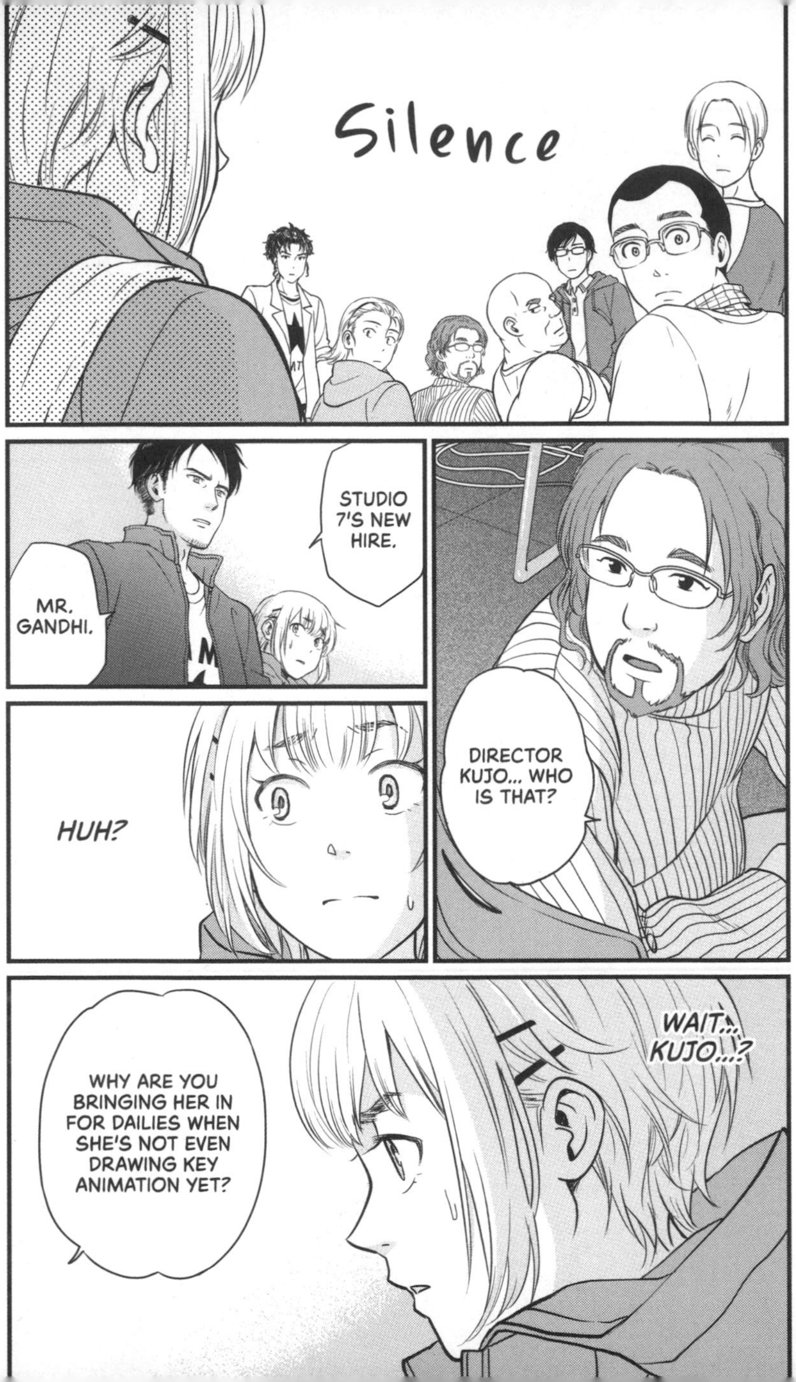
Silence
DIRECTOR KUJO... WHO IS THAT?
STUDIO 7'S NEW HIRE.
MR. GANDHI.
HUH?
WAIT... KUJO...?
WHY ARE YOU BRINGING HER IN FOR DAILIES WHEN SHE'S NOT EVEN DRAWING KEY ANIMATION YET?

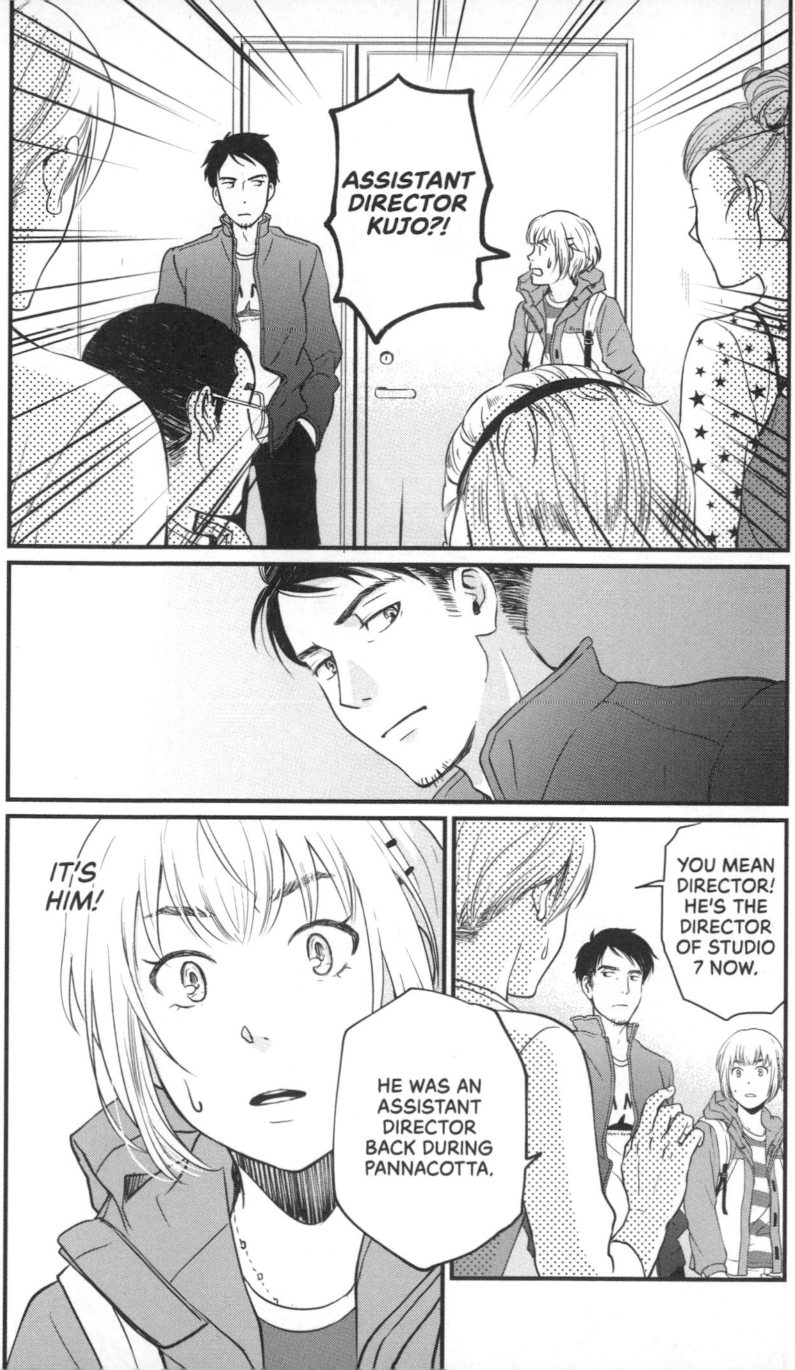
ASSISTANT DIRECTOR KUJO?!
YOU MEAN DIRECTOR! HE'S THE DIRECTOR OF STUDIO 7 NOW.
HE WAS AN ASSISTANT DIRECTOR BACK DURING PANNACOTTA.
IT'S HIM!

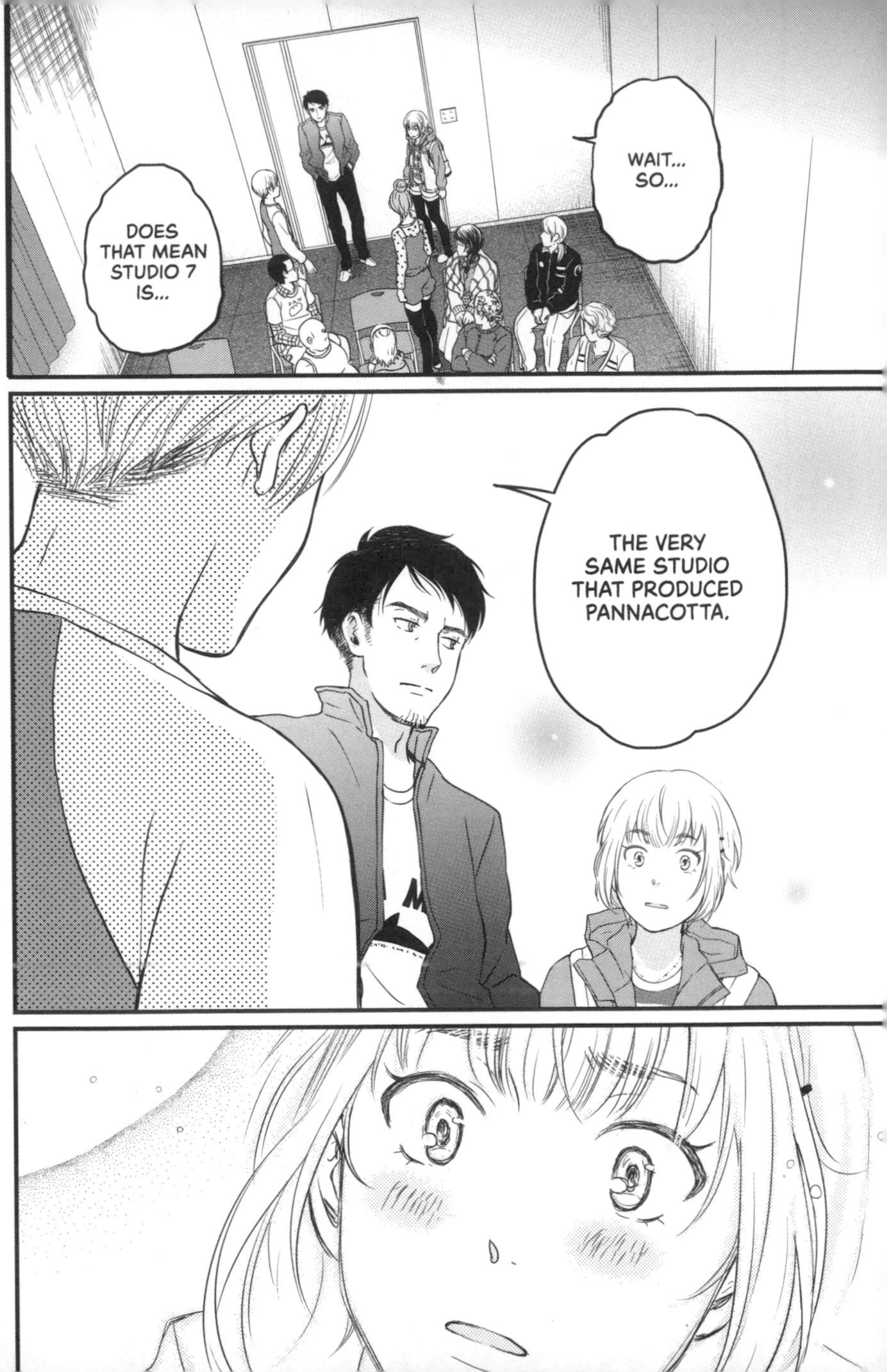
WAIT... SO...
DOES THAT MEAN STUDIO 7 IS...
THE VERY SAME STUDIO THAT PRODUCED PANNACOTTA.

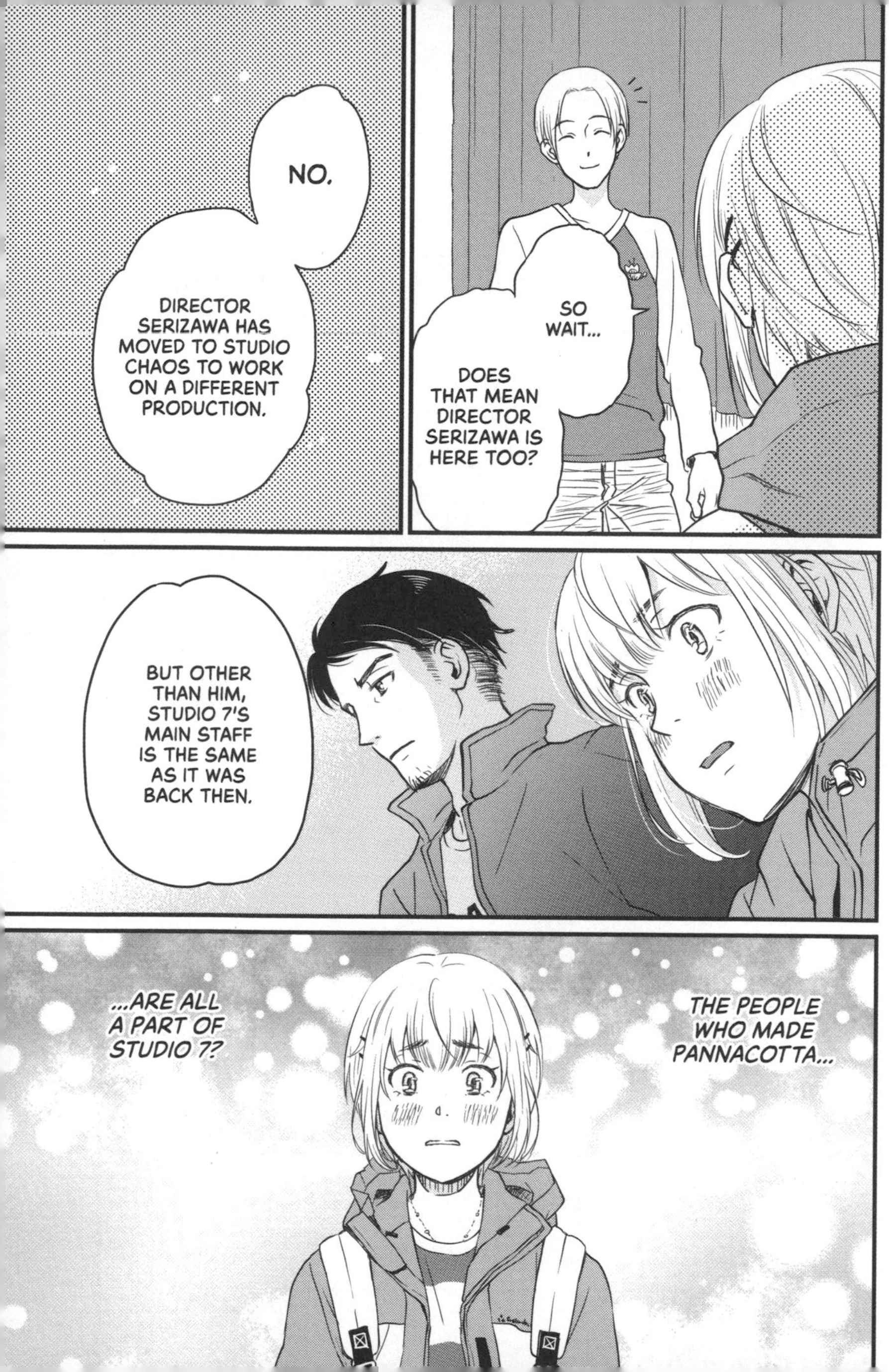
SO WAIT...
DOES THAT MEAN DIRECTOR SERIZAWA IS HERE TOO?
NO.
DIRECTOR SERIZAWA HAS MOVED TO STUDIO CHAOS TO WORK ON A DIFFERENT PRODUCTION.
BUT OTHER THAN HIM, STUDIO 7'S MAIN STAFF IS THE SAME AS IT WAS BACK THEN.
THE PEOPLE WHO MADE PANNACOTTA...
...ARE ALL A PART OF STUDIO 7?

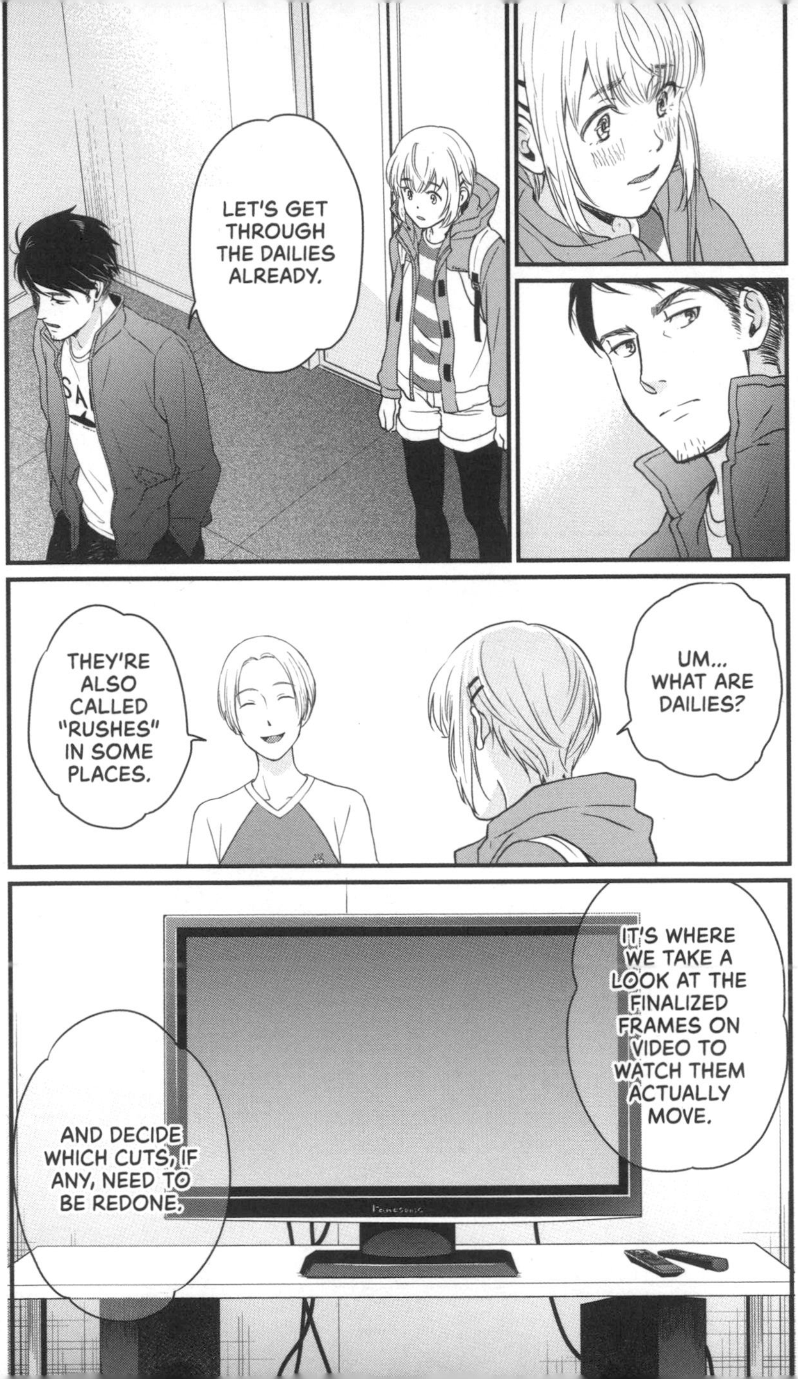
LET'S GET THROUGH THE DAILIES ALREADY.
UM... WHAT ARE DAILIES?
THEY'RE ALSO CALLED "RUSHES" IN SOME PLACES.
IT'S WHERE WE TAKE A LOOK AT THE FINALIZED FRAMES ON VIDEO TO WATCH THEM ACTUALLY MOVE.
AND DECIDE WHICH CUTS, IF ANY, NEED TO BE REDONE.

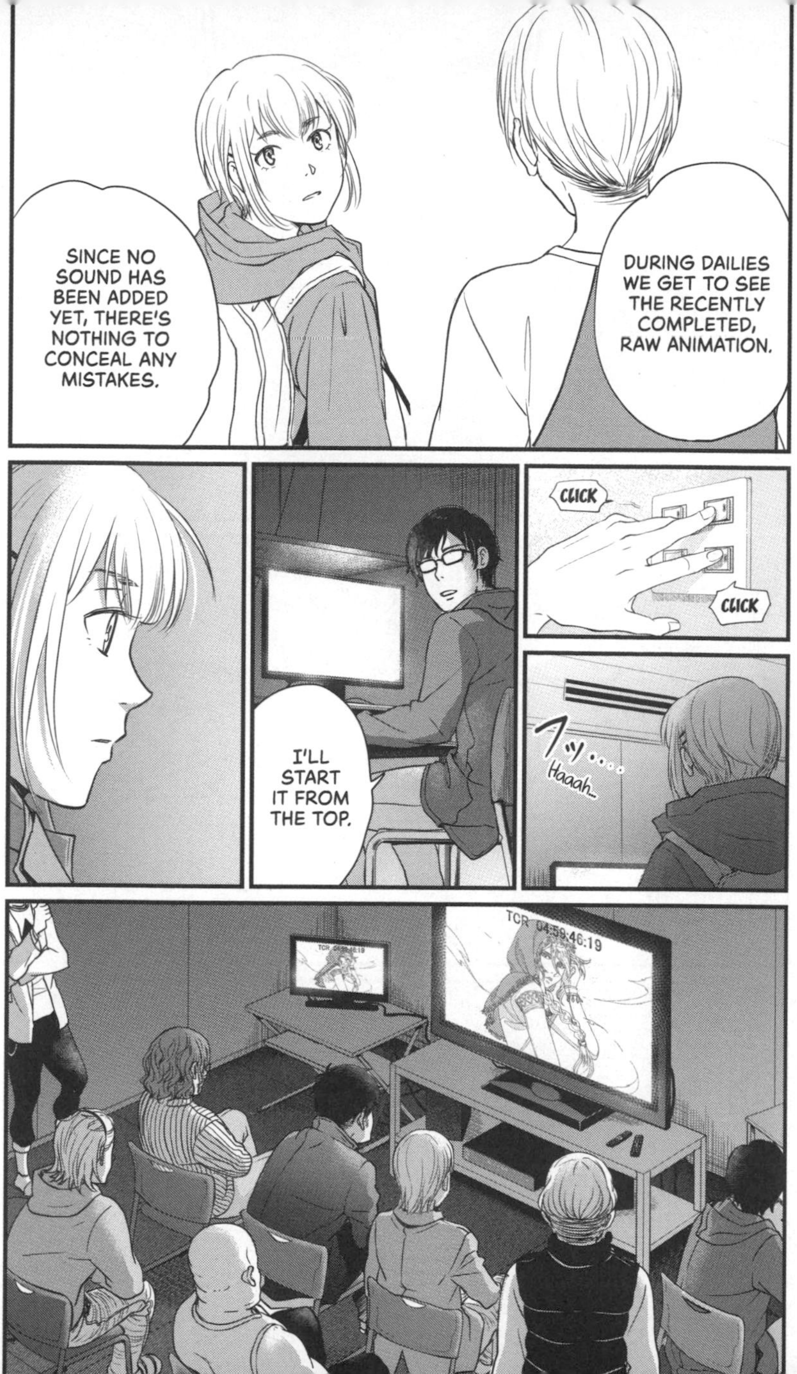
DURING DAILIES WE GET TO SEE THE RECENTLY COMPLETED, RAW ANIMATION.
SINCE NO SOUND HAS BEEN ADDED YET, THERE'S NOTHING TO CONCEAL ANY MISTAKES.
CLICK
CLICK
フッ....
Haaah...
I'LL START IT FROM THE TOP.
TCR 04:59:46:19

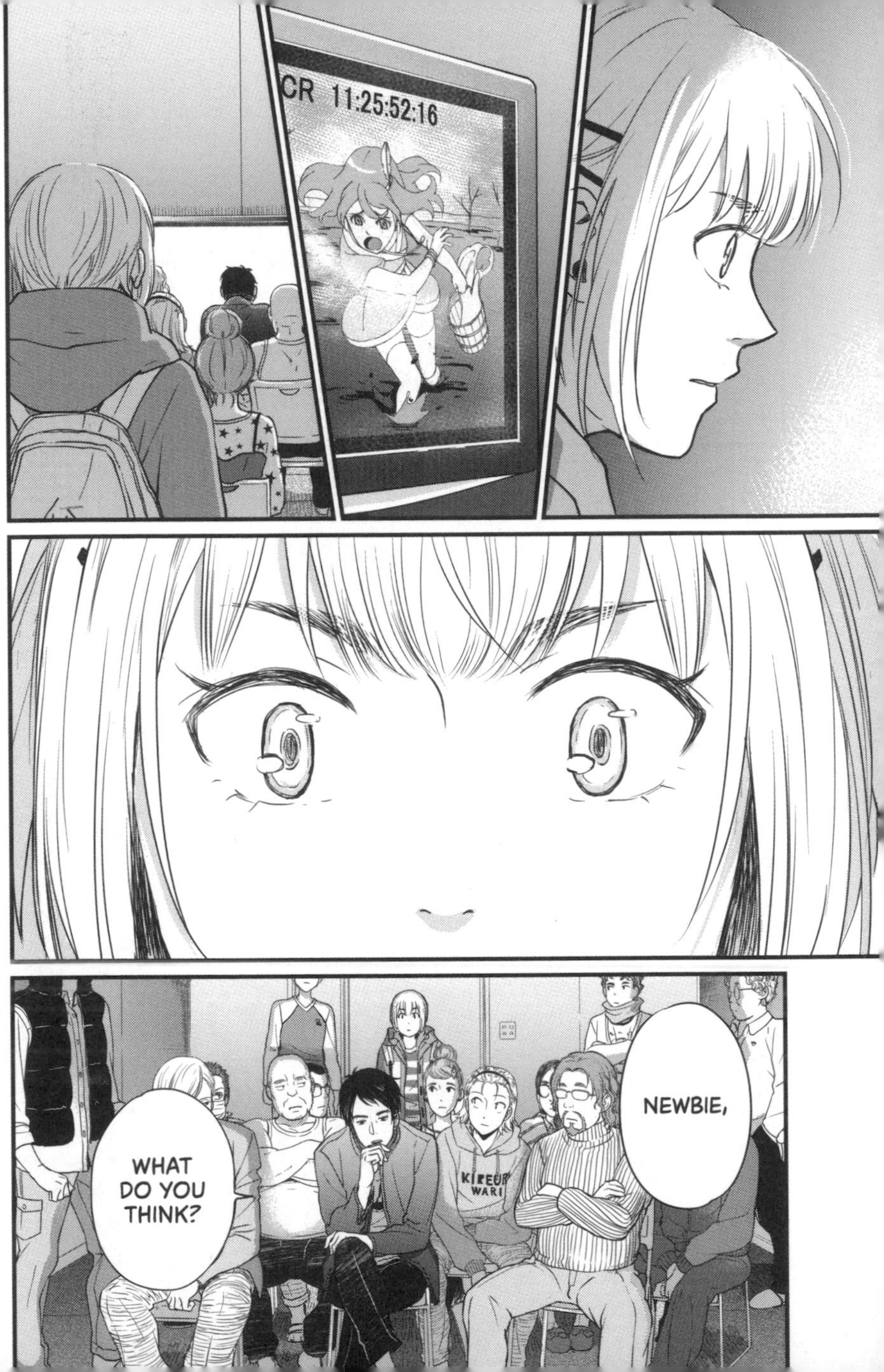
CR 11:25:52:16
NEWBIE,
WHAT DO YOU THINK?

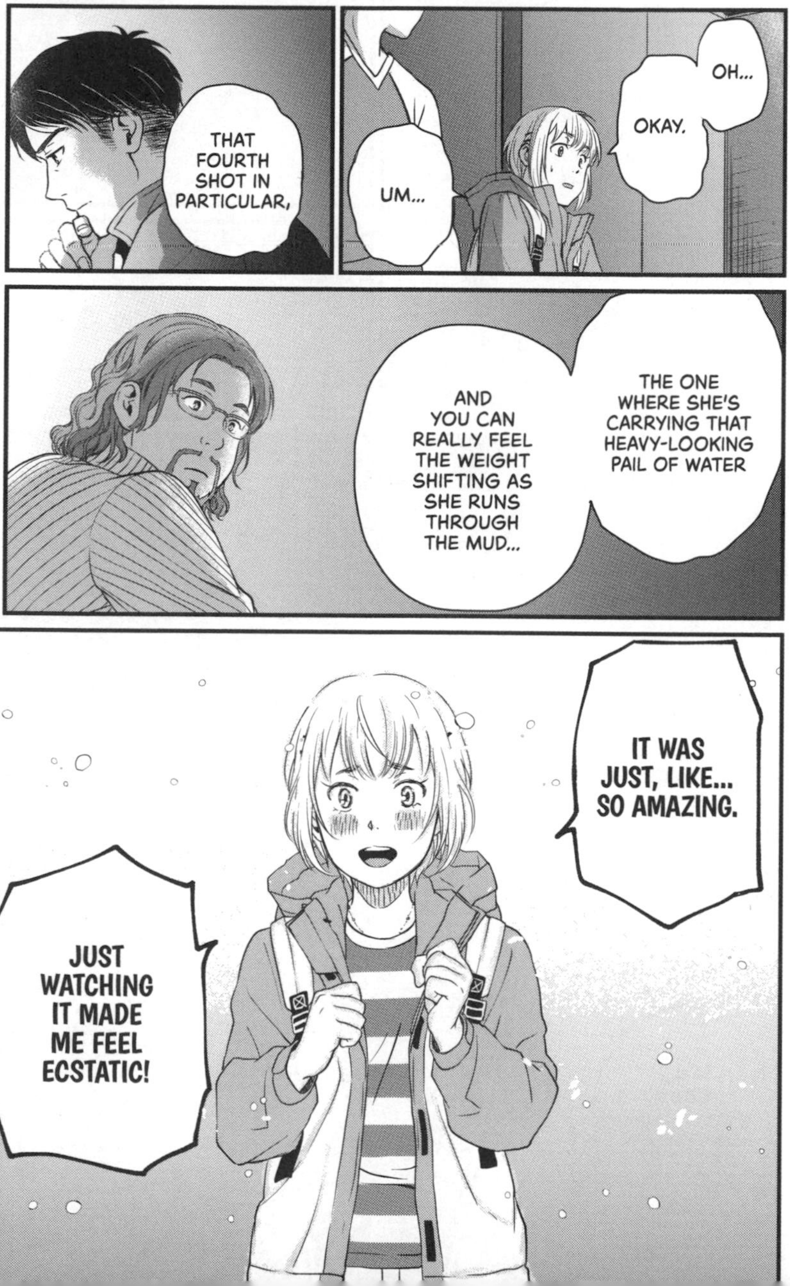
OH... OKAY.
UM...
THAT FOURTH SHOT IN PARTICULAR,
THE ONE WHERE SHE'S CARRYING THAT HEAVY-LOOKING PAIL OF WATER
AND YOU CAN REALLY FEEL THE WEIGHT SHIFTING AS SHE RUNS THROUGH THE MUD...
IT WAS JUST, LIKE... SO AMAZING.
JUST WATCHING IT MADE ME FEEL ECSTATIC!

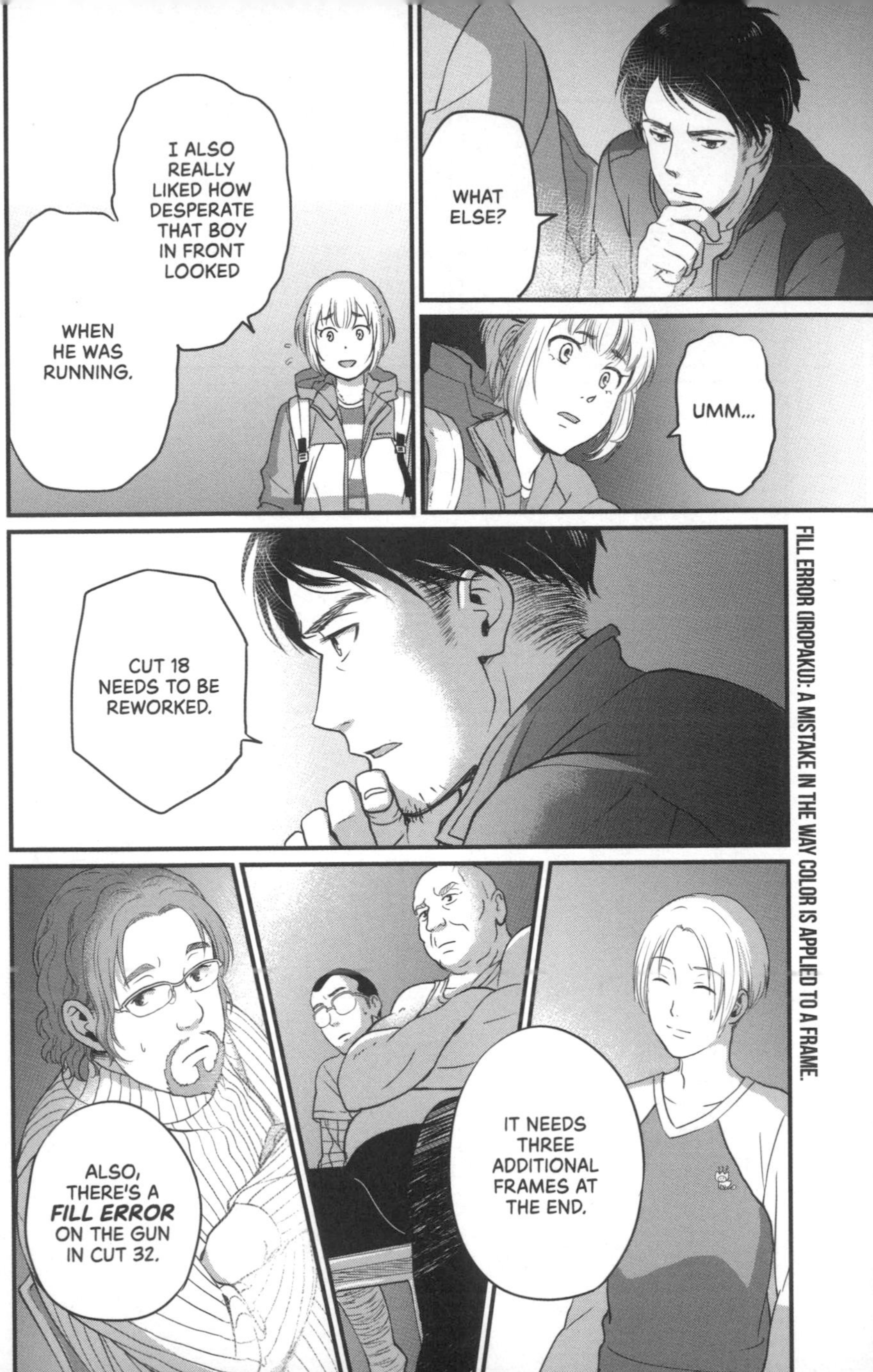
WHAT ELSE?
UMM...
I ALSO REALLY LIKED HOW DESPERATE THAT BOY IN FRONT LOOKED
WHEN HE WAS RUNNING.
CUT 18 NEEDS TO BE REWORKED.
IT NEEDS THREE ADDITIONAL FRAMES AT THE END.
ALSO, THERE'S A ***FILL ERROR*** ON THE GUN IN CUT 32.

FILL ERROR (IROPAKU): A MISTAKE IN THE WAY COLOR IS APPLIED TO A FRAME.

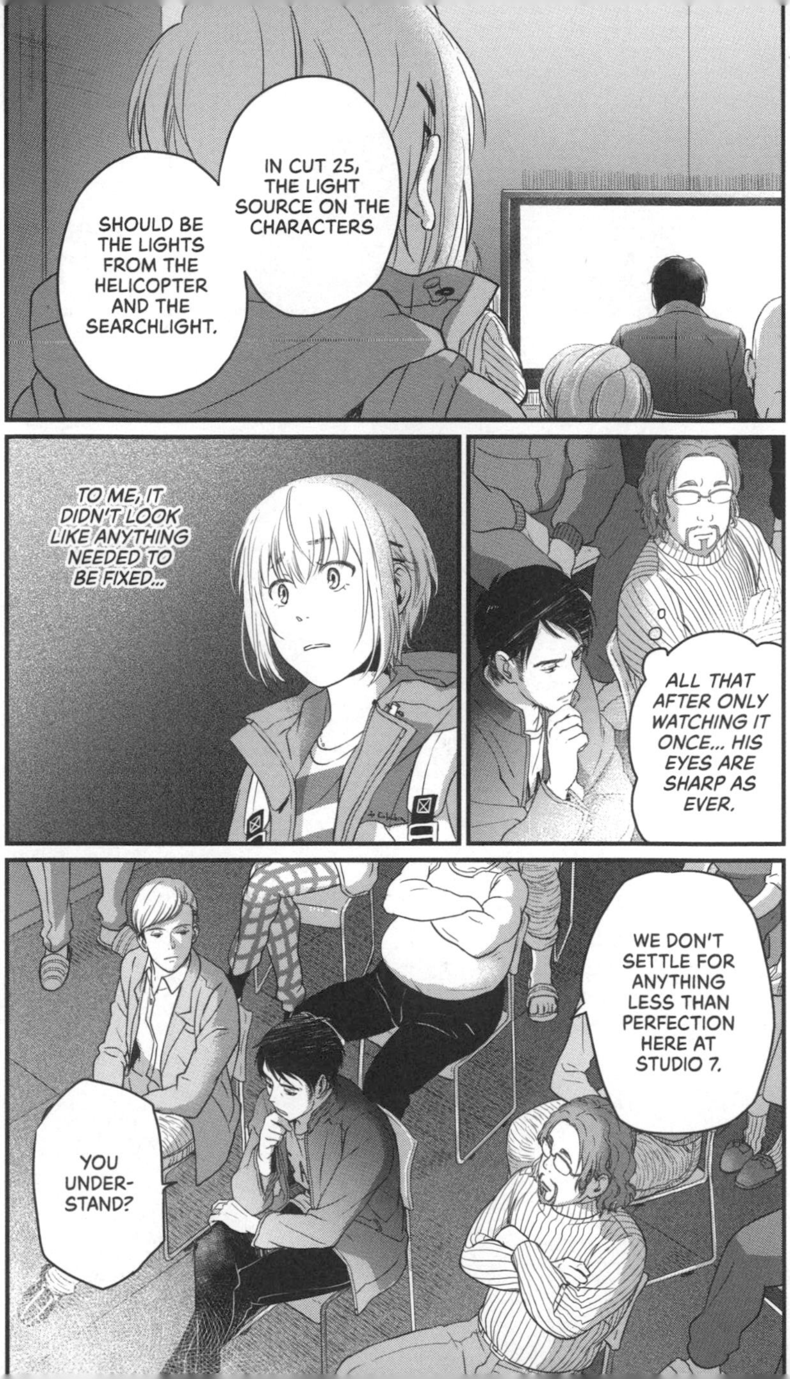
IN CUT 25, THE LIGHT SOURCE ON THE CHARACTERS
SHOULD BE THE LIGHTS FROM THE HELICOPTER AND THE SEARCHLIGHT.
ALL THAT AFTER ONLY WATCHING IT ONCE... HIS EYES ARE SHARP AS EVER.
TO ME, IT DIDN'T LOOK LIKE ANYTHING NEEDED TO BE FIXED...
WE DON'T SETTLE FOR ANYTHING LESS THAN PERFECTION HERE AT STUDIO 7.
YOU UNDER-STAND?

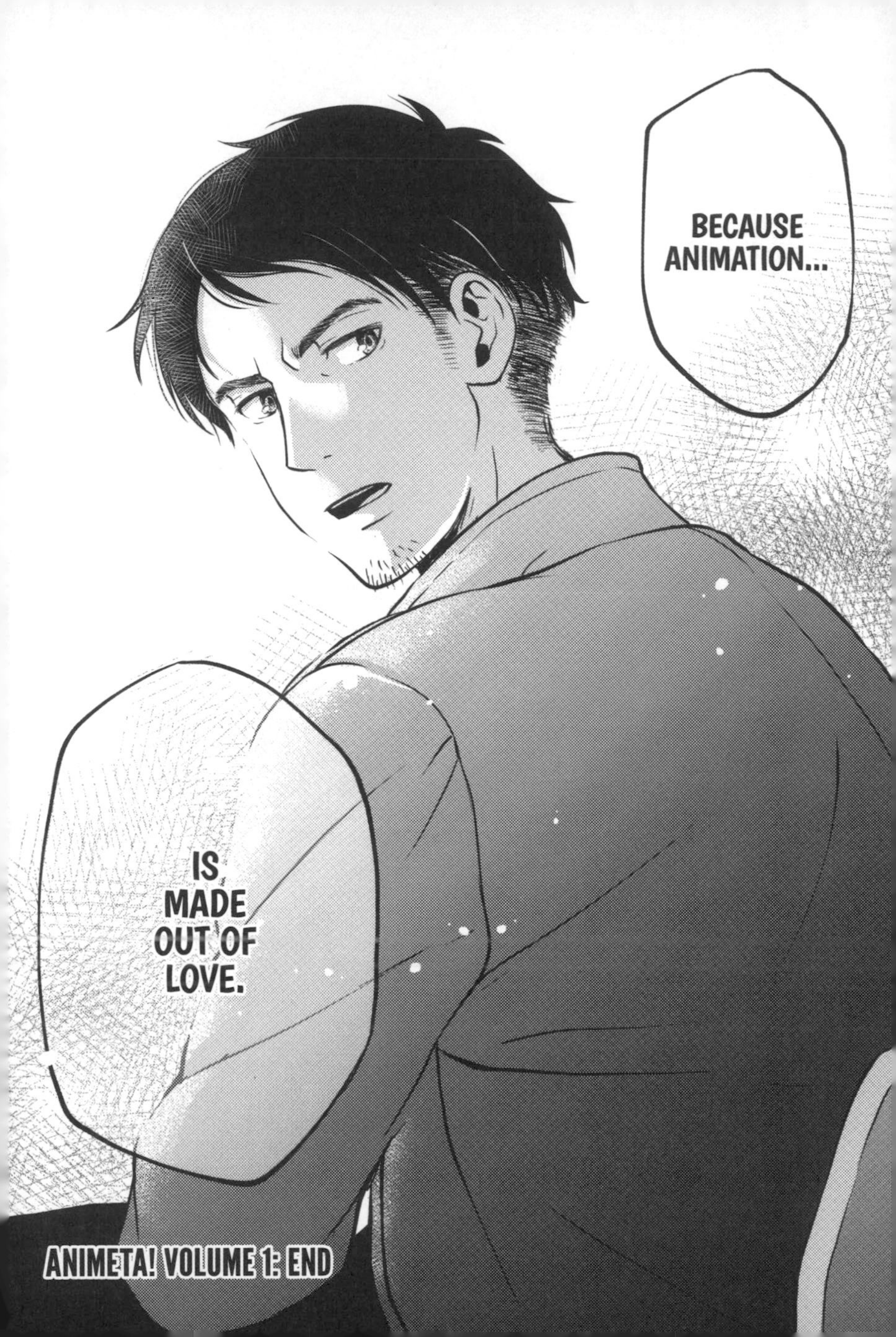
BECAUSE ANIMATION...
IS MADE OUT OF LOVE.
ANIMETA! VOLUME 1: END

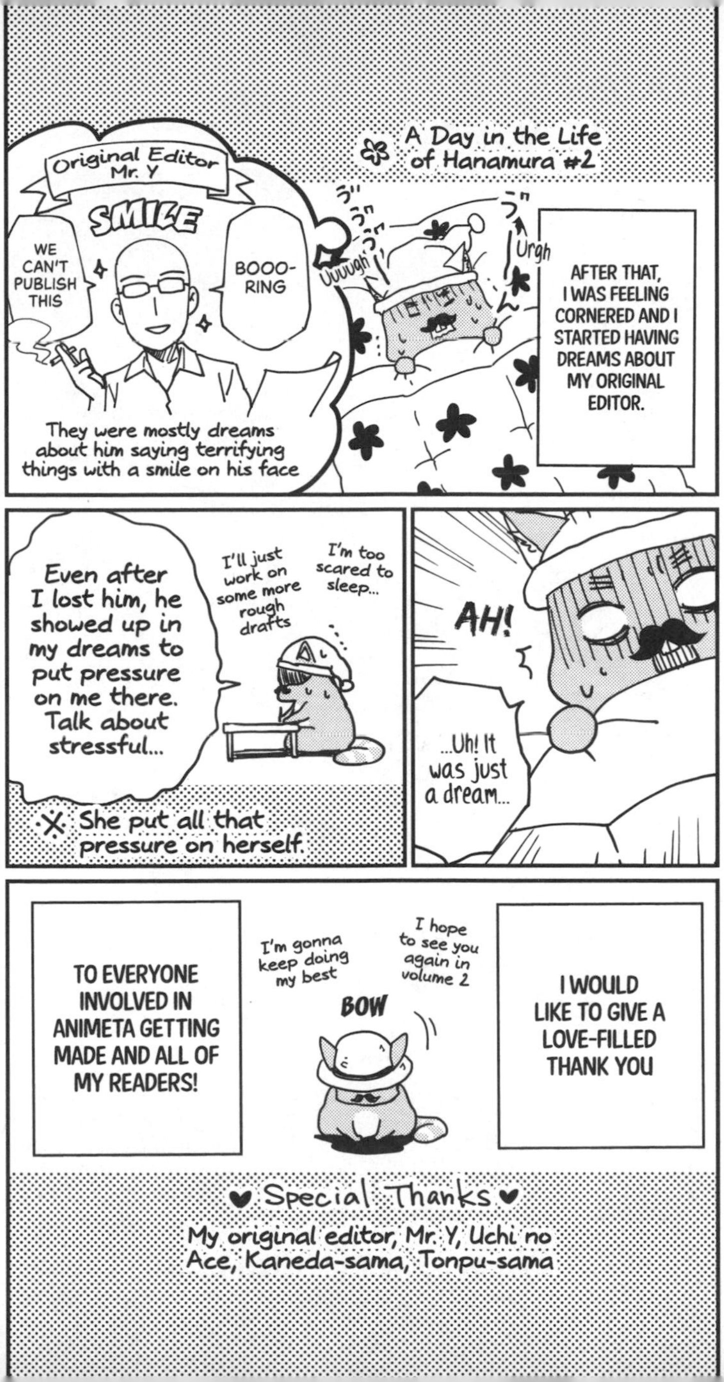
A Day in the Life of Hanamura #2
AFTER THAT, I WAS FEELING CORNERED AND I STARTED HAVING DREAMS ABOUT MY ORIGINAL EDITOR.
Urgh
Uuuugh
Original Editor Mr. Y
SMILE
BOOO-RING
WE CAN'T PUBLISH THIS
They were mostly dreams about him saying terrifying things with a smile on his face
AH!
...Uh! It was just a dream...
I'm too scared to sleep...
I'll just work on some more rough drafts
Even after I lost him, he showed up in my dreams to put pressure on me there. Talk about stressful...
※ She put all that pressure on herself.
I WOULD LIKE TO GIVE A LOVE-FILLED THANK YOU
I hope to see you again in volume 2
I'm gonna keep doing my best
BOW
TO EVERYONE INVOLVED IN ANIMETA GETTING MADE AND ALL OF MY READERS!
♥ Special Thanks ♥
My original editor, Mr. Y, Uchi no Ace, Kaneda-sama, Tonpu-sama

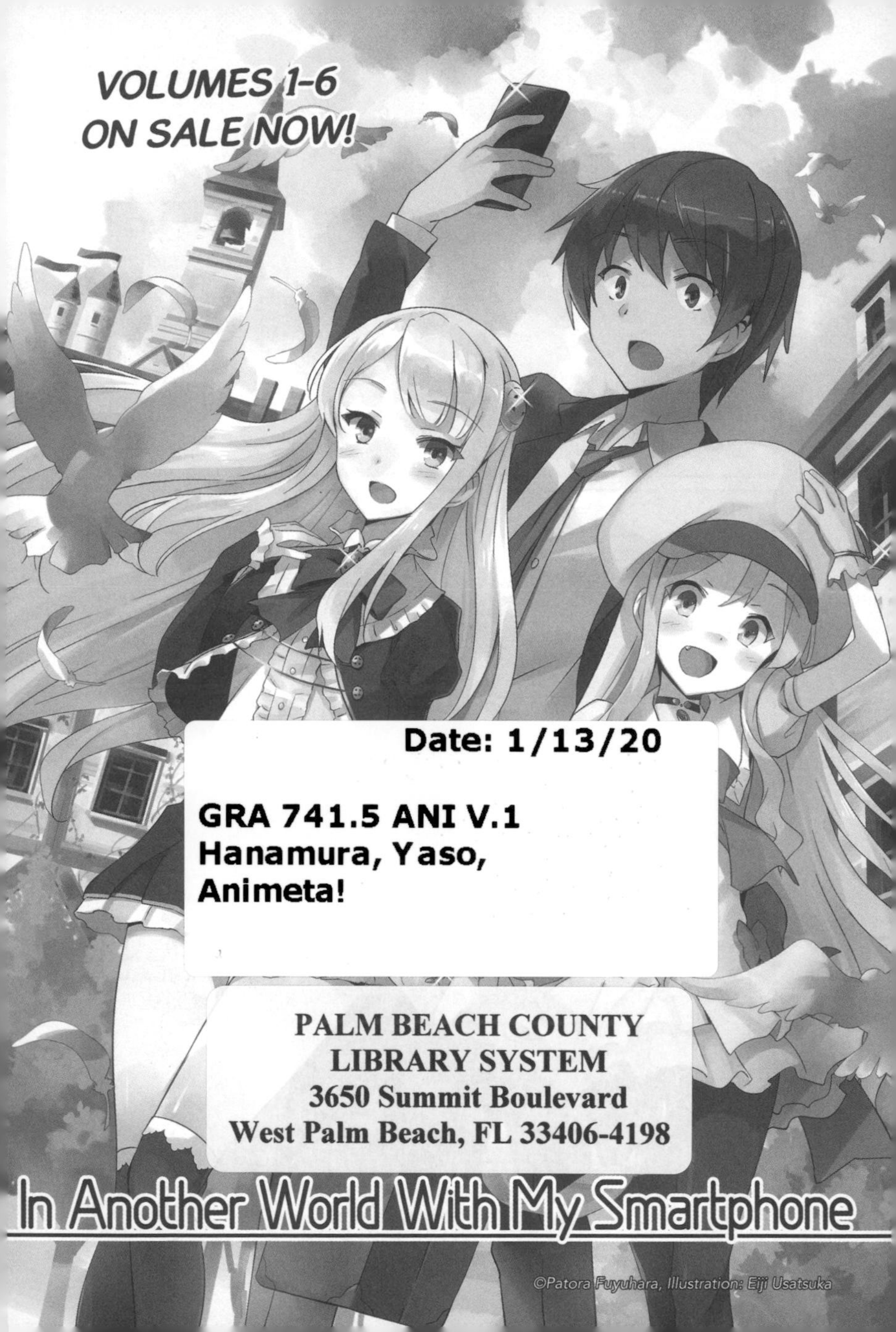
VOLUMES 1-6
ON SALE NOW!
In Another World With My Smartphone
©Patora Fuyuhara, Illustration: Eiji Usatsuka

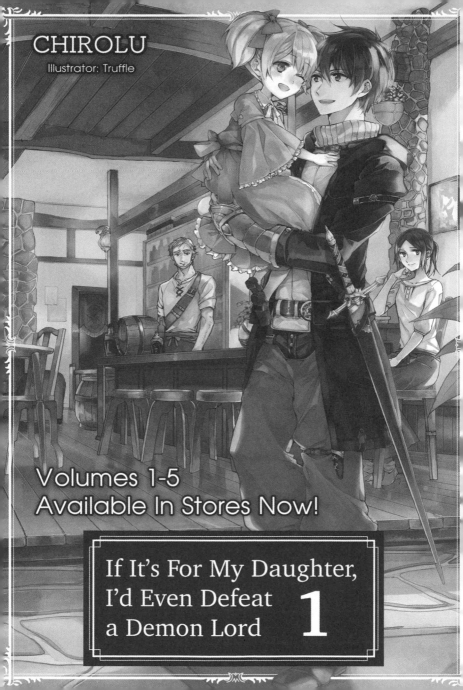

CHIROLU

Illustrator: Truffle

Volumes 1-5
Available In Stores Now!

If It's For My Daughter,
I'd Even Defeat
a Demon Lord **1**

ANIMETA! VOLUME 1
by Yaso Hanamura

Translated by T. Emerson
Edited by Maneesh Maganti
Lettered by Kai Kyou

First published in Japan in 2015 by Kodansha Ltd., Tokyo.
Publication rights for this English edition arranged through Kodansha Ltd., Tokyo.

Find more books like this one at www.j-novel.club!

President and Publisher: Samuel Pinansky
Managing Editor: Aimee Zink
Manga Editor: J. Collis

ISBN: 978-1-7183-5800-3
Printed in Korea
First Printing: October 2019
10 9 8 7 6 5 4 3 2 1

J-Novel Club Lineup

Ebook Releases Series List

Amagi Brilliant Park
An Archdemon's Dilemma: How to Love Your Elf Bride
Ao Oni
Arifureta Zero
Arifureta: From Commonplace to World's Strongest
Bluesteel Blasphemer
Brave Chronicle: The Ruinmaker
Clockwork Planet
Demon King Daimaou
Der Werwolf: The Annals of Veight
ECHO
From Truant to Anime Screenwriter: My Path to "Anohana" and "The Anthem of the Heart"
Gear Drive
Grimgar of Fantasy and Ash
How a Realist Hero Rebuilt the Kingdom
How NOT to Summon a Demon Lord
I Saved Too Many Girls and Caused the Apocalypse
If It's for My Daughter, I'd Even Defeat a Demon Lord
In Another World With My Smartphone
Infinite Dendrogram
Infinite Stratos
Invaders of the Rokujouma!?
JK Haru is a Sex Worker in Another World
Kokoro Connect
Last and First Idol
Lazy Dungeon Master
Me, a Genius? I Was Reborn into Another World and I Think They've Got the Wrong Idea!
Mixed Bathing in Another Dimension
My Big Sister Lives in a Fantasy World
My Little Sister Can Read Kanji
My Next Life as a Villainess: All Routes Lead to Doom!
Occultic;Nine
Outbreak Company
Paying to Win in a VRMMO
Seirei Gensouki: Spirit Chronicles
Sorcerous Stabber Orphen: The Wayward Journey
The Faraway Paladin
The Magic in this Other World is Too Far Behind!
The Master of Ragnarok & Blesser of Einherjar
The Unwanted Undead Adventurer
Walking My Second Path in Life
Yume Nikki: I Am Not in Your Dream